Martha's QUILTS

by Martha Campbell Pullen, Ph.D.

May God Bless You
Martha Pullen

Martha Pullen Company, Inc.

Book Team

Editor
Martha Campbell Pullen, Ph.D.

Construction Editors
Dody Baker, Louise Baird, Linda Mann, Kathy McMakin,
Claudia Newton, Charlotte Potter, Martha Pullen, Patty Smith

Quilt Designs
Louise Baird, Cheri Collins, Carol Ingram, Diane Marr,
Kathy McMakin, Sue Pennington, Gail Settle, Janice Stewart

Cover Design
Jon Scull

Book Design
Laura Beth Yates

Photography
Jennifer & Company

Photo Stylist
Claudia Newton

Illustrations
Kris Broom, Angela Cataldo Pullen

Printed in the United States of America.

Martha Pullen Company, Inc., 149 Big Cove Road, Brownsboro, AL 35741
Phone (256) 533-9586 • Fax (256) 533-9630 • info@marthapullen.com

ISBN 1-878048-26-0
Library of Congress Control Number: 2001012345

Introduction

Martha's Quilts is the newest book by Martha Pullen and her first book completely dedicated to the art of quilting. Inside, you'll find a variety of quilts from fancy to fun and an illustrated section including the techniques featured on these beautiful quilts. Written with variety in mind, *Martha's Quilts* contains quilt patterns for beginner to advanced quilters. There are quilts to commemorate special events, quilts with "Block of the Month" clubs in mind, and quilts that are just fun to make! Also, matching wallhanging and pillow instructions are included with select projects. The detailed instructions, color photography, and beautiful designs in *Martha's Quilts* are sure to have you as excited about quilting as Martha is - and we know you'll have fun quilting together!

Table of Contents

Noah's Ark Wave Quilt 1
Noah's Ark Wall Hanging 8
"Welcome to our Family" Heart Quilt 12
Mother Goose Quilt 18
Springtime in Paris Quilt 24
Lighthouse Wall Hanging 37
Simple Star Block Quilt 40
Simple Star Block Pillow 46
Heirloom Classics 7 Stippled Quilt 49
Tapestry of Hearts Quilt 52
Serger Quilt 67
Joanna's Memory Quilt 70
Crazy Patch Doll Quilt & Pillow 76
Blue Danube Quilt 80
Crayon Art Heart Quilt 93
Bunnies by the Bay® Quilt 96
Mommy's Helpers Wall Panel 101
Mommy's Helpers Wing Needle Entredeux Quilt 105
Extra Stable Lace Finishing Technique 108
Beginning French Sewing Techniques 108
Lace Shaping Techniques 109
Stipple Stitching Technique 111
Appliqué Techniques 112
Shadow Appliqué 115

ABOUT Martha Campbell Pullen, Ph.D.

Martha Campbell Pullen didn't invent heirloom sewing — the art of joining laces to create fabric has survived for centuries — but she and her fabulous staff can take some of the credit for turning this age-old art into a hobby that's approaching "all the rage" proportions.

Martha personally learned how to smock and French sew by machine over 20 years ago when she was making clothes for her baby daughter. She realized if she could be drawn in so passionately, other women could be as well.

Today, she fronts her own heirloom sewing empire, which grew out of a tiny shop in Huntsville, Alabama. In 1981, two months after opening that shop, she began importing laces and fabrics to sell mail-order both wholesale and retail. Next, came Martha Pullen Heirloom Sewing Schools, which now attract more than 600 women to Huntsville twice a year. Their success prompted Pullen to venture out of her local market, conducting full scale Martha Pullen schools in Australia, England, Sweden, Canada, New Zealand and Texas. She has done mini-schools in almost every state in the United States.

An accomplished author, she has more than 25 books to her credit including three hardback manuals in excess of 400 pages. "You Can Make Money From Your Hobby," her most recent book has been published by Broadman and Holman, an arm of the Baptist Sunday School Board. It is available in Christian and mainstream bookstores nationally.

Adding to that list of successes, and probably the project of which she is most proud, is *Sew Beautiful*, a magazine she founded and began publishing over a decade ago. The publication focusing on heirloom and other classic sewing arts has an international following and distributes in excess of 90,000 copies bi-monthly. Four years ago, she began sharing her love of heirloom sewing with public television audiences around the country through her *Martha's Sewing Room* series.

To encourage heirloom sewn garments in cooler climates, Martha expanded the range of materials used from traditional batistes and other lightweight materials to wool challis, corduroys, flannels and home decorating fabrics. She has even come up with a name for these heirloom garments — love clothes.

"I call them 'love clothes' because I quickly realized that they are the special garments we make with love for the people we love," she explained. "With sewing, it almost seems that the love goes right from the machine or stitching needle into whatever we are making, especially where children are involved. It means so much more than just purchasing something ready made. Best of all, the classic, beautifully-sewn heirloom garments can carry that love from one generation to another."

Annually, Martha presents *Martha's Sewing Market* at the Arlington Convention Center in Arlington, Texas and in Orlando at the Tupperware Convention Center. Her consumer exhibitions feature top international sewing instructors, more than 50 free class choices per day, a vendor arena, fashion shows, and displays. All of these activities are available after paying a low admission fee.

"Sewing makes memories that are passed on from generation to generation through the actual garments but also through the stitches learned," said Martha, who is on the road promoting the art of sewing many weeks out of every year.

A native of Scottsboro, Alabama, Martha is an internationally-known lecturer and teacher in the heirloom sewing field. After graduating with a degree in speech and English from the University of Alabama, she taught those subjects at almost every level of middle school and high school. Later, her studies led to a Ph.D in educational administration and management from the University of Alabama.

She has been named Huntsville Madison County Chamber of Commerce Executive of the Year, the second woman in the history of the organization to receive this award. She has been a nominee for *Inc,* magazine's executive of the year. She is a member of Rotary International and Optimist International. She has served on the board of directors of the Smocking Arts Guild of America and has presented workshops in French sewing by machine throughout the United States, Australia, England, Canada, Sweden and New Zealand. She is the wife of Joe Ross Pullen, an implant dentist and president of her company, mother of five and grandmother to ten! An active member of her church, she also volunteers with the Southern Baptist International Mission Board.

Noah's Ark Wave Quilt

Using pink, ecru, blue and white linen/cotton blend fabric, this quilt is beautiful. The waves of the quilt (the outside border) are made of blue linen; the inside of the waves is ecru. The sashing around the squares is pink and the squares with machine embroidery are white. Different characters from the Martha Pullen Embroidery Card, Noah's Ark, are stitched inside each of the white squares which measure seven inches by seven inches. Blue stars are found in each corner between the embroidered squares. The back of the quilt is ecru linen/cotton blend and the binding is blue. "Created by Cheri Collins, Kennesaw, GA, August, 1999" is found on the back of the quilt stitched with a beautiful machine-embroidered script. A pretty green machine-embroidered bow is at the top of the machine-embroidered section.

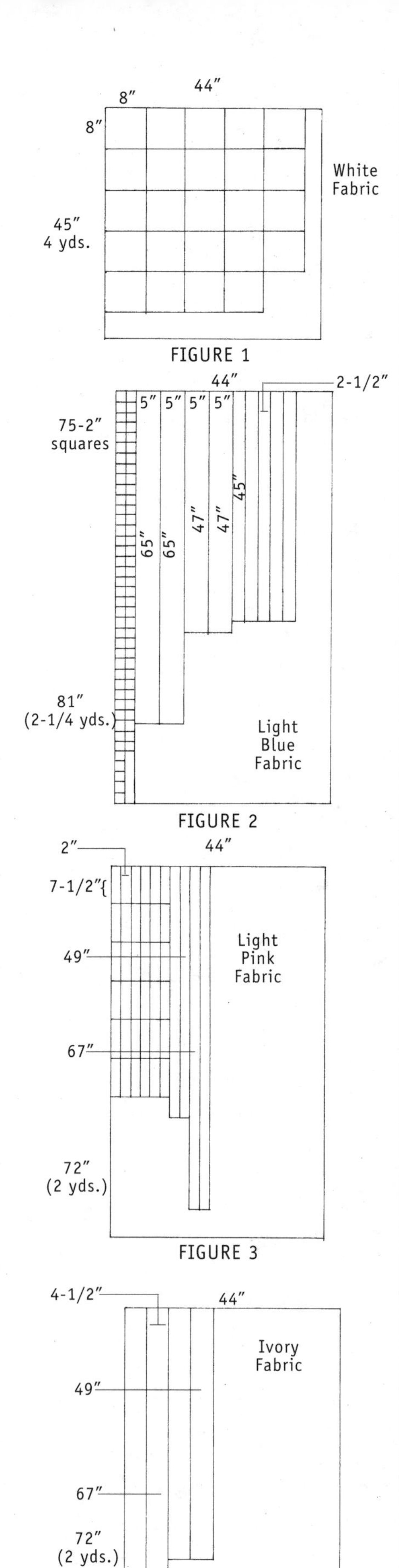

Please read these instructions before beginning your quilt. All sashing strips and border pieces will be cut from the lengthwise grain of the fabric to reduce the chance of stretching during construction. This is reflected in the yardages below, but you may wish to buy smaller amounts and cut the strips from the crosswise grain. Especially when using linens, I prefer to pull threads and use the resulting "run" as a guide to cut strips, rather than using a rotary cutter, but this is up to you. You may also tear the strips.

Supplies

All measurements are based on 45" wide fabric. Yardages given are ample amounts to avoid piecing of strips.

For best results, use heavy weight linen, cotton/linen blend, or 100% cotton such as Kona Cotton. These fabrics should be pre-shrunk before beginning.

- 2-1/4 yards light blue - pinwheel stars, wave border and binding
- 1-1/4 yards white - embroidered squares
- 2 yards light pink - sashing strips and first border
- 2 yards ivory - second border
- 2 yards – color of your choice for quilt back (or you may piece the scraps from the top, and add enough to make one piece big enough for the back of the quilt)
- 3/4 yard of scrap fabric similar in weight to the fabrics above
- Size #18 denim or embroidery needle
- Wash-away pen
- Tear-away type stabilizer for embroidery
- Twin size cotton batting
- Rayon threads for embroidery as called for in design pack
- White thread for assembling quilt
- Safety pins or a quilt tack gun
- Wave Template
- Noah's Ark embroidery disk from Martha Pullen Company
- Point turner
- Wash-away basting thread

Cutting

Cut the following pieces and label all sets of pieces. Remove all selvages before cutting the pieces.

1. From the white fabric, cut twenty-four 8" squares. Each square should be lightly spray-starched and ironed. While ironing, make certain each piece is, in fact, square. If it is slightly off, simply tug gently on opposite corners to straighten, then press *(fig. 1)*

2. From the light blue, cut or tear two strips, each 2" wide and the length of the piece. Each strip is then cut into 2" squares– you will need a total of 75 of these squares *(fig. 2)*.

3. From the light blue, cut two strips 5" by 47" for the top and bottom wave strips and two strips 5" by 65" for the side wave strips *(fig. 2)*.

4. From the light blue fabric, cut 5 strips 2-1/2" by 45" for the binding *(fig. 2)*.

5. From the light pink, cut or tear six strips, each 2" wide and the length of the piece. Each strip is then cut into 7-1/2" long pieces – you will need a total of 36 pink strips *(fig. 3)* .

6. From the light pink fabric, cut two strips 2" by 49" for the top and bottom borders and two strips 2" by 67" for the side borders *(fig. 3)*. The extra length is added to allow room for the miter at each corner.

7. From the ivory fabric, cut two strips 4-1/2" by 49" for the top and bottom borders and two strips 4-1/2" by 67" for the side borders *(fig. 4)*.

8. From the scrap fabric, cut five 5" by 44" strips. Stitch the strips together along the short ends to create one long strip. Press the seams open. From this long strip cut two strips 5" by 47" for the top and bottom wave strips and two strips 5" by 65" for the side wave strips.To find the center of each white square, fold in half, and then in half

again, finger pressing the folds. Hoop each square, and with a piece of stabilizer underneath, center then embroider each of the 23 designs. For the 24th design, part of the quote from Genesis "And of every living thing . . . two of every sort" was embroidered (*fig. 5*). The recipient's name and the date could be used, or you may choose to embroider one of the other designs twice to fill this square.

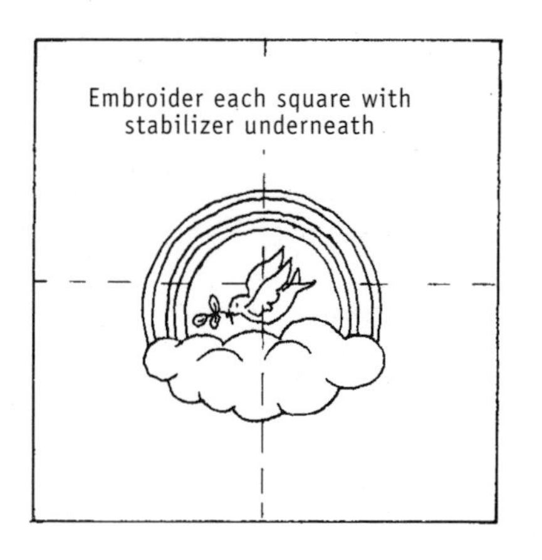

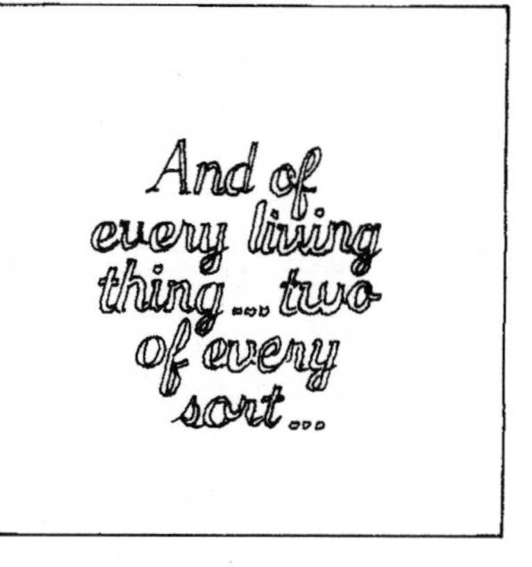

FIGURE 5

Sashing Strips

Divide the pink sashing strips (2" by 7-1/2") into two piles – 16 strips in one pile, 20 in the other.

1. On each of the blue squares, use a pencil or other marker to draw a diagonal line from corner to corner. Now place a square at one end of a pink strip, having all raw edges even, and having the diagonal line running from upper left to lower right, as shown *(fig. 6)*. Stitch on the drawn line.

2. Sew squares to one end only of 16 strips, and to both ends of 20 strips. When that is complete, trim each seam down to 1/4" *(fig. 7)* and press the seam allowance toward the blue. This results in a triangle at the end of the strip, without the worry of dealing with bias seams *(fig. 8)*.

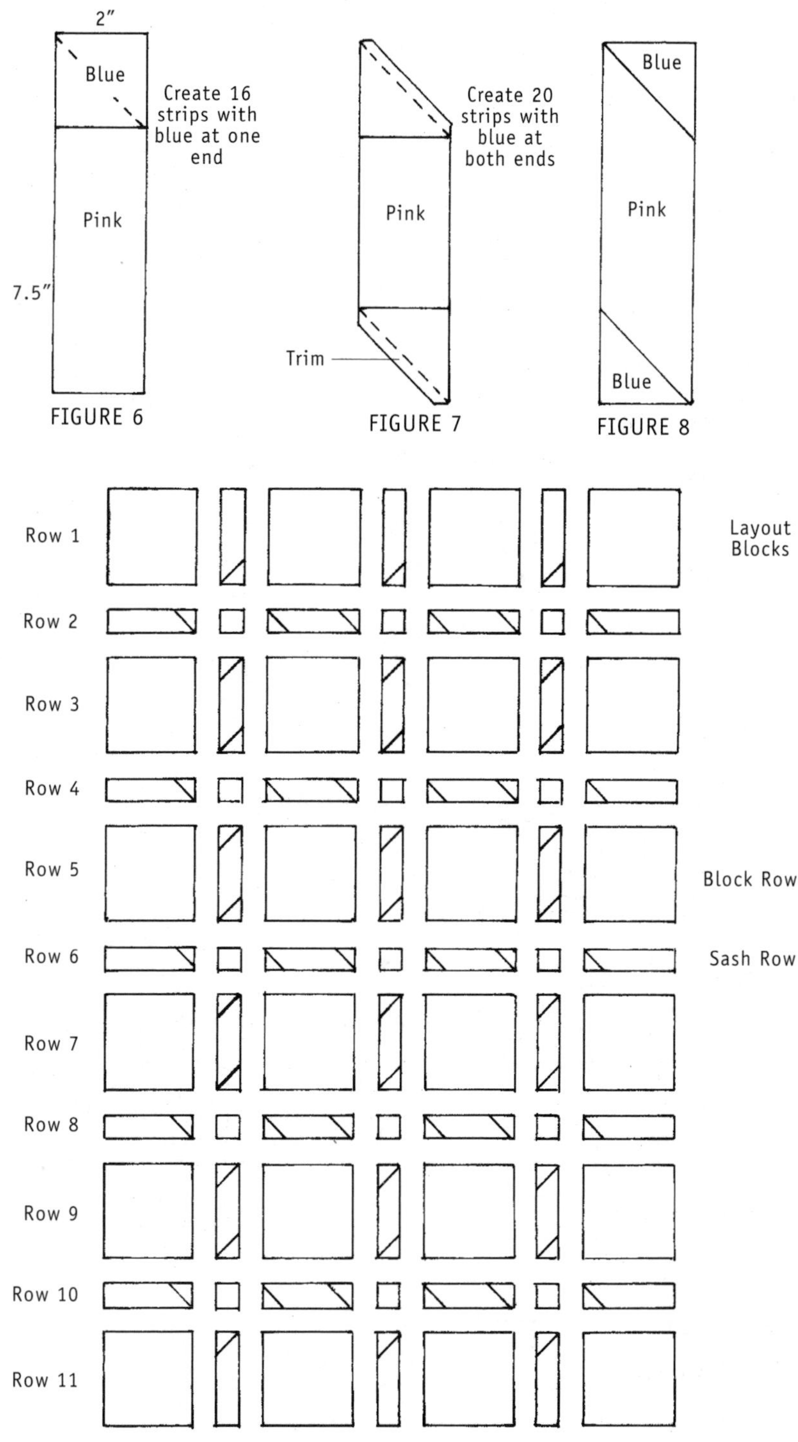

FIGURE 6

FIGURE 7

FIGURE 8

FIGURE 9

Construction of the Quilt Top

All seam allowances are stitched precisely 1/4". Please be accurate with these seam allowances, as each one affects the overall size of the quilt top and the way the pieces fit together. Also, take care that you maintain the layout as shown in figure 9.

1. After all the squares are embroidered and sashing strips are complete, you're ready to begin piecing the quilt top. On a large flat surface, lay the blocks out in the desired arrangement. Between each of the squares, place a 2" by 7-1/2" pink/blue strip, as shown *(fig. 9)*.

2. To construct the quilt top, you will be working first on the horizontal rows. Begin by stitching together the first block and the first sashing strip, and so on, until you have all 4 blocks and the 3 sashing strips joined.

3. The second horizontal row consists of 4 sashing strips and 3 corner stones (the blue 2" squares).

4. Continue as above until all 11 horizontal rows are joined. On the block rows, press seam allowances toward the blocks. On sashing rows, press the seams toward the 2" blue squares.

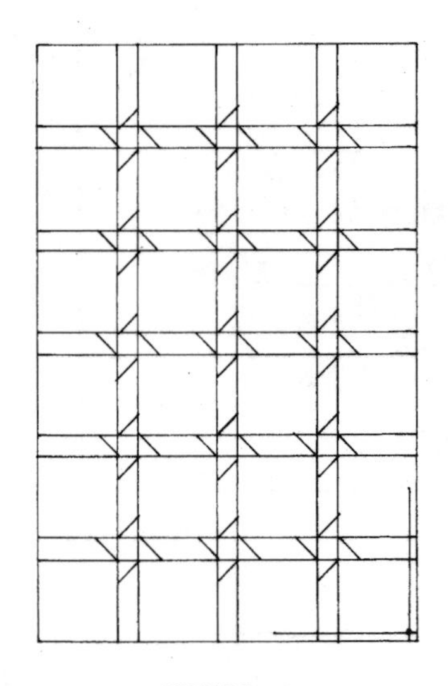

FIGURE 10

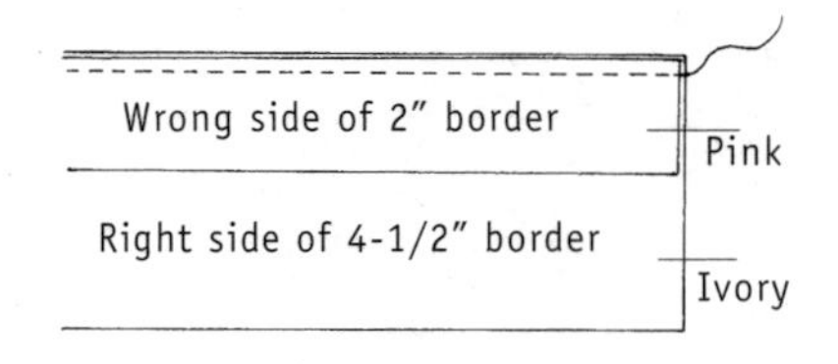

FIGURE 11

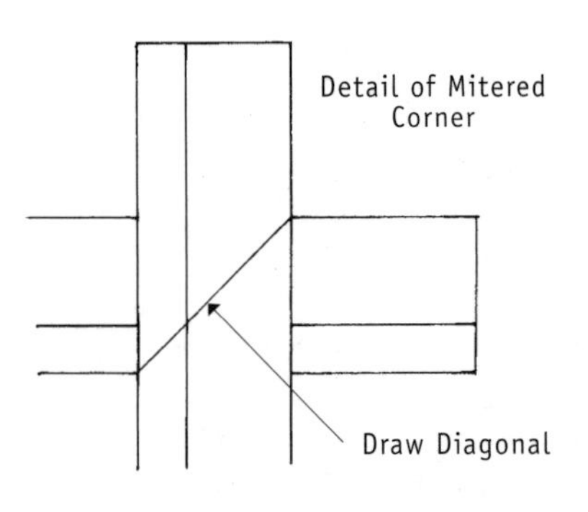

FIGURE 12

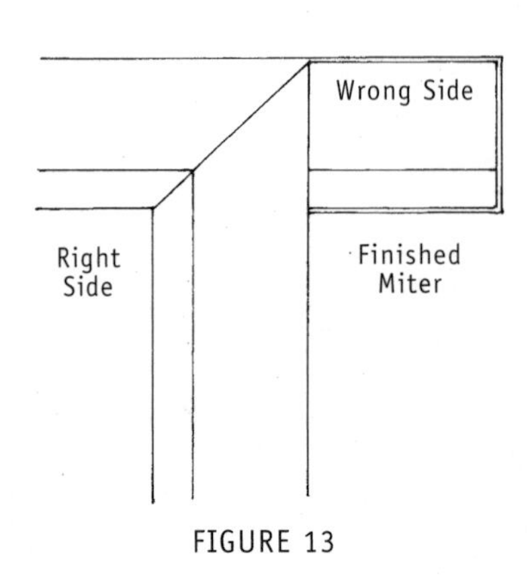

FIGURE 13

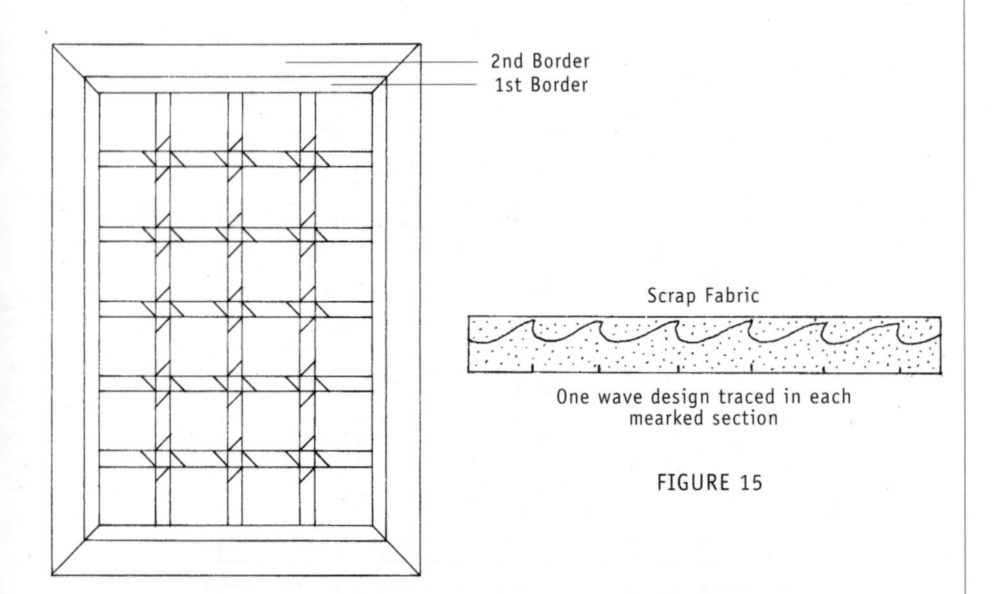

FIGURE 14

FIGURE 15

5. To complete the construction of the top, stitch the first block row to the first sashing row. Add the next block row, sashing row, block row, etc., until all 11 have been stitched together, and you have one big piece *(fig. 10)*. Carefully press the remaining seams, pressing seam allowances toward the block rows.

Completing the Quilt

1. Lay the quilt top out on a large flat surface and carefully smooth it out. Measure the length and width of the top. The quilt top so far should measure 35" wide by 53" long.

2. Draw a line 1/4" from each side near all four corners. Place a dot where the lines intersect *(fig. 10)*.

3. Stitch the 2" light pink border to the 4-1/2" ivory border matching the respective lengths *(fig. 11)*. Press the seam allowances towards the darker color.

4. Attach the 2" border edge of the shorter strips to the top and bottom of the quilt top, beginning and ending at the dot. Allow equal amounts of the borders to extend beyond the quilt top.

5. Attach the 2" border edge of the longer strips to the sides of the quilt top beginning and ending at the dot. Allow equal amounts of the borders to extend beyond the quilt top.

6. Overlap the border pieces, draw a diagonal line on each piece *(fig. 12)*. Carefully flip the pieces right sides together. Match and stitch along the diagonal line *(fig. 13)*. Trim the seam to 1/8". Complete the miters on all four corners *(fig. 14)*.

7. Fold each of the wave strips in half to find the center. Trace the wave template onto the wrong side of the scrap fabric strips (*fig. 15*). You should be able to trace 7 complete waves on the top and bottom strips (3-1/2 waves on each side of the center fold) and 10 complete waves on the side strips (5 waves on each side of the center fold). Adjust the template as necessary to meet the diagonal miters of the borders.

8. Place the right side of the scrap fabric to the right side of the blue wave strip, matching the lengths respectively. Pin the layers together.

9. Using wash-away basting thread in the needle, the bobbin or both, stitch along the traced line through the scrap fabric and wave fabric *(fig. 16)*.

10. After the stitching is complete, trim the seam to a scant 1/4" and clip all curves, placing the clips about 1/4" to 1/2" apart, and clipping up to the stitching line(*fig. 17*). Turn right side out, taking care not to poke through the fabrics when poking out the corners. Press the border strip *(fig. 18)*. Spray the edge of the wave heavily with starch. The dampness of the starch will dissolve the wash-away thread. Press the border strip until it is totally dry. Pull the layers apart. If they do not come apart easily, re-spray the border edges and press until dry. Pull the layers apart and discard the scrap fabric. Complete all four wave borders.

NOTE: Replace the wash-away thread with lightweight sewing thread before continuing.

11. Matching the centers, pin one wave border in place on top of the ivory border, matching the raw edges and aligning the tops of the waves in a straight line, about 1/4" away from the seam line where the pink and ivory borders are joined. Make certain that there is no gap between the ivory border and the lowest parts of the waves.

12. Pin all four borders in place on the quilt top. Draw a diagonal line at each corner of the quilt on both layers of the wave border. Un-pin at the corner, flip the wave border pieces right sides together and stitch along the drawn diagonal lines, mitering the corners. Press well. When you are satisfied with the positioning of the wave border, stitch the edge of the wave in place using a pinstitch (L=2.5, W=2.5). The straight portion of the pinstitch will be on the ivory fabric and the "fingers" of the pinstitch will catch the blue wave. You may wish to adjust the length and/or width – always do a test stitch before beginning on your project *(fig. 19)*.

13. Mark the quilting lines on the top, unless you plan to free-motion quilt. Choose a design that will complement the top, keeping in mind the size limitations. Also choose a marking method that will not be permanent. Again, test the marker for ease of removal before marking the entire top.

14. Now that the top is completed, we're ready to put the layers together and quilt! This is when you piece the backing if that is what you've chosen to do. You can create a simple design as you piece, or simply stitch together strips – either wide or narrow. Now is also a good time to sign your work. Embroider by hand or machine, or use

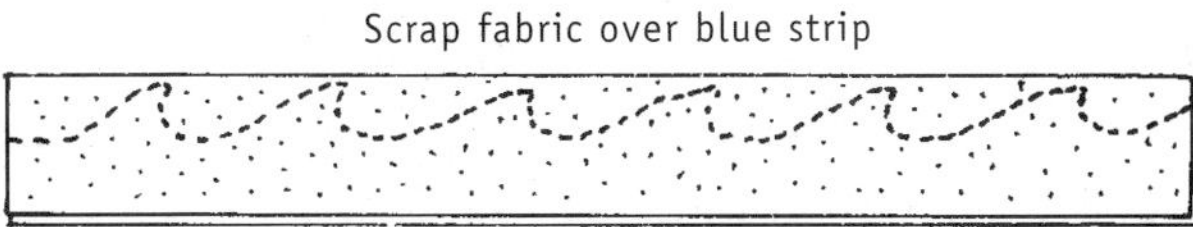

FIGURE 16

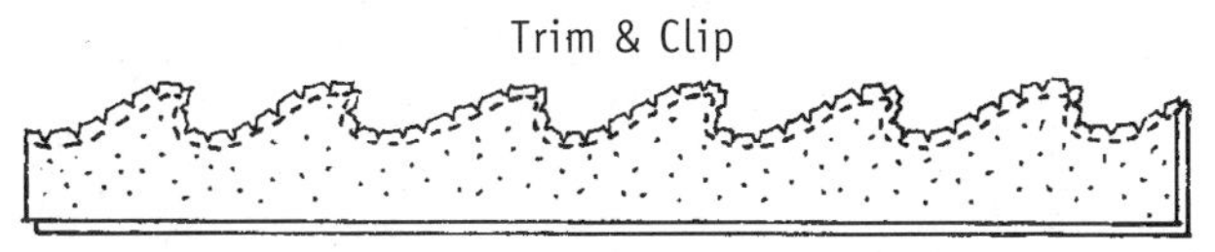

FIGURE 17

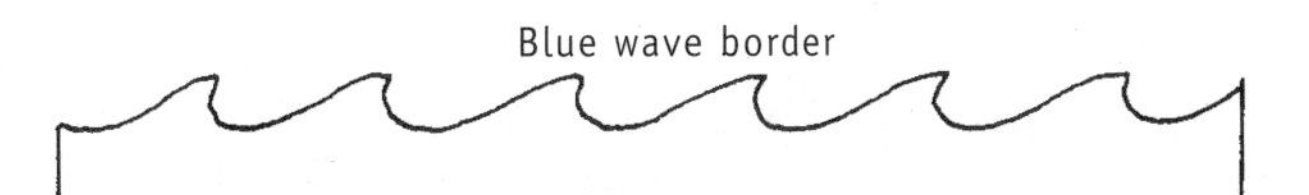

FIGURE 18

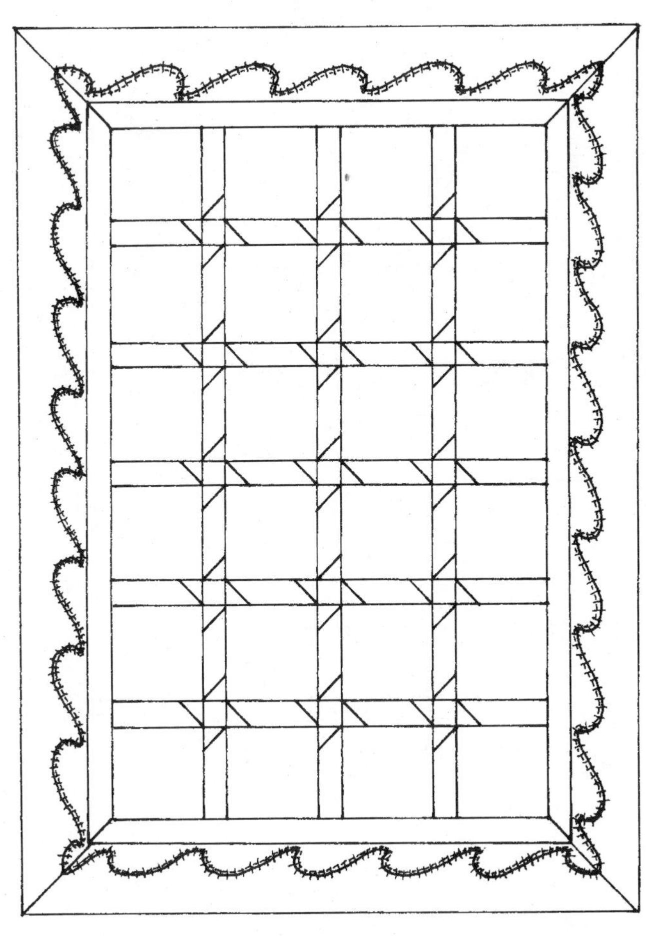
FIGURE 19

Signed on back of quilt

FIGURE 20

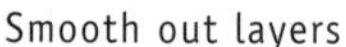

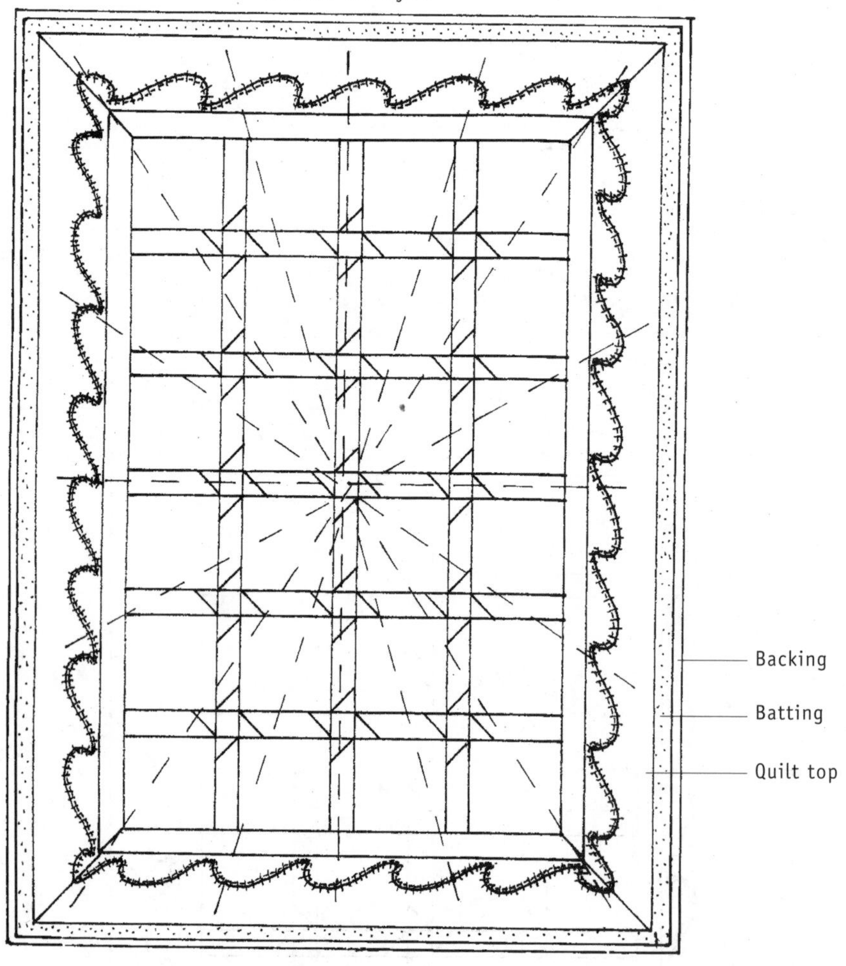

Needle baste quilt as shown (or use safety pins)

FIGURE 21

indelible ink to sign the piece, including your name, then date (month and year is fine), and the city and state where you live. This is usually done on the back of the quilt. You may also include the name of the recipient if you wish. Signing your work at this time ensures that it will be "quilted in", and thus more difficult to remove in case of theft *(fig. 20)*.

15. Place the backing fabric wrong side up on a large flat surface, and smooth it out. Lay the batting on top of the backing, and make sure both layers are smooth. Any wrinkles in the backing must be smoothed out before basting, or they may end up as tucks when the piece is quilted.

16. Place the quilt top on the backing/batting layers, and center it so that there is batting and backing exposed on all sides of the top. The easiest way to baste the layers together for quilting is to use 1" safety pins, placed so as not to interfere with the quilting lines. It takes a lot of pins, but they are necessary to prevent the layers from shifting as you manipulate the quilt again and again to do the quilting. If you prefer, you can baste the layers with needle and thread (taking long stitches) or use a quilt tack gun. Which ever method you choose, begin the basting in the center, and stitch out to 3:00 position, then to the 12:00 position, 9:00 and so on. Then place more basting lines between the first lines, always working from the center out. Don't skimp here – it's very important to have enough basting in place so that the layers cannot shift *(fig. 21)*.

17. After the basting is complete, begin quilting – again working from the center outward. Free-motion quilting was used 1/4" inside of the blue stars. A quarter inch foot was used to quilt around the inside of each embroidered square and the inside of the pink border. Free-motion quilting was used along the blue border, echoing the shape of the waves *(fig. 22)*.

18. After all quilting is complete, trim the backing and batting even with the edges of the top.

19. Using the 2-1/2" blue fabric for the binding, place two strips right sides together. Stitch the layers together with a diagonal seam *(fig. 23)*.

20. Trim the excess fabric 1/4" beyond the stitched seam. Press the seam open or to one side.

21. Continue stitching the strips together until you have one long continuous strip of binding.

22. Fold the strip lengthwise, wrong sides together and press.

23. Draw miter lines along each corner of the quilt. Beginning along one long edge of the quilt, pin the raw edges of the quilt binding to the edges of the right side of the quilt top.

24. Stitch using a 3/8" seam allowance, starting about 1" from the end of the strip. Stop stitching at the miter line and backstitch.

25. Fold a 3/4" pleat in the binding at the corner and begin stitching again along the second side of the binding, starting at the miter line *(fig. 24)*.

26. Continue stitching, using this same technique at each corner. Stitch through all layers. Stop stitching about 2" from the beginning. Overlap the beginning and the end 1/2" and trim away any excess. Fold one edge of the binding to the inside 1/4". Place the straight end into the folded end and continue stitching *(fig. 25)*.

27. Fold the binding over the edges of the quilt, enclosing the seam allowance. The folded edge of the binding should be placed just past the seam line. At the corner, the binding will be folded into a miter. Stitch the binding in place by machine using a straight stitch or whipstitch in place by hand *(fig. 26)*.

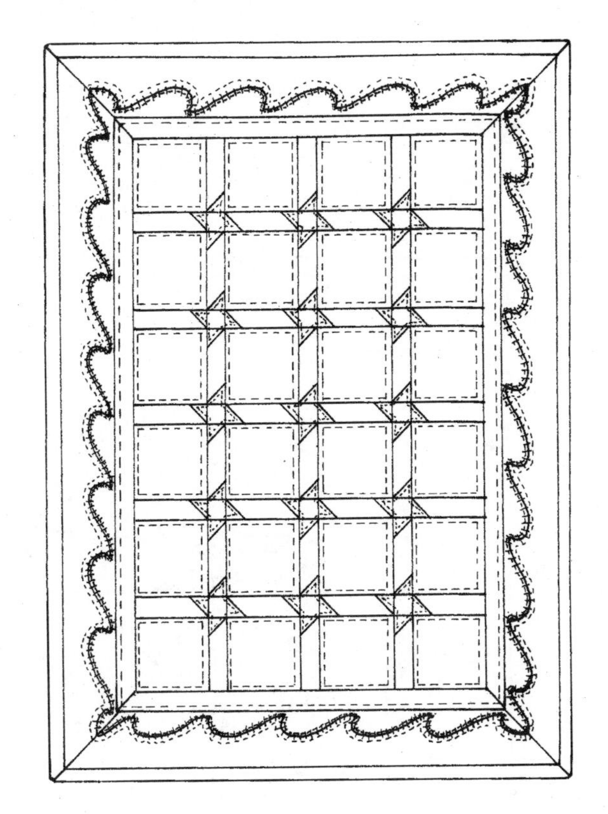

FIGURE 22

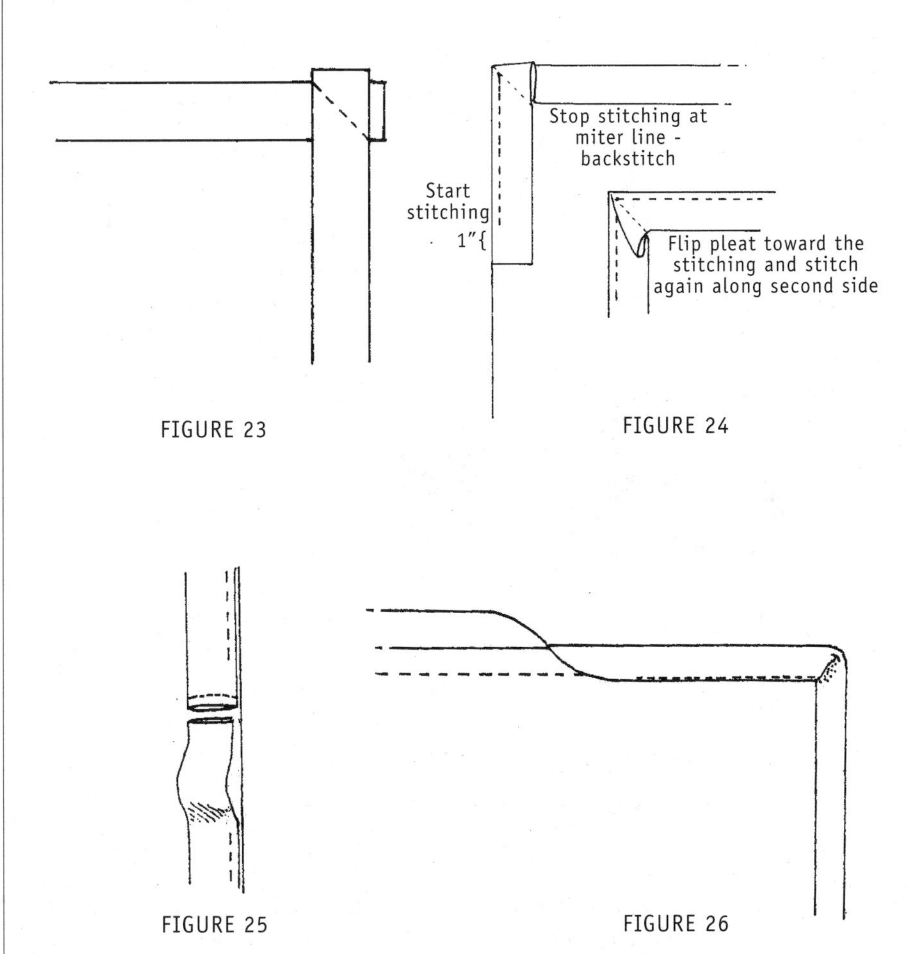

FIGURE 23

FIGURE 24

FIGURE 25

FIGURE 26

Noah's Ark Wall Hanging

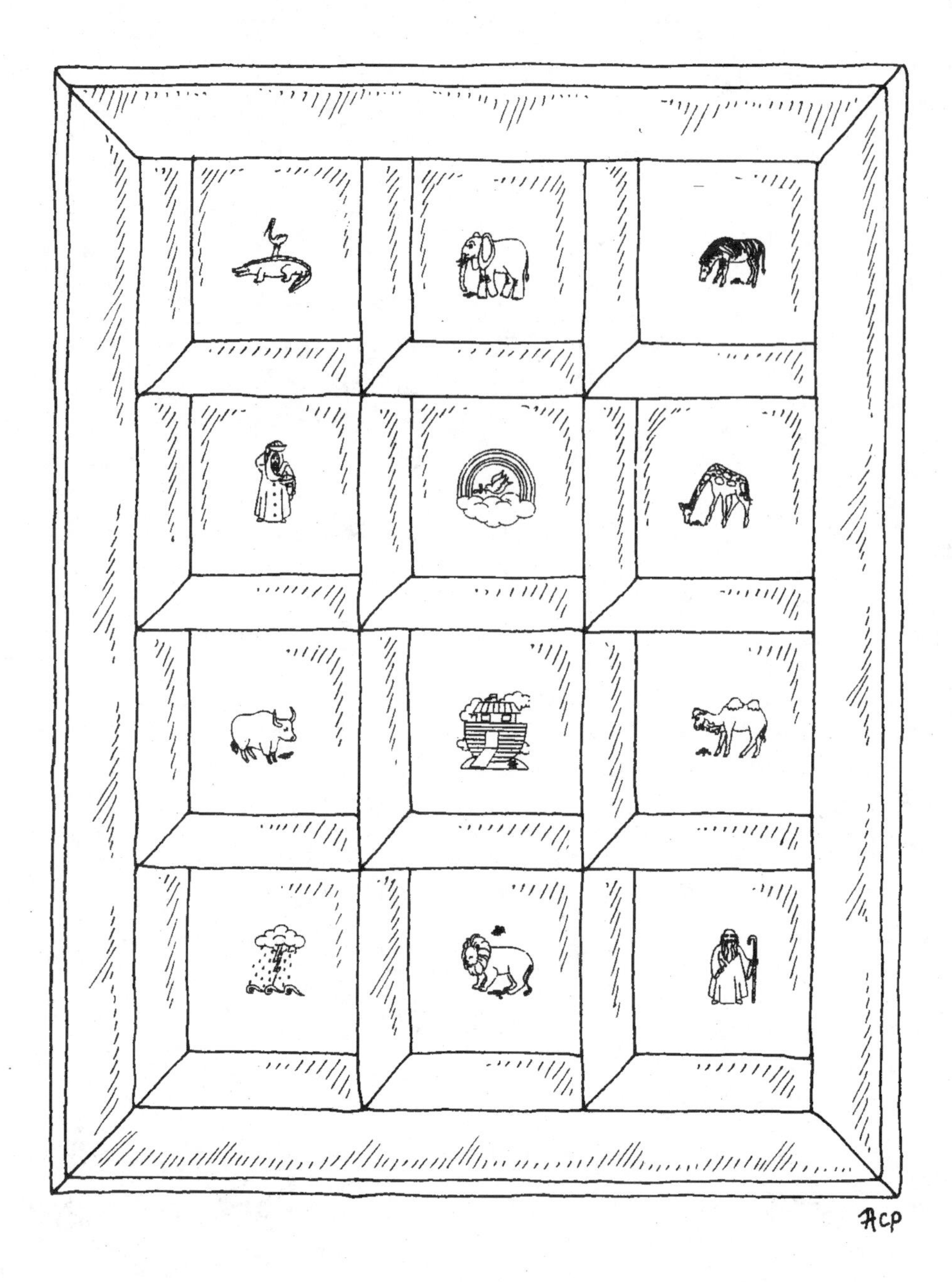

Using twelve of the designs from Martha Pullen's Noah's Ark embroidery CD, this wallhanging is a wonderment of color and design. A bright red printed fabric is used for the outside border. Printed on this fabric are animals of every bright color including red, orange, blue, yellow, black, white, green and turquoise. The binding is made of the same red print fabric. There are twelve white squares, each with a different design embroidered on it. The sashings around the white squares are purple, yellow, green and dusty blue. The finished wallhanging measures 24 by 31 inches.

The backing of the wallhanging is made from the red fabric with the animals scattered all over. This Noah's Ark embroidery CD was used for Joanna's nursery for both her little girl and little boy. It is the perfect nursery embroidery card, because Noah's Ark is great for a baby but can be used in a child's room as well. This wallhanging is a great learning tool for little ones interested in naming the animals. Sunday School teachers would love to have this wallhanging on the wall of their classroom to tell the story of Noah and the Ark.

SUPPLIES

- 1/2 yard of white fabric for embroidered squares
- 1/8 yard of six different colored solids for inner sashing
- 1-1/4 yard printed fabric for outer sashing, backing and binding
- Optional: 1/8 yard printed fabric for rod pocket
- Batting 26" by 33"
- Martha Pullen's Noah's Ark Embroidery Designs
- Stabilizer
- Decorative thread for embroideries
- Machine embroidery thread
- Invisible thread
- Safety pins or quilt tacks and quilt tack gun
- Optional: Rod for hanging

Cutting

- Cut four strips 2" by 8" from each of the six solid fabric pieces for the inner sashings
- Cut twelve 7" squares from white fabric to be embroidered
- Cut one backing piece 26" by 33" from printed fabric
- Cut two pieces 2-3/4" by 26" from the printed fabric for the outer sashing - top and bottom
- Cut two pieces 2-3/4" by 33" from the printed fabric for the outer sashing – sides
- Cut three binding strips 2-1/2"wide by 45" from the printed fabric Remove the selvages from both ends of each strip
- Optional: Cut one strip 4-1/2" by 23-1/2" from the printed fabric (rod casing)

Embellishing and Creating the Quilt Top

1. Stabilize, hoop and embroider the center of each square with the desired Noah's Ark embroidery design. Remove the stabilizer and press.

2. Center the designs and trim each block to 5-1/2" square *(fig. 1)*.

3. Lay out the blocks in the desired order on a flat surface (refer to the finished drawing).

4. Draw a line 1/4" from the left edge and bottom edge of each block. Place a dot where the two lines intersect *(fig. 2)*. The sashing strips will be added to the left edge and bottom edge of each block. Each block will require two sashing strips that are the same color. Arrange the placement of each sashing pair.

5. Place one sashing strip to the left side of the block. The upper edge of the strip should be even with the block and the lower edge of the strip should extend beyond the block. Stitch the strip to the block, beginning the stitching at the upper corner and stopping at the lower corner on the marked dot *(fig. 3)*. Backstitch to secure the seam.

6. Press along the seam line. Open the sashing/block and press again with the seam allowance toward the sashing.

7. Place the other sashing strip to the lower edge of the block with the right edges even and the sashing strip extending beyond the left side of the block. Begin stitching at the right lower edge and stitch to the marked dot at the left lower edge *(fig. 4)*. Backstitch to secure the seam. The end of this seam should meet the end of the first seam.

8. Press the seam flat and then toward the sashing.

9. Place the block with two extended sashing strips on the ironing surface, right side up. The side sashing strip should be flat with the bottom sashing strip on top.

10. Fold the top sashing strip under

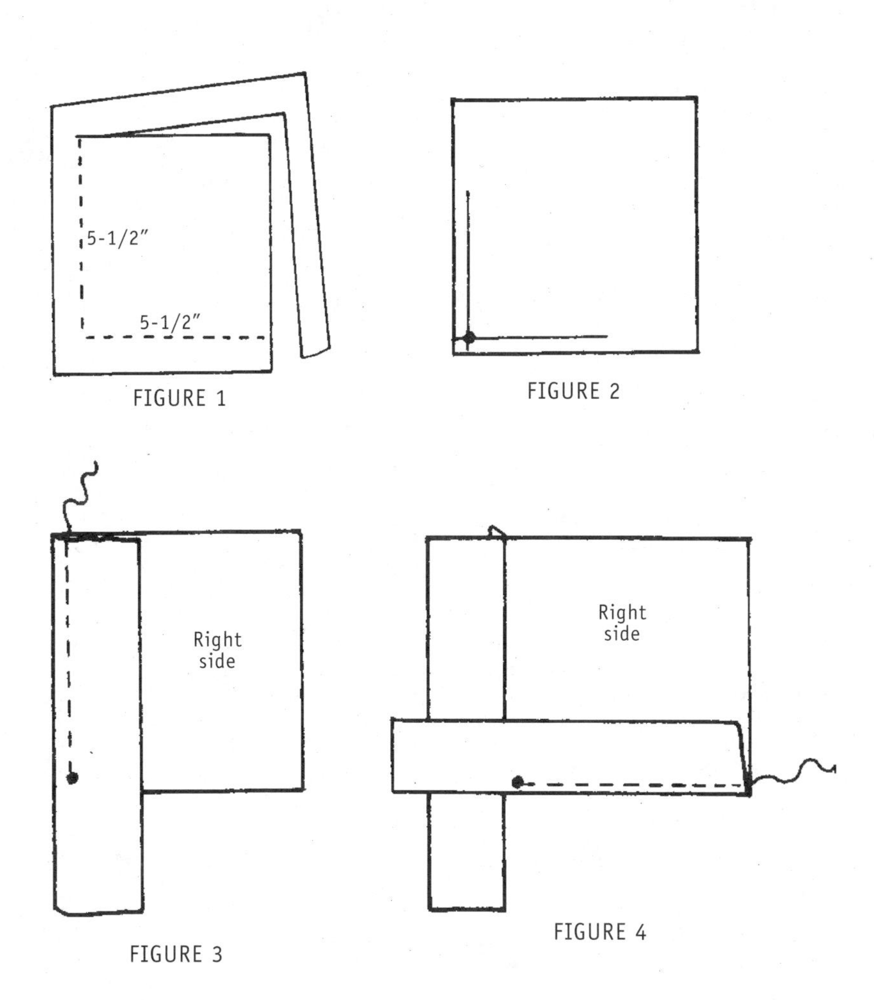

FIGURE 1

FIGURE 2

FIGURE 3

FIGURE 4

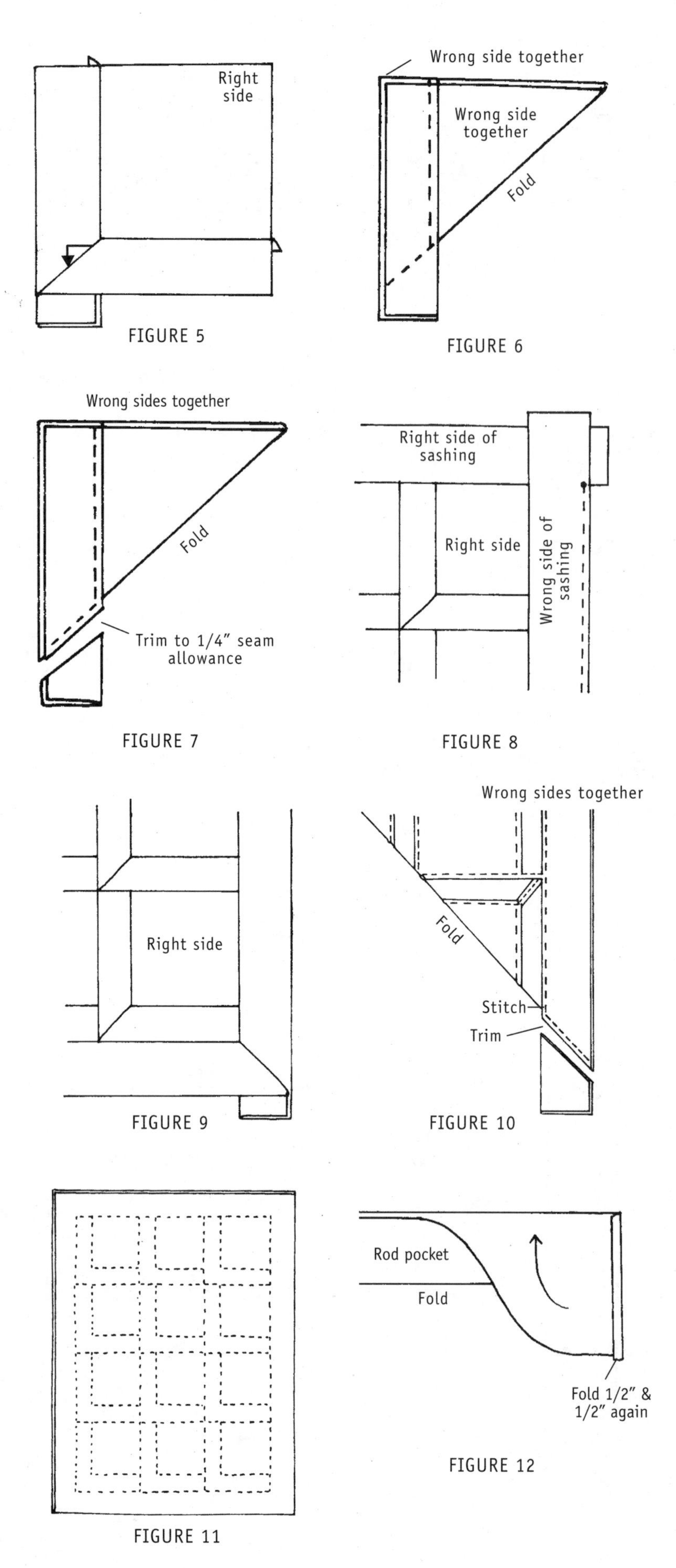

until there is a diagonal fold beginning at the seam line and extending in a diagonal line to the outer edges of the sashing strips. The short ends of the sashing strips should meet. Press the fold to mark the crease *(fig. 5)*.

11. Lift off the ironing surface and match the ends and raw edges of the two sashing strips right sides together. Pin along the diagonal fold.

12. Stitch on the fold line, beginning where the seam lines meet, stitching toward the outer edges *(fig. 6)*. When stitching is complete, finger press the seams open and lay on a flat surface right side up. The diagonal seam should begin exactly where the two previous seams ended. If they do not and a tuck is formed, remove the stitching until it is smooth and flat. Restitch. Trim the seam to 1/4" *(fig. 7)* and press open.

13. Repeat for all block and sashing pieces.

14. The quilt top is stitched together in four horizontal rows consisting of three blocks in each row. Stitch blocks 1, 2, and 3 together for row 1. Stitch blocks 4, 5, and 6 together for row 2. Stitch blocks 7, 8, and 9 together for row 3. Stitch blocks 10, 11, and 12 together for row 4.

15. Stitch row 1 to row 2, row 2 to row 3 and row 3 to row 4, matching the sashing seams. This completes the inner quilt top (refer to finished drawing).

16. Place a line 1/4" on both sides of each corner of the inner quilt top. Place a dot where the two lines intersect (*refer to fig. 2)*.

17. Center and stitch the top and bottom sashing strip from corner dot to corner dot. Backstitch to secure the seam.

18. Press along the seam line. Open the sashing/inner quilt top and press again with the seam allowance toward the sashing.

19. Center and stitch the side sashing strip from corner dot to corner dot *(fig. 8)*. Backstitch to secure the seam.

20. Press along the seam line. Open the sashing/inner quilt top and press again with the seam allowance toward the sashing.

21. Place the quilt top on an ironing surface, right side up. Fold the top sashing strip under until there is a diagonal fold beginning at the seam line and extending in a diagonal line toward the outer edges of the sashing strips. Press the fold to mark the crease *(fig. 9)*.

22. Lift off the ironing surface and match the raw edges of the two sashing strips right sides together. Pin along the diagonal fold.

23. Stitch on the fold line, beginning where the seam lines meet, stitching toward the outer edges *(fig. 10)*. When stitching is complete, finger press the seams open and lay on a flat surface right side up. If a tuck is formed, remove the stitching until it is smooth and flat. Restitch.

24. Trim the seam to 1/4" *(fig. 10)* and press open.

Constructing the Quilt

1. Place the backing onto a table top with the wrong side up.

2. Center the batting onto the backing.

3. Center the quilt top onto the batting. The backing and batting should be slightly larger than the quilt top.

4. Pin the layers together with safety pins approximately 2" to 3" apart. Pin the layers together along the raw edges of the quilt top. A quilt tack gun, hand basting or machine basting can be used to hold the layers together.

5. Trim away the excess batting and backing even with the edge of the quilt top, being very careful not to cut away any of the quilt top.

Quilting

NOTE: Machine embroidery thread to match the backing is used in the bobbin for all quilting. Machine embroidery thread to match the part of the quilt top being stitched is used in the needle. Invisible thread can be used in the needle when "stitching in the ditch".

Stitch in the ditch along the top and bottom of each horizontal row and on each side of the vertical rows *(fig. 11)*. This can be stitched free-motion or stitched using a walking foot.

Optional: Adding A Rod Pocket For Hanging

1. Fold each end of the strip for the rod pocket 1/2" and 1/2" again and press. Fold the strip in half lengthwise and press *(fig. 12)*.

2. Pin in place along the top edge of the back of the quilt, matching the raw edges.

Binding

1. Using the 2-1/2" printed fabric for the binding, place two strips right sides together and stitch the layers together with a diagonal seam *(fig. 13)*.

2. Trim the excess fabric 1/4" beyond the stitched seam. Press the seam open or to one side.

3. Continue stitching the strips together until you have one long continuous strip of binding.

4. Fold the strip lengthwise, wrong sides together and press.

5. Draw miter lines along each corner of the quilt. Beginning along one long edge of the quilt, pin the raw edges of the quilt binding to the edges of the right side of the quilt top.

6. Stitch using a 3/8" seam allowance, starting about 1" from the end of the strip. Stop stitching at the miter line and backstitch.

7. Fold a 3/4" pleat in the binding at the corner and begin stitching again along the second side of the binding, starting at the miter line *(fig. 14)*.

8. Continue stitching, using this same technique at each corner. Stitch through all layers (including the rod casing layers along the top of the quilt). Stop stitching about 2" from the beginning. Overlap the beginning and the end 1/2" and trim away any excess. Fold one edge of the binding to the inside 1/4". Place the straight end into the folded end and continue stitching *(fig. 15)*.

9. Fold the binding over the edges of the quilt, enclosing the seam allowance. The folded edge of the binding should be placed just past the seam line. At the corner, the binding will be folded into a miter. Stitch the binding in place by machine using a straight stitch or whipstitch in place by hand *(fig. 16)*.

Finishing the Rod Pocket

1. Press the rod pocket flat to the back of the quilt.

2. Hand whip the lower fold and the inside of the opening to the quilt back *(fig. 17)*.

3. Insert the rod through the casing for hanging.

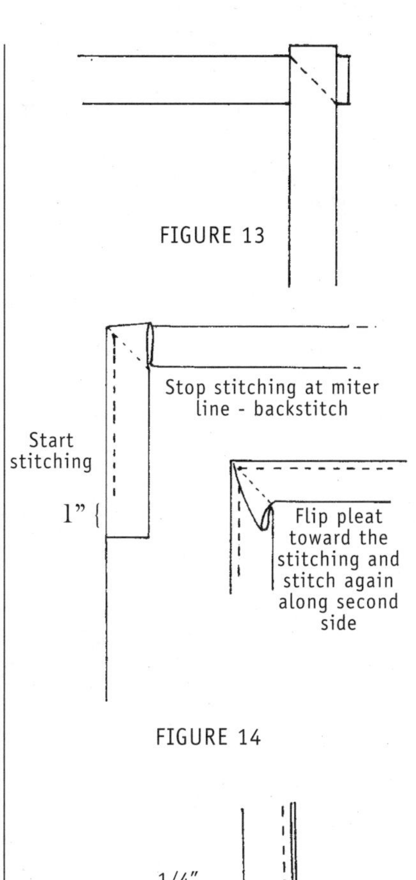

FIGURE 14

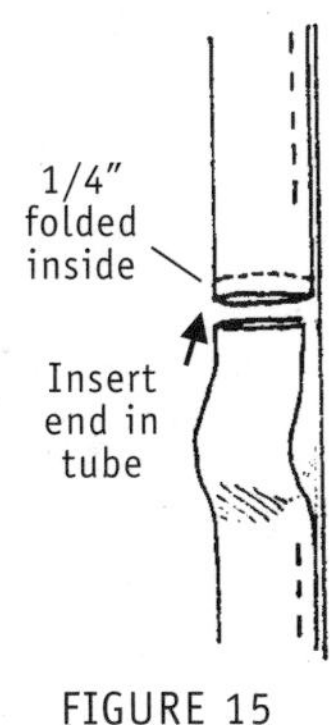

FIGURE 15

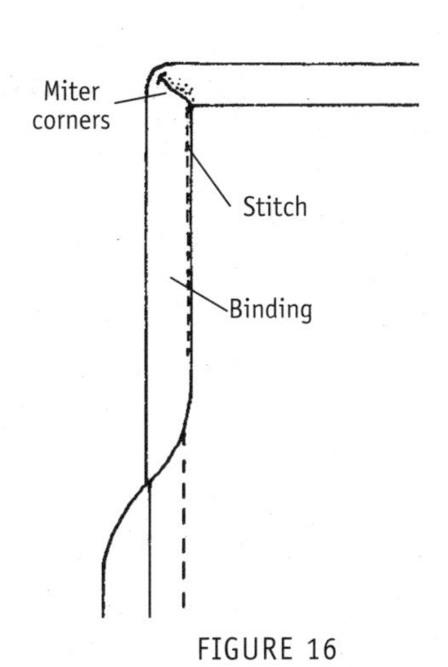

FIGURE 16

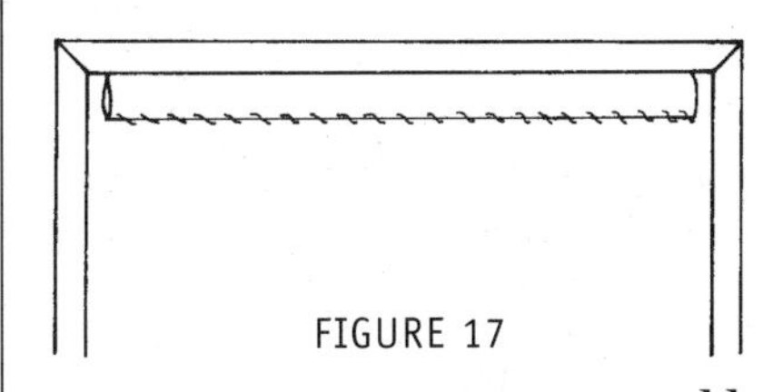

FIGURE 17

"Welcome to Our Family" Heart Quilt

Welcoming a new baby to the extended family is always joyful! When Gail Settle had a new great-niece coming, she made this precious heart "family tree" quilt. The base fabric is white with white stars. Machine Madeira appliquéd hearts are found all over the quilt using different 1930's fabrics, all in children's prints. On each heart is machine embroidered a family member's name such as Meme, Uncle Robert, Aunt Jeannette, Aunt Erica and Uncle Roger, Nana and Papa, and Mommy and Daddy and Maddie. Of course the baby's name, Allyson, is embroidered in a pink heart in the very middle of the quilt. The quilting is done around each heart with straight stitching in heart shapes. The double row of sashing is done in yellow and white gingham fabric; the inside sashing is little squares of the heart fabrics pieced together. The binding is done in the yellow gingham fabric with piping in one of the pink fabrics. A pretty baby print with little handprints and hearts is used for the backing of the quilt. On the back of the quilt is another heart made of the yellow sashing fabric which says, "So many people love you, Some near-some far away, We're sending you our happy thoughts, We wish you laughter every day." "This quilt celebrates the birth of Allyson Mae Dube to Michael and Adrienne Dube on November 16, 2000." It then gives the place of the birth and that it was made by Great-Aunt Gail Settle, Huntsville, Alabama.

Supplies

- 2 yards of cotton fabric for the quilt top (white)
- 2 yards of cotton fabric for the back of the quilt (baby print)
- 1-3/4 yards of cotton for the small sashing strips, the binding and the strip-pieced border **(color 5)** (yellow micro check print)
- 1/4 yard each of a variety of colors of reproduction 30's fabrics. This quilt used 13 different pastel prints. Three of these prints (**colors 1, 2 and 3** for the strip-pieced border) need to be in the same color family as the binding fabric (yellow)
- 1/2 yard of one color of reproduction 30's fabrics. This color will be for the piping and also used for one or more hearts and will be **color 4** for the strip-pieced border (the quilt illustrated uses a pink mini stripe).
- Threads for names and blanket stitching (or fabric marking pens if you wish to write names instead of embroidering)
- Machine Quilting Thread (Mettler silk finish, 50 wt. 3 ply) for construction stitching and in the bobbin while quilting
- Soft invisible thread for quilting
- 1 cotton crib-size batting - remove from package to de-wrinkle
- 1/2 yard very lightweight fusible tricot interfacing (mark the fusible side)
- Butcher or tracing paper - 36" by 63" (or size of quilt top)
- Colored paper similar to the colors of the fabrics you have chosen for the hearts (anything will do - old envelopes - computer paper - this is to save fabric while designing the quilt)
- Quilt tack gun or safety pins for basting the quilt
- Wash-out marking pen
- Teflon-coated pressing sheet
- Mini iron (optional)
- Walking foot (optional)
- Heart Template

NOTE: None of the fabric for the quilt shown was pre-washed, in order to increase shrinkage of the finished quilt to give it an antique look. Expect this quilt to shrink approximately 1/8" per inch lengthwise and crosswise when washing. The yardages listed below are sufficient to make a quilt for a standard baby bed. Due to variations in shrinkage of the cotton fabrics and batting we can not list a finished size. If you use bright colors instead of pastels, check for colorfastness before using.

Read complete instructions before beginning the quilt.

Designing

Decide how many relatives' names will be on the quilt. This will determine how many hearts you will need. The smallest hearts were used for children who lived at home and these were overlapped onto the parents' larger heart. The honoree's name was placed on the largest heart in the center of the quilt with her parents and sister centered above. The maternal relatives are on the left side of the quilt, and paternal relatives on the right side. There are more hearts on the right than the left. The grandparents are placed between the main heart and the parents' heart, toward each side. Closer relatives were placed toward the top (close to the baby's heart and head) and the more distant relatives nearer the foot. Feel free to choose your own placement and heart sizes. Cut several hearts of each size from each color of paper. Place the butcher or tracing paper on your cutting table. Draw off the size of the mattress top. Crib mattresses are usually 28" x 52". Arrange the hearts in a way that pleases you. Embroider a test of some of the longer names, since this may affect the size of this person's fabric heart. Change the sizes and colors as you wish. Tape the hearts to the paper when you are happy with the placement. This is your master plan template. Once you are sure the hearts are in the position you want them to be, quilting lines can be added to this master plan template, echoing out from each heart approximately 1". Arched lines of quilting can be added to "connect" the echoes of each heart where needed *(fig. 1)*.

FIGURE 1

Cutting

Remove all selvages from the fabric before cutting the pieces. Label the groups of pieces and lay aside until needed.

1. From the white cotton fabric cut a panel 31" by 59" and three 4-1/4" by 72" sashing strips.

2. From color 5 (yellow micro check) cut

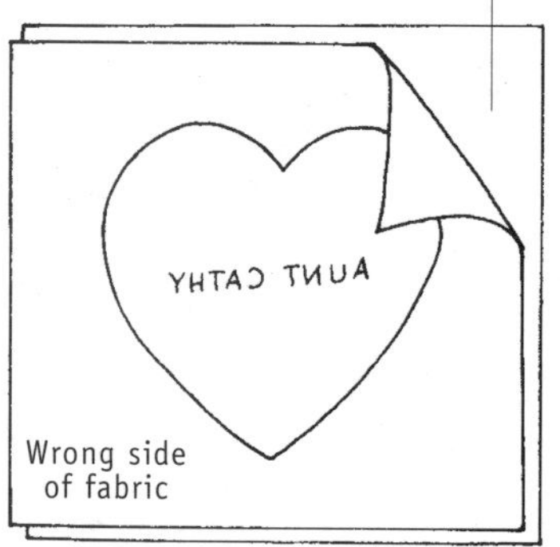

FIGURE 2

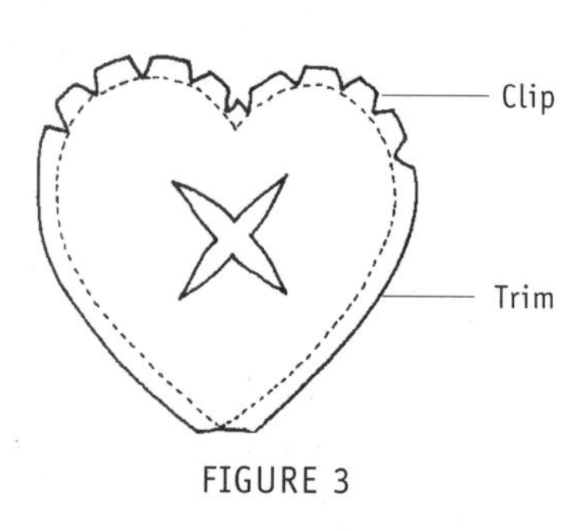

FIGURE 3

FIGURE 4

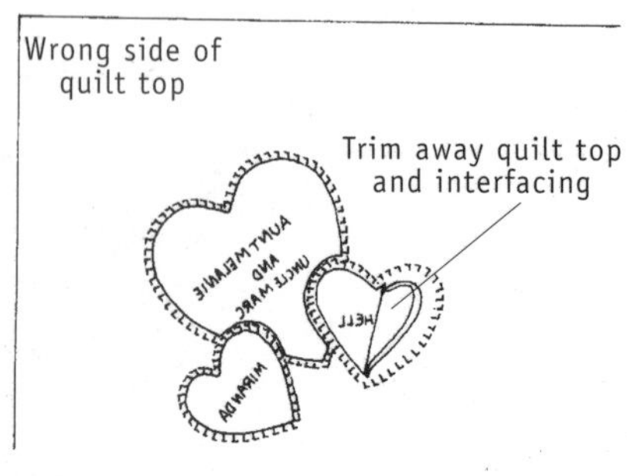

FIGURE 5

four 6" by 45" binding strips, one 3" by 45" facing strip, eight vertical strips 1-1/2" by 9" for the strip pieced border and six 1-1/2" by 30"+/- for the sashing strips.

3. From colors 1, 2 and 3 of the print fabrics cut eight vertical strips 1-1/2" by 9" (24 strips total). Lay the remaining fabric aside with the other prints for the hearts.

NOTE: Other prints will be used for the hearts only.

4. From color 4 of the mini stripe cut five strips 1" by the width of the fabric for the "piping" and eight 1-1/2" by 9" strips for the strip pieced border. Lay the remaining fabric aside with the other prints for the hearts.

Embroidering the Names

1. Trace the various sized hearts onto the wrong side of the remaining print fabrics, grouping coordinating colors together by families. Choose a thread color that will show up on each fabric.

2. Stabilize, hoop and embroider the names on all the hearts in all the sizes and colors chosen.

NOTE: The hearts which overlap will need to be drawn separately, then overlapped when fused to the quilt.

Constructing the Hearts

1. Cut a square of fusible interfacing just larger than each drawn heart *(fig. 2)*.

2. Pin the fusible side of the interfacing square against the right side of the drawn heart on the printed fabric; do not iron. (When you turn the heart right side out, the fusible side will be fused to the quilt top and will keep your heart appliqué in place.)

3. Stitch along the drawn line using a stitch length of 1.5. This small stitch length makes the curves much smoother when they are turned. Trim the heart approximately 1/4" outside the stitching line, clipping the curves and points *(fig. 3)*.

4. Cut an X in the interfacing *(fig. 3)* and turn the heart right side out *(fig. 4)*. Push out the points and curves and finger press the edges.

5. Repeat with the remaining hearts.

6. Lightly press the outer edge using a Teflon coated pressing sheet on your ironing board. A mini iron works great for this.

Placing the Hearts on the Quilt Top

1. Iron the quilt top fabric. Mark the center and the mattress top edges. Pin the hearts as you arranged them on your master plan. Check to make sure that you are still happy with the arrangement.

2. Press the hearts to the quilt top when satisfied.

3. Stitch the hearts to the quilt top, using a blanket stitch and a contrasting thread color. Stitch the larger hearts with a larger size width and length, and the smaller hearts with a smaller size blanket stitch. Changing the stitch size on different sized hearts contributes to the antique look of this quilt, but it is a matter of personal preference (see finished drawing).

Trimming Behind Hearts (Optional)

1. Carefully trim the quilt top and interfacing from behind the hearts. Do not cut the blanket stitching. This reduces bulk in the finished quilt and makes it look a little softer *(fig. 5)*.

Strip-pieced border 1

(All seams 1/4")

1. Collect the 1-1/2" by 9" strips cut from the printed fabrics (colors 1, 2, 3, 4 and 5) (40 strips total).

2. Stitch colors 1 and 2 together along the 9" length (Unit 1).

3. Stitch colors 3, 4 and 5 together along the 9" length (Unit 2).

4. Stitch unit 1 and unit 2 together *(fig. 6)*.

5. Repeat steps 2 – 4 for the other 7 strips of each color.

6. Press seams open.

7. Cut crosswise into six 1-1/2" strips producing six strips with 5 different color squares in them *(fig. 7)*.

8. Stitch the strips together to make a strip the same length as the side of the quilt top (be sure to sew color 1 square to color 5 square so there is a color pattern to the strip) *(fig. 7)*. Repeat for the other side.

9. Stitch the strip to each side of the quilt, narrow raw edge even with the lower edge of the quilt top. The horizontal strip across the lower edge of the quilt top will need to measure 1-1/2" by the width of the quilt,

including the pieced strips just added. Stitch this strip along the lower edge, overlapping the side borders and matching the overlapping squares *(fig. 8)*. Press.

10. Place a line 1/4" on both sides of each bottom corner of the quilt top (on the pieced printed border). Place a dot where the two lines intersect *(fig. 8)*.

11. Stitch the six 1-1/2" by 30" strips (color 5) together at the short ends to make one continuous strip.

12. Measure the side of the quilt panel and cut two strips this measurement plus 6" from two of the 4-1/4" by 72" white strips, discarding the remaining length of the strips. Stitch the color 5 strip to one side of each 4-1/4" strip. Cut the ends even. This will create an outside sashing for each side of the quilt top *(fig. 9)*.

13. Stitch the 1-1/2" (color 5) strip to the remaining 4-1/4" white strip. The lengths will not come out equal. Cut away the excess white strip and discard. Press the strip well.

14. Beginning at the top edge of the quilt, stitch the strips from step 12 to each side of the quilt top placing the printed strips together. Stop stitching and back stitch at the dot marked in step 10. Note that there is excess sashing extending beyond the lower edge of the quilt on each side *(fig. 10)*. Press well.

15. Center and stitch the printed/white strip to the bottom edge of the quilt top, attaching the printed strip to the pieced, printed border of the quilt top. Begin and end at each corner dot and backstitch to secure. This will create a sashing along the bottom edge of the quilt top. Note that there is excess sashing extending on each side of the quilt top *(fig. 11)*. Press well

16. Place the quilt top on an ironing surface, right side up. At one lower corner of the quilt top, fold the sashing strip which is on top under until there is a diagonal fold beginning at the dot and extending in a diagonal line toward the outer edges of the sashing strips. The bottom sashing strip will lay directly on top of the side sashing strip right sides together. Press the fold to mark the crease *(fig. 12)*.

17. Lift off the ironing surface and pin along the diagonal fold.

18. On the wrong side of the quilt, stitch on the fold line, beginning where the seam lines meet, stitching toward the outer edges *(fig. 13)*. When stitching is complete, finger press the seams open and lay on a flat surface right side up. If a tuck is formed, remove the stitching until it is smooth and flat. Restitch.

19. Trim the seam to 1/4" *(fig. 13)* and press open.

20. Repeat steps 16-19 for the other lower corner of the quilt top.

Marking

The quilt is echo quilted approximately 1" apart. The hearts are not arranged symmetrically, so you will have to space the quilting more than 1" apart in some areas,

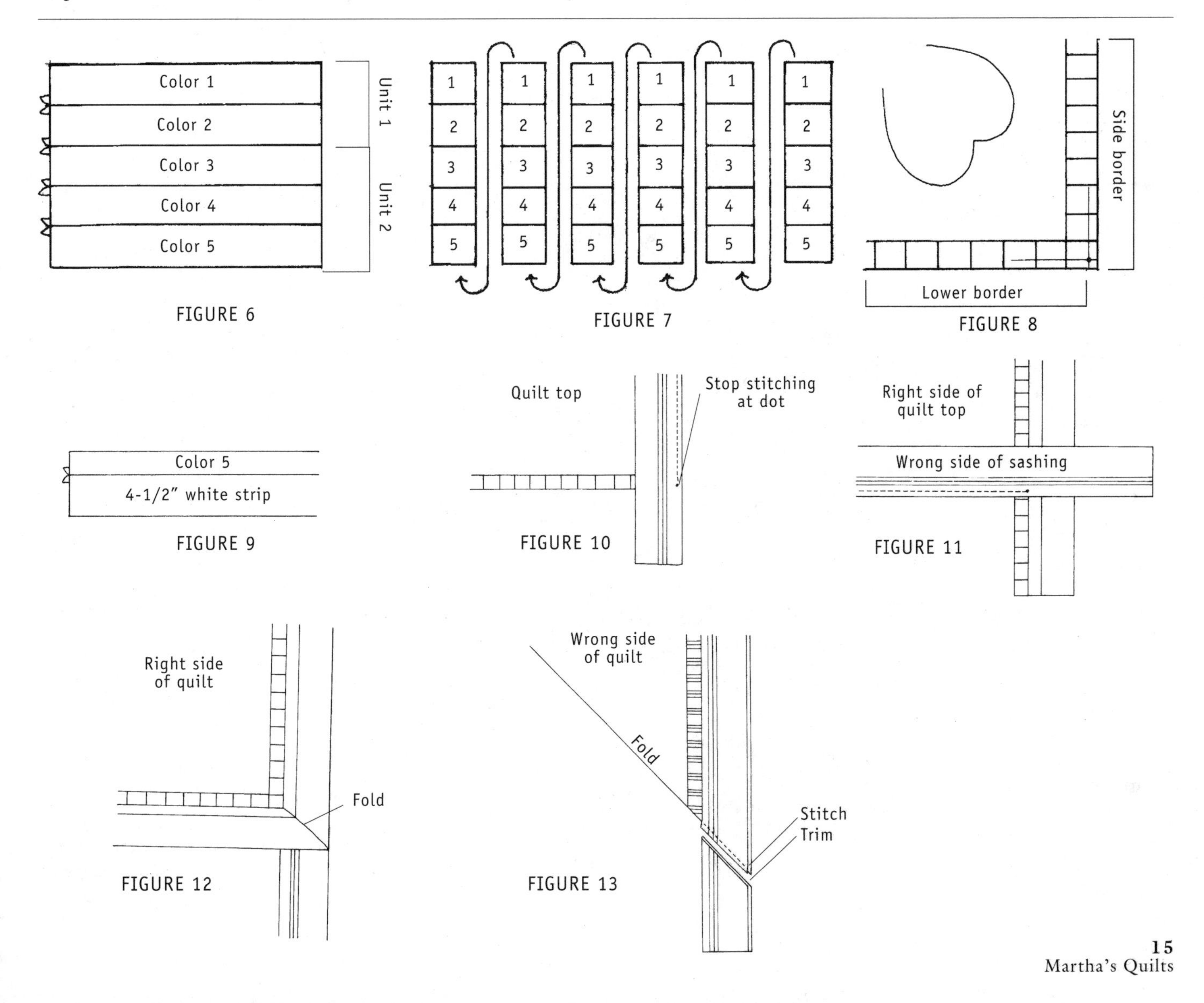

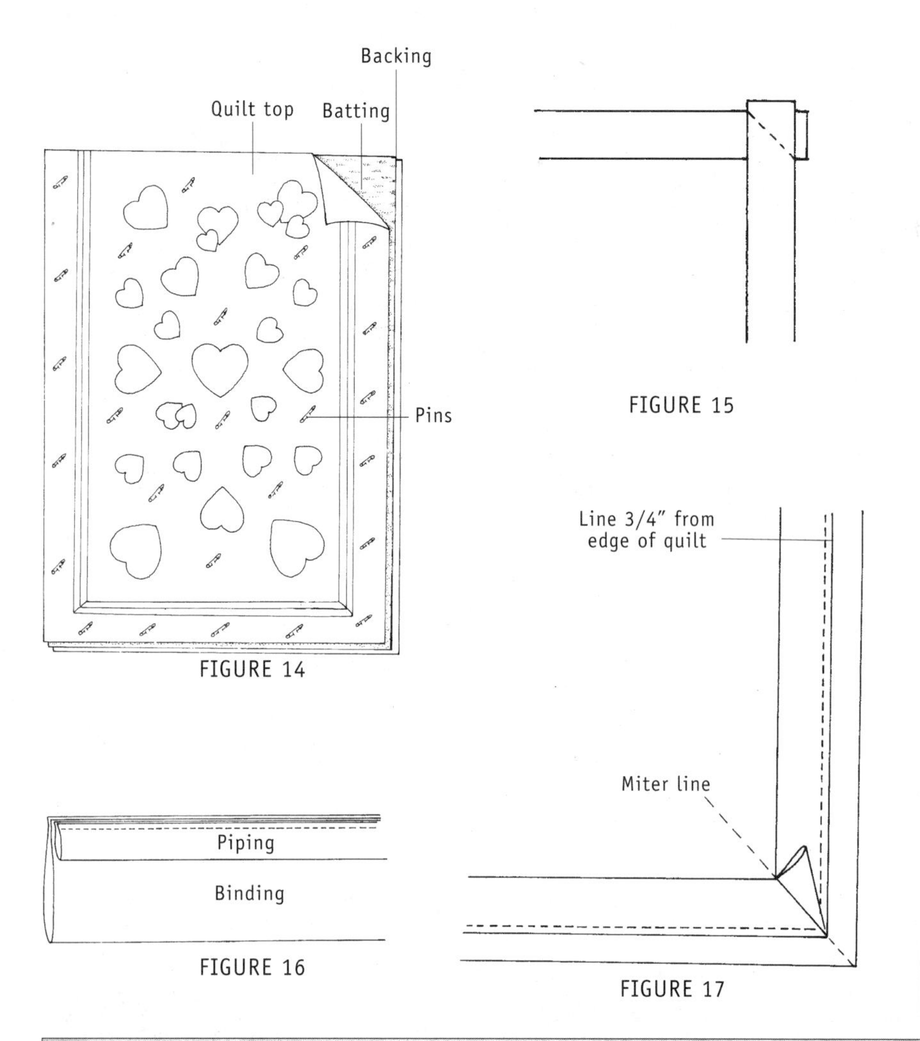

FIGURE 14

FIGURE 15

FIGURE 16

FIGURE 17

and less in others. This adds to the charm of the quilt. Place the ironed quilt top over the master plan template. Using a light box or a lamp under a glass table, trace the quilting design on the quilt top using a blue pen or your favorite method of quilt marking. The quilt is stitched in the ditch at the pieced border, the solid border and quilted in rows spaced 1" apart to the outer edges.

Basting

1. Iron the backing fabric smooth. Place it wrong side up on the cutting table.

2. Place the batting smoothly on top of it and smooth it out.

3. Place the quilt top right side up on top of the batting.

4. Baste with the basting gun, safety pins or your favorite method of quilt basting *(fig. 14)*.

Quilting

Thread the sewing machine with invisible thread on the top and silk finish in the bobbin. It is easier to stitch the design free motion, but it could be stitched with the feed dogs up. The straight line quilting at the sides and foot is stitched with the feed dogs up, using a walking foot if available. Start in the center and work your way to the outside to minimize the chance of tucks in the back. When you are finished quilting, check to make sure the quilt edges are straight and even, trimming if necessary.

Bindings, facing and inner contrast strip "piping"

1. Remove the selvages and stitch the four 6" binding strips (color 5) together along the short ends with a diagonal seam to reduce seam bulk *(fig. 15)*. Trim and press the seams open. Fold the continuous strip lengthwise wrong sides together and press well.

2. Remove the selvages and stitch the "piping" strips (color 4) together with diagonal seams to create a continuous strip *(see fig. 15)*. Fold the "piping" strip in half lengthwise wrong sides together and press well.

3. Match the raw edges of the "piping" and the binding. Stitch all layers together with a 1/4" seam *(fig. 16)*. Continue stitching the strips together until you have one long continuous strip of binding with piping attached.

4. Measure and draw a line 3/4" from the outer raw edge of the quilt on the two sides and the bottom edge *(fig. 17)*. Draw miter lines at the two lower corners of the quilt.

5. Add three rows of quilting around three sides of the quilt, evenly spaced between the yellow micro check border and the drawn line (refer to the finished drawing).

6. To bind the sides and bottom of the quilt, place the binding right sides together to the quilt top with the raw edge of the binding even with the line drawn in step 4. The "piping" will be sandwiched between the binding and the quilt top.

7. Stitch the binding to the quilt using the previous stitching as a guide. Fold a pleat at each turn to miter the two corners *(fig. 17)*. Stop stitching at the miter line and backstitch.

8. Fold the binding over the edges of the quilt, enclosing the 3/4" portion of the quilt which extends past the seam. The folded edge of the binding should be placed just past the seam line on the back of the quilt. At the corner, the binding will be folded into a miter. Stitch the binding in place by machine using a straight stitch or whipstitch in place by hand *(fig. 18)*.

9. Fold the 2-1/2" by 44" strip for the facing in half lengthwise wrong sides together and press *(fig. 19)*.

10. Place the facing along the upper edge on the right side of the quilt, matching the raw edges and allowing the same amount to extend on each side of the quilt. Stitch with a 1/4" seam.

11. Trim the facing 1/2" longer than the edge of the outermost binding on each side of the quilt. Press the seam toward the quilt and fold in the 1/2" extension *(fig. 20)*.

12. Fold the facing completely to the back. None of the facing shows on the front. Pin in place *(fig. 21)*.

13. Hand stitch this facing to the back of the quilt along each end and the length of the facing *(fig. 21)*.

14. Don't forget to sign your quilt, and it is nice to make a label with the baby's full name and place of birth. This can be hand stitched to the back of the quilt *(fig. 22)*.

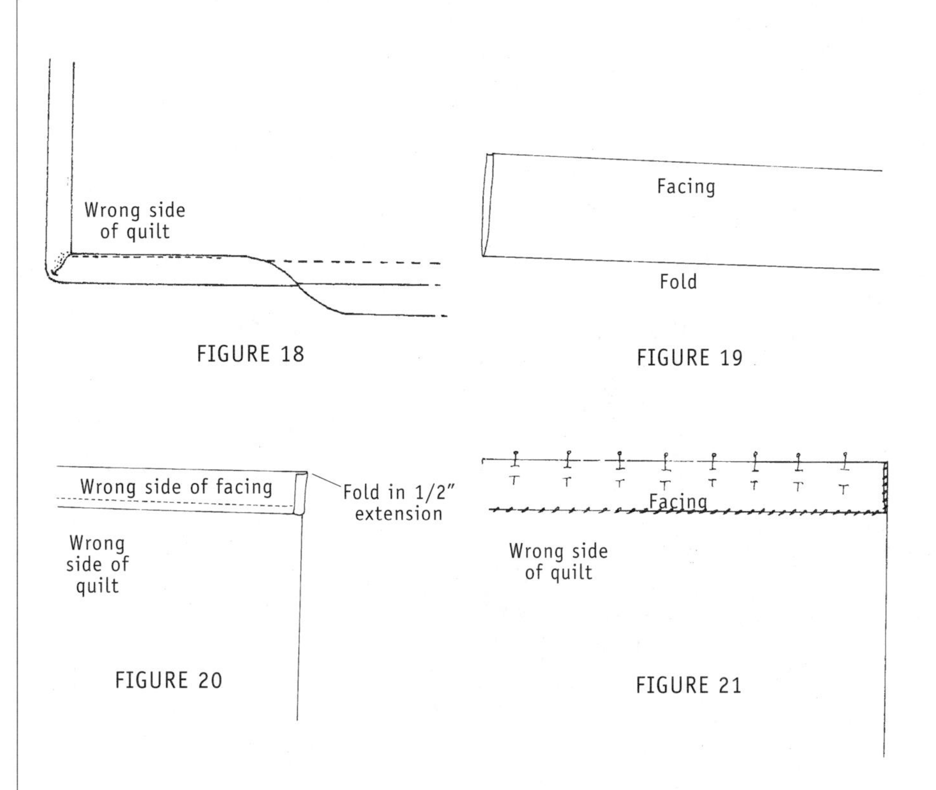

FIGURE 18

FIGURE 19

FIGURE 20

FIGURE 21

FIGURE 22

Mother Goose Quilt

What a precious gift to make for your special baby! Everybody's favorite nursery rhymes are appliquéd to the quilt squares and muted/brightly colored sashes attach the quilt. Using nearly every color in the rainbow, the nursery rhymes certainly do stand out on the white squares. In-between each sash which joins the sections there are four -color corner blocks. The name of the nursery rhymes are simply stitched in with zigzag stitching in beautiful colors. A delicious variety of fabrics was used for this appliqué from calico, to solid, to lamé and to other shiny fabrics. The colors of the sashing are red, gray, teal green, purple, flesh, tan, brown, gray, orange, forest green, rust, dusty pink, blue and yellow. All of these sashing colors are used in the various squares making this indeed a quilt of many colors.

Given next is a description of each block including the color families. Remember, your choices of fabrics and colors will be what makes your quilt personally yours. Have fun making this quilt for any baby you love whether he or she is a newborn, an unborn or a grown child who would love a baby quilt. Since my boys didn't have baby quilts made especially for them, I think the next four quilts that I make will be for them. Joanna's Grandmother Pullen had a baby quilt made for her before she was born, so she has her heirloom already.

Block #1
Itsy Bitsy Spider

The sun is yellow poplin, the water spout is gray poplin, and the flower is pink poplin. Yellow zigzags radiate out from the sun and a permanent pen is used to draw that happy mouth and eyebrows. Zigzag green stems are around the water spout. Shiny white material makes the puddle of water and the drips from the faucet are of metallic white thread. The spider is made of black ultrasuede. The letters are in dark dusty pink stitching.

Block #2
Hey Diddle Diddle

The cat is made of two fabrics; one which looks like brown cat fur and one which is plain tan. The fiddle is rusty poplin, the cow is brown poplin with a beige udder, the moon is yellow poplin and the dish is dark teal blue poplin. The spoon is silver lamé; the legs of the spoon and the dish are gray straight stitch. The Hey Diddle Diddle is in medium blue zigzag. The faces on the dish, the spoon, the moon, and the cow are painted on with a permanent pen. The eyes of the cat are satin stitch; the nose is painted on with a permanent pen. The strings of the fiddle are brown embroidery floss. The spots on the cow are beige zigzag.

Block #3
Three Blind Mice

The mice are made of gray poplin; their tails are gray thread zigzag. The face features and the glasses are painted on with a permanent pen. Their canes are zigzagged on with dark brown thread with a red tip on the end. The letters of "Three Blind Mice" are zigzagged in dark brown.

Block #4
There Was An Old Lady Who Lived In A Shoe

The shoe is chocolate brown poplin with three different brown and tan prints. The first print is for the toe and the door on the shoe; the second actually looks like a roof; and the third is on the inside open part of the upper part of the shoe. Blue "drapes" are inside the door and the window; a white shoestring is draped across the tie portion of the shoe; there is a gray smokestack at the top of the shoe. Black ultrasuede makes the sole of the shoe.

Block #5
Jack and Jill

The grass portion is medium green and the trail leading down from the well is medium brown poplin. The well is made of a print fabric which looks like rocks. The crank in the well is straight stitched in brown. Jill is wearing a calico print dress in beige, pink and green; her sleeves are pink poplin; her face is flesh poplin and her hair is zigzagged brown thread. Jack's shirt is blue poplin and his pants are brown poplin. His hair is appliquéd brown poplin. Both Jack and Jill have drawn-in faces and flesh tone poplin for their hands and faces. Both of their shoes are black ultrasuede. Cluny lace in beige is gathered at the bottom of Jill's dress. Her bucket is gray poplin and the water drops splashing out are of shiny white thread. A red flower with green leaves are satin stitched in the proper place. The words "Jack and Jill" are written in red zigzag.

Block #6
Hickory Dickory Dock

The cute clock is made of brown poplin with beige poplin for the inside of the bottom and the face of the clock. The pendulum is gold lamé and the stitching holding the pendulum is gold thread in a straight stitch. The face and the hands on the clock are drawn on in permanent pen. The mouse at the top is ultrasuede and the features are drawn on with permanent pen. The little knob on the clock is painted with a permanent pen also. The words beside the clock are "Hickory Dickory Dock The Mouse Ran Up The Clock".

Block #7
Peter Peter Pumpkin Eater

A bright orange pumpkin with a little yellow window and a stem of green form the cutest square. All fabrics on this square are poplin. A little gray mouse sits looking out the window. The vine and stem are green zigzag stitching. The words "Peter Peter Pumpkin Eater" are stitched in green.

Block #8
Humpty Dumpty

The absolute cutest fabric is used for the rock wall for Humpty. It is various shades of white to gray and actually looks like a rock wall. The top strip on the rock wall is gray poplin. Humpty Dumpty's body is the color of a yellowish egg. His suit is a checked fabric in black, teal green, purple and blue. The bow tie is teal green as is his hat. His eyes are zigzagged in white with the black permanent pen used to make the lashes and the other features of the eye. His mouthis in pink satin stitch. His socks are teal green poplin and his shoes areultra-suede. The words"Humpty Dumpty" are purple.

Block #9
Jack Be Nimble

Jack, in this interpretation of the nursery rhyme, is a gray poplin mouse. His "jump line" is a straight stretch stitch done on the machine, of course. The candle holder is silver lamé; the candle is red poplin and the flame is gold lamé. The words "Jack Be Nimble" are in zigzag.

Block #10
Mary And Her Lamb

The sun is yellow poplin and the rays running out from it are yellow zigzag. Mary's lamb is a gray print fabric which actually looks like lamb's wool. The eyes, mouth, and ear features are drawn using a permanent pen. Mary's dress is a green and orange print; her bonnet is orange poplin. Her legs and hands are flesh poplin and her shoes are brown poplin. Her staff is wide satin stitch in dark brown thread.

Block #11
Patty Cake, Patty Cake, Baker Man

This baker is carrying a very pretty birthday cake. His jacket and hat are bright yellow poplin; his buttons are satin stitched in black. His collar and pants are black poplin and his hair is brown poplin. His facial features are drawn on with a permanent pen; his face and hands are flesh colored poplin. The cake is blue poplin with pink poplin icing. The tray is silver zigzagged thread; the candle is blue satin stitch. The candle flame is gold lamé thread. The words "Patty Cake, Patty Cake, Baker Man" are stitched in blue zigzag.

Block #12
London Bridge Is Falling Down

The towers of London Bridge are a material which actually looks like rocks in shades of brown and beige. The tops of the tower and the underside of the bridge are brown poplin. The flags are gold lamé. The actual bridge is tan poplin and the door and windows of the largest tower are beige also. The words "London Bridge is Falling Down" are stitched in green.

Supplies

- 3 yards of 45" white cotton fabric for blocks and backing
- Scraps of fabric for the appliqué
- 17 pieces of 2" x 15" fabric strips for sashing between blocks and multicolored corner blocks
- 2 pieces of 2" x 38" pieces of fabric for top and bottom borders
- 2 pieces of 2" x 51" pieces of fabric for side borders
- Crib-size quilt batting
- Machine embroidery thread to match appliqué fabrics
- Very fine, permanent, black marking or paint pen, such as a Pigma pen
- Wash-out marking pencils
- Wonder Under or other fusing agent
- Totally stable iron on stabilizer
- Open-toe appliqué foot
- Size 80 needle
- Safety pins or quilt tack gun and tacks
- Mother Goose templates

Directions

All seams 1/4" unless otherwise indicated.

1. Cut 12 white squares 10-1/2" by 10-1/2" excluding the selvages.

2. Spray starch and fold into fourths to mark the center and quarter points.

3. Trace the patterns onto the paper side of the Wonder Under and add the underlap (dotted lines) on the pieces where indicated.

NOTE: Reverse the designs when copying onto the Wonder Under to keep from getting a mirror image (fig. 1).

4. Fuse to the wrong side of the desired appliqué fabric.

5. Cut out all of the pieces, remove the paper backing, assemble the design, and fuse to the background square.

6. Place stabilizer under the background squares and iron in place.

7. Appliqué the designs using the directions for Appliqué found on page 112.

8. Use the fine, black permanent marker to add detail lines. A light box is very helpful in seeing the detail lines.

9. Stitch the words with a narrow satin stitch (W = 1-1.5) or use the built-in alphabet from the machine.

10. Remove the stabilizer.

11. Cut 2" strips of the sashing fabric to 10-1/2". The sashing strips do not extend into the corners of the blocks.

12. Decide the arrangement of blocks to have 3 blocks across by 4 blocks down. Stitch the sashing to the tops and/or bottoms of the squares to make three long strips of four blocks each. The sashing should not be on the top of the first block or the bottom of the last block of each strip of blocks at this time *(fig. 2)*.

13. To make the corner blocks, cut 1-1/4" squares from the remaining sashing fabric. The four colors used are the same as the sashing on the adjoining blocks. Look at the diagram, then stitch the 4 small blocks together to make a 2" block (six total) for each corner *(fig. 3)*. Stitch the short end of the side sashing to the finished 4-fabric block. Continue to add the sashing fabric and four fabric blocks to make one long strip of sashing. Stitch this sashing strip to the side of the blocks in row 1. Add row 2 blocks, the next row of sashing and row 3. Be careful to match all seams *(fig. 4)*.

14. For outside sashing, use fabric strips 2" wide by the length of the outside edges plus about 4" for mitering the corners.

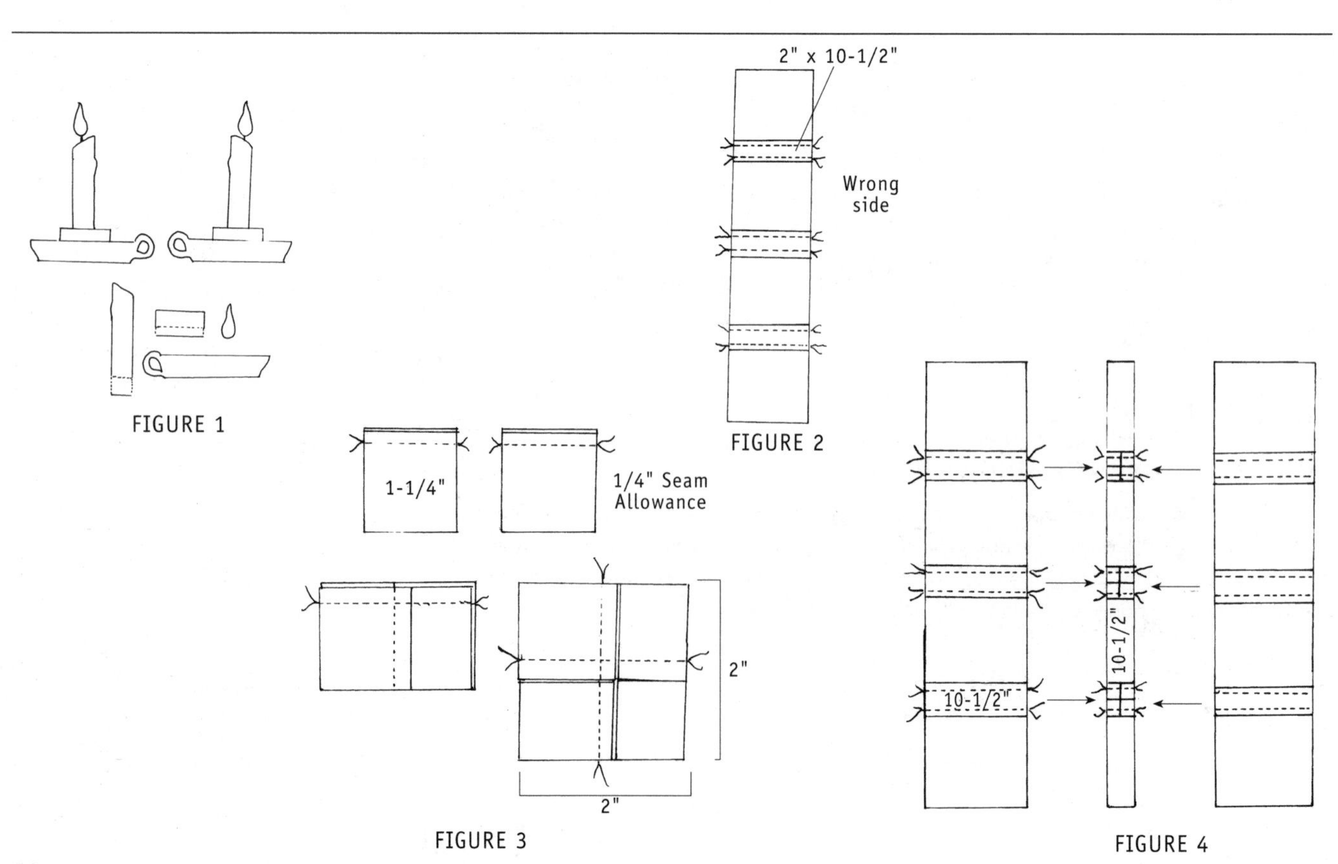

FIGURE 1

FIGURE 2

FIGURE 3

FIGURE 4

15. Stitch the outside sashing strips to the quilt, starting and stopping 1/4" from the corners *(fig. 5)*.

16. Miter the corners. Hand stitch or machine stitch in place. Trim away any excess sashing fabric *(fig. 6)*.

17. Measure the quilt top. Cut a backing piece 4" larger than the quilt top. Make the quilt sandwich by placing the backing fabric right side down on a flat surface, then smooth the quilt batting over the backing, then the quilt top right side up. Pin baste or use the quilt tacks to tack the layers together. The backing will extend 2" beyond the outside edges of the quilt top which will be used as the binding *(fig. 7)*.

18. Quilt as desired, using the machine and a medium stitch length.

19. Trim the edges of the backing and batting to extend 1" beyond the quilt top *(fig. 8)*.

20. Fold the extended backing and batting in half, then fold again to cover the raw edges of the quilt. Miter the corners.

21. Hand blind stitch or machine edge-stitch the binding in place.

22. Remove the pins or the quilt tacks.

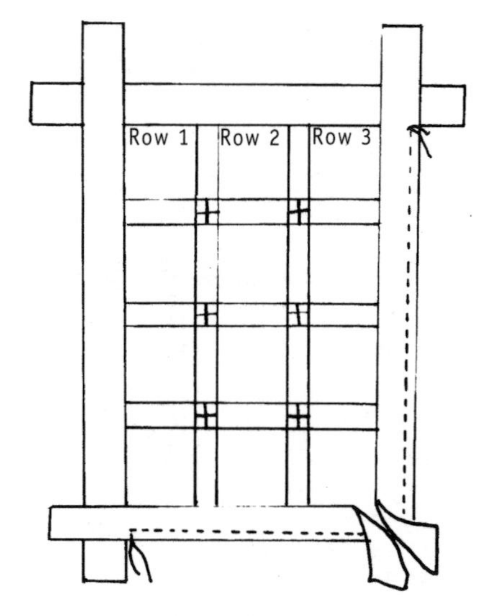

FIGURE 5

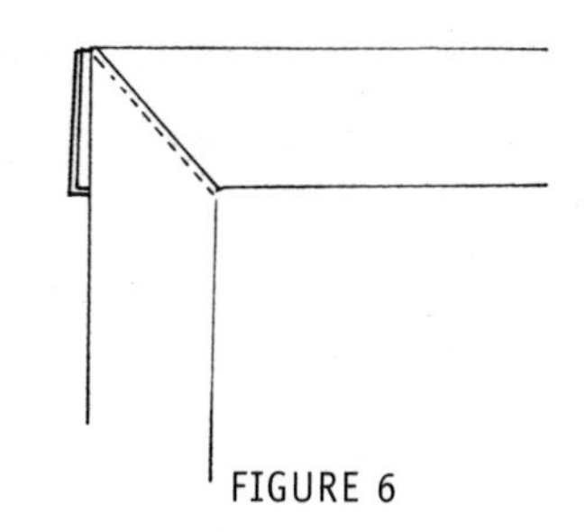
FIGURE 6

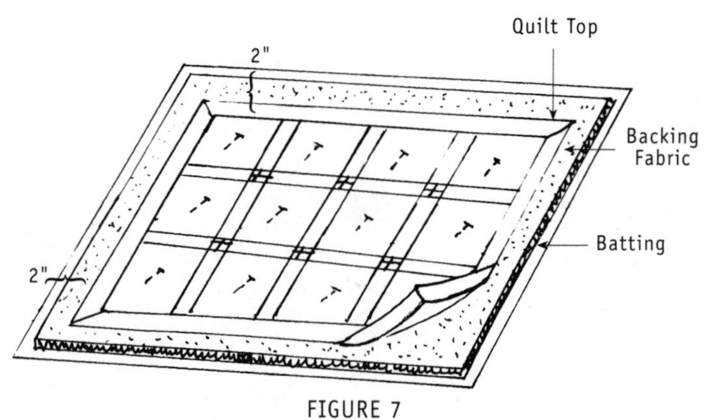

FIGURE 7

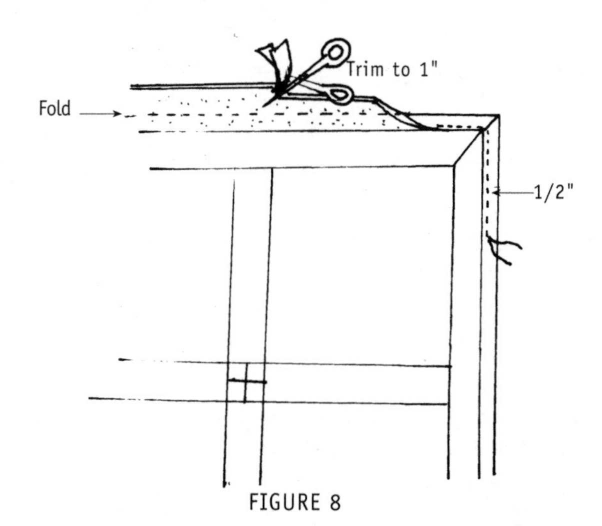

FIGURE 8

Springtime in Paris Quilt

Green and yellow Swiss Nelona batistes are used for the sashings in between beautiful ecru quilt squares. Baby blue Swiss Nelona batiste is used for the binding. Doesn't this just seem like springtime in Paris? Flowers, flowers everywhere dance across the quilt in shades of yellow, green and blue. Totally made and embellished by machine, this quilt is a dream of French sewing, another word for heirloom sewing. Presented on the 1200 and 1300 series of Martha's Sewing Room, our television series for PBS, we delighted in sharing the French sewing techniques used on each square as well as the construction of the quilt. All of the squares are embellished on ecru Swiss Nelona background fabric.

NOTE: Pfaff (P) and Viking (V) embroidery cards were used for all enbroidery designs. Other embroidery designs may be used within the dimensions allotted.

Beginning in the upper left hand corner, the first square features a beautiful ecru puffing oval shape with ecru French lace insertion on the outside and inside of the puffing. A beautiful blue bow with yellow, ecru and pink flowers finishes this delicate square. The oval is quilted with two lines of straight stitching with ecru thread around the outside of the oval. Moving to the right, the next square has shadow appliqué by machine with a beautiful design in blue for the base of the flowers and yellow tulips with green leaves. An ecru outline straight stitch follows around the whole design in two rows. The upper right hand square has a Seminole patchwork strip, surrounded on either side with ecru lace insertions and a blue Nelona strip inside the two lace strips. Three rows of tiny feather stitching run vertically beside the lace and Nelona strips. The colors on these featherstitched strips are blue, green and yellow.

The middle row is fabulous also. Beginning on the left hand side in the middle, there is a wonderful design using yellow bias linen strips shaped in a Celtic pattern. The linen is pinstitched to the batiste square. A straight line of stitching travels around the shaping to quilt the piece. The middle square features the technique French waterfall. What is French waterfall? Scallops of lace create an outline for the center panel, which is machine embroidered with blue, yellow, green and ecru. Two blue Swiss Nelona strips with three rows of pintucks are on either side of this center strip. Two more rows of French scallops outline the blue strips. The quilting is done on all edges of the lace insertion using a straight stitch with ecru thread. The right hand square has an interesting use of medium ecru linen with pale ecru batiste. The technique is Madeira borders and Madeira motifs accented with a tiny blue feather stitching around the center Madeira motif section of ecru linen. The blue feather stitching is also found around the four Madeira borders on each corner. The little silk ribbon flowers can be stitched by either hand or machine.

The bottom left square has three rows of shark's teeth on either side of a wonderful diamond shaped machine embroidery in green. This square almost looks Native American in its design. On either side of the shark's teeth section are rows of diamond machine embroidery in shades of green, yellow and blue. The center bottom square is just plain fun. There are many sections of crazy patch. Some of the crazy patchwork is done on ecru Swiss batiste. Some of the squares have machine-embroidered decorative stitches in shades of yellow, green, blue and ecru. Some of the squares have combinations of antique laces with machine-embellished stitches. A couple of the squares have machine embroidered flowers in green, blue and yellow. One of the green squares has ecru lace stitched over green satin ribbon along with green machine decorative stitches. One of the pieces has a portion of Swiss embroidered collar edging with lace stitched at the bottom. All of the crazy patch stitching lines are covered with green silk ribbon stitched down with feather stitching. The bottom right hand square is pretty as can be. The technique, Australian windowpane, is used for the four blue bows with organdy inside the bows. The yellow and green flowers in the center use Australian windowpane also. There is a circle of Australian windowpane with ecru decorative stitching; wing needle entredeux surrounds the circle of Australian windowpane. A pretty ecru machine scallop is stitched on the outside of the circle. The piece is quilted to the back by using a straight stitch surrounding the outline of the quilt embellishment. A row of ecru straight stitching is on each side of the circle in the square. The center of the flower is stitched in ecru.

The long strips of sashing around each square are green. Yellow squares are found in each corner of each square. The backing of the quilt is white Nelona.

Supplies

- 2 yards of ecru Nelona
- 3/8 yard of yellow Nelona
- 7/8 yard of green Nelona
- 7/8 yard of blue Nelona
- 1/2 yard of yellow linen
- 1/2 yard of ecru linen
- 1/3 yard of white cotton organdy
- 5 yards of 4mm green silk ribbon
- Scraps of insertion laces
- 27 yards ecru 5/8-inch insertion lace
- Backing fabric: 1-3/4 yards if 60" wide; 3-1/4 yards if 45" wide (ecru Nelona)
- Optional underlining, same amount as backing
- 54" square of batting
- Rotary cutter, ruler and mat
- 1/2-inch bias tape maker
- Water-soluble fabric glue
- Decorative machine embroidery thread: green, blue, yellow, ecru
- Blue wash-out marking pen
- Paper-backed fusible web
- Twin needle #1.6 or #2.0
- Two spools of ecru fine cotton thread
- Clear nylon thread
- Water-soluble stabilizer (WSS)
- Lightweight tear-away stabilizer
- #70/10 embroidery needle
- #100 or #110 universal needle
- Safety pins or quilt tack gun
- Open-toe appliqué foot
- Gathering foot
- Viking (V) cards 11, 24, 25, library #711068415, cassette L45 (optional)
- Pfaff (P) card 48 (optional)

Cutting

- Ecru Nelona
  Seven 15" squares
  One 15" x 21" rectangle
  Two 2-1/4" x 45" strips
  Two 3-1/2 x 15" strips
  Two 4" x 15" strips
  The remaining ecru fabric will be used for the Heirloom Crazy Patch Block.
- Ecru Linen
  One 15" linen square
- Yellow Nelona
  Two 2-1/4" x 11-1/2" strips
  One 5" square
  The remaining yellow fabric will be used for assembling the quilt top.
- Green Nelona
  Two 1-3/4" x 11-1/2" strips
  One 3-1/2" x 15"
  One 5" square
  The remaining green fabric will be used for assembling the quilt top.
- Blue Nelona
  One 1-3/4" x 11-1/2" strip
  Two 1" x 15" strips
  Two 5" x 15" strips
  One 4" x 9" piece
  The remaining blue fabric will be used for the quilt binding.
- Yellow Linen
  2-1/2 yards of 1-1/16" wide bias strips
- White Cotton Organdy
  One 12" square

Shaped Puffing

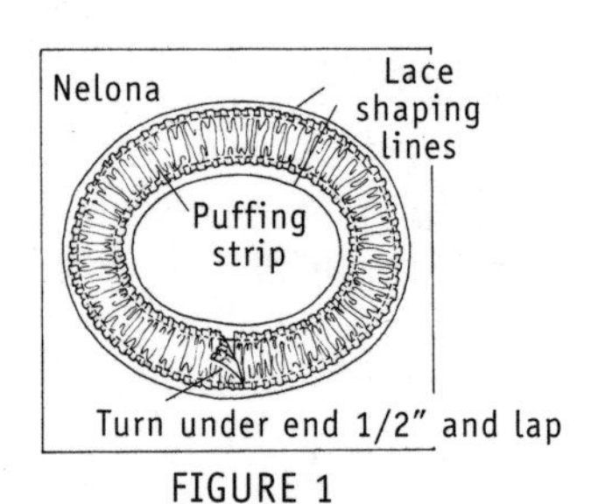

FIGURE 1

FIGURE 2

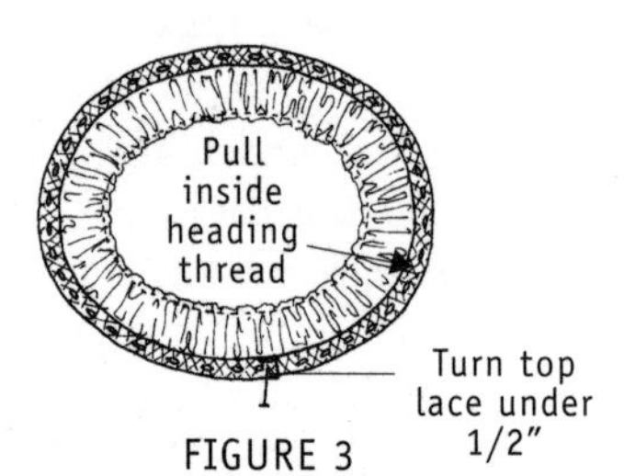

FIGURE 3

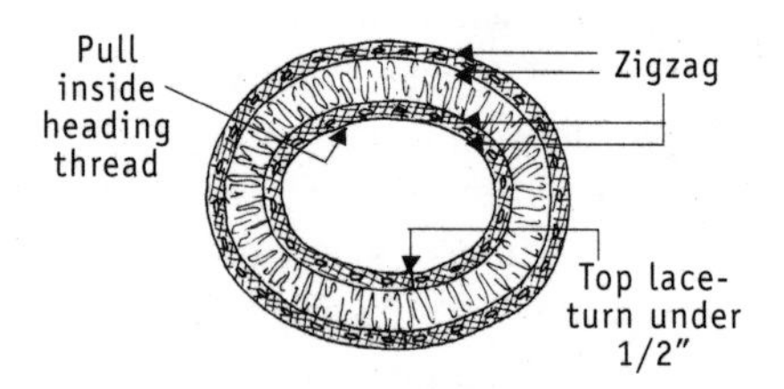

FIGURE 4

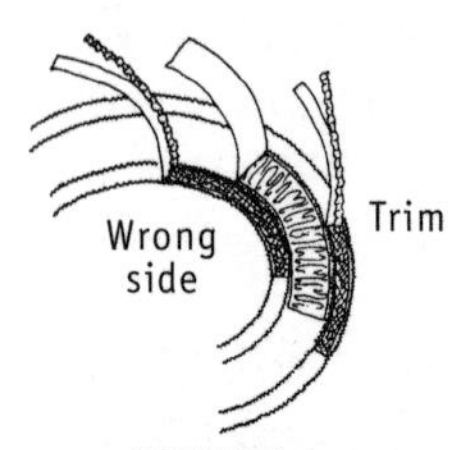

FIGURE 5

FIGURE 6

FIGURE 7

Block #1
Shaped Puffing

Supplies

- One 15" square of ecru Nelona
- Two strips of ecru Nelona, each 2-1/4" x 45"
- 2 yards of 5/8" insertion lace
- #70/10 Embroidery needle
- Gathering foot
- V card 25, design #3 (optional)
- Machine embroidery threads
- Oval lace shaping template

1. Starch and press the Nelona square. With the blue wash-out marking pen, trace the oval lace shaping template lines onto the Nelona.

2. Seam the narrow fabric strips together at one short end, creating one long strip for puffing. Gather both long edges with a gathering foot, using a 1/2" seam allowance. Trim each seam allowance to 1/8" – 1/4".

3. Position the puffing strip between the two inner lace shaping lines with the gathering stitch lines on top of the inner lace shaping lines. Pin the outer edge in place, or use water-soluble fabric glue to tack the raw edges of the puffing strip to the background fabric. Adjust the puffing so the inner edge lies flat and the gathers are perpendicular to the lace shaping lines. Trim excess puffing, allowing ends to overlap 1". Fold under the top piece 1/2" and lap *(fig. 1)*.

4. Shape the lace insertion along the outer edge of the puffing by holding the inner edge of the lace insertion along the outer gathering line with your finger. Pin along the outer edge of the lace *(fig. 2)*. Allow the ends to overlap 1" and trim the excess. Pull the inside heading thread, causing the lace to lay flat. Fold the top piece of lace under 1/2" and pin *(fig. 3)*.

5. Shape the lace insertion along the inside edge of the puffing by pinning the outer edge of the lace along the inside gathering line *(fig. 4)*. Pull the inside heading thread, causing the lace to lay flat. Allow the ends to overlap 1" and trim the excess. Fold the top piece of lace under 1/2" and pin *(fig. 5)*.

6. Zigzag (L = 0.6 - 0.8; W = 2.0) along both edges of the lace insertion *(fig. 5)*. On the wrong side, trim away fabric from behind the puffing, and trim away both flat fabric and gathered seam allowances from behind the insertion *(fig. 6)*.

7. Zigzag (L = 1.0; W = 2.0) over the folded ends where laces were joined *(fig. 7)*. Rinse, starch, and press the block. Hand or machine monograms or other embroidery may be stitched inside the oval. V card 25, design #3 was used for the pictured quilt. Trim the square to 14".

Easy Shadow Appliqué

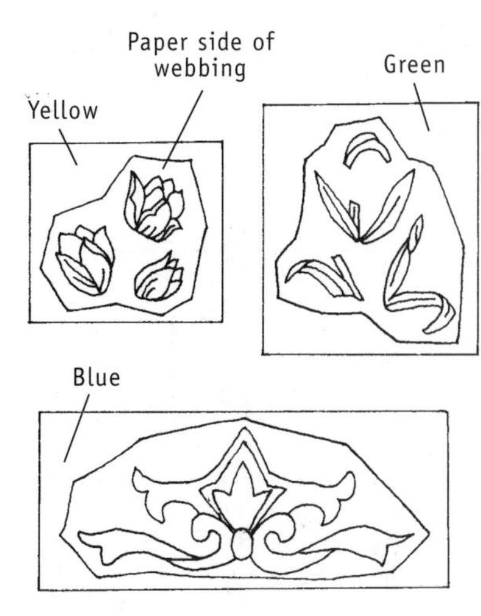

FIGURE 1

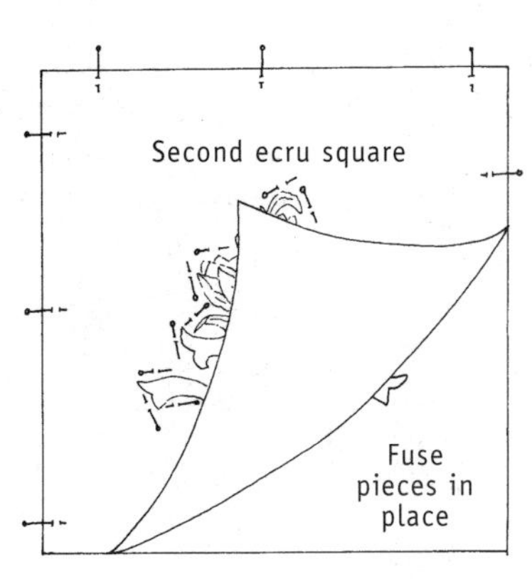

FIGURE 2

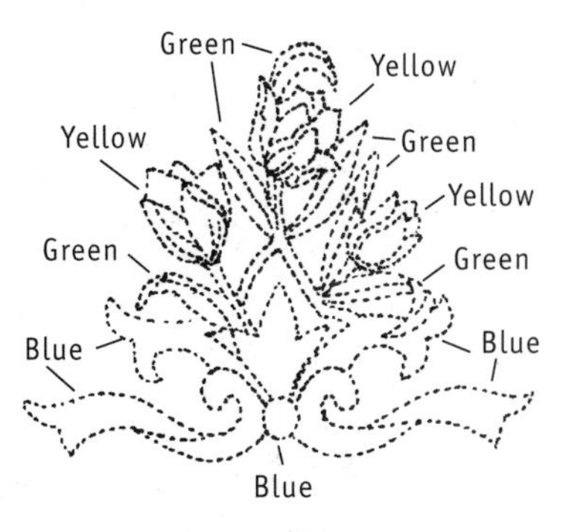

FIGURE 3

Block #2
Easy Shadow Appliqué

Supplies

- Two 15″ squares of ecru Nelona
- One piece of blue Nelona, 4″ x 9″
- One 5″ square of yellow Nelona
- One 5″ square of green Nelona
- #70/10 embroidery needle
- Open-toe appliqué foot
- Shadow appliqué template
- Wash-out marker
- Machine embroidery thread
- Fusible web

1. Trace the scroll, flowers, and leaves onto the paper side of the fusible web. Cut around the pieces so that the scroll, flowers and leaves are separated from each other. Press the traced scroll onto the wrong side of the blue fabric, flowers onto the wrong side of the yellow fabric, and leaves onto the wrong side of the green *(fig. 1)*. Cut out the traced shapes.

2. Starch and press both ecru squares. Before you remove the paper backing from the appliqué pieces it would be helpful to trace the lines, exterior and interior, onto the fabric. You can use a light table or place the pieces on a window, paper side on the glass and let the light help you see through the fabric to trace all lines. Cut out the appliqué pieces. Remove the paper backing from the appliqué pieces; arrange the pieces right side up on one square, referring to the template and photograph for placement. Press to fuse the shapes in place. Place the second ecru square over the first and pin both layers together around the appliqués *(fig. 2)*.

3. Use decorative thread to match or slightly darker than the appliqué pieces, ecru cotton thread in the bobbin,#70/10-75/11 Embroidery or Metafil needle, tension slightly loosened, straight stitch (L = 1.0), and an open-toe appliqué foot if available.

4. If the appliqué outlines are hard to see, use a sharp pencil to trace over the outlines. Straight stitch along the design lines of the appliqué pieces, changing colors of thread as noted. Instead of backstitching to start and stop, hold the fabric firmly against the machine bed to prevent feeding for a few stitches, allowing the machine to stitch in place and tie-off.

5. Repeat for all pieces, stitching close to the shape outlines and along design lines; areas do not have to be enclosed shapes as in shadow embroidery, but can be partial lines. Just be sure each appliqué has stitching around the entire outer edge *(fig. 3)*. Wash the block to remove any visible marks, then starch, press, and trim to 14"square.

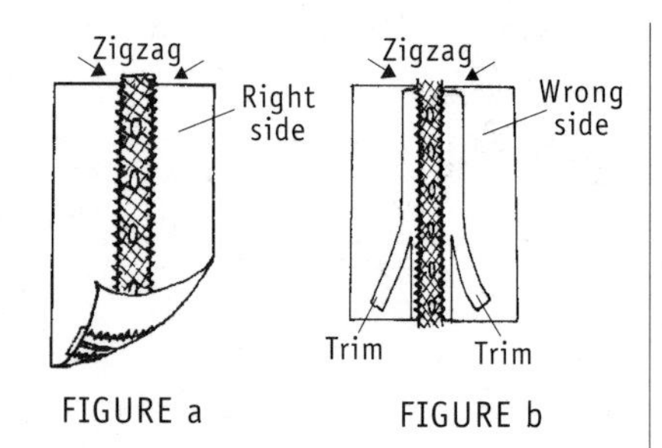

FIGURE a FIGURE b

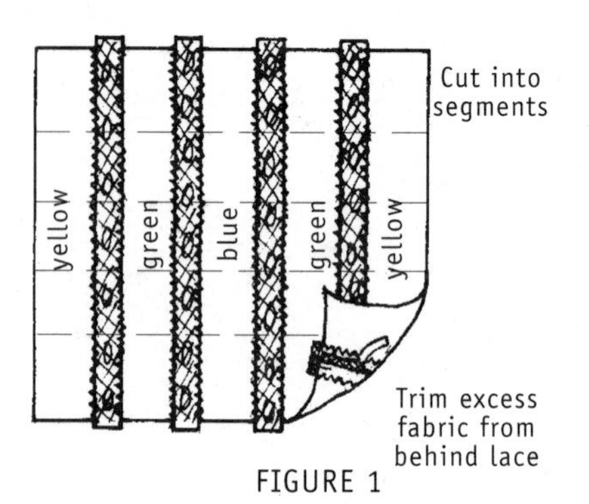

FIGURE 1

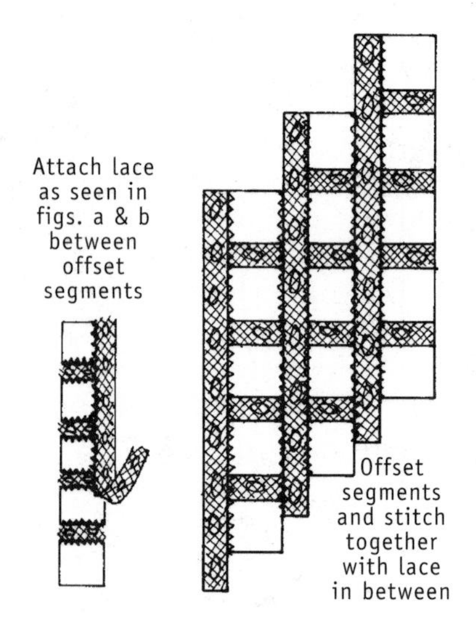

FIGURE 2a FIGURE 2b

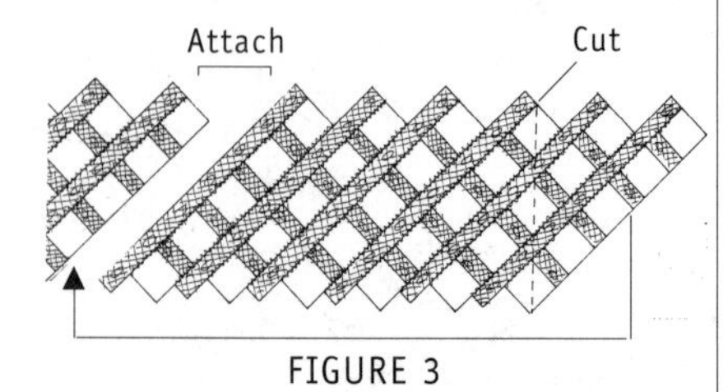

FIGURE 3

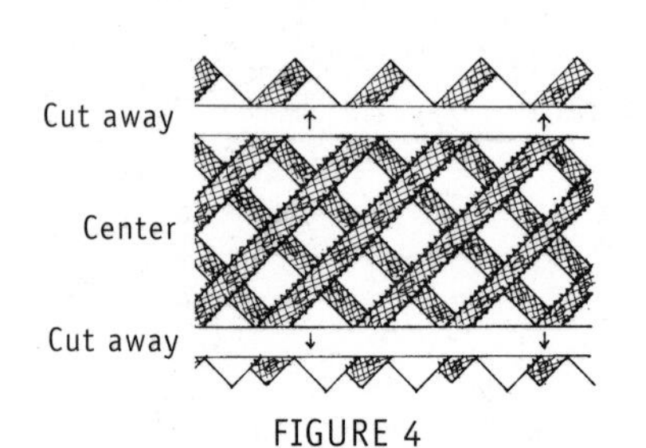

FIGURE 4

Seminole Lacework

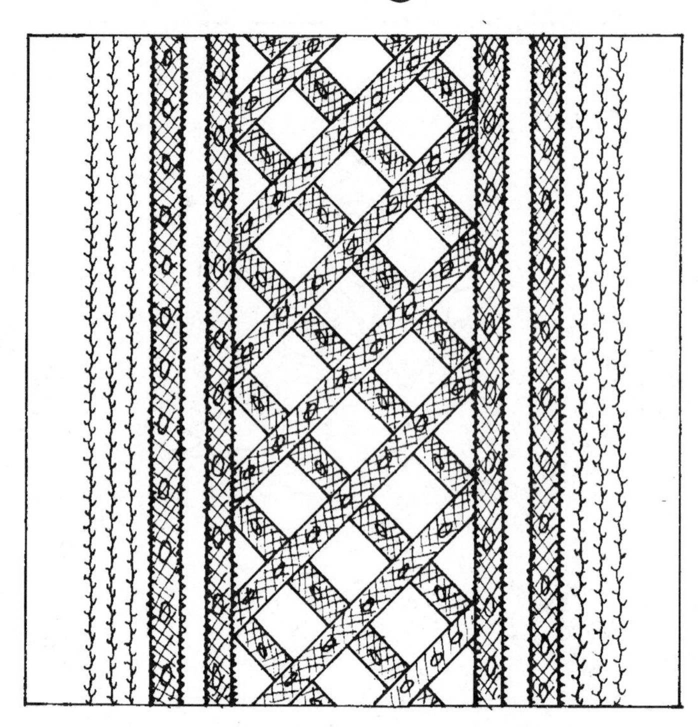

Block #3
Seminole Lacework

Supplies

- Two strips of yellow Nelona, each 2-1/4″ x 11-1/2″
- Two strips of green Nelona, each 1-3/4″ x 11-1/2″
- One strip of blue Nelona, 1-3/4″ x 11-1/2″
- Two strips of blue Nelona, each 1″ x 15″
- Two strips of ecru Nelona, each 3-1/2″ x 15″
- 5 yards of 5/8″ insertion lace
- #70/10 embroidery needle
- Machine embroidery threads

General procedure for attaching lace:

Step 1) Use fine ecru thread, #70 needle, and zigzag (W = 0.8; L = 2.0). Center lace insertion over the fabric raw edge; zigzag over lace heading. Zigzag the next fabric strip to the other side of the lace insertion. Fabric raw edges will meet at center under the lace (fig. a).

Step 2) Press the fabric raw edges away from the lace. Zigzag (W=1.5 – 2.0, L=1.5) along the lace heading and trim away the excess fabric from behind the lace(fig. b).

1. Join the five 11-1/2" fabric strips at long edges with lace between the strips: yellow, lace, green, lace, blue, lace, green, lace, yellow *(fig. 1)*.

2. Square one short end of the striped block; use the rotary cutter to cut six 1-3/4" segments *(see fig. 1)*. Zigzag insertion to one long side of each segment *(fig. 2a)*. Offset segments and zigzag them together in a stairstep panel *(fig. 2b)*.

3. To square the ends of the panel, make a perpendicular cut through the strip; join the angled ends of the two pieces just as the segments were joined *(fig. 3)*.

4. Using the rotary cutter, trim off the sawtooth points along both long edges, making sure the cut is a consistent distance from the center of the strip on both sides *(fig. 4)*.

5. Zigzag insertion to both long edges of each 1" x 15" blue strip; zigzag one strip to each long edge of the lacework strip. Zigzag the ecru rectangles to the remaining edge of each border strip. Trim fabric from behind the lace, starch, and press the block; trim to 14" square (*see finished drawing*).

6. Stitch yellow, green, and blue rows of featherstitching (W = 2.0; L = 2.0) on ecru fabric, using presser foot width as a guide along lace and between rows of feather stitching (*see finished drawing*).

Shaped Bias

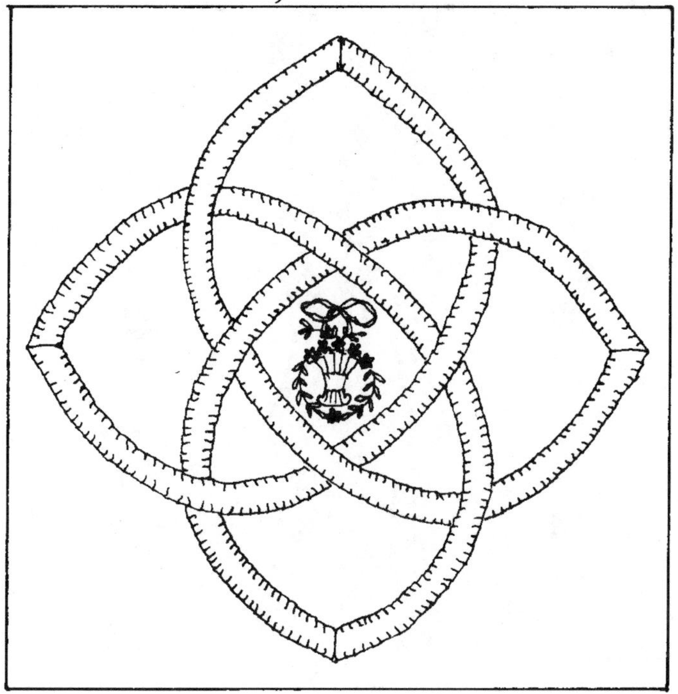

Block #4
Shaped Bias

Supplies

- One 15″ square of ecru Nelona
- 2-1/2 yards of yellow linen bias strips, 1-1/16″ wide
- #100-110 universal needle
- Water-soluble fabric glue
- 1/2" Bias tape maker
- Lightweight tear-away stabilizer
- V card 11, design #27 (optional)
- Shaped bias template
- #70/10 embroidery needle
- Machine embroidery threads

1. Starch and press Nelona; fold in quarters and finger press along foldlines. With blue wash-out marker, trace template onto each quarter of square *(fig. 1)*.

2. Use the 1/2" bias tape maker to press the bias strips; it is not necessary to seam the strips together.

3. Cut one end of a bias strip straight across. Starting at an intersection, sparingly apply water-soluble fabric glue along several inches of the template line on the Nelona. Center the bias strip over the template line; press briefly to dry glue. Apply glue and center bias another few inches; continue. Leave about 1" un-glued at intersections to allow weaving over and under, like a Celtic design. Look at the finished drawing to see the under and over weaving pattern. Shape and miter the points of the bias as you would lace insertion. Hide the cut ends of the bias strips under intersections *(fig. 2)*. If you prefer working without glue, pin the bias in place every 1" to 2".

4. Turn the block over and very lightly starch and press on the wrong side.

5. Place fine ecru thread in the machine, insert a #100 or #110 universal needle, and select a pinstitch (L = 2.0 – 2.5; W = 1.5). Place lightweight tear-away stabilizer to the wrong side of the block. Stitch along both sides of the linen strips so that the backward and forward stitches go into the batiste just beside the linen strips and the side-to-side stitches "bite" into the bias linen strips. Do not sew across intersections when a strip goes under; backstitch a few stitches or tie-off *(fig. 3)*.

6. After all pinstitching is complete, soak the block in warm water for a few minutes to remove fabric markings and dissolve glue. Roll the block in a towel and press dry on the wrong side.

7. Machine or hand embroidery may be added to the center of the block. V card 11, design #27 was used for the pictured quilt. Trim the block to 14" square.

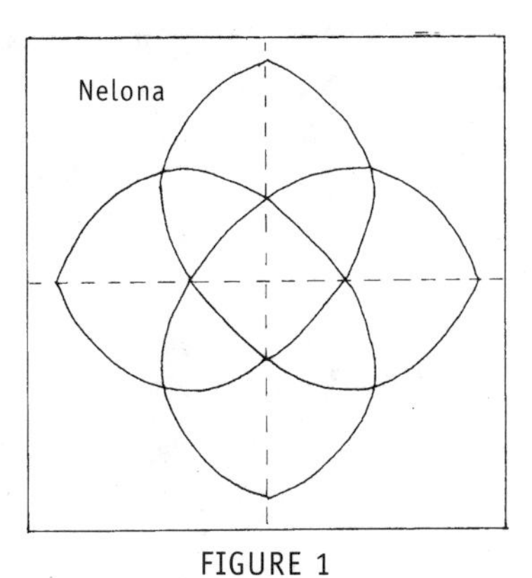

FIGURE 1

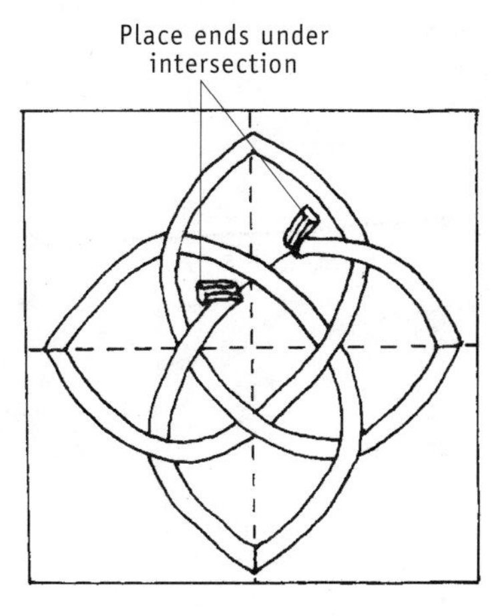

FIGURE 2

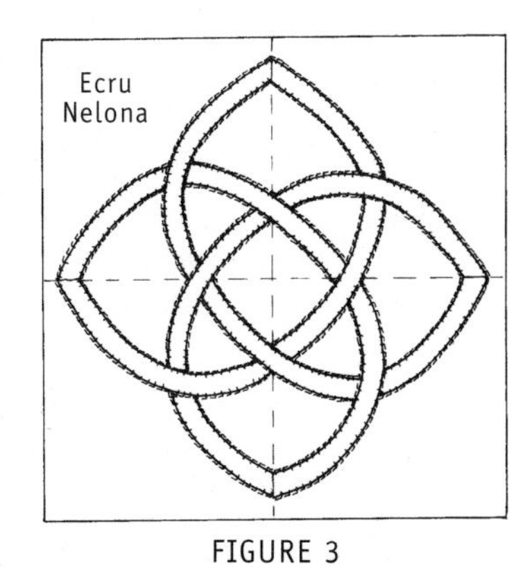

FIGURE 3

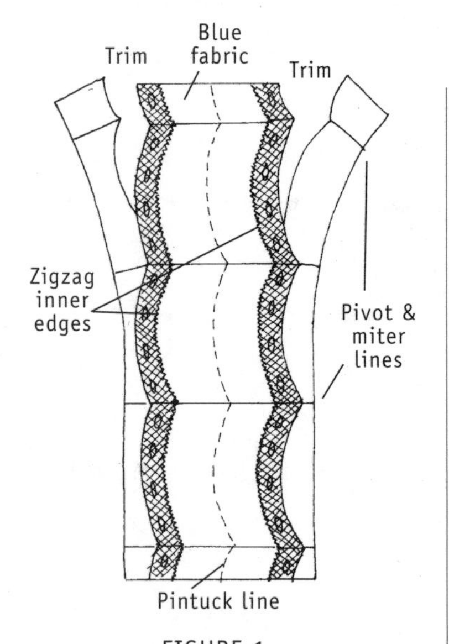

FIGURE 1

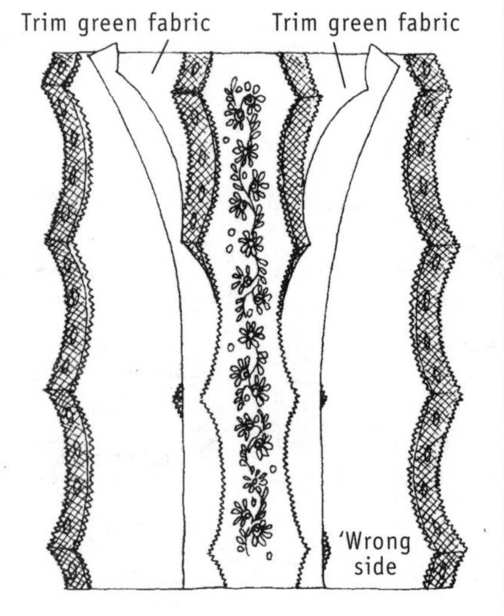

FIGURE 2

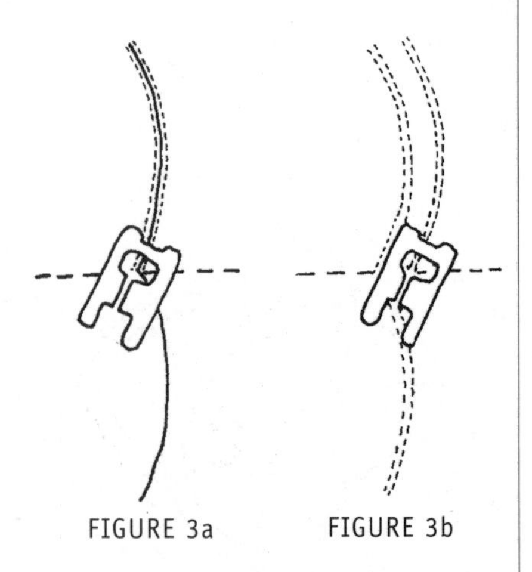
FIGURE 3a FIGURE 3b

French Waterfall

Block #5
French Waterfall

Supplies

- One strip of green Nelona, 3-1/2" x 15"
- Two strips of blue Nelona, each 5" x 15"
- Two strips of ecru Nelona, each 4" x 15"
- 2-1/2 yards of 5/8" insertion lace
- Twin needle #1.6 or #2.0
- Two spools of ecru fine cotton thread
- P card 48, design #3 (optional)
- Lightweight tear-away stabilizer
- #70/10 embroidery needles
- Machine embroidery threads
- French waterfall template

1. Lightly starch and press all fabric pieces (not lace). Trace the lace shaping template, pintuck lines, and pivot lines onto the blue Nelona pieces. Center the template on the fabric and extend the scallops to the ends of the fabric.

2. Stabilize the fabric and stitch a machine or hand embroidery design down the length of the green strip. P card 48, design #3 was used for the pictured quilt.

3. Shape lace insertion along the template lines on the blue fabric strips. Refer to Lace Shaping (page 109). Zigzag (L = 0.8; W = 2.0) along the inner edges (closest to center of fabric) of the lace scallops. Trim away excess fabric along the edges behind the lace *(fig. 1)*.

4. Place the scalloped lace edge of the blue fabric over the raw edges of the green embroidered strip, so that the scallops point away from the center and are symmetrical. Zigzag the insertion onto the center fabric strip. Trim the fabric away from behind the lace *(fig. 2)*.

5. Place the raw edges of the ecru rectangles underneath the remaining unstitched edges of the lace scallops. Zigzag the lace to the fabric and trim away fabric from behind the lace as before.

6. For double needle pintucks, use two spools of ecru thread, increase the needle tension slightly, and choose a short straight stitch (L = 1.5). Stitch a test on a fabric scrap and adjust the tension until the tucks pull up but do not pucker. If the fabric is too stiff from spray starch, rinse and press dry, then re-trace pintuck lines.

7. Stitch along the curved pintuck line until the pivot line is reached, stop needle-down with the double needles straddling the pivot line, raise the foot, turn the fabric, and continue stitching along the drawn line, creating a scalloped pintuck *(fig. 3a)*. Stitch another pintuck on each side of the first one by placing the outer edge of the foot along the pintuck, pivoting as before at the pivot lines *(fig. 3b)*. Rinse, press, and trim the block to 14".

Madeira Applique

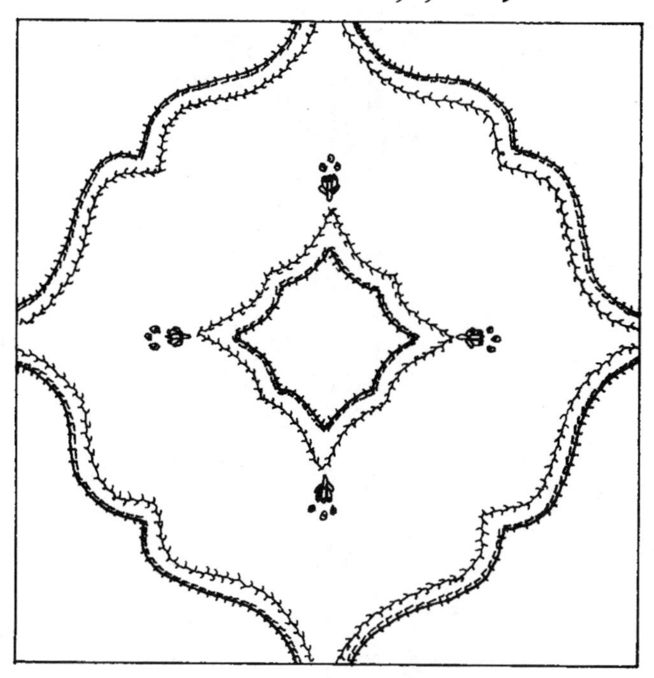

Block #6
Madeira Appliqué

Supplies

- One 15″ square of ecru Nelona
- One 15″ square of ecru linen
- Water-soluble stabilizer (WSS)
- Lightweight tear-away stabilizer
- #100 or #110 universal needle
- #70/10 embroidery needle
- Machine embroidery threads
- Madeira appliqué template
- Point turner

1. Starch and press both fabric squares. Trace four corner templates and one center template onto the right side of the linen.

2. Place water-soluble stabilizer (WSS) in strips about 2" wide over the template lines on the right side of the linen; use a 5" square of WSS over the center medallion. Straight stitch with a short (L =1.5) stitch length directly along the traced lines through both the WSS and the linen (refer to *fig. 2a*). Do not leave openings for turning *(fig. 1)*.

3. Trim to 1/8" outside the stitching lines; clip the curves *(fig. 2b)*. Turn the WSS facing to the wrong side *(fig. 2c)*; for the center medallion, just make a slit in the WSS and turn the medallion right side out *(fig. 2d)*. Push out the points, finger press, and then press from the linen side *(fig. 2e)*.

4. Place the linen appliqué pieces on the corners and at the center of the Nelona square. Very lightly spray starch and press; this will bond the WSS to the base fabric, essentially gluing the appliqué pieces to the Nelona.

5. Set up the machine for pinstitch (L = 2.0 – 2.5; W = 1.5), with a #100 or #110 universal needle. Pinstitch the linen pieces in place using the same technique as for the Shaped Bias Square *(fig. 3)*.

6. Using a #70 needle and decorative embroidery thread, featherstitch (L = 2.0; W = 2.0) on the Nelona, tracing along the edges of linen pieces by using the foot as a spacing guide. If desired, stitch little silk ribbon flowers at the points. Soak the block in warm water to dissolve the WSS, press dry, and trim to 14" square.

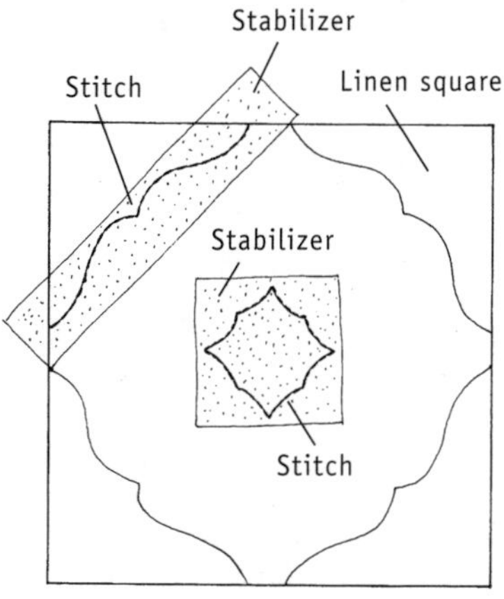

FIGURE 1

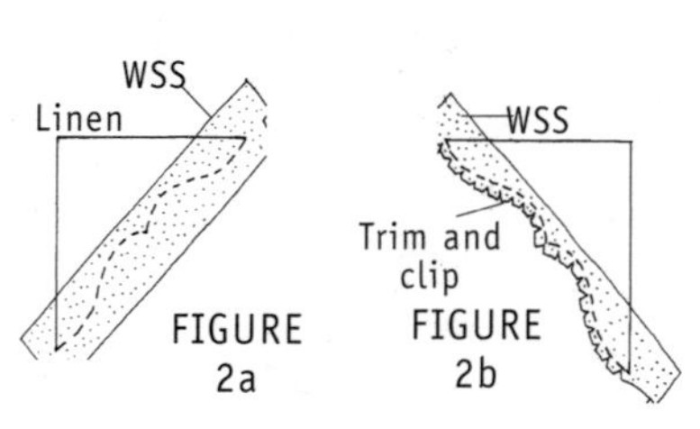

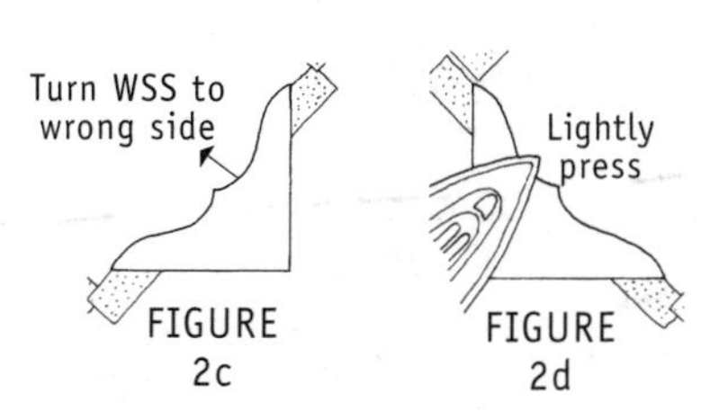

Complete all 4 corners

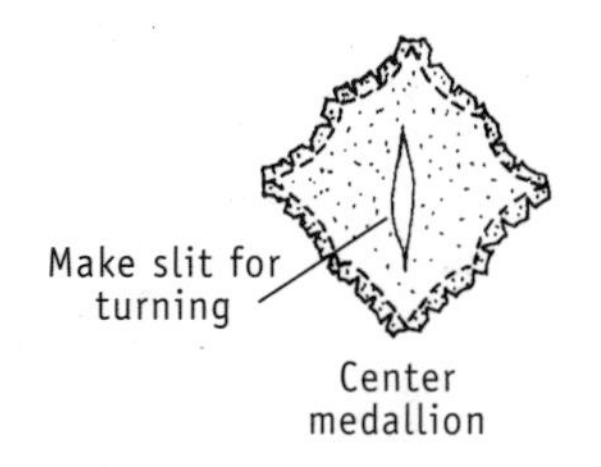

FIGURE 2e

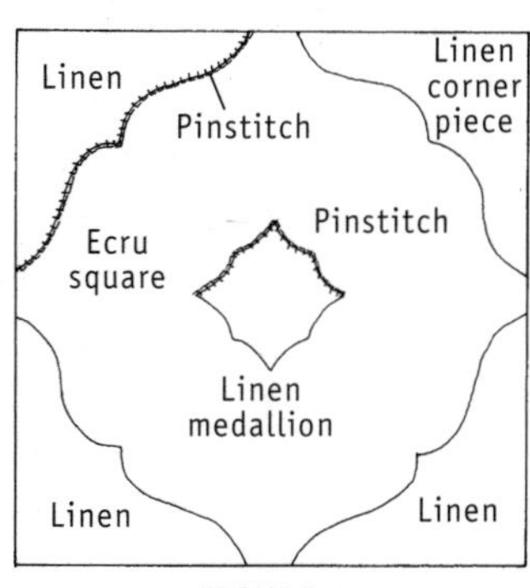

FIGURE 3

Shark's Teeth

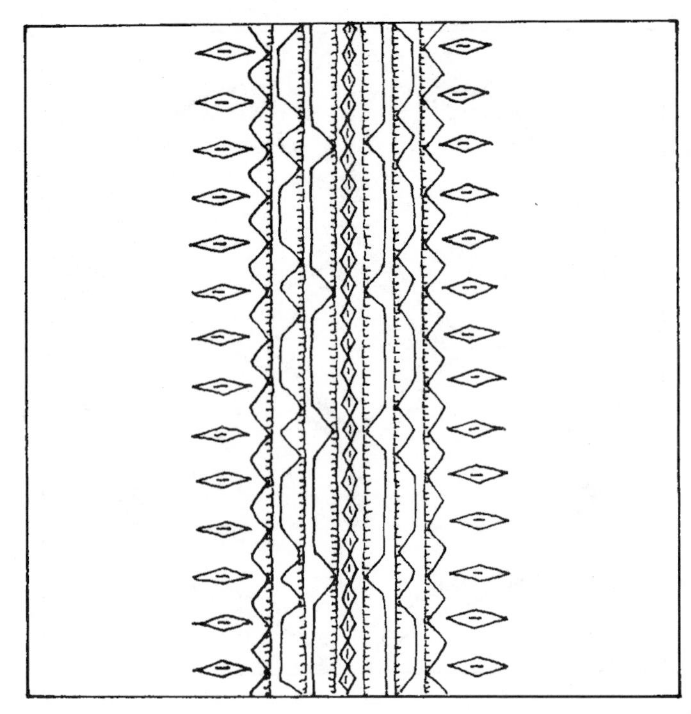

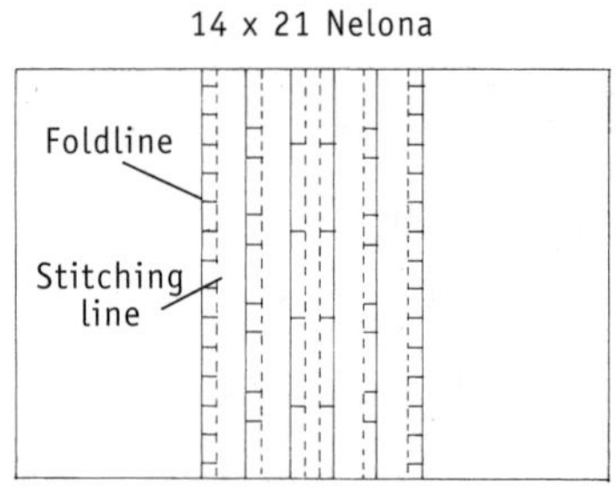

FIGURE 1

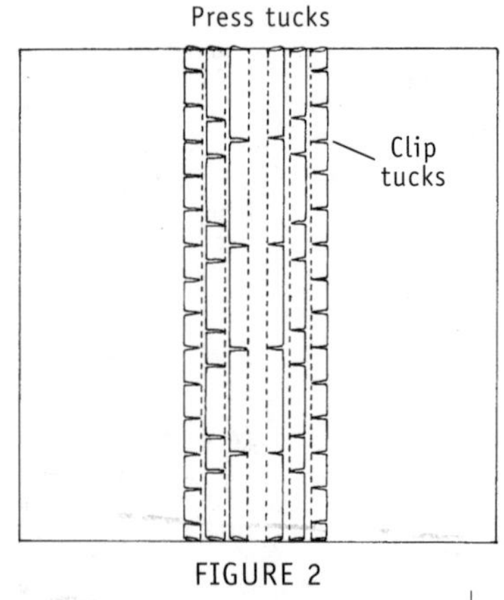

FIGURE 2

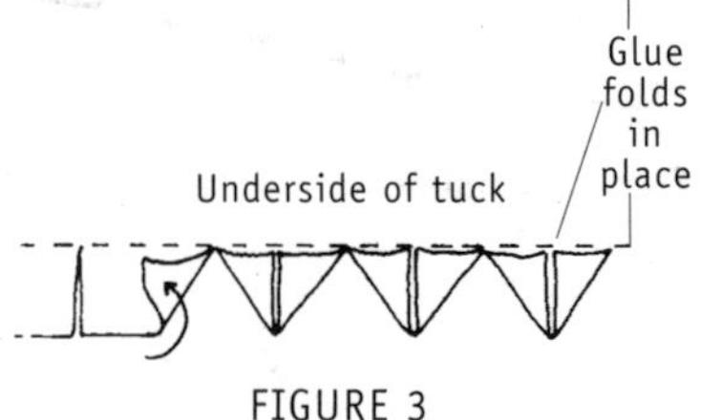

FIGURE 3

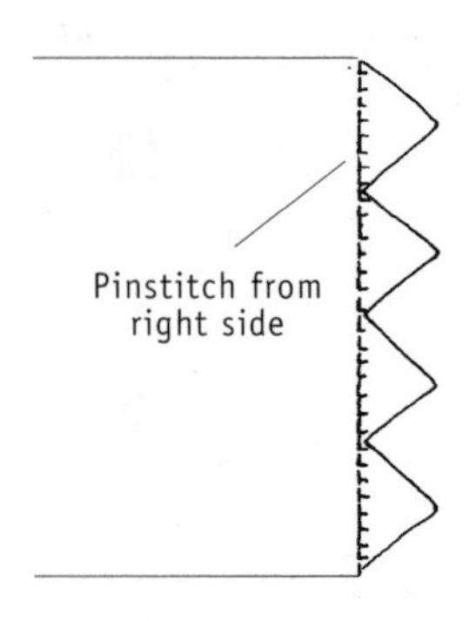

FIGURE 4

Block #7
Shark's Teeth

Supplies

- One rectangle of ecru Nelona, 15" x 21"
- #70/10 embroidery needle
- Water-soluble fabric glue
- Shark's teeth template
- Machine embroidery thread

1. Starch and press the Nelona. Use the water-soluble marking pen to trace the shark's teeth template along the full length of the strip *(fig. 1)*. Press a fold directly along each marked foldline (solid lines).

2. Using a #70 needle and fine ecru cotton thread, straight stitch (L = 1.5 - 2.0) along the marked stitching lines (dashed lines) to form 1/2" tucks. Press the tucks away from center.

3. Clip the tucks, one row at a time, on the short solid lines perpendicular to the fold, just to, but not through, the stitching line *(fig. 2)*. At the ironing board, place the fabric so you are looking at the underside of the tuck, with the fabric below the tuck folded out of the way. At each clip, fold the fabric so the raw edge of the clip lies directly along the stitching line *(fig. 3)*. You are making V's, or upside down triangles. Press firmly; use a very tiny bit of water-soluble fabric glue to secure the little flaps if necessary.

4. Set up the machine for zigzag (L = 1.0; W = 2.0), a picot stitch (L = 2.0, W = 2.0), or a blanket stitch (L = 1.0; W = 2.0). Stitch along previous stitching lines from the right side, keeping all the little clips folded under. Stitch so that the left swing of the needle (straight stitching) is directly on top of the previous stitching, and the right swing of the needle bites into the tuck *(fig. 4)*.

5. If desired, stitch a machine or hand-embroidered motif on the fabric between each "tooth" in the outer rows, and down the center of the block. The sample shows machine satin stitched diamonds.

6. Soak the square in warm water to remove markings and any glue. Roll the block in a towel, starch, and press. Trim the block to 14" square.

Heirloom Crazy Patch

Block #8
Heirloom Crazy Patch

Supplies

- One 15" square ecru Nelona
- 1/4 yard ecru Nelona
- 5 yards 4mm silk ribbon, green
- Small bits of lace insertions
- Water-soluble (WSS) or lightweight tear-away stabilizer
- Water-soluble fabric glue
- V card 24, design #4; V-embroidery library #711068415; V cassette, L45 (optional)
- #70/10 embroidery needle
- Machine embroidery thread

1. Starch and press the Nelona. Cut the 1/4 yard of Nelona into 7 pieces about 6" by 9". Stabilize the pieces with water-soluble stabilizer or tear-away stabilizer.

2. Completely cover each 6" piece with machine embroidery; the sample shows single-color embroidery on each piece. Use the suggested cards and stitches above and your machine's built-in stitches or varied embroideries from your machine. Alternate rows with two or three different stitches look nice, as do mirror image rows. Some stitches can be worked over bits of silk ribbon, or between strips of lace. Try to create an overall pattern that resembles a tapestry or jacquard. Make six to eight pieces with different stitches in desired colors. Remove the stabilizer and press the pieces.

3. Cut an odd-shaped piece with four or five straight sides, about 2" or 3" in size. Place the first piece somewhere on the Nelona square. Cut other pieces to fit like jigsaw puzzle pieces, keeping all sides straight. Pin a few pieces in place or glue in place with water-soluble fabric glue. With ecru thread, zigzag (L = 1.5; W = 2.5) over raw edges to hold the pieces in place. Try to get a nice, tight fit between patches without overlapping *(fig. 1)*.

4. When the entire block is covered with patches, use a tiny feather stitch to stitch both edges of silk ribbon in place over the seams between patches *(fig. 2)*. The ribbon can be held in place with a very small amount of fabric glue if needed. When possible, plan stitching so the raw ends of the ribbons are tucked under other ribbons; when this is not possible, fold under and secure the raw ends of the ribbon with a feather stitch. The ribbon can be bent around shallow angles, but do not try to miter or bend around sharp angles.

5. Rinse away the stabilizer and glue if necessary; press and starch the square. Trim the block to 14".

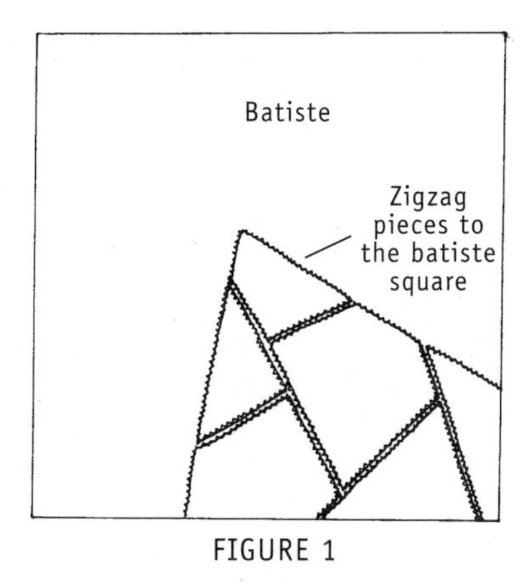

FIGURE 1

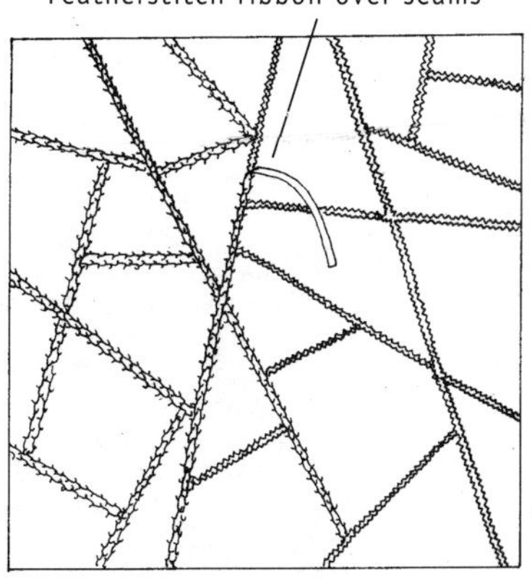

FIGURE 2

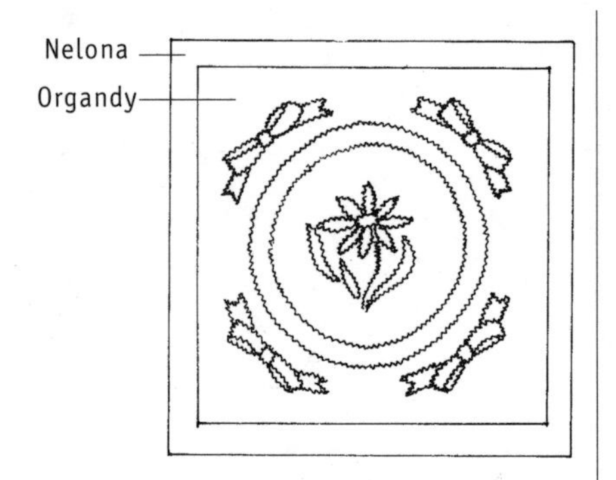

FIGURE 1

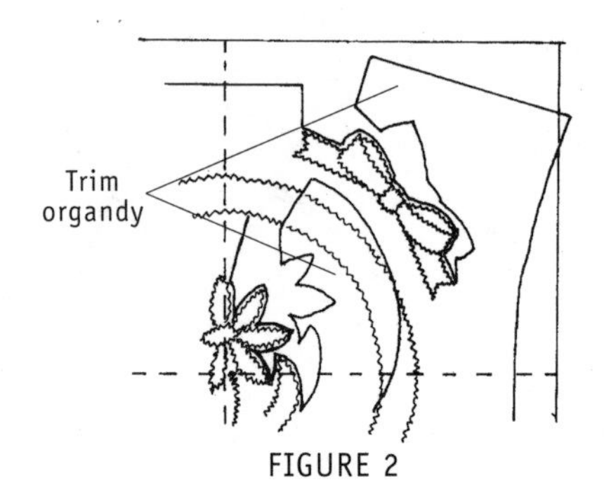

FIGURE 2

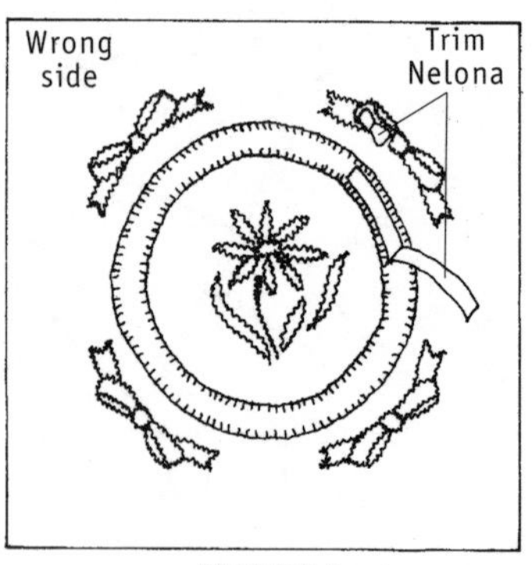

FIGURE 3

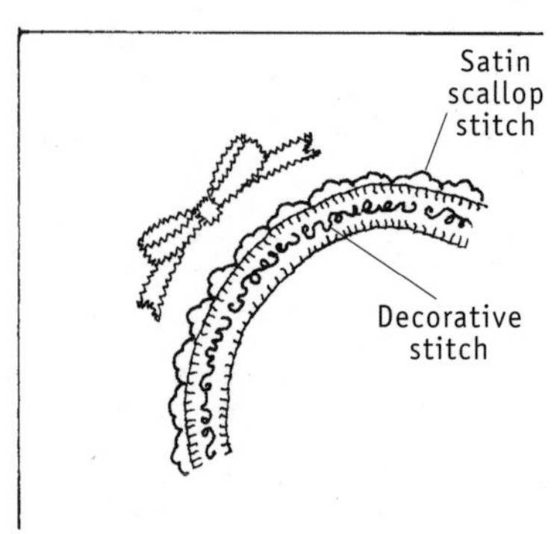

FIGURE 4

Australian Windowpane

Block #9
Australian Windowpane

Supplies

- One 15″ square of ecru Nelona
- One 12″ square of Swiss cotton organdy
- #70/10 Embroidery needle
- #100 or #110 Universal needle
- Machine embroidery threads
- Australian windowpane template
- Tear-away stabilizer

1. Starch and press the Nelona and press the organdy. Use the blue wash-out marking pen to trace the circle, flower/ leaves and bow motifs centered on the Nelona block.

2. Place the organdy over the traced design and pin in place. Use fine ecru thread, #70 needle, and zigzag (L = 1.0; W = 1.0) over all outer lines of the flower/leaves and bow motifs and both circle lines. *(fig. 1)*. Trim away the organdy from **outside** the lines, leaving the organdy inside the circle and flower/leaves and bow motifs *(fig. 2)*.

3. Set up for satin stitch (L = about 0.3; W = 2.0). Using decorative embroidery thread and tear-away stabilizer, satin stitch over all design lines for the flower, leaves, and bows; increase the satin stitch width where the stem joins the flower. Tie-off satin stitching each time the stitching is started or stopped. Use ecru thread and #100 or #110 universal needle to work the pinstitch (L = 2.0 – 2.5, W = 1.5) around the inner and outer edges of the circle. The "fingers" of the pinstitch should go into the organdy and the straight part of the stitch is on the marked lines.

4. On the wrong side, trim the Nelona away from behind the organdy, very, very close to satin stitching, being careful not to cut the stitches or organdy. Use blunt end scissors where possible, but pointed scissors will be needed to trim in some areas *(fig. 3)*.

5. Using ecru decorative embroidery thread, stitch a decorative stitch in the center of the organdy of the circle. Use water-soluble stabilizer if necessary to stabilize.

6. Using tear-away stabilizer behind the block, add a satin scallop stitch along the outer edge of the circle *(fig. 4)*.

7. Rinse the block to remove markings, starch, and press; trim to 14" square.

Assembling the Quilt Top

NOTE: Refer to assembly diagram (Figures 1-4).

Supplies

- 3/4 yard of green Nelona
- 1/4 yard of yellow Nelona
- 16 yards of 5/8-inch lace insertion

1. Starch and press the green and yellow Nelona. Measure all blocks; if any are less than 14" square, trim all squares to the size of the smallest block. It doesn't matter if the blocks don't measure a full 14", it just matters that all blocks are the same size.

2. Cut 24 rectangles from the green Nelona, each 3" x 14" (or the length of the finished blocks). For example, if the blocks are 13-1/2" square, the green strips should measure 3" x 13-1/2".

3. Cut sixteen 3" squares from the yellow Nelona.

4. Zigzag (L = 0.8; W = 2.0) lace insertion along one long side of six green rectangles and along both sides of six more. Place the raw edge of the fabric halfway under the width of the insertion, as in the Seminole Lacework Block.

5. Lay out the blocks as they will be positioned in the quilt top, making a three-by-three grid. Stitch the blocks together in three vertical rows with green rectangles between the blocks. The rectangles with lace on both sides will be between blocks; the rectangles with lace on one side only will be stitched at the top and bottom of the rows. There will be lace between each block and rectangle, with no lace on the outer edges of the quilt top *(fig. 1)*. Trim the fabric from behind the lace.

6. Zigzag lace insertion to one side of eight yellow squares and to two opposite sides of the remaining eight yellow squares.

7. Zigzag the yellow squares and the short ends of the remaining green rectangles together to form four narrow strips to fit between the vertical rows of blocks. The sequence from top to bottom will be: square with lace on one side; rectangle; square with lace on both sides; rectangle; square with lace on both sides; rectangle; square with lace on one side *(see fig. 2)*. Lace is between all fabric pieces. Trim the fabric from behind the lace.

8. Zigzag insertion along one long edge of two rectangle/square strips and along both edges of the remaining two strips *(fig. 3)*.

9. Stitch the block strips to the rectangle/square strips, matching the insertion at intersections. Again, there is lace between fabric pieces, and no lace along the outer edge *(fig. 4)*. Trim the fabric from behind the lace. Press the quilt top.

FIGURE 1

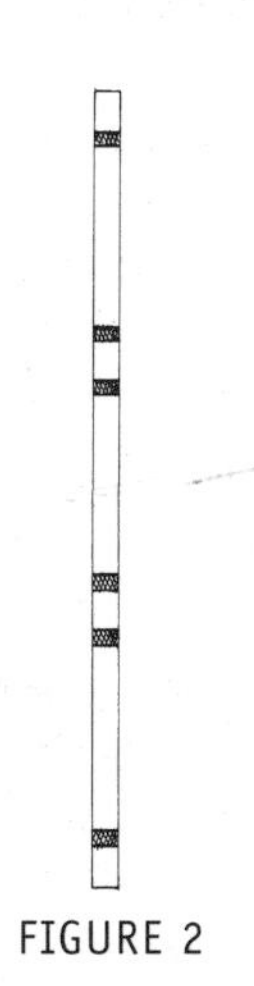

FIGURE 2

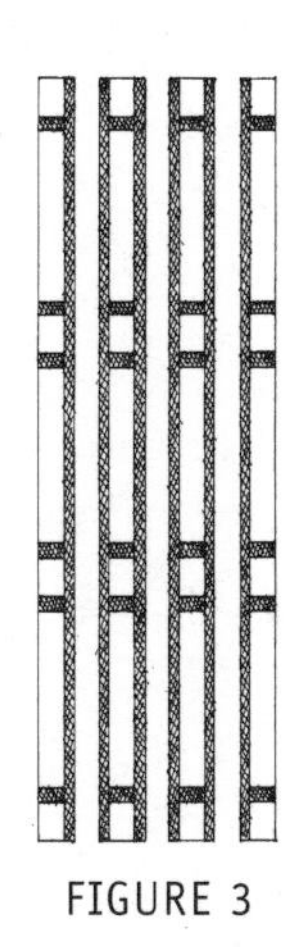

FIGURE 3

FIGURE 4

Final Quilt Assembly

Supplies

- Backing fabric:
  1-3/4 yards if 60 inches wide; 3-1/4 yards if 45″ wide
- Optional underlining, same amount as backing
- 54″ square of batting
- 1/2 yard of blue Nelona for binding
- Clear invisible thread
- Safety pins or quilt tack gun and tacks

1. Prepare the backing by lightly starching and pressing. Piece the backing fabric as necessary to form a backing about 2" larger than the quilt top on all sides. Prepare optional underlining in the same way.

2. On a large, flat surface (like the floor!) place the backing wrong side up, then smooth the batting over the backing. If an underlining is to be used, place it over the batting; place the quilt top right side up over the other layers. Use safety pins or quilt tacks to baste all layers together.

3. Hand quilt or machine quilt with clear invisible thread. Refer to the drawing of the quilt showing quilting lines *(fig. 1)*. Quilt along each edge of the lace insertion pieces between rectangles and squares.

4. Stitch close to the outer edge of the quilt top, then trim away any excess batting and backing.

5. Cut 6-1/2 yards (six crossgrain strips) of blue fabric 2" wide. Remove the selvages from both ends of each strip. Place two strips right sides together and stitch the layers together with a diagonal seam *(fig. 2)*.

6. Trim the excess fabric 1/4" beyond the stitched seam. Press the seam open or to one side.

7. Continue stitching the strips together until you have one long continuous strip of binding.

8. Fold the strip lengthwise, wrong sides together and press.

9. Draw miter lines along each corner of the quilt. Beginning along one long edge of the quilt, pin raw edges of the quilt binding to the edges of the right side of the quilt.

10. Stitch, using a 1/4" seam allowance, starting about 1" from the end of the strip. Stop stitching at the miter line and backstitch.

11. Fold a 1/2" pleat in the binding at the corner and begin stitching again along the second side of the binding, starting at the miter line *(fig. 3)*.

12. Continue stitching, using this same technique at each corner. Stop stitching about 2" from the beginning. Overlap the beginning and the end 1/2" and trim away any excess. Fold one edge of the binding to the inside 1/4". Place the straight end into the folded end and continue stitching *(fig. 4)*.

13. Fold the binding over the edges of the quilt, enclosing the seam allowance. The folded edge of the binding should be placed just past the seam line. At the corners, the binding will be folded into a miter. Stitch the binding in place using machine straight stitch, pinstitch (L = 2.0 – 2.5, W = 1.5) or stitch by hand *(fig. 5)*.

FIGURE 1

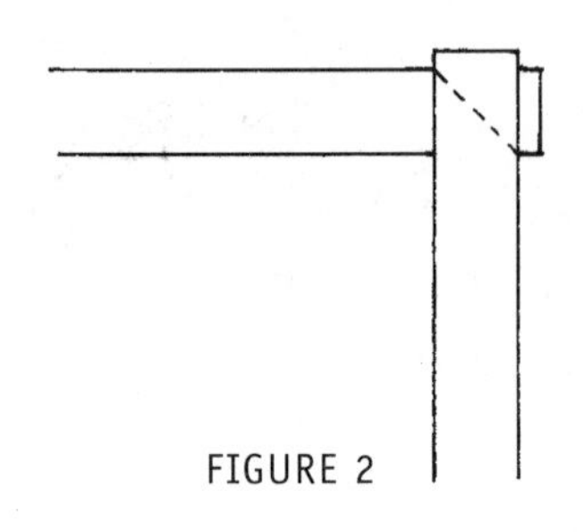

FIGURE 2

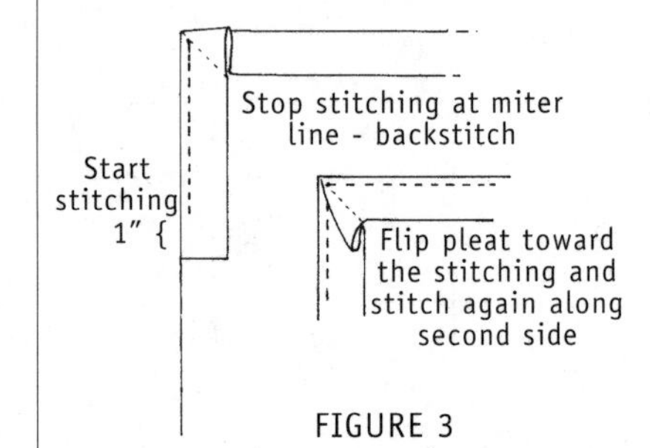

FIGURE 3

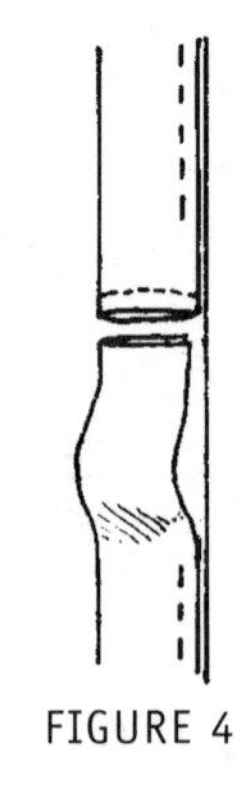

FIGURE 4

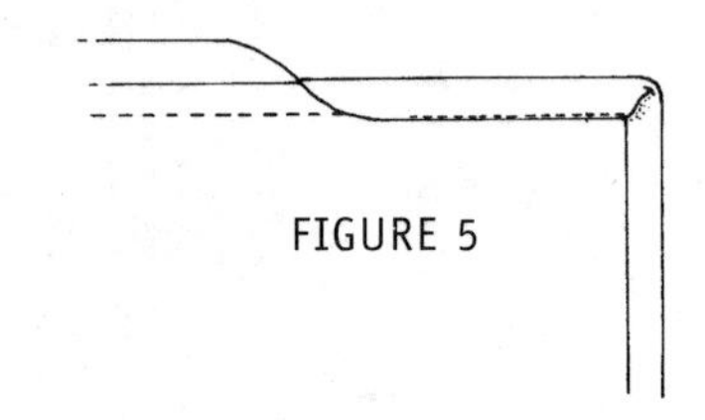

FIGURE 5

Lighthouse Wall Hanging

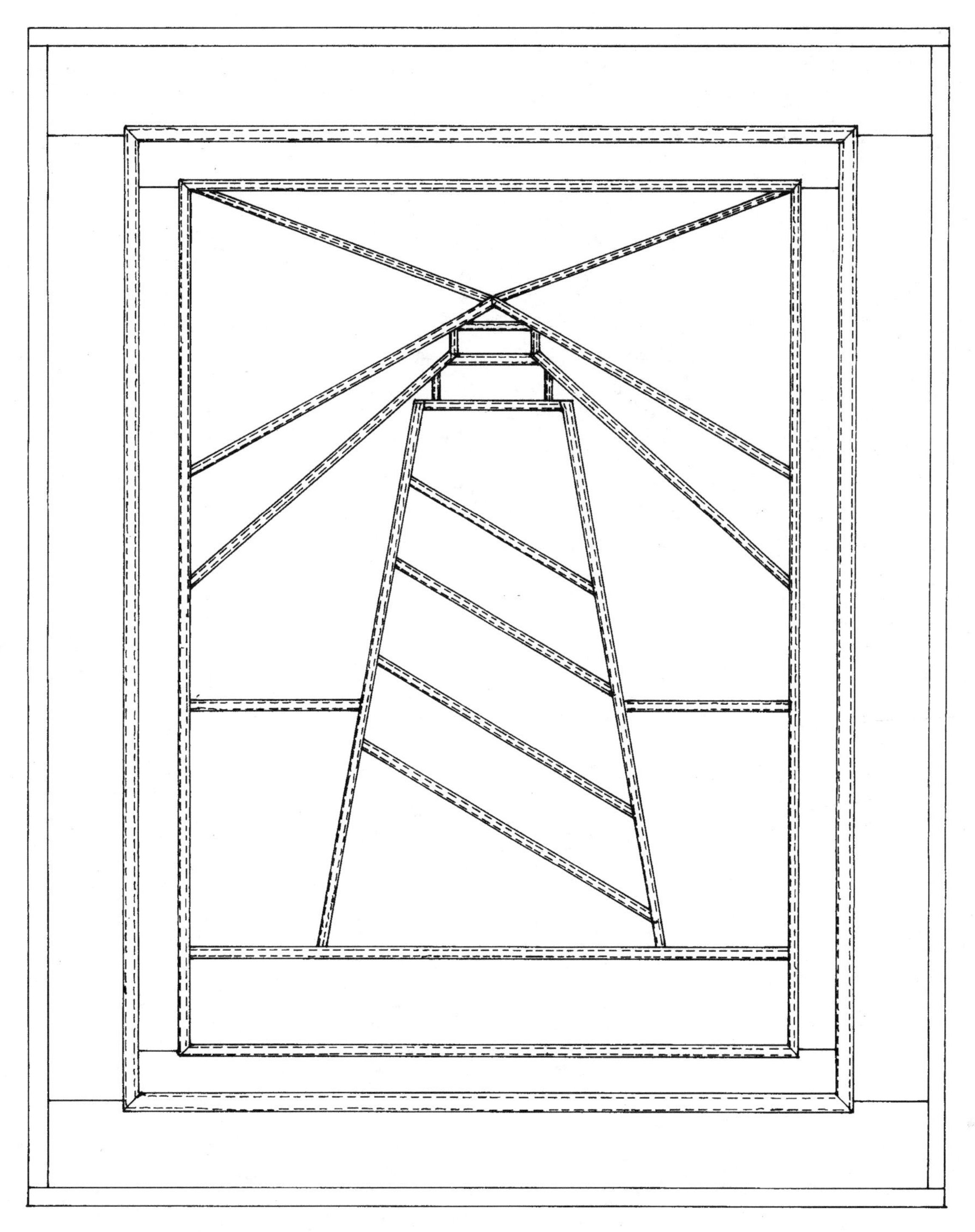

This wonderful wall hanging measures 29 inches wide by 36 inches long. It has four different shades of blue with a pale yellow. The lightest shade is almost white and the darkest is a wonderful royal blue. The lighthouse outlines are made with fusible 1/4 inch bias tape. The bias tape also outlines the yellow stream of light and borders with 1/4 inch bias on the outer border. Fabric that matches the fusible bias is used to finish the edge of the wall hanging. This wall hanging can be attached to a decorative rod or hung with simple hooks by adding loops to the top edge. What a great gift idea for a little boy's room with a nautical theme. It would also be great for a beach house or a lake house made in the colors of the room.

SUPPLIES

NOTE: The blue fabric colors need to blend well together beginning with the palest blue for the background behind the lighthouse to a royal blue for the outer edge binding.

- 20"x 26-1/2" rectangle of pale blue for center of wall hanging (color #1) marking the vertical center
- 1/2 yard of light blue for border and lighthouse (color #2)
- 1-1/2 yards of medium light blue for border, lighthouse, and backing (color #3)
- 3/4 yard of blue fabric to match the fusible bias for the edge binding (color #4)
- 1/4 yard of pale yellow for light stream
- 1/2 yard of fusible web
- 3 yards of 1/2" fusible bias tape - Royal Blue
- 7-1/2 yards of fusible 1/4" bias tape - Royal Blue
- Two spools of lightweight sewing thread to match the fusible bias or invisible thread
- #4.0/80 twin needle for stitching 1/4" bias tape
- #70 universal needle
- Ruler
- Wash-away marker
- Temporary spray adhesive
- Low Loft Batting

Templates

Lighthouse templates A,B,C,D,E,F,G,H,I

All seams are 1/4" unless otherwise noted.

Cutting

1. Cut a rectangle of fabric just larger than each of the lighthouse template pieces in the color stated on the template. Trace the templates onto the back of the fusible web.

NOTE: Reverse the designs when tracing onto fusible web to keep from getting a mirror image. Tracing as is will reverse the lines on the lighthouse.

Fuse the webbing to the back of each rectangle following the directions included with the webbing. Cut out each shape along the template lines.

2. From color #2, cut two strips 2" by 26-1/2" and two strips 2" by 23-1/2".

3. From color #3, cut two strips 3-1/2" by 30" and two strips 3-1/2" by 29-1/2".

4. From color #3, cut a rectangle 29" by 36" for back of wall hanging.

5. From color #4, cut two strips 2-1/4" by 37" and two strips 2-1/4" by 30" for the binding on the outer edge.

Construction

1. Mark the vertical center of the 20" x 26-1/2" piece (color #1). Place marks on the vertical center 3-1/4" from the bottom and 3-5/8" from the top.

2. Remove the paper backing and center the lighthouse pieces onto the 20" x 26-1/2" rectangle of color #1 beginning 3-1/4" from the bottom edge *(fig. 1)*. Following the instructions for the fusible web, adhere the pieces to the rectangle.

3. With a wash-away marker and ruler, draw the lines extending from either side of the lighthouse, the lines coming from the top of the lighthouse and the line following the bottom edge of the lighthouse *(fig. 2)*.

4. Sew the two 26-1/2" strips of color #2 to each side of the rectangle *(fig. 3)*. Press the seams toward the strips.

5. Sew the two 23-1/2" strips of color #2 to the top and bottom of the rectangle *(fig. 4)*. Press the seams toward the strips.

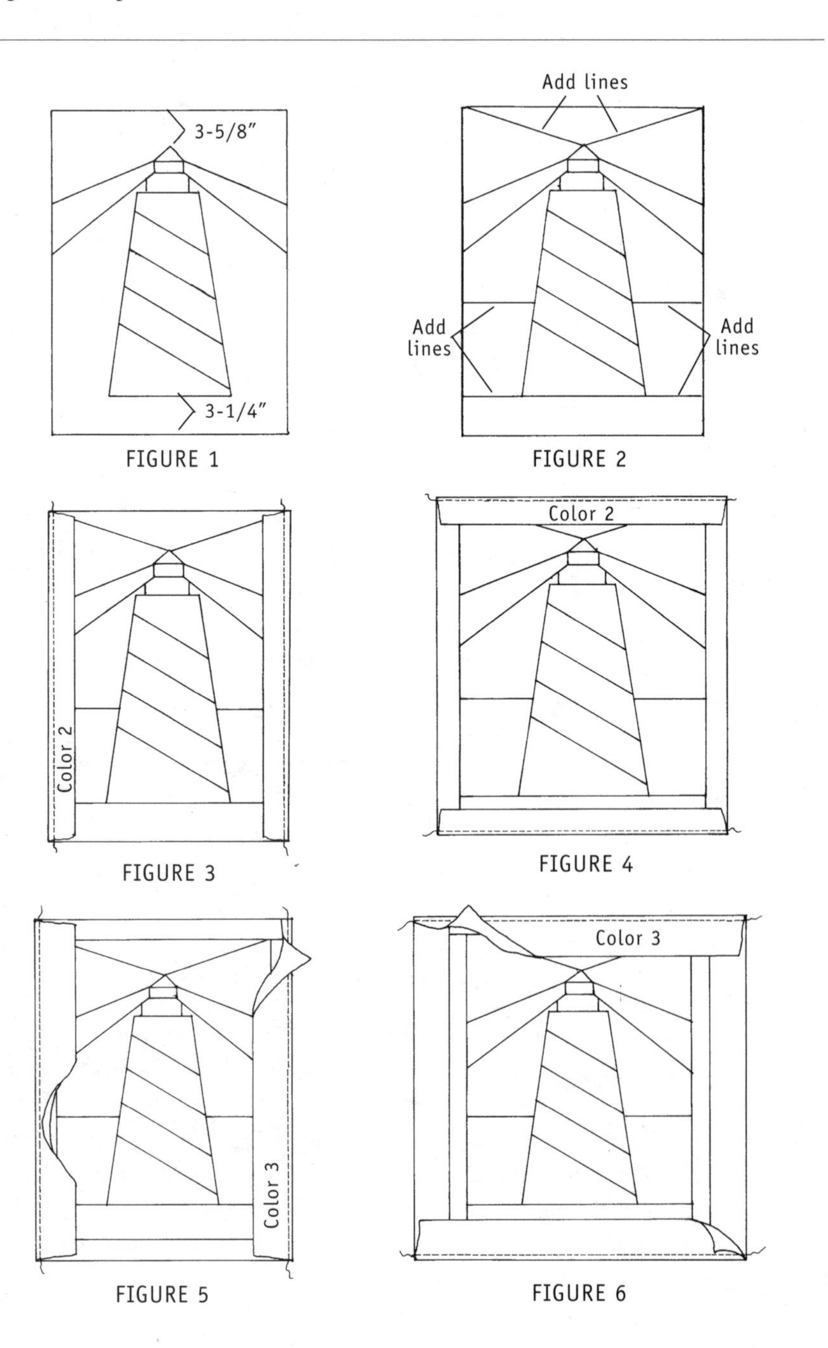

FIGURE 1 FIGURE 2 FIGURE 3 FIGURE 4 FIGURE 5 FIGURE 6

6. Sew the two 29-1/2 " strips of color #3 to the sides of the rectangle *(fig. 5)*. Press the seams towards the strips.

7. Sew the two 30" strips of color #3 to the top and bottom of the rectangle *(fig. 6)*. Press the seams toward the strips.

8. Press the completed wall hanging top. Fuse the bias to the wall hanging top following the directions with the bias and referring to the diagram *(fig. 7)* for order of application.

9. Spray the wrong side of the 29" by 36" rectangle of color #3 with temporary spray adhesive. Place the wrong side of the top rectangle to the batting and the batting to the wrong side of the backing making sure edges are even. The three layers will now be treated as one.

10. Stitch each section of bias in place with the twin needle, pivoting at the miters and corners. Begin stitching the bias at a place that will be covered by another piece of bias. The bias around the border begins and ends at a corner. You may use either the lightweight thread to match the bias or clear or smoke invisible thread in both the needle and bobbin.

NOTE: If a twin needle is not available, use a single needle and straight stitch each side of the bias.

11. When stitching is complete, press the rectangle well.

12. Fold the two 30" strips and the two 37" strips (color #4) in half and press well.

13. Place a 37" strip on each side of the wall hanging with the raw edges even, matching raw edges with the bias on the right side. Stitch the strip to the wall hanging with a 1/2" seam. Trim the excess strip even with the top and bottom of the wall hanging *(fig. 8)*.

14. Fold the strip away from the rectangle and to the back, enclosing the raw edges. The folded edge of the strip should be just beyond the stitching line. Pin in place. On the front, stitch in the ditch of the seam connecting the strip. This stitching should catch the strip on the back of the wall hanging near the fold *(fig. 9)*.

15. Place the two 30" strips on the top and bottom of the wall hanging with the raw edges even. Fold up 1/4" on each end of the strip *(fig. 10)*. Trim away any excess strip. Stitch in place with a 1/2" seam.

16. Fold the strip away from the rectangle and to the back. The folded edge of the strip should be just beyond the stitching line. Pin in place. On the front of the rectangle, stitch in the ditch of the seam connecting the strip. This stitching should catch the strip on the back of the rectangle near the fold. Hand whip or machine stitch the openings at the end of the strip *(fig. 11)*.

17. Optional: Add fabric loops or ribbon loops to tie or hang onto rod or hooks.

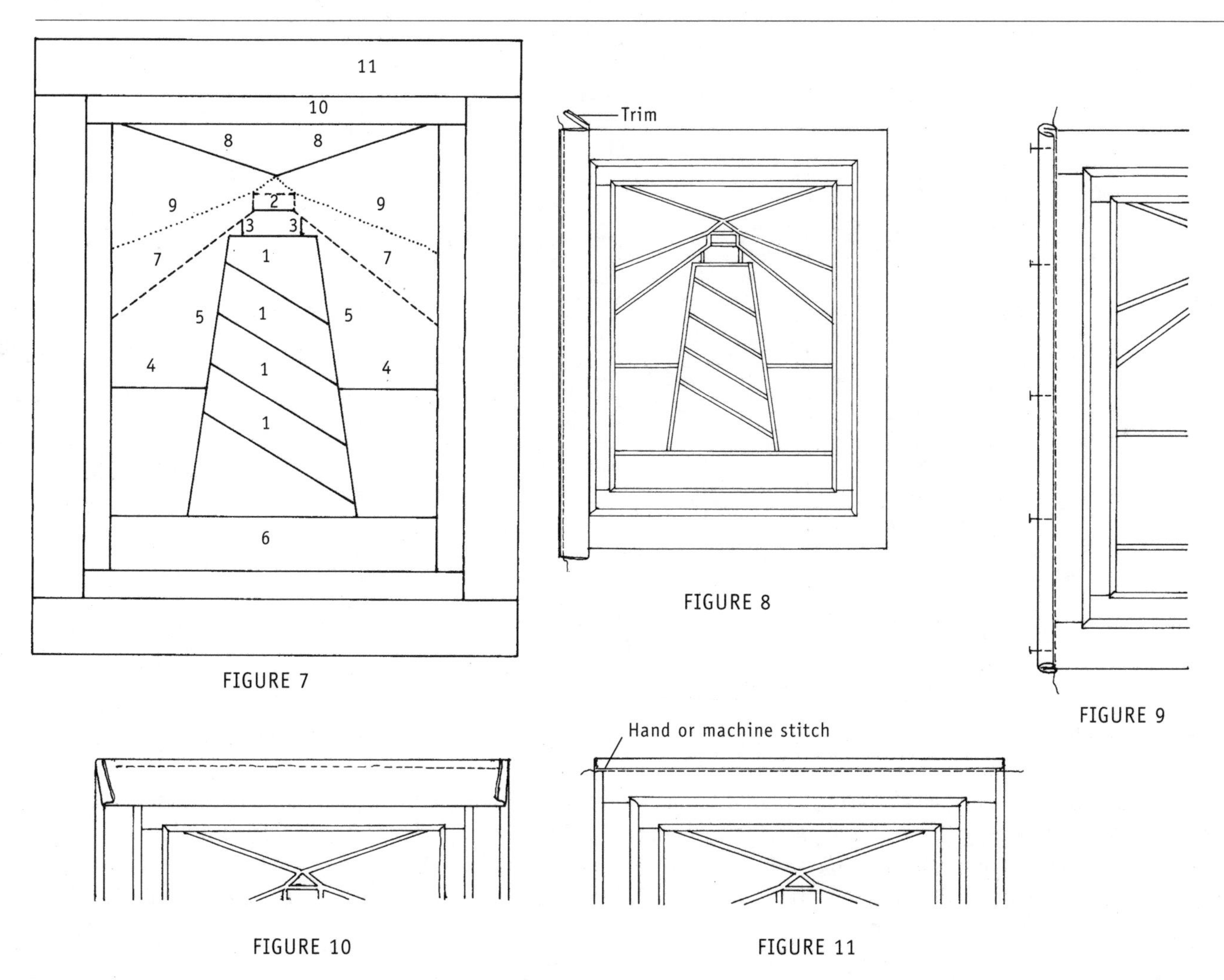

FIGURE 7

FIGURE 8

FIGURE 9

FIGURE 10

FIGURE 11

Simple Star Block Quilt

This beautiful wall quilt features the popular simple star block design, which frames floral inspirational verses. The designs are available from Amazing Designs and include several flower selections. The block is bordered with embroidered sashings and butterfly cornerstone blocks. The selection of mottled print fern and leaf fabric compliments the floral designs. This fabric is available in an assortment of colors from your local quilting supply shop. A beautiful pillow featuring the same star pattern and another floral embroidery is the perfect companion piece for the quilt. It has the same embroidered sashing and cornerstone blocks and is bordered by a wide ruffle in a complimentary leaf design. We are sure you will love these projects incorporating both embroidery and quilting techniques.

The quilt pictured was made using a mottled fabric such as Fossil Ferns (available in many colors at quilting shops).

Supplies

• 2/3 yard pale lavender fabric (*color* 1)
• 1/3 yard lavender fabric (*color* 2)
• 7/8 yard purple fabric (*color* 3)
• 2 yards coordinating lavender print fabric (*color* 4)
• Low-loft batting
\- • Sewing thread for construction
• Machine embroidery thread for quilting: lavender, purple and off-white
• Machine embroidery thread in desired colors for the embroidery designs
\- • Invisible thread
\- • Quilter's Ruler
\- • 1-1/2" Half Square Triangle Paper (available at quilting shops) (optional)
\- • Rotary cutter and mat
• 3-1/2 yards of tear-away stabilizer
\- • Temporary spray adhesive (KK2000)
\- • Quarter-inch sewing foot
\- • Free-motion quilting or embroidery foot
\- • Walking foot (optional)
\- • Computerized Embroidery Card #AD3000 "Inspirational Concepts in Sulky" available from Amazing Designs: Joyce Drexler, designer
\- • Quilting templates
• Optional: 27" rod (not including decorative ends) for hanging

(-) *Indicates supplies needed to create the Simple Star Block pillow*

Cutting

(Refer to cutting guide)

1. Cut three 10" squares (or large enough to fit into your hoop) from the pale lavender *(color 1)* fabric to be embroidered.

2. Cut twenty-four 3-1/2" squares from pale lavender *(color 1).*

3. Cut twelve 3-1/2" by 6-1/2" rectangles from the lavender fabric *(color 2).*

4. Cut twelve 3-1/2" squares from the lavender fabric *(color 2).*

5. Cut ten sashing strips 3-1/2" by 12-1/2" from the purple fabric *(color 3).*

6. Cut twelve pieces of tear-away stabilizer the same size as the squares cut in step 1 above. Mark the vertical grain of each piece of stabilizer.

7. For the butterfly cornerstones cut eight 2-3/8" squares from the pale lavender *(color 1)* and eight 2-3/8" squares from the purple fabric *(color 3). NOTE: If you are using triangle paper, cut rectangles of colors 1 and 3 large enough to produce sixteen 1-1/2" finished half squares instead of cutting the 2-3/8" squares. Refer to the instructions for the triangle paper.*

8. Cut sixteen 2" squares from the purple fabric *(color 3)* for the solid blocks in the butterfly cornerstones.

9. Cut two strips 2" by 18-1/2" and two strips 2" by 51-1/2" from the coordinating lavender print fabric *(color 4)* for the narrow sashings.

10. Cut two strips 3-1/2" by 21-1/2" and three strips 3-1/2" by 44" from the purple fabric (*color 3*) for the outermost sashings.

11. Cut a piece of batting 28" by 58".

12. Cut a piece of lavender print fabric *(color 4)* 28" by 58" for the quilt backing.

13. Cut four 2-1/2" by 44" strips from the lavender print *(color 4)* for the quilt binding.

14. Cut one 4" by 27" strip from the lavender print *(color 4)* for the rod casing *(optional).*

NOTE: All seams need to be stitched precisely at 1/4" unless otherwise noted.

CUTTING GUIDE

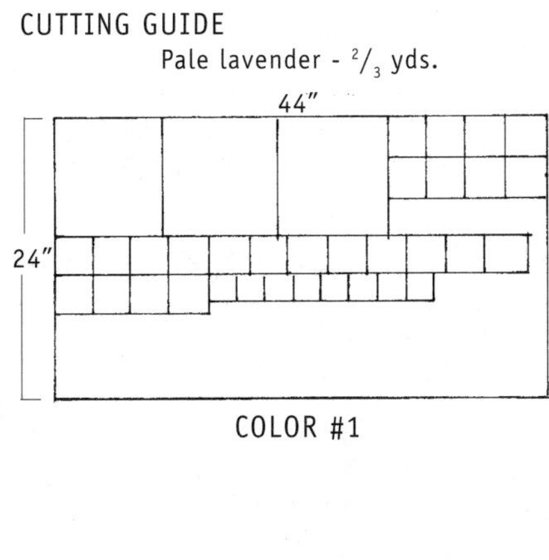

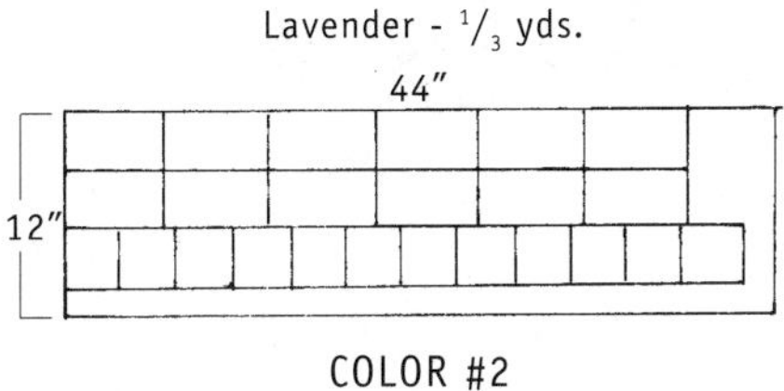

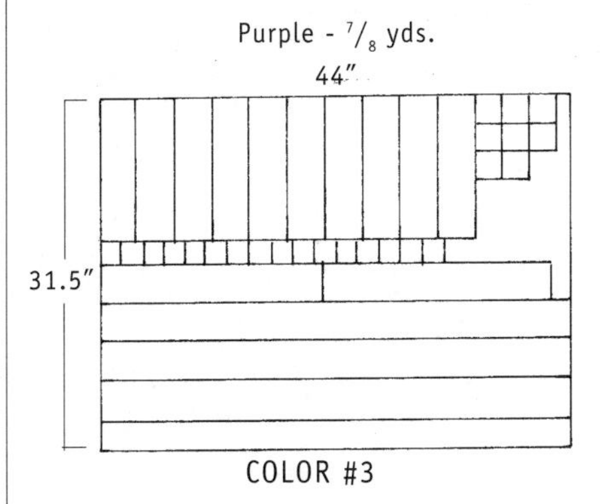

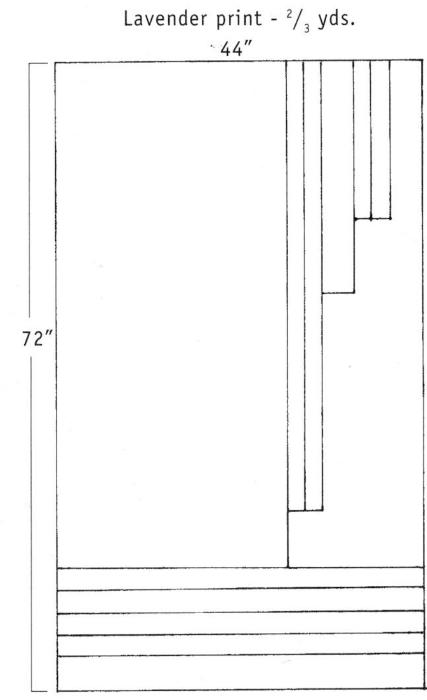

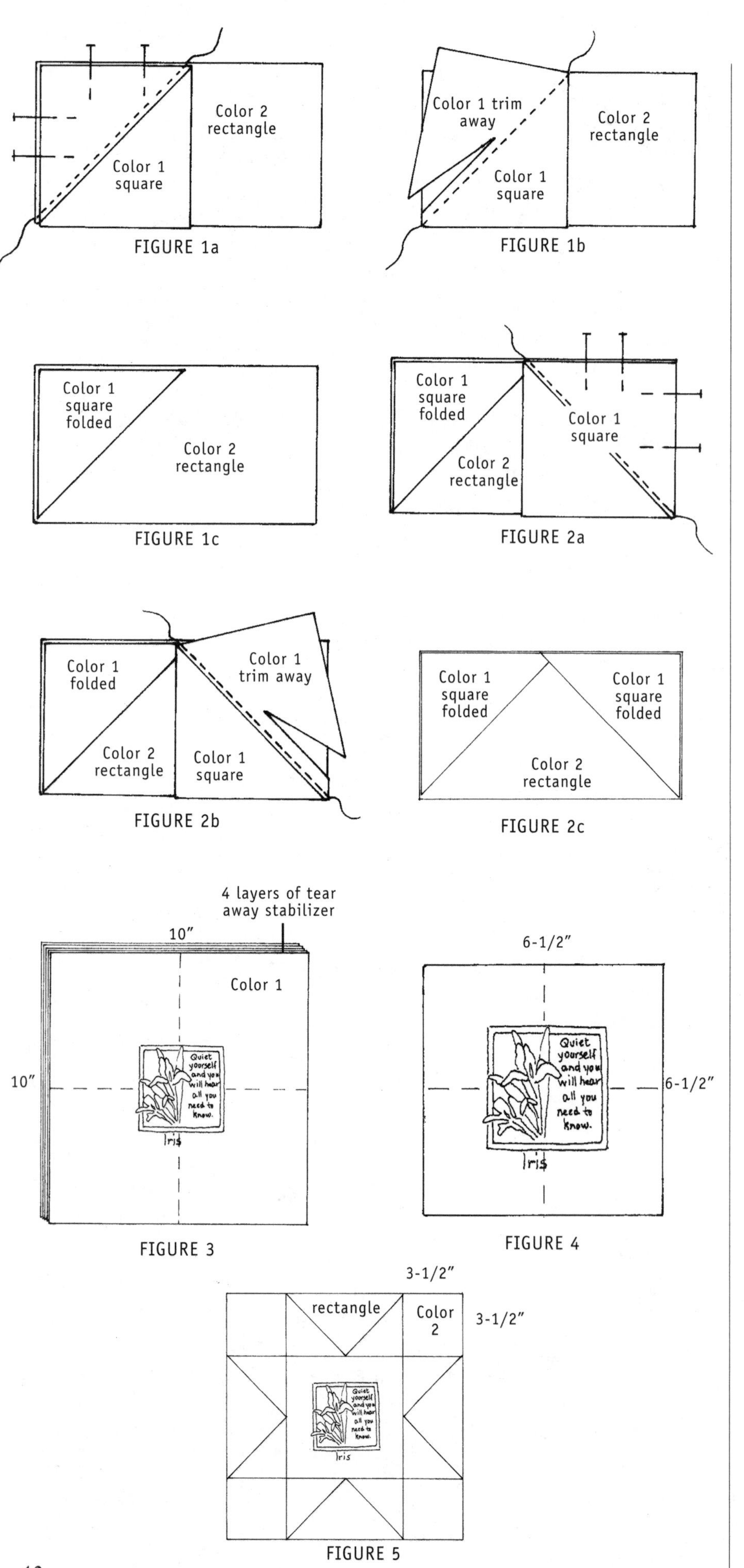

Constructing the Simple Star Block(s)

1. Place one of the color 2 rectangles right side up onto a protected flat surface.

2. Place a 3-1/2" square of color 1 on the left hand side of the rectangle right sides together. Pin in place *(fig. 1a)*.

3. Using the small ruler and a wash-out marker, draw a line from corner to corner of the 3-1/2" square as shown *(fig. 1a)*.

4. Sew a straight line just outside the drawn line (not on it) *(fig. 1a)*. Trim away the upper triangle leaving a 1/4" seam allowance *(fig. 1b)*.

5. Fold the square back on itself to create the triangle *(fig. 1c)*.

6. Repeat steps 2-5 placing a square of color 1 on the right hand side of the rectangle *(fig. 2a, 2b and 2c)*.

7. Repeat steps 1 – 6 with the remaining color 2 rectangles and color 1 squares. You should have a total of 12 completed rectangles.

8. Lay all rectangles aside.

9. Fold one of the 10" squares of color 1 into quarters and mark the center.

10. Place the square right side down onto a protected flat surface.

11. Using temporary spray adhesive, adhere four layers of tear-away stabilizer to the back of the fabric square, alternating grain direction.

12. Hoop and embroider the square. The embroidery needs to be no larger than 3-1/4" by 3-1/4". The sample quilt contains embroideries measuring 3-1/4" by 3-1/4" plus the flower name in 1/4" lettering just below the embroidery *(fig. 3)*.

13. Repeat steps 10 - 12 for the two remaining 10" squares.

14. Remove the stabilizer from behind the squares one layer at a time to avoid stretching the fabric or distorting the embroidery.

15. Centering the embroidery, cut each embroidered piece to measure 6-1/2" square *(fig. 4)*. Set embroidered squares aside.

16. Place the pieces right side up for one star block onto a flat surface as shown in figure 5.

17. On the top horizontal row, with right sides together, stitch the 3-1/2" square (color *2)* to each end of the rectangle being careful that the points of the star are toward the outside of the square. Press the seams

toward the rectangle *(fig. 5)*.

18. Repeat step 17 for the bottom horizontal row.

19. On the center horizontal row, with right sides together, stitch the rectangles to each side of the center embroidered square making certain that the points of the star are facing outward. Press the seams toward rectangles *(fig. 5)*.

20. With right sides together, stitch the top horizontal row to the center horizontal row matching the seams. Press the seam toward the center block *(fig. 5)*.

21. With right sides together, stitch the bottom horizontal row to the center horizontal row matching the seams. Press the seam toward the center block.

22. Repeat steps 17 - 21 to construct the remaining two squares.

23. Lay the blocks aside.

Constructing the Butterfly Cornerstones

1. If using triangle paper, follow the instructions with the paper to produce sixteen half squares of colors 1 and 3.

2. If not using triangle paper, follow the instructions below:

a. Place a 2-3/8" square of color 1 and color 3 right sides together *(fig. 6a)*. Repeat for the remaining seven pairs of squares.

b. On each of the eight sets, draw a diagonal line from corner to corner with a ruler and wash-out marker on the lighter color *(fig. 6a)*.

c. On each of the eight sets, stitch with a straight stitch 1/4" on each side of the drawn line *(fig. 6b)*.

d. Cut each set on the line drawn in step 2b. There are sixteen double layer triangles *(fig. 6c)*.

e. Open each of the triangles and press the seam to the darker fabric creating sixteen half squares *(fig. 6d)*.

f. Stitch one color 3 (2") square to each of the half squares. Press the seam toward color 3 square *(fig. 6e)*.

g. Stitch two of the rectangles created in step f together to form the butterfly cornerstone, making sure that color 1 is as in figure 6f.

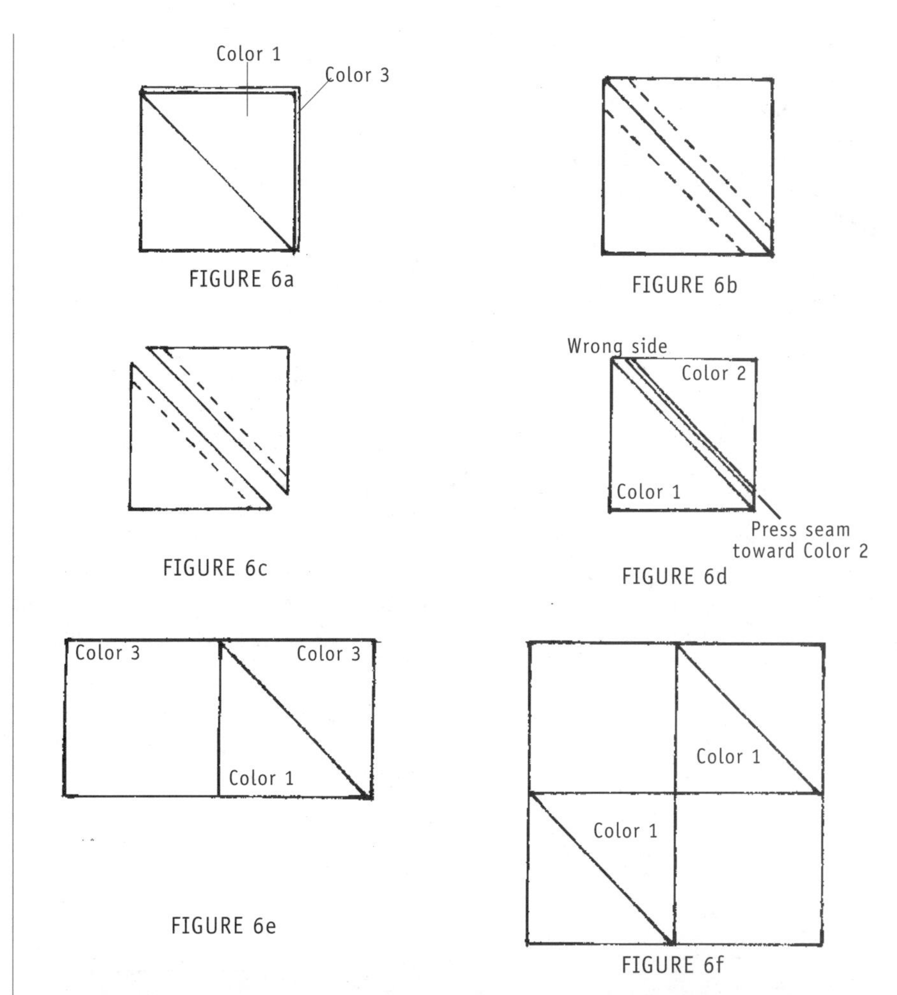

Constructing the Sashings and Center Panel

1. Lay out each star square with sashing strips and cornerstone squares (*as in figure 7*) being careful that all butterfly cornerstone squares are in the correct position.

2. Create the four sashing strips by stitching together two butterfly cornerstones with a sashing strip in the center for each sashing cornerstone strip as illustrated. Press seams toward the purple sashings (*fig. 8*).

3. Stitch a sashing strip to each side of the star blocks. Press seams toward sashing strips (*fig. 9*).

4. Matching seam intersections, stitch the completed sashing strips to the completed sashing/block strips to create the center panel. Press seams toward the center of the block (*fig. 10*).

5. Straight stitch the 2" by 18-1/2" lavender print (*color* 4) strips to the top and bottom edge of the created panel. Press the seams toward the strips (see fig. 11).

6. Straight stitch the 2" by 51-1/2" lavender print (*color* 4) to each side of the panel. Press the seams toward the strips (*fig. 11*).

7. Straight stitch the 3" by 21-1/2" purple (*color* 4) strip to the top and bottom of the newly created panel. Press the seams toward the strips (*see fig. 12*).

8. Stitch the short ends of the three 3" by 45" purple (*color* 4) strips together to make one continuous strip. Cut the strip into two strips 3" by 56-1/2". Straight stitch the 3" by 56-1/2" purple (*color 4*) strip to each side of the newly created panel. Press the seams toward the purple strips (*fig. 12*).

Layering the Quilt

1. Press the entire quilt top very well.

2. Place the backing onto a table top with the wrong side up.

3. Center the batting onto the backing.

4. Center the quilt top onto the batting. The backing and batting should be slightly larger than the quilt top.

5. Pin the layers together with safety pins or use a quilt tack gun approximately 2" to 3" apart. Pin the layers together along the raw edges of the quilt top.

6. Trim away the excess batting and backing beyond the raw edge of the quilt top, being very careful not to cut away any of the quilt top (*fig. 13*).

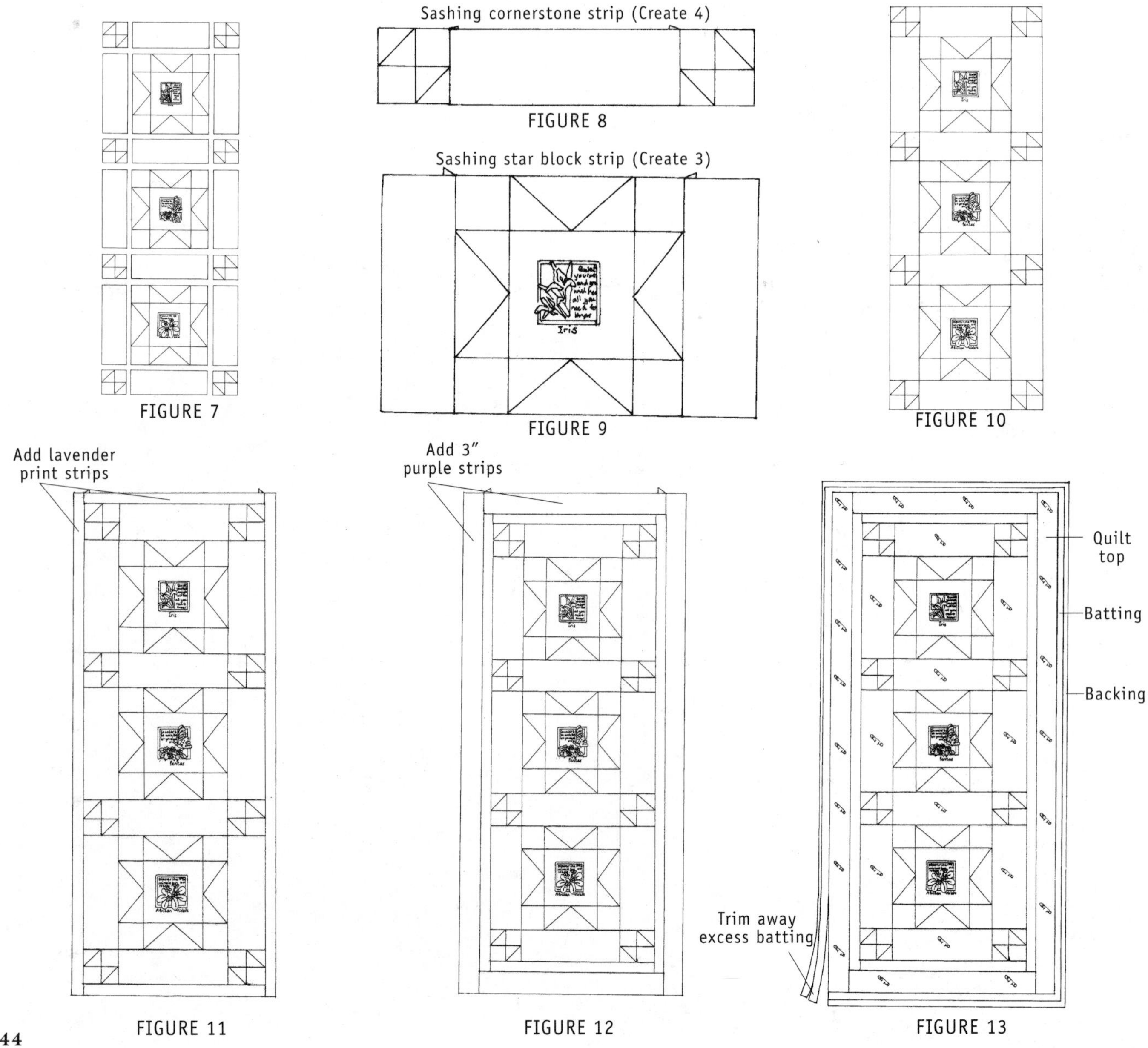

FIGURE 7

FIGURE 8

FIGURE 9

FIGURE 10

FIGURE 11

FIGURE 12

FIGURE 13

Quilting

NOTE: Machine embroidery thread to match the backing is used in the bobbin for all quilting.

1. Leave the quilt pinned well.

2. Using invisible thread in the needle and thread to match the quilt backing in the bobbin, stitch in the ditch along the lines shown in figure 14. This can be done free-motion or using a walking foot. Straight stitch quilting using invisible thread may also be added where desired in the embroidery designs of each square.

3. On the lavender squares and triangles, stitch 1/8" in from the seam line using a straight stitch (L = 2.5) and 30-weight dark purple thread (refer to the finished drawing).

4. The center block is stitched using loose stipple stitching with lavender thread in the needle. Refer to the technique for Stipple Stitching, page 111.

5. In the pale lavender triangles, stipple stitch tightly with lavender thread in the needle (refer to the finished drawing).

6. Transfer the flower design randomly around the outermost sashing, placing a flower in each corner.

7. Transfer the quilting design around the outermost sashing, repeating the design.

8. Transfer the inside sashing quilting design onto each of the quilt sashings bordering the three star blocks.

9. Transfer the quilting lines for the butterfly in each butterfly cornerstone square.

10. Using 30-weight off-white thread, stitch along the lines drawn in steps 7 - 10 to complete the quilting (refer to the finished drawing).

Optional (Part 1): Adding A Rod Pocket For Hanging

1. Fold each short end of the strip for the rod casing 1/2" and 1/2" again and press. Hand whip the hem in place. Fold the strip in half lengthwise wrong sides together and press *(fig. 15)*.

2. Pin in place along the top edge of the back of the quilt matching the raw edges *(fig. 16)*.

Refer to "Finishing the Rod Pocket" after the *binding is completed to finish the rod pocket.*

Binding

1. Using the 2-1/2" lavender print fabric for the binding, place two strips right sides together as shown in *figure 17* and stitch the layers together with a diagonal seam.

2. Trim the excess fabric 1/4" beyond the stitched seam. Press the seam open or to one side.

3. Continue stitching the strips together until you have one long continuous strip of binding.

4. Fold the strip lengthwise, matching raw edges, wrong sides together and press.

5. Draw miter lines along each corner of the quilt. Beginning along one long edge of the quilt, pin the raw edges of the quilt binding to the edges of the right side of the quilt top *(fig. 18)*.

6. Stitch using a 3/8" seam allowance, starting about 1" from the end of the strip. Stop stitching at the miter line and backstitch *(fig. 18)*.

7. Fold a 3/4" pleat in the binding at the corner and begin stitching again along the second side of the binding, starting at the miter line *(fig. 18)*.

8. Continue stitching, using this same technique at each corner. Stitch through all layers (including the rod casing layers, if a rod pocket is used) along the top of the quilt. Stop stitching about 2" from the beginning. Overlap the beginning and the end 1/2" and trim away any excess. Fold one edge of the binding to the inside 1/4". Place the straight end into the folded end and continue stitching *(fig. 19)*.

9. Fold the binding over the edges of the quilt, enclosing the seam allowance. The folded edge of the binding should be placed just past the seam line. At the corner, fold the binding into a miter. Stitch the binding in place using a straight machine stitch or whip stitch by hand *(fig. 20)*.

Optional (Part 2): Finishing the Rod Pocket

1. Press the rod pocket flat to the back side of the quilt.

2. Hand whip the lower fold of the rod pocket to the quilt back *(fig. 21)*.

3. Insert the rod through the casing for hanging.

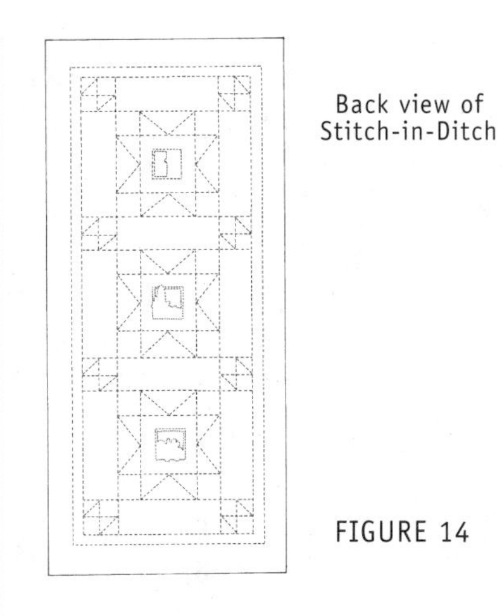

FIGURE 14

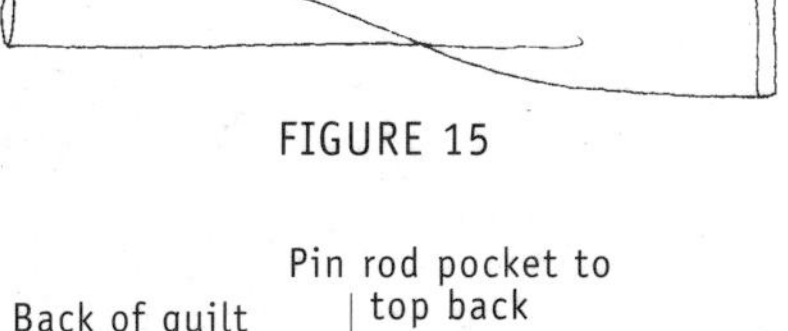

FIGURE 15

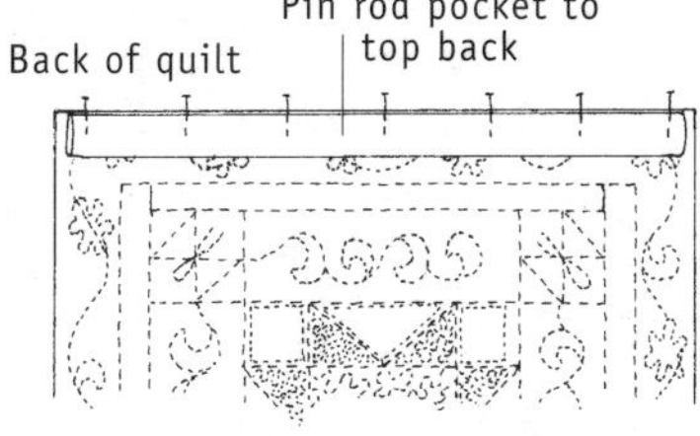

FIGURE 16

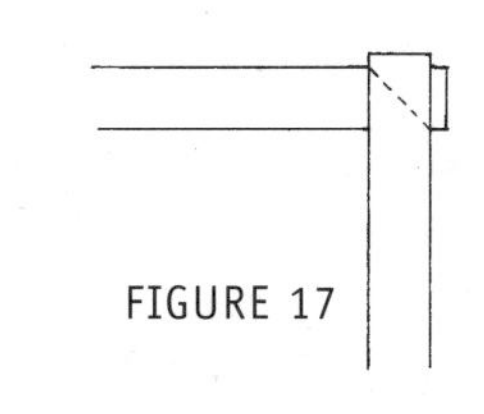

FIGURE 17

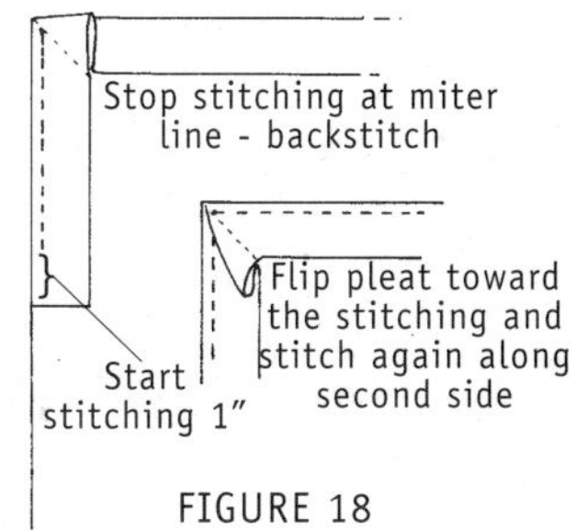

FIGURE 18

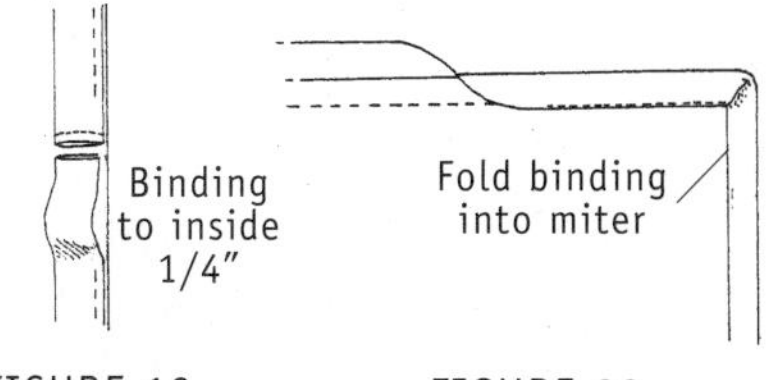

FIGURE 19 FIGURE 20

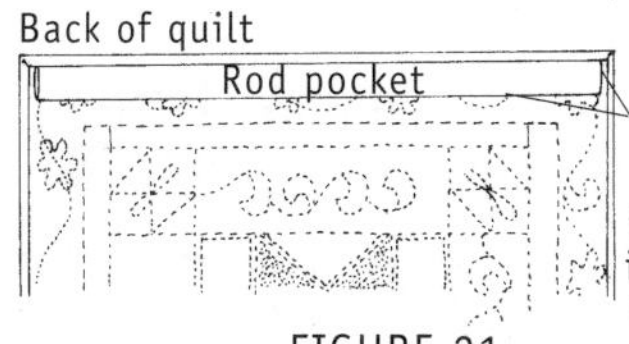

FIGURE 21

Simple Star Pillow

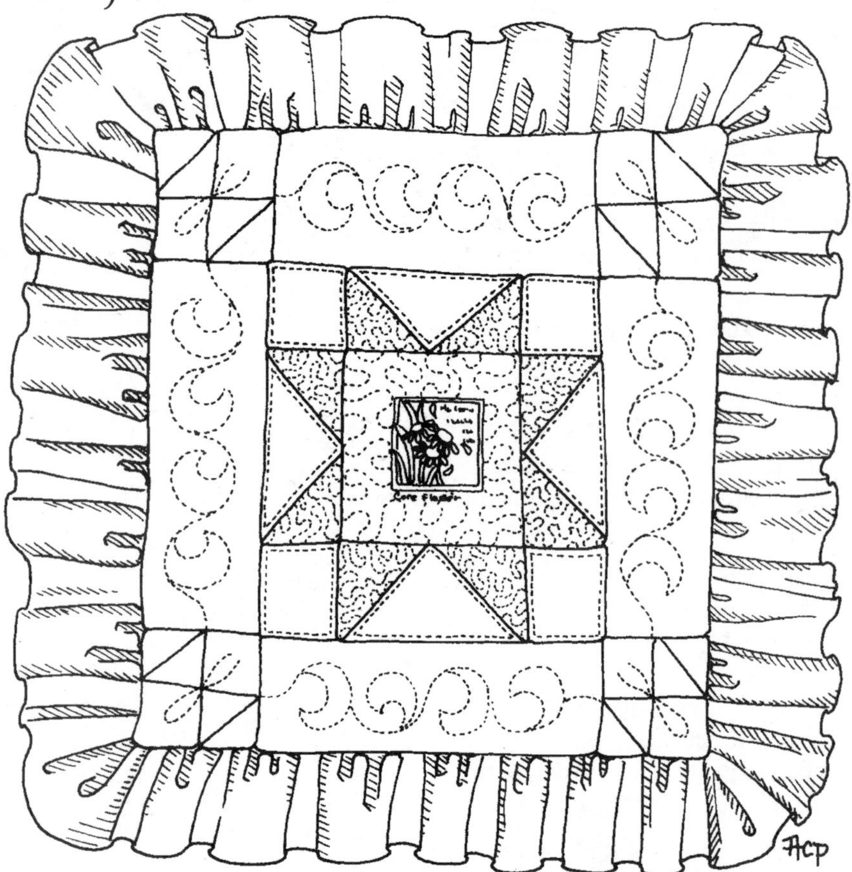

Supplies

- 1/3 yard pale lavender fabric (color 1)
- 1/4 yard lavender fabric (color 2)
- 1/4 yard purple fabric (color 3)
- 7/8 yard coordinating lavender print fabric (color 4)
- 19" square low loft batting
- 19" square muslin for backing of pillow top
- 18" pillow form
- 2/3 yard of tear-away stabilizer
- Quilting templates

(-) *Refer to quilt supply list for additional supplies needed for the pillow*

Cutting

(see cutting guide)

1. Cut one 10" square (or large enough o fit into your hoop) from the pale lavender *(color 1)* fabric to be embroidered.

2. Cut eight 3-1/2" squares from pale lavender *(color 1).*

3. Cut four 3-1/2" by 6-1/2" rectangles from the lavender fabric *(color 2).*

4. Cut four 3-1/2" squares from the lavender fabric *(color 2).*

5. Cut four sashing strips 3-1/2" by 12-1/2" from the purple fabric *(color 3).*

6. Cut four pieces of tear-away stabilizer the same size as the square cut in step 1 above. Mark the vertical grain of each piece of stabilizer.

7. For the butterfly cornerstones cut four 2-3/8" squares from the pale lavender (color 1) and four 2-3/8" squares from the purple fabric *(color 3). NOTE: If you are using triangle paper, cut two pieces of colors 1 and 3 large enough to produce eight 1-1/2" half squares instead of cutting the 2-3/8" squares. Refer to the instructions for the triangle paper.*

8. Cut eight 2" squares from the purple fabric *(color 3)* for the solid blocks in the butterfly cornerstones.

9. Cut two 13-1/2" by 18" pieces from the lavender print *(color 4)* for the pillow back.

10. Cut two strips 7-1/2" by 44" from the lavender print *(color 4)* for the pillow ruffle.

NOTE: All seams need to be stitched precisely at 1/4" unless otherwise noted.

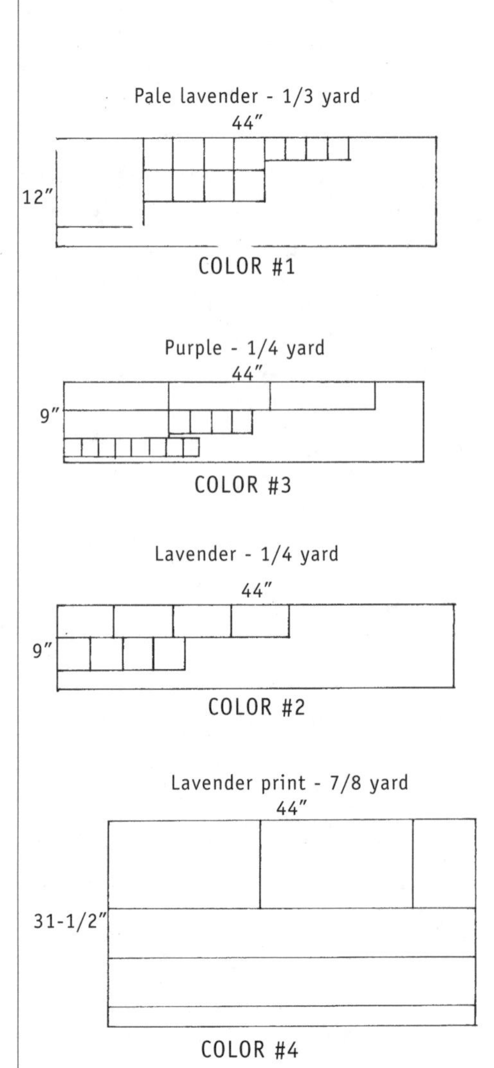

Construction of the Star Square Quilt Block

1. Refer to Simple Star Block Quilt, Constructing the Simple Star Block, steps 1-21.

2. Refer to Constructing the Butterfly Cornerstones, steps 1-2g to create four corner pieces for the pillow.

3. Using off-white thread, stitch along the design, completing the quilting *(fig. 7).*

4. Cut the muslin and batting even with the edges of the pillow top.

5. Mark the center of each side of the square.

Constructing the Sashings and Adding to the Star Square

1. Place all of the star block pieces right side up on a flat surface as shown in *figure 1.*

2. The top and bottom horizontal rows consist of one cornerstone on each side of the 3–1/2" by 12-1/2" sashing strip, note correct direction of "butterflies" on cornerstone blocks. Press the seams toward the sashing *(fig. 2).*

3. On the center horizontal row, with right sides together, stitch the sashings strips to the star square. Press the seams toward the sashing *(fig. 3).*

4. With right sides together, stitch the top and bottom horizontal rows to the center horizontal row, completing the Star Square Block *(fig. 4).*

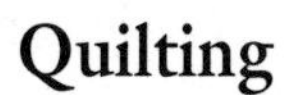

Quilting

1. Place the muslin square, wrong side up, on a flat surface and spray lightly with a temporary spray adhesive.

2. Center the batting square on top of the muslin square. Spray the batting lightly with the temporary spray adhesive.

3. Center the completed star block on top of the batting. Baste all layers together by hand, a long machine stitch, the "Quilt Tack" gun or safety pins *(fig. 5).*

4. Place invisible thread in the needle with 30-weight machine embroidery thread to match the backing in the bobbin. A regular foot, quarter-inch foot or walking foot may be used. Straight stitch-in-the-ditch at all seams *(fig. 6).*

5. Place purple machine embroidery thread in the needle. Using a straight stitch, stitch 1/8" from the seam lines in the squares and triangles of color 2 *(fig. 7).*

6. Place lavender thread in the needle. Stipple stitch in a loose pattern around the center embroidered square *(fig. 7).* Refer to Stipple Stitching, page 111.

7. Stipple stitch in a tighter pattern in the color 1 triangles *(fig. 7).*

8. Transfer the quilting lines for the butterfly in each butterfly cornerstone square.

9. Transfer the quilting design onto the sashing pieces bordering the star block.

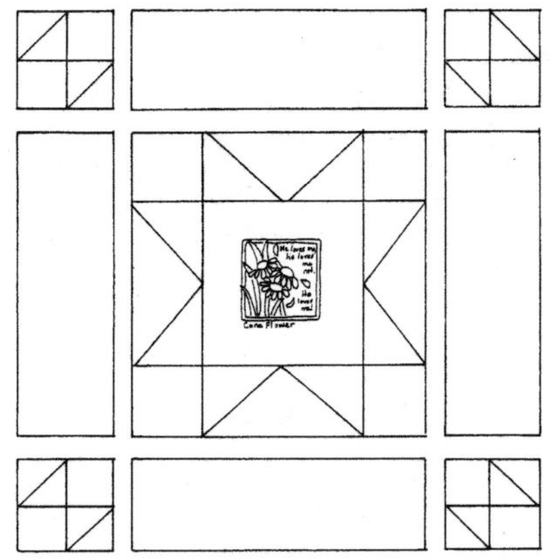

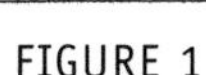

FIGURE 1

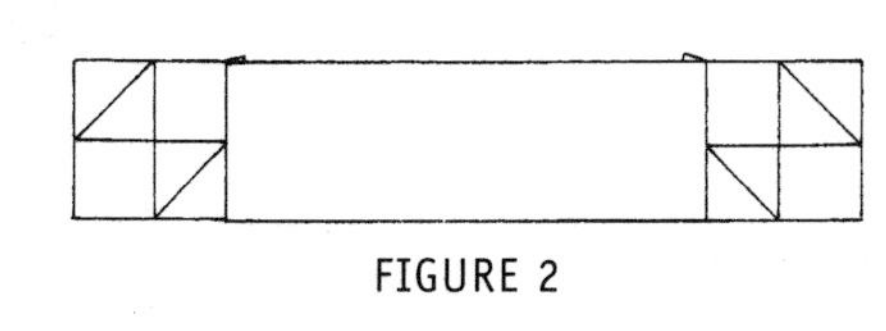

FIGURE 2

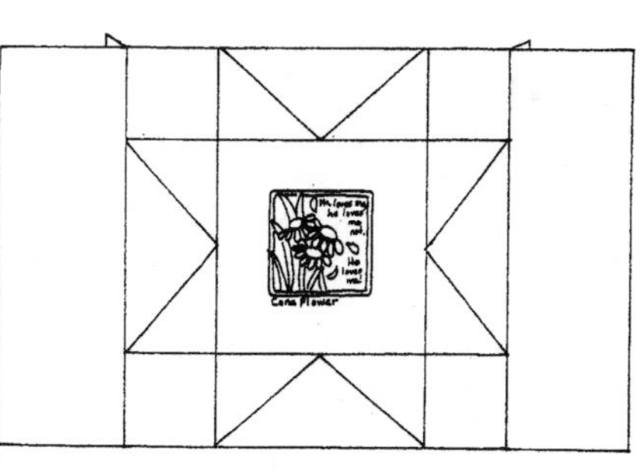

FIGURE 3

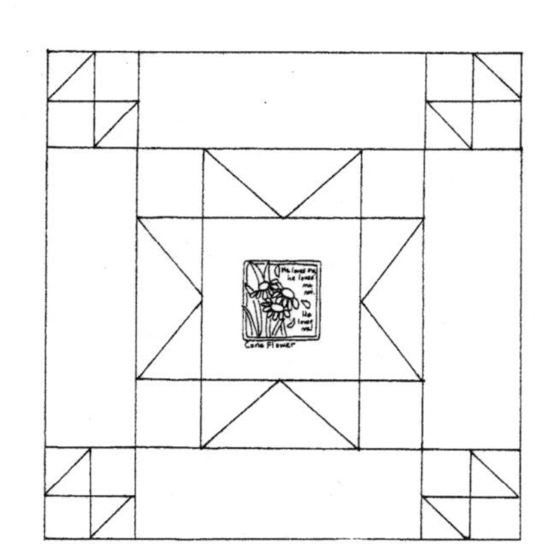

FIGURE 4

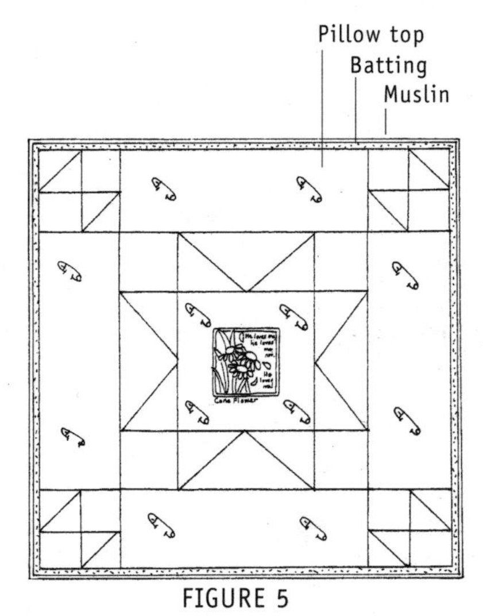

FIGURE 5

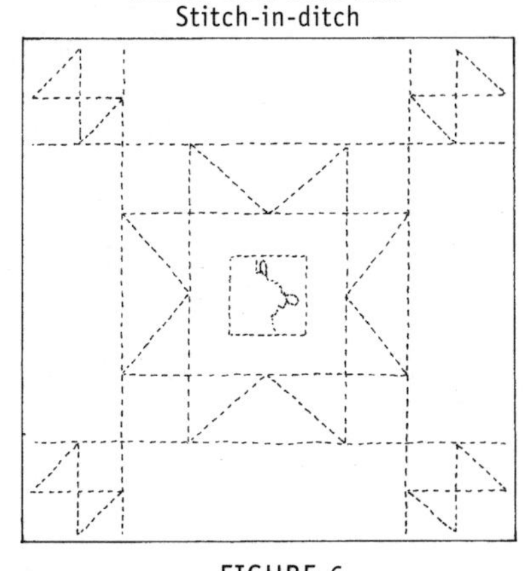

FIGURE 6

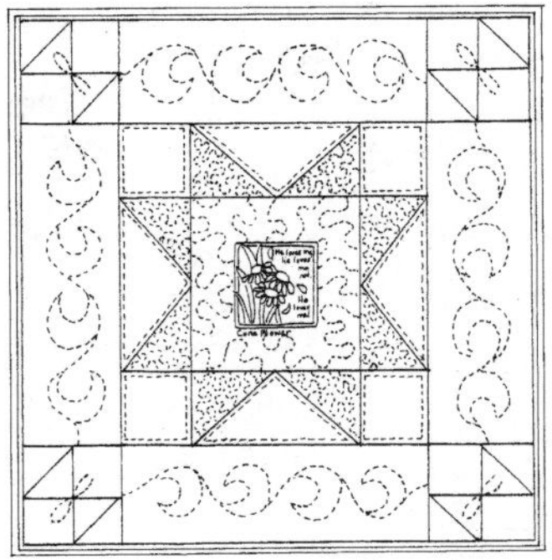

FIGURE 7

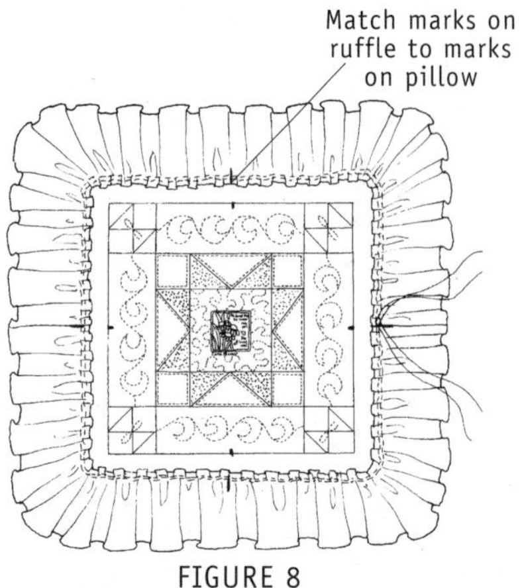

FIGURE 8

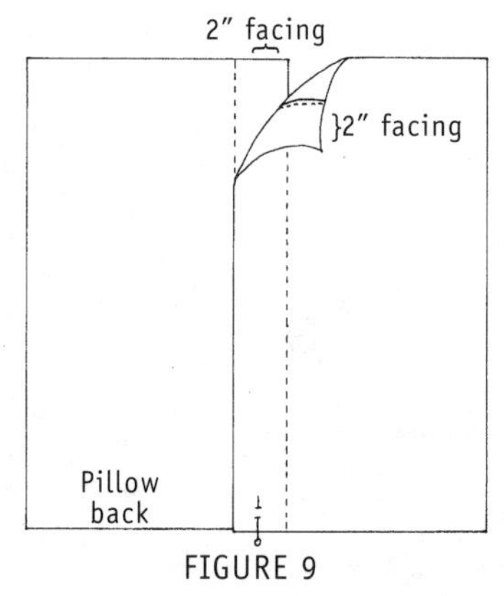

FIGURE 9

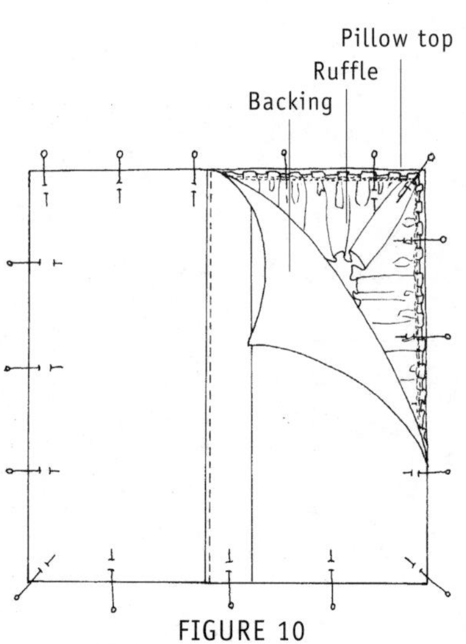

FIGURE 10

Constructing the Pillow

1. Stitch the two ruffle strips right sides together along the short ends to create a circle. Fold into quarters and mark the folds with a wash-out marker.

2. With wrong sides together, fold the ruffle piece in half, matching the raw edges and press well.

3. Stitch two rows of lengthened machine stitching at 1/8" and 3/8" from the raw edge. Pull the gathers up to fit the outside edge of the pillow square, matching the marks on the ruffle to the marks on the pillow square *(fig. 8)*. Evenly distribute the gathers, placing extra at the corners. Pin the ruffle in place.

4. On the two pieces cut for the pillow back, fold under 1/4" along one 18" side of each piece. Press well.

5. Fold under a 2" facing along the same side of each backing square and pin in place.

6. Top stitch the hem in place to secure with a color of thread to match the backing.

7. Lap one facing over the other and pin in place *(fig. 9)*.

8. Measure the lapped pillow back and trim if necessary so that it measures 18" square.

9. Place the pinned pillow back right sides together to the pillow top with the ruffle sandwiched between. Pin in place *(fig. 10)*.

10. Stitch around the pillow top, clip the corners and finish the seam with a zigzag or serge.

11. Remove the pins from the lap and turn the pillow through the lap, pushing the corners out.

12. Insert the pillow form into the completed pillow (see finished drawing).

Heirloom Classics 1 Stippled Quilt

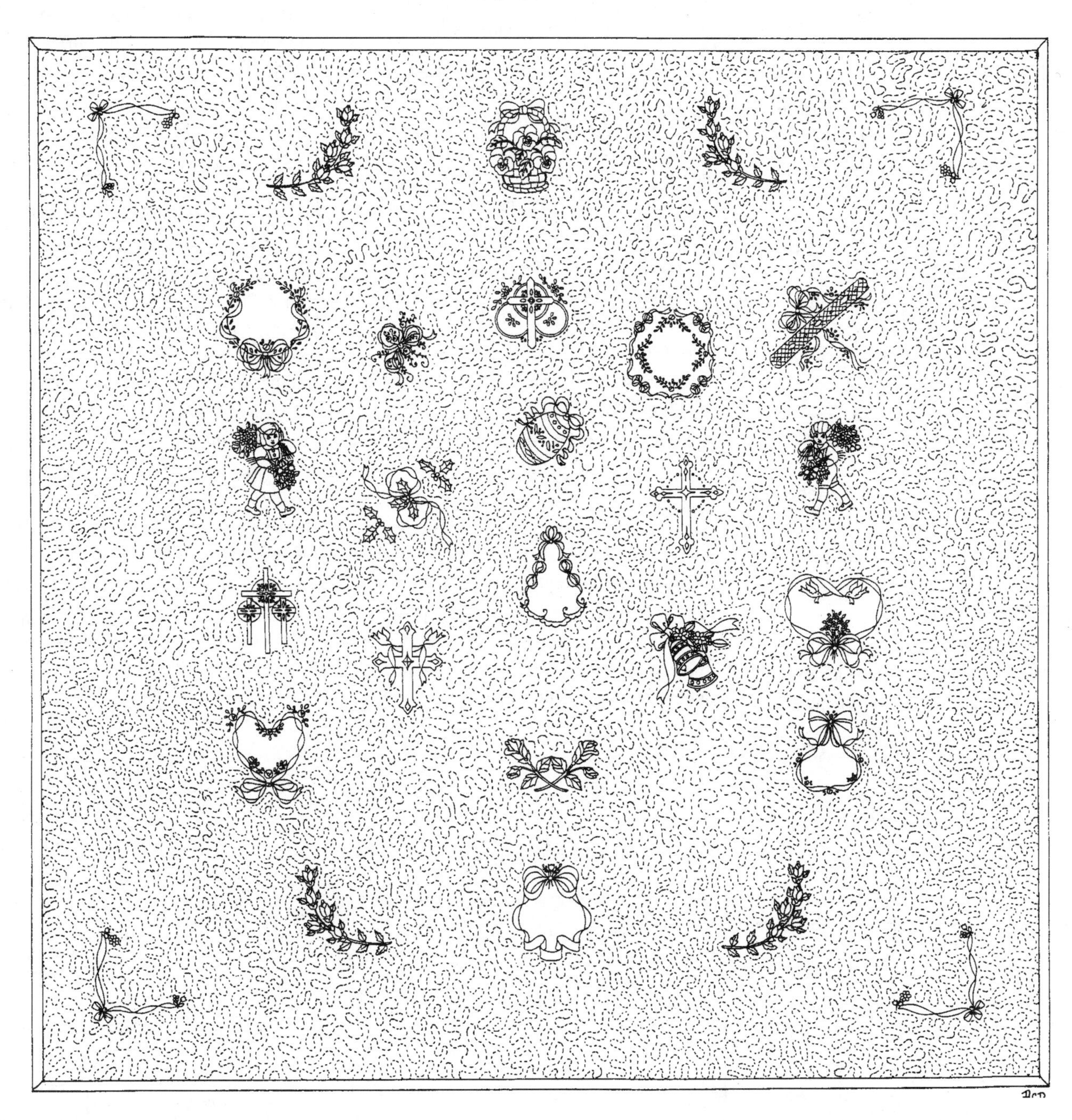

Made of white linen/cotton blend with blue linen/cotton blend binding, this quilt is elegant and easy to make. We used designs from Martha Pullen's embroidery CD, Heirloom Classics I. The quilt has one piece of white linen blend for the top; the lining is the same. All of the embroideries on the CD are spaced over the quilt and stitched using the color suggestions which come on the CD. The quilt is stippled with white on the white linen background. The stippling goes around each machine embroidered design. Thin, traditional batting is used between the quilt top and quilt back.

This quilt is the perfect one to use for your favorite embroidery card. The finished quilt measures 42 by 38-1/2 inches.

SUPPLIES

- 2-1/4 yards of white linen/cotton blend (top and backing)
- 3/8 yard of blue linen/cotton blend (binding)
- Low-loft quilt batting
- Martha Pullen's Heirloom Classics I Embroidery Design CD
- Machine embroidery threads for embroidery
- White machine embroidery thread for stippling
- Stabilizer
- Safety pins or quilt tacks and quilt tack gun
- Optional: Temporary spray adhesive

Construction

1. Cut or tear two pieces of fabric 44" wide by 40" long. One piece will be for the quilt top and one piece will be for the quilt back.

2. For the embroidery placement, mark the quilt top as follows:

a. Fold the 44" width of the quilt top in half to find the center. Draw a line along the fold *(fig. 1)*.

b. Measure 5" down from the top and place a mark on the center line.

c. Place 5 additional marks on the center line 6" from the first mark and 6" apart. This will place the last mark on the center line 5" from the lower edge *(fig. 1)*.

d. Extend the two 5" markings horizontally across the top and bottom of the quilt top *(fig. 1)*.

e. On the top and bottom horizontal lines, place two markings 8" apart on each side of the center mark *(fig. 1)*.

f. From the marks made step e, measure over 8-1/2" and mark *(fig. 1)*.

g. Place shorter vertical lines 5-1/2" from each side of the center line. Place marks on these vertical lines that fall in between the 6" marks on the center line *(fig. 1)*.

h. Place shorter vertical lines 11" from each side of the center line. Place marks on these vertical lines that are even with the 6" marks on the center line *(fig. 1)*.

3. The Heirloom Classic I embroideries always start in the center of the hoop. The "plus marks" indicate the center of each embroidery. Hoop, stabilize and stitch the embroideries on each "plus mark". Refer to the finished drawing for specific embroideries.

4. Remove the stablizer and press the quilt top.

Layering and Quilting

1. Make a quilt sandwich by placing the quilt backing, wrong side up on a flat surface. Place the batting on top of the quilt backing. Center the quilt top on top of the batting, right side up. Baste all layers together with safety pins, hand or machine basting, or quilt tack gun *(fig. 2)*.

2. Using the white machine embroidery thread in the needle and bobbin, stipple stitch the quilt in a loose meandering pattern. Refer to the technique for Stipple Stitching on page 111.

3. Place a line 4" above the center line of the upper embroideries and 4" below the center line of the lower embroideries. Place lines 4" from the center of the corner embroideries along each side of the quilt *(fig. 3)*. Evenly trim all layers along these lines.

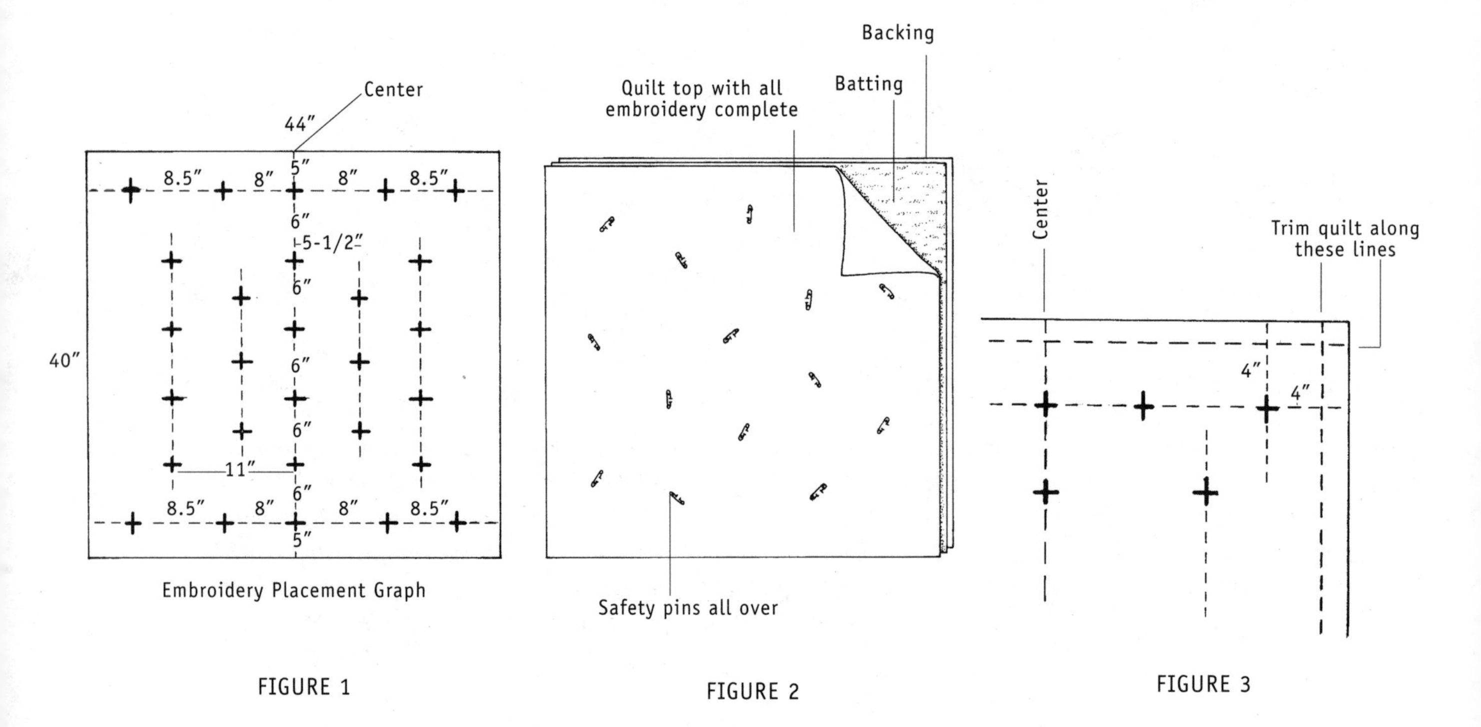

FIGURE 1 FIGURE 2 FIGURE 3

Binding

1. Cut 3 strips of blue fabric for the binding, each 2-1/2" wide. Place two strips right sides together. Stitch the layers together with a diagonal seam *(fig. 4)*.

2. Trim the excess fabric 1/4" beyond the stitched seam. Press the seam open or to one side.

3. Continue stitching the strips together until you have one long continuous strip of binding.

4. Fold the strip lengthwise, wrong sides together and press.

5. Draw miter lines along each corner of the quilt. Beginning along one long edge on the quilt, pin the raw edges of the quilt binding to the edges of the right side of the quilt top.

6. Stitch using a 3/8" seam allowance, starting about 1" from the end of the strip. Stop stitching at the miter line and backstitch.

7. Fold a 3/4" pleat in the binding at the corner and begin stitching again along the second side of the binding, starting at the miter line *(fig. 5)*.

8. Continue stitching, using this same technique at each corner. Stitch through all layers. Stop stitching about 2" from the beginning. Overlap the beginning and the end 1/2" and trim away any excess. Fold one edge of the binding to the inside 1/4". Place the straight end into the folded end and continue stitching *(fig. 6)*.

9. Fold the binding over the edges of the quilt, enclosing the seam allowance. The folded edge of the binding should be placed just past the seam line. At the corner, the binding will be folded into a miter. Stitch the binding in place by machine using a straight stitch or whipstitch in place by hand *(fig. 7)*.

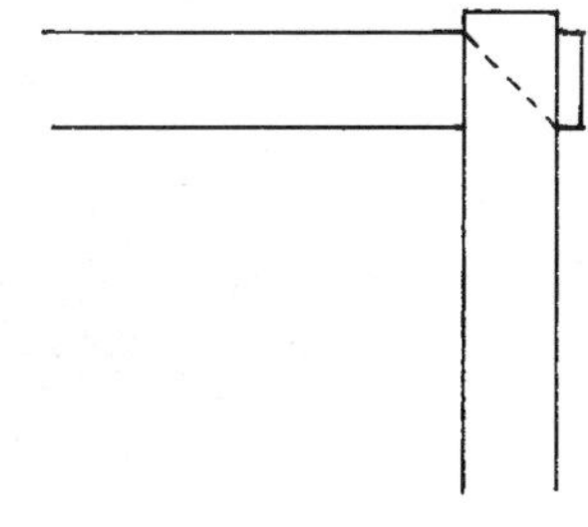

FIGURE 4

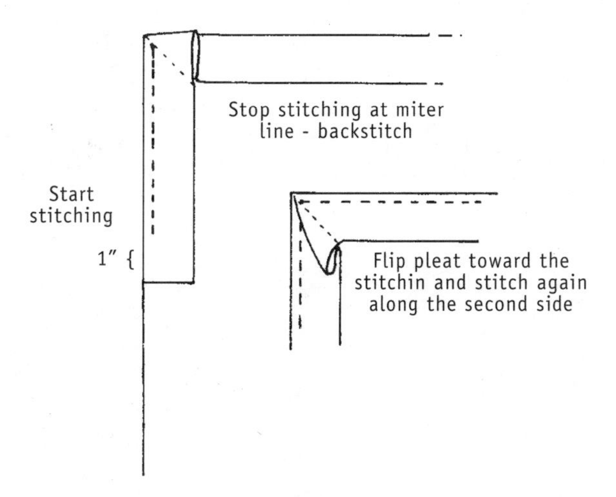

FIGURE 5

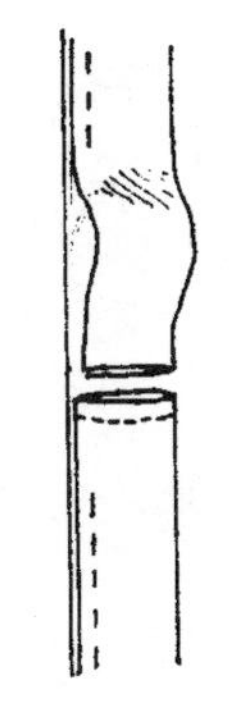

FIGURE 6

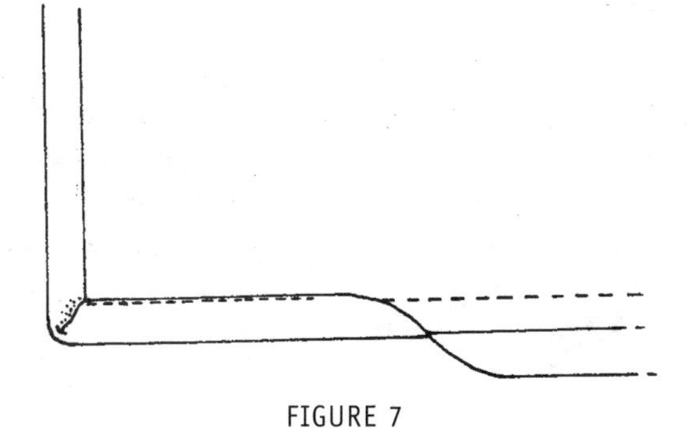

FIGURE 7

Tapestry Of Hearts Quilt

What a joy to stitch a heart quilt for someone you love-completely by machine! This would be the perfect memory quilt if you stitch in names and places underneath each heart. Using so many of our beloved heirloom techniques, this heart quilt is a wonderment of machine work. This quilt was stitched completely on a Pfaff machine (7570) and all of the machine embroidery is from Pfaff. As always, any machine can be used to make a heart quilt like this and you can use the machine embroidery that you have available.

All of the background squares of the quilt are made of pink Swiss Nelona batiste. The sashing pieces with the cross stitch on them are ecru Swiss Nelona batiste. The green squares in-between each of these cross-stitched sashing pieces are mint green Swiss Nelona batiste. The backing of the quilt is made of white Swiss Nelona batiste and the binding is made of pink Swiss Nelona batiste. In each square two lines of straight machine stitching have been made from corner to corner in an "x" shape. This is a pink, green and ecru quilt.

The upper left hand corner begins this "heart journey." It has a lace shaped heart using ecru French lace insertion. The roses embroidered in the middle are a machine cross stitch design.

The next square features the technique, "Normandy Lace." Ecru French edging is around the heart with ecru 100% cotton English netting inside the heart. Pretty machine embroidery designs have been stitched around this heart and on the two upper sections of the heart. An ecru lace shaped diamond is in the center of the heart and a tiny ecru machine embroidery design is in the center.

The upper right hand corner has a wonderful ribbon and lace insertion treatment stitched within the ecru lace insertion shaped heart. Pink, ecru and multicolored purchased ribbons have been joined together with ecru French lace insertion. The created ribbon/ lace fabric has been turned sideways to give it a pretty effect.

Row two has on the far left side an ecru stippled design inside the heart. The actual stippled piece has been stitched down with a wide satin stitch. There is a row of ecru machine scallops around the heart.

The middle square of this row has crazy patch in the center of the ecru French lace insertion shaped heart. Pieces of ribbon in solid pink and green are crazy patched to other pieces of ribbon which are multicolored and ecru tone-on-tone ribbon. Machine featherstitch embellishes the crazy patch sections.

Block 6 has a very pretty technique called "Organdy Madeira Windows". Inside the Madeira window is ecru Swiss organdy or organza on which a beautiful hemstitched, machine appliquéd rose has been stitched. Some of the leaves are lacy in appearance and are connected to a satin-stitched stem. Two rows of ecru pinstitching outline the heart shape. The square is quilted to the back of the quilt with straight stitching along the outermost pinstitching line and radiating lines from the heart to each corner of the square.

The left hand corner of the bottom of the quilt has a wonderful Seminole patchwork interior inside the ecru lace-shaped heart. Two shades of pink batiste and one shade of ecru are the colors for the Seminole patchwork.

The next heart also has a beautiful ecru lace- shaped heart as the frame for a magnificent center treatment. Puffing is used for the whole piece and this puffing is divided with rows of pink, green and gold purchased ribbon stitched down inside the puffing piece. It looks as if there are four rows of very narrow puffing when indeed it is one piece of puffing with the ribbon stitched to make it look like four rows of skinny puffing.

The last square is a Madeira appliqué motif made of ecru Swiss Nelona batiste with a beautiful green, pink and dark pink cross stitch motif stitched in the center.

This quilt is a dream come true for those who love romance and cross stitch. Don't tell anyone that your cross stitch was done entirely on the sewing machine.

Supplies

- 4-1/4 yards of ecru Nelona Swiss batiste
- 1 yard of dusty pink Nelona Swiss batiste
- 1-1/2" by 24" strip of pale pink Nelona Swiss batiste
- 1/4 yard of green Nelona Swiss batiste
- One 11" square of cotton netting
- Two 11" squares of organdy
- One 11" square of muslin or light-weight cotton fabric
- 5-1/3 yards of 5/8" lace insertion
- 1 yard of 1/4" lace insertion
- 3/4 yard of 5/8" lace edging
- 1-1/4 yards of 45" wide batting
- 1-1/2 yards of tear-away stabilizer
- 1 yard of water-soluble stabilizer (WSS)
- Temporary spray adhesive (KK2000)
- Pfaff cards 1, 7, 49 and MP1004 for the embroideries shown
- Glass head pins
- Lace shaping board
- Wash-away basting thread
- Lightweight sewing thread
- Decorative thread in the following colors: (Sulky numbers given below)
  #1047 - Mint Green
  #1046 - Teal
  #1207 - Sea Foam Green
  #1082 - Ecru
  #1127 - Medium Ecru
  #1034 - Burgundy
  #1117 - Mauve
  #1119 - Dark Mauve
- 1/2 yard of 1/2" wide embroidered ribbon for block #8
- 8" pieces of several different ribbons (7/8" to 1-1/4") to coordinate with the decorative thread colors listed above

Notions

Wash-out marker, #100 wing needle or #120 universal, 1.6/70 twin needle, #70 universal needle, white lightweight sewing thread, wash-away thread, invisible thread, glass head pins, a lace shaping board, open-toe appliqué foot, 7-groove pintuck foot, gathering or shirring foot, embroidery foot, a point turner, rotary cutter, ruler and mat

Templates

Heart Template, Normandy Lace Template, Crazy Patch Template and the Organdy Madeira Window Template

Specific supplies for each block are listed under the specific directions.

Pfaff cards were used for all embroidery designs. Other embroidery designs may be used within the dimensions given under each specific block.

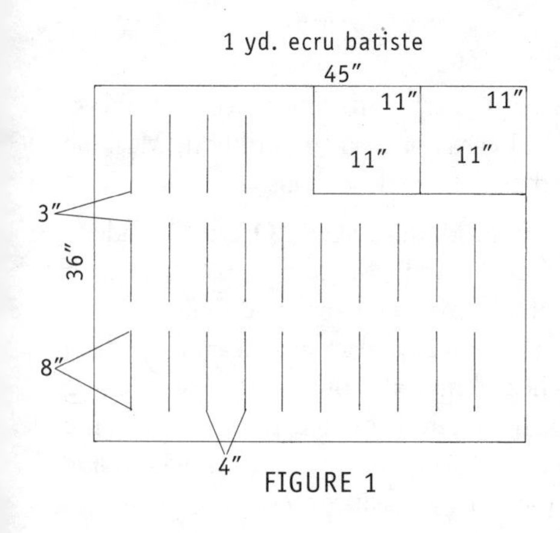

FIGURE 1

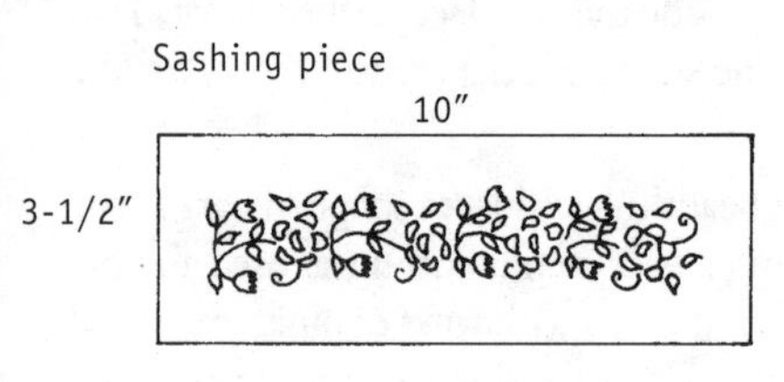

FIGURE 2

A zigzag stitch can be used instead of a pinstitch.

NOTE: If the fabric is too small to fit into the desired hoop use the following steps:

1. Hoop a piece of stabilizer.

2. Spray the hooped stabilizer with a temporary spray adhesive.

3. Secure the fabric to the stabilizer, aligned as needed. If an area is not secure, remove the fabric, spray again and secure the fabric.

4. Stitch the embroidery.

Cutting Directions

Cut and label the following pieces for the quilt:

1. Cut nine pink 11" squares for blocks 1 - 9.

2. Cut one piece of ecru batiste one yard by the width of the fabric. This piece will be used for the 24 embroidered sashings and the two ecru 11" squares for blocks 1 and 9.

3. Cut one ecru rectangle 11" by 39" for puffing (block 8).

4. Cut one 11" square of netting for block 2.

5. Cut two 11" organdy squares for blocks 4 and 6.

6. Cut two 45" batiste squares, one for the backing and one for the lining.

7. Cut sixteen 3-1/2" squares of green batiste for the intersecting blocks between the sashings.

8. Cut six pink batiste strips 1-3/4" by 33" for the binding. (Straight of grain, not bias.)

9. Cut a piece of batting 45" square.

10. Reserve scraps of ecru and dusty pink Nelona for cutting strips for the Seminole Lacework.

Preparation of Blocks

1. Press and starch each of the squares for the blocks. Press but do not starch the rectangle for block 8 (puffing).

2. Fold all squares into quarters and crease. Mark the creases to determine placement of the templates.

3. Complete each square and set aside until all 9 blocks are completed. The 9 pink blocks will be trimmed to measure 10" when all are completed.

4. Please refer to the technique section for the lace shaping techniques.

5. When a #120 universal needle is required, a #100 wing needle can be used if a larger hole is desired.

NOTE: Stitch settings given are approximate settings and may be adjusted as desired.

Embroidering the Sashings

Card 49, design #4 was used to embroider the sashings on the pictured quilt.

1. Choose an embroidery no larger than 1-3/4" by 8". Two or more embroideries may be combined to create an embroidery this size.

2. On the one yard by 45" piece of ecru batiste, draw 24 lines 8" long. Draw the outline of the two 11" blocks in one corner. The lines will be placed 4" apart and have 3" above and below the lines (see *figure 1).*

3. Hoop, stabilize and embroider the design onto each of the 24 lines.

4. Remove the stabilizer and press the piece well.

5. Cut the two 11" blocks from the piece and lay them aside for blocks 1 and 9.

6. Cut the 24 embroideries into sashing pieces measuring 3-1/2" by 10", centering the embroidery on each strip. Lay the sashing pieces aside *(fig. 2).*

Lace Heart

Block #1
Lace Heart

Supplies

- One 11" pink batiste square
- Tear-away stabilizer
- One 11" ecru batiste square
- #70 universal needle
- #120 universal or #100 wing needle
- Embroidery foot
- Burgundy, mauve, dark mauve, and sea foam green decorative threads
- Wash-out marker
- Ecru lightweight sewing thread
- Glass head pins
- Lace shaping board
- Basic sewing supplies
- Heart template
- Pfaff card 1, design #9 was used to embroider the design for this block
- 5/8" lace insertion

Constructing Block #1

1. Place the 11" ecru square and a square of stabilizer (cut stabilizer to fit into the hoop) into the machine's embroidery hoop.

2. Choose an embroidery no larger than 2-1/4" wide by 2-1/2" high. Complete the embroidery in the center of the square using the pinks for the flower and the green for the leaves and stem. When the embroidery is complete, remove the stabilizer and press the piece well. Set the piece aside *(fig. 1)*.

3. Place the pink square onto the heart template (aligning the centers) and trace the heart template line *(fig. 2)*.

4. Shape the lace around the inside of the template, mitering at the points. Pin the lace in place.

5. Place stabilizer beneath the square and pinstitch (W=2.0, L=2.0) the **outside edge** of the lace to the pink square *(fig. 3)*.

6. Remove the stabilizer and trim the fabric from behind the lace, leaving a heart-shaped opening in the center of the pink fabric *(fig. 4)*.

7. Center the embroidered ecru square behind the heart opening. Pin in place.

8. Place stabilizer beneath the square and pinstitch (W=2.0, L=2.0) the **inside edge** of the lace insertion to the embroidered ecru piece *(fig. 5)*.

9. Remove the stabilizer and trim the excess ecru fabric from behind the lace.

10. Set the square aside.

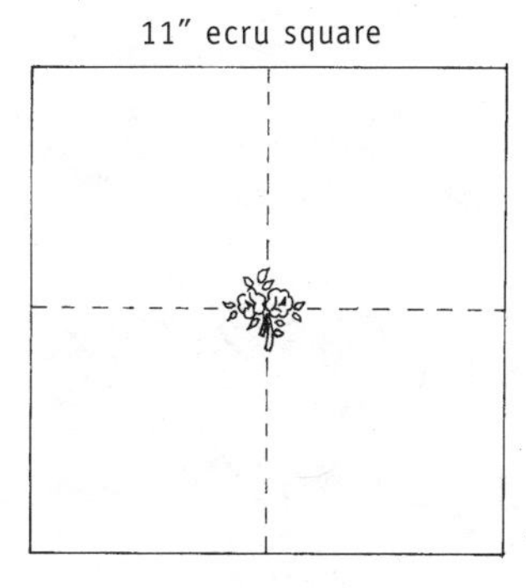

FIGURE 1

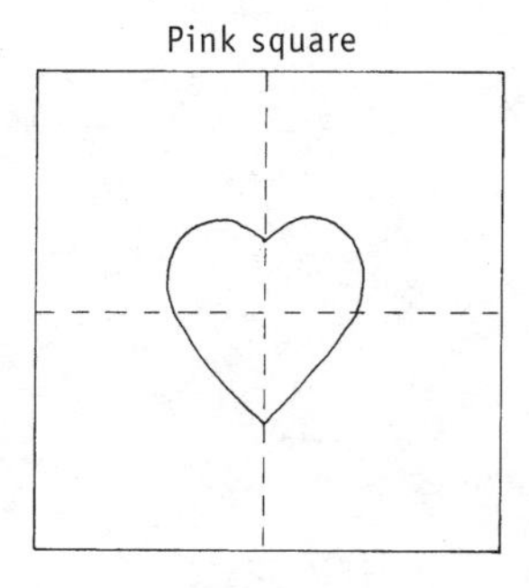

FIGURE 2

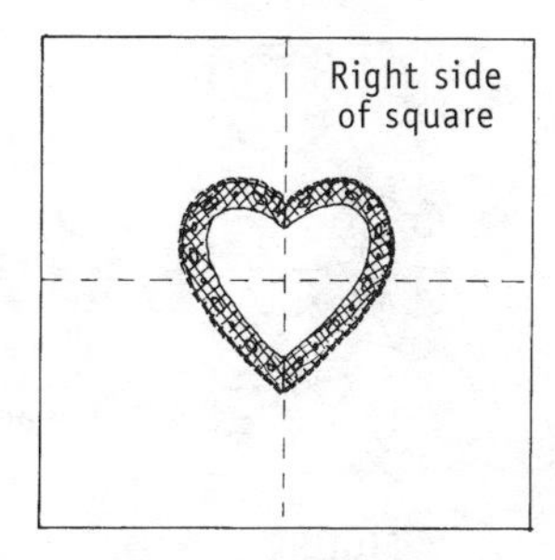

FIGURE 3

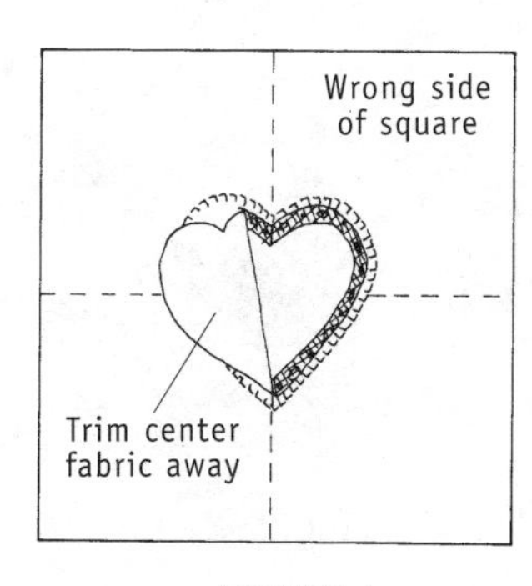

FIGURE 4

FIGURE 5

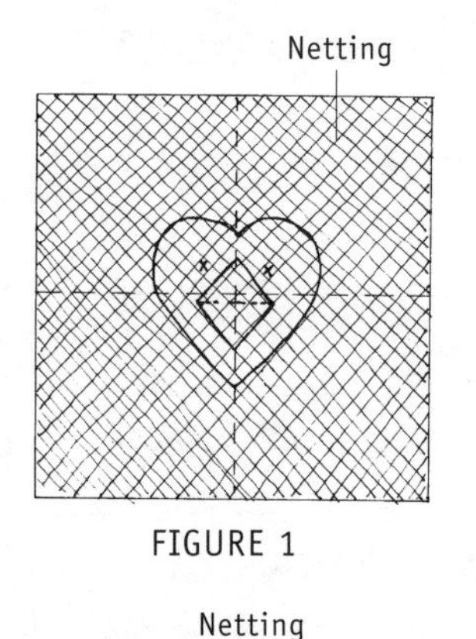

FIGURE 1

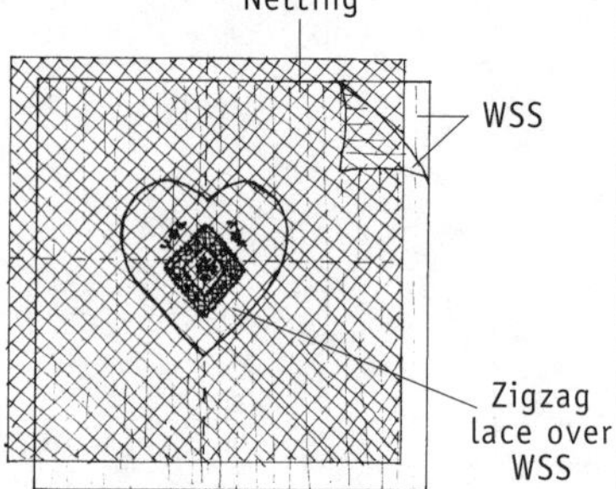

FIGURE 2

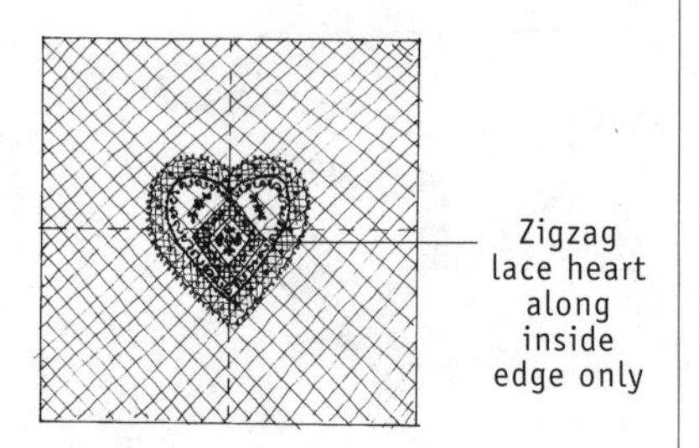

FIGURE 3

FIGURE 4

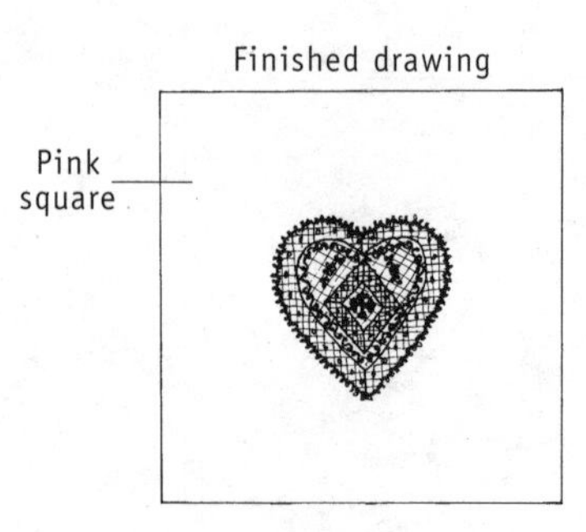

FIGURE 5

Normandy Heart

Block #2
Normandy Lace Heart

Supplies

- One 11" pink batiste square
- One 11" square of netting
- Lace insertion (5/8")
- Lace edging (5/8")
- Tear-away stabilizer
- Water-soluble stabilizer (WSS)
- #70 universal needle
- Embroidery foot
- Ecru decorative thread
- Wash-out marker
- Lightweight sewing thread
- Glass head pins
- Lace shaping board
- Basic sewing supplies
- Normandy Lace template
- Pfaff card MP 1004, designs #8 and #11 were used to embroider this block

Constructing Block #2

Refer to Lace Shaping Directions found on page 109.

1. Spray starch the netting and press until dry several times to pre-shrink. Fold the netting into quarters and mark the center.

2. Trace the lace shaping lines and the embroidery placement lines. *NOTE: if you are using embroideries other than the ones listed, the embroideries need to be small. The embroidery inside the diamond must be contained within the center of the diamond. (fig. 1).*

3. Sandwich the 12" square of netting between two layers of water soluble stabilizer, hoop and complete the embroidery designs, using ecru decorative thread. Remove from the hoop.

4. Shape the lace insertion between the lace shaping lines of the diamond.

5. Zigzag (W=1.5 – 2.0, L=1.5) the lace to the netting on top of the WSS *(fig. 2)*. Zigzag along the miter lines.

6. Shape the scalloped edge of the lace edging along the heart shape, mitering at the top and bottom of the heart *(fig. 3)*.

7. Zigzag only the inside heading of the lace.

8. Select stitch #188 (W=9.0, L=48) if using the Pfaff 7570 machine or choose another decorative stitch no wider than 3/8" and stitch this design inside the shaped heart. The foot of the machine should run along the zigzagged heading of the lace edging. *NOTE: One or two more layers of WSS may be needed when stitching the decorative stitch (fig. 3).*

9. Trim close to the zigzag to remove the excess netting and WSS from around the heart *(fig.4)*. Zigzag over miter lines and trim away excess lace.

10. Rinse to remove the WSS from the netting. Press the heart until dry, taking care not to distort the shape.

11. Place the Normandy lace heart onto the 11" pink square, aligning the centers. Pin in place. Stitch around the outside edge of the lace edging with a tiny zigzag (W=1.5 – 2.0, L=1.5) *(fig. 5)*.

12. Press the square well and set aside.

Joanna's Memory Quilt

Blue Danube Quilt

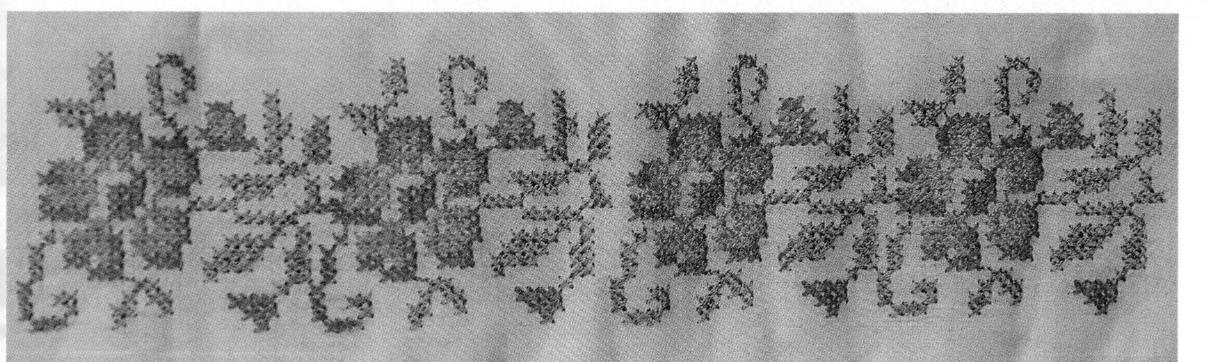

Tapestry of Hearts

Springtime in Paris Quilt

Top:
Heirloom Classics I Stippled Quilt

Top Right:
"Welcome to Our Family" Heart Quilt

Below Left:
Bunnies by the Bay Quilt

Below Right:
Crayon Art Heart Quilt

TOP LEFT: *Crazy Patch Doll Quilt*

TOP RIGHT: *Mommy's Helpers Wing Needle Entredeux Quilt*

BELOW LEFT: *Simple Star Block Quilt and Pillow*

BELOW RIGHT: *Noah's Ark Wallhanging*

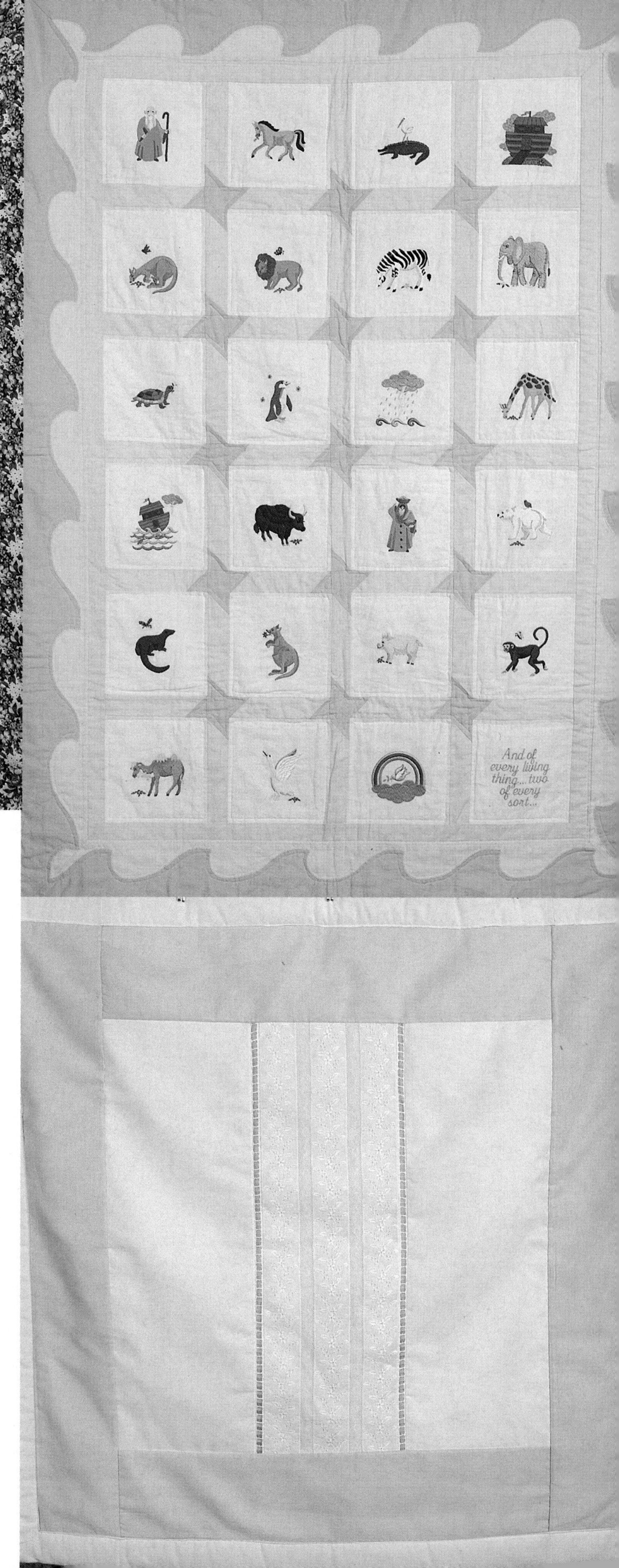

Top Left: *Mommy's Helpers Wall Panel*

Top Right: *Noah's Ark Wave Quilt*

Below Left: *Lighthouse Wallhanging*

Below Right: *Serger Quilt*

Mother Goose Quilt

Lace & Trim Heart

Block #3
Lace and Trim Heart

Supplies

- One 11" pink square
- 1/4" lace insertion
- 5/8" lace insertion
- Assorted decorative ribbons
- Tear-away stabilizer
- #70 universal needle
- #120 universal or #100 wing needle
- Wash-out marker
- Lightweight sewing thread
- Glass head pins
- Lace shaping board
- Basic sewing supplies
- Heart template

Constructing Block #3

1. Trace the heart template onto a square of tear-away stabilizer.

2. Place a piece of decorative ribbon diagonally across the heart, trimming away the excess ribbon beyond the drawn line.

3. Lay a piece of narrow lace insertion beside the decorative ribbon, trimming the excess lace away beyond the drawn line *(fig. 1)*.

4. Remove the ribbon and lace from the stabilizer and stitch together with a small zigzag (W=1.5 – 2.0, L=1.5) *(fig. 2)*.

5. Place the piece onto the stabilizer again and cut another piece of decorative ribbon to be attached to the remaining edge of the lace insertion.

6. Remove the pieces from the stabilizer and stitch the ribbon and the lace together with a small zigzag (W=1.5 – 2.0, L=1.5) *(fig. 3)*. Repeat steps 5 and 6, alternating ribbon and lace until a ribbon/lace panel is created as large as the heart shape. Set the piece aside *(fig. 4)*.

7. Place the pink square onto the heart template (aligning the centers) and trace the template lines.

8. Shape the lace around the inside of the template, mitering at the points. Pin the lace in place.

9. Place stabilizer beneath the square and pinstitch (W=2.0, L=2.0) the **outside edge** of the lace to the pink square *(fig. 5)*.

10. Remove the stabilizer and trim the fabric from behind the lace, leaving a heart-shaped opening in the center of the pink fabric.

11. Place the ribbon/lace panel behind the open heart shape. Pin in place *(fig. 6)*.

12. Stitch the inside of the lace heart with a small zigzag (W=1.5 – 2.0, L=1.5) to secure the lace to the ribbon/lace panel. Trim the excess panel away from behind the lace heart.

13. Press the square well and set aside.

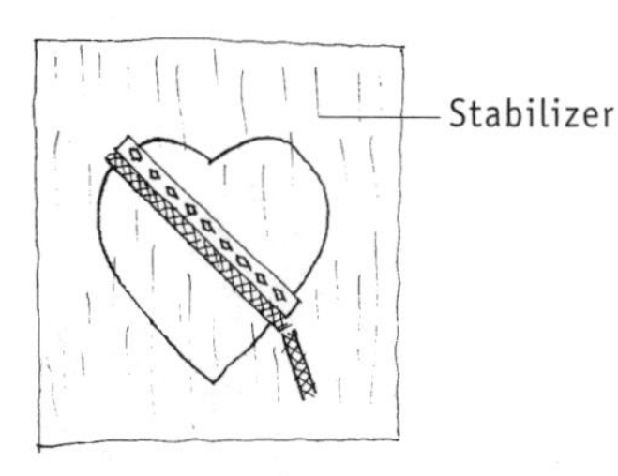

FIGURE 1

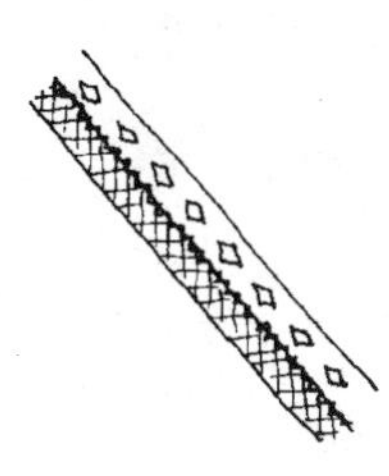

FIGURE 2

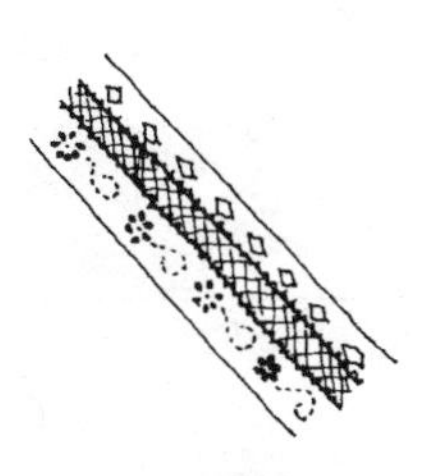

FIGURE 3

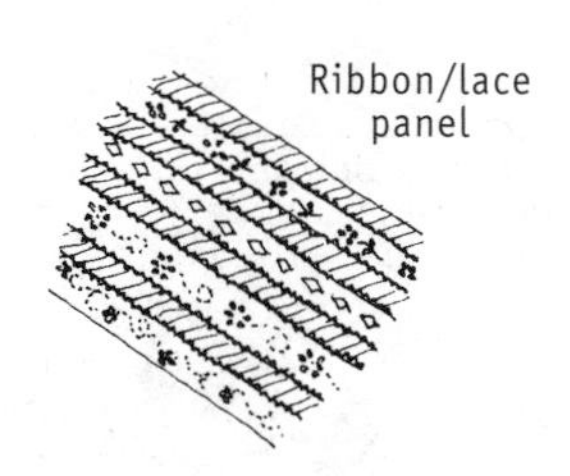

FIGURE 4

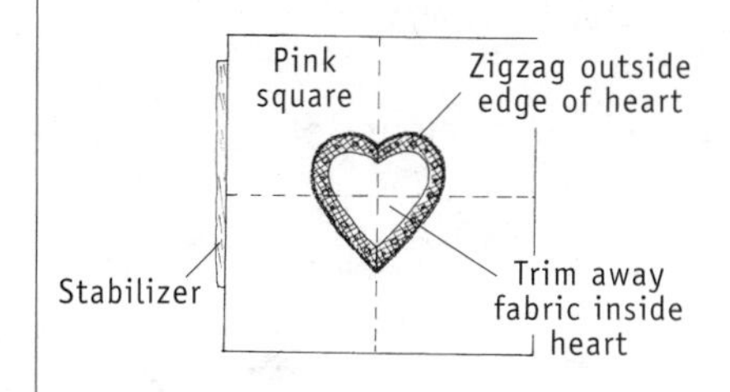

FIGURE 5

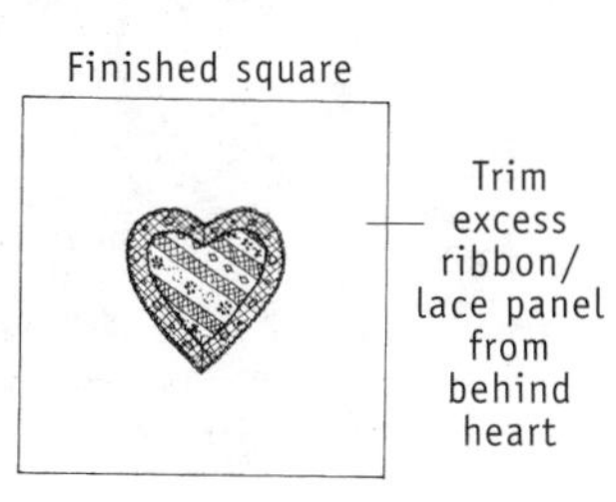

FIGURE 6

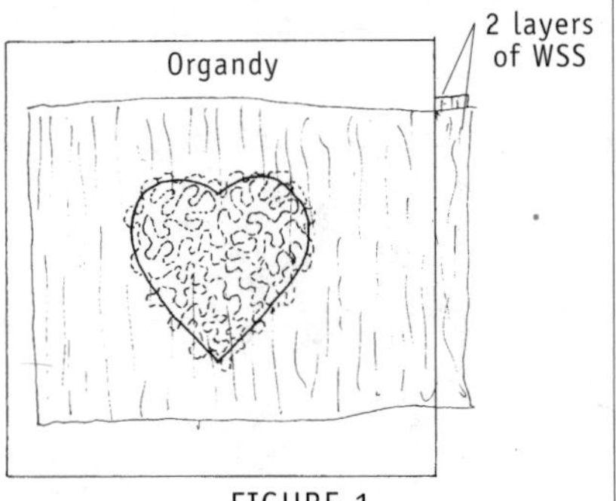

FIGURE 1

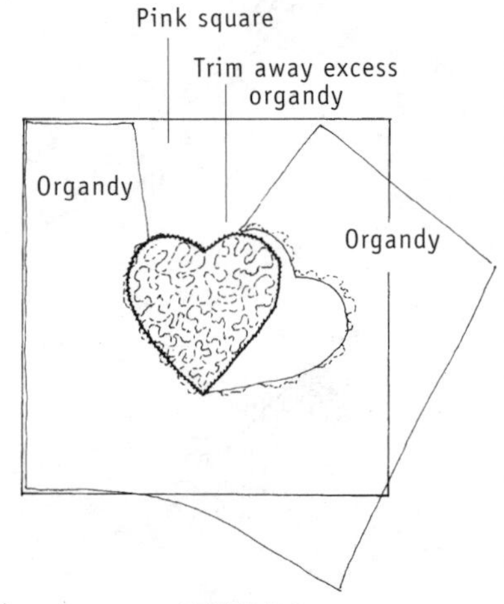

FIGURE 2

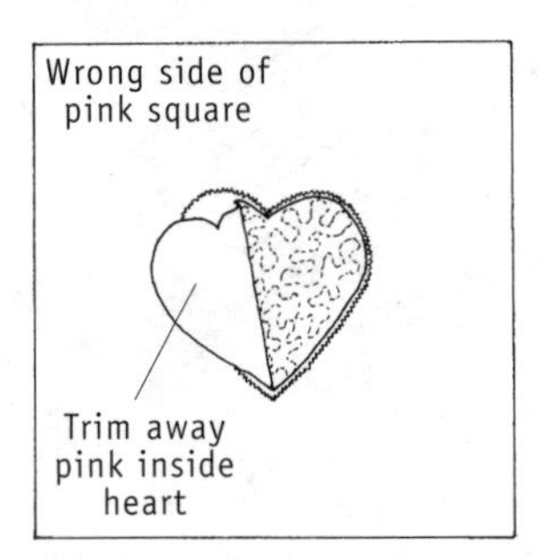

FIGURE 3

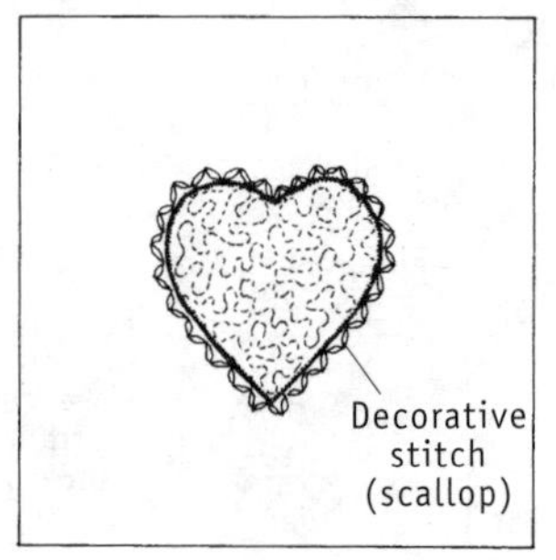

FIGURE 4

Embroidered Organdy Heart

Block #4
Embroidered Organdy Heart

Supplies

- One 11" pink batiste square
- One 11" organdy square
- Tear-away stabilizer
- WSS
- #70 universal needle
- Embroidery foot
- Medium ecru 30 wt. decorative thread
- Wash-out marker
- Lightweight sewing thread
- Glass head pins
- Lace shaping board
- Temporary spray adhesive
- Basic sewing supplies
- Heart template

Constructing Block #4

1. Trace the heart template onto the center of the organdy square.

2. Sandwich the organdy between two layers of WSS, adhering the layers with a light spray of temporary spray adhesive.

3. Stipple stitch (page 111) the heart shape, extending just beyond the drawn line of the heart. Pfaff 7570 stitch #220 (L=91, W=40) was used for the floral decorative stitch on the pictured quilt *(fig. 1)*.

4. Cut away the excess WSS and rinse away the remaining WSS. Allow the piece to dry and press well.

5. Trace the heart template onto the center of the pink square.

6. Place the embroidered organdy piece onto the pink square, centering the embroidery in the heart. Pin in place.

7. Stitch a tiny zigzag (W=1.5 – 2.0, L=1.5) around the drawn outline of the heart through both layers of fabric *(fig. 2)*.

8. Trim away the excess organdy beyond the stitching *(fig. 2)*.

9. Turn the piece over and trim away the pink fabric from inside the heart shape *(fig. 3)*.

10. Place a piece of tear-away stabilizer beneath the square and stitch a satin stitch (L=0.5, W-2.5-3.0) over the zigzag around the heart shape. Remove the stabilizer.

11. Place another piece of tear-away stabilizer beneath the square and stitch a decorative scallop around the outside edge of the heart shape. Pfaff 7570 stitch #56 (L=16, W=9.0) was used for the decorative scallop on the pictured quilt. Remove the stabilizer *(fig. 4)*.

12. Press the square well and set aside.

Crazy Patch

Block #5

Crazy Patch

Supplies

- One 11″ pink batiste square
- One 11″ square of muslin or lightweight cotton fabric
- Tear-away stabilizer
- #70 universal needle
- #120 universal or #100 wing needle
- Embroidery foot
- Burgundy decorative thread
- Assorted ribbons 7/8″ - 1-1/4″ wide (approximately 8″ of 7 or 8 different colors)
- Wash-out marker
- Lightweight sewing thread
- Glass head pins
- Basic sewing supplies
- Crazy Patch template
- Lace shaping board
- 5/8″ lace insertion

Constructing Block #5

1. Trace the lace shaping lines and the crazy patch lines from the template onto the center of the 11" muslin square *(fig. 1)*.

2. Keep the template handy for reference to the order of placing the crazy patches.

3. Each patch will be cut as it is placed.

4. Cut a piece of ribbon large enough to cover area #1 with at least 1/4" extending beyond the lines for a seam allowance *(fig. 2)*. Pin in place.

5. With the patch for area #1 in place, cut a patch from the next ribbon for area #2 that will cover area #2 with the finished edge of the #2 ribbon on the stitching line overlapping ribbon #1. With invisible thread stitch a tiny zigzag (W=1.5 – 2.0, L=1.5) along the finished edge of ribbon #2 where it overlaps ribbon #1. Do not stitch past the overlapping line *(fig. 3)*.

6. Flip ribbon #2 up so that the portion of ribbon #1 which is underneath can be seen. Trim ribbon #1 close to the zigzag stitching line and continue cutting straight across the ribbon *(fig. 4)*.

7. Place ribbon #3 on top of the first two ribbons with the finished edge of the ribbon along the drawn line and the rest of the ribbon extending beyond the #3 area *(fig. 5)*.

8. Zigzag (W=1.5 – 2.0, L=1.5) with the invisible thread along the line which overlaps. Lift up ribbon #3 and trim away the excess of ribbons #1 and #2.

9. Repeat this procedure for the remaining ribbons in the order given on the template until all areas are covered with ribbon.

10. Pin well around the outside edge of the heart shape to secure the patches.

11. Stitching on the wrong side, baste between the two lace shaping lines.

12. On the right side, trim the ribbon extensions about 1/8" from the stitching line *(fig. 6)*.

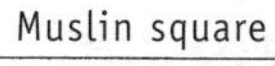

FIGURE 1

FIGURE 2

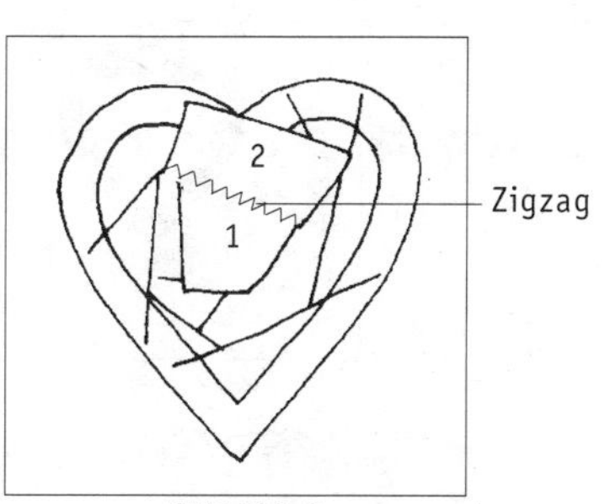

FIGURE 3

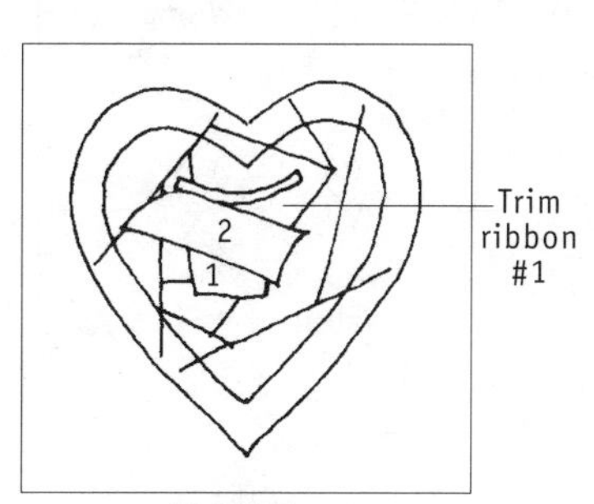

FIGURE 4

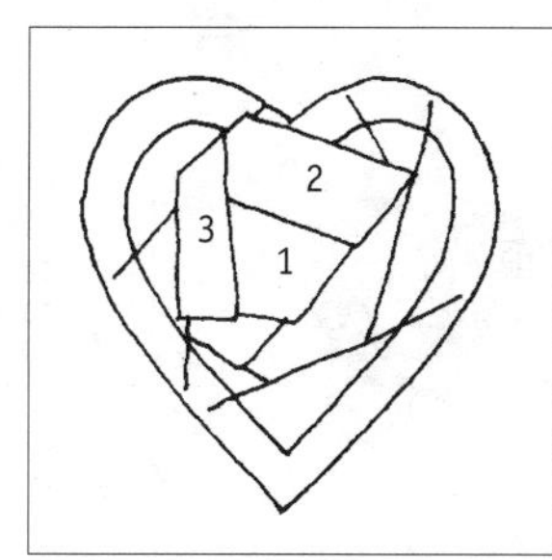

FIGURE 5

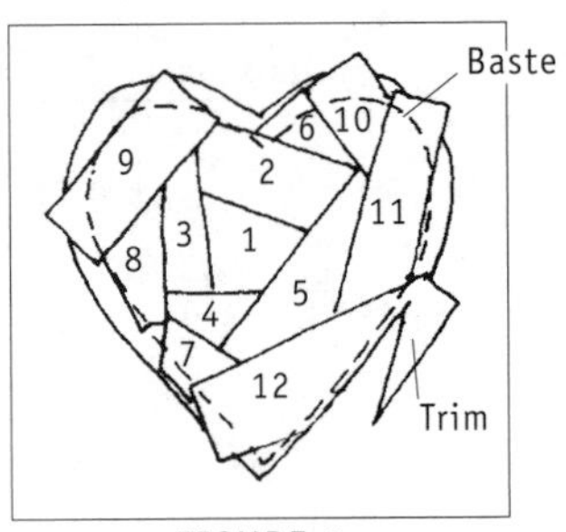

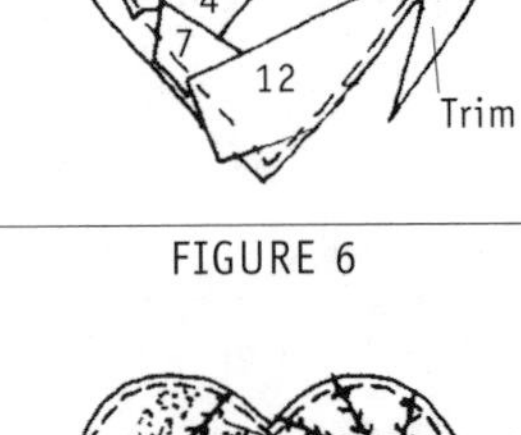

FIGURE 6

FIGURE 7

Pinstitch outer edge only

Stabilizer

FIGURE 8

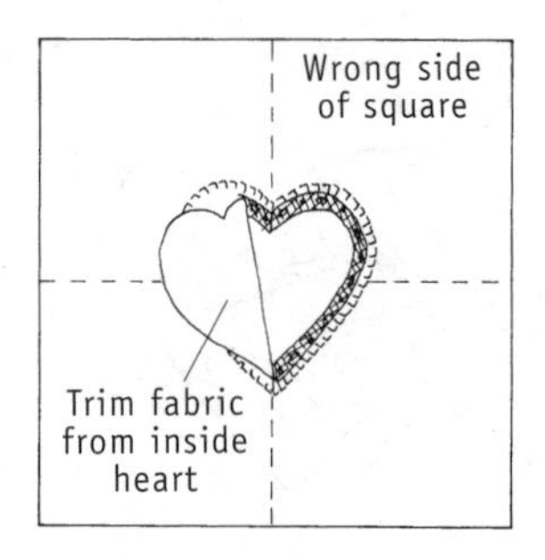

FIGURE 9

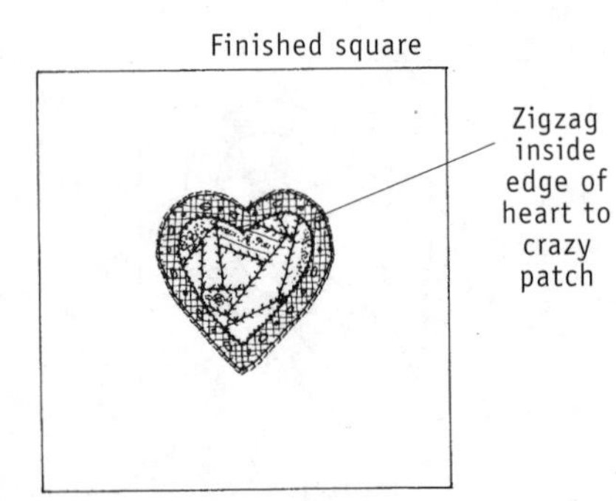

FIGURE 10

13. Embellish each "seam" of the crazy patch with a machine featherstitch using decorative thread. Set the patchwork piece aside *(fig. 7)*.

14. Trace the heart shape of the template onto the center of the pink square. Shape the lace around the heart shape, mitering where necessary.

15. Place stabilizer beneath the square and pinstitch (W=2.0, L=2.0) the **outside edge** of the lace to the pink square *(fig. 8)*.

16. Remove the stabilizer and trim the fabric from behind the lace, leaving a heart-shaped opening in the center of the pink fabric *(fig. 9)*.

17. Place the patchwork piece behind the heart opening and pin to secure.

18. With a small zigzag (W=1.5 – 2.0, L=1.5), stitch the inside heading of the lace insertion to the patchwork piece *(fig. 10)*.

19. From the wrong side, trim the excess patchwork piece from behind the lace, discarding it and the remaining muslin.

20. Press the piece well and set aside.

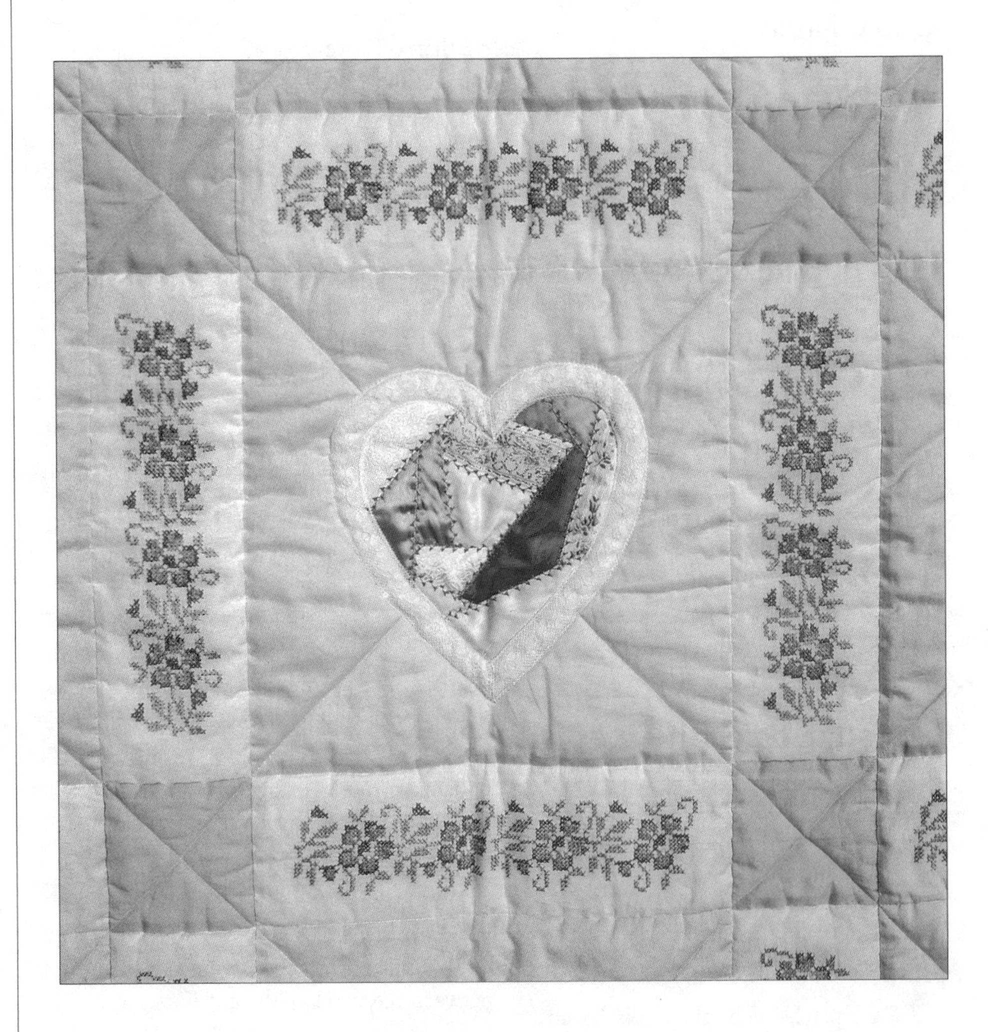

Organdy Madeira Windows

Block #6
Organdy Madeira Windows

Supplies

- One 11″ pink square
- One 11″ square of organdy
- Tear-away stabilizer
- WSS
- #70 universal needle
- #120 universal or #100 wing needle
- Embroidery foot
- Medium ecru decorative thread
- Wash-out marker
- Point turner
- Lightweight sewing thread
- Glass head pins
- Basic sewing supplies
- Wash-away basting thread
- Organdy Madeira Window template
- Pfaff card 7, design #10 was used to embroider the flower for this block. Inside the flower is stitch #116 (L=1.5,W=5.0) stitched with a big needle on a block of fabric, then inserted as an appliqué as directed in hoop embroidery.

Constructing Block #6

1. Using medium ecru decorative thread and three layers of WSS, stitch a design onto the center of the organdy square, to fit within the template lines of the heart. Remove the stabilizer and set the piece aside *(fig. 1)*.

2. Place the pink square onto the template, matching the centers, and trace one-half of the Madeira Window template lines onto the wrong side of the pink fabric *(fig. 2)*.

3. Fold the square in half so that the template lines can be seen. Using wash-away basting thread in the bobbin, the needle, or both, stitch the two layers of the quilt block together along the template line using a short straight stitch *(fig. 3)*.

4. Trim away the inside 1/4" from the edge. Clip corners and curves of the seam allowance *(fig. 4)*.

5. Turn the square right side out, "punch out" all curves and corners and press well. Starch and press several times, concentrating most of the starch along the seam edge. Press until dry *(fig. 5)*.

6. Gently pull the two layers apart. If the two layers will not pull apart easily, starch and press again.

7. Place the wrong side of the square to the right side of the embroidered organdy. Center the embroidery in the opening. Pin the organdy and the square together in several places and especially around the opening.

8. Stitch the organdy to the square along the edge of the opening, using a large needle or wing needle and a pinstitch (W=2.0, L=2.0). The "fingers" of the stitch should stitch into the batiste and the straight side of the stitch should fall on the organdy *(fig. 6)*.

9. Using a wash-out marker, extend the miter lines on the batiste at the top and bottom of the heart.

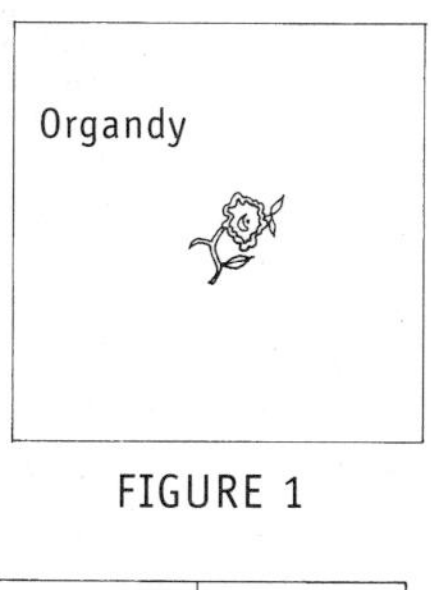

FIGURE 1

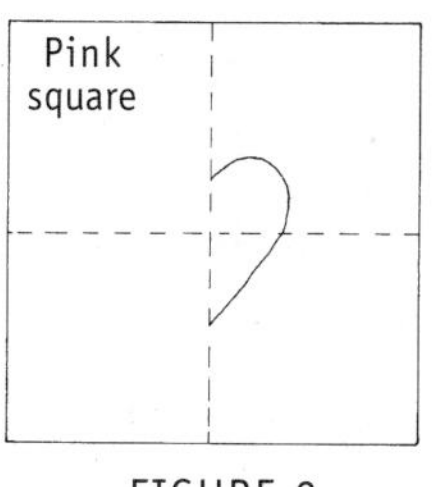

FIGURE 2

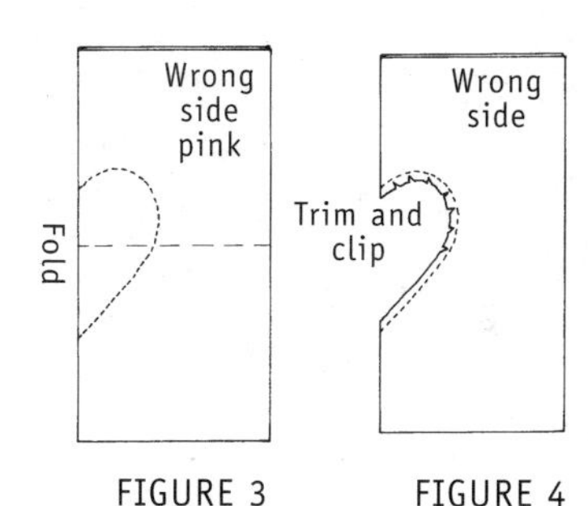

FIGURE 3 FIGURE 4

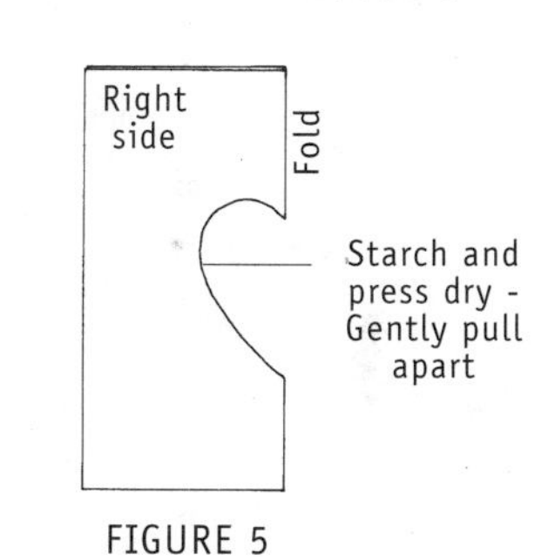

FIGURE 5

Finished square

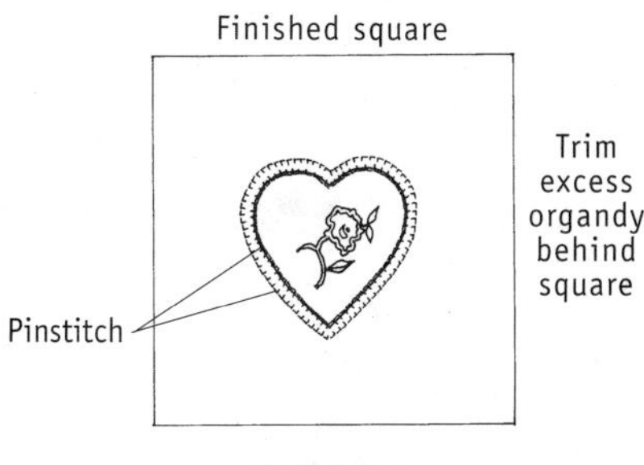

FIGURE 6

10. Stitch a second row of pinstitching 1/4" from the first stitch, pivoting at the miter lines. The "fingers" of the stitch should point to the first row of stitching *(fig. 6)*.

11. From the wrong side, carefully trim the excess organdy just beyond the second row of pinstitching.

12. Press the square well and set aside.

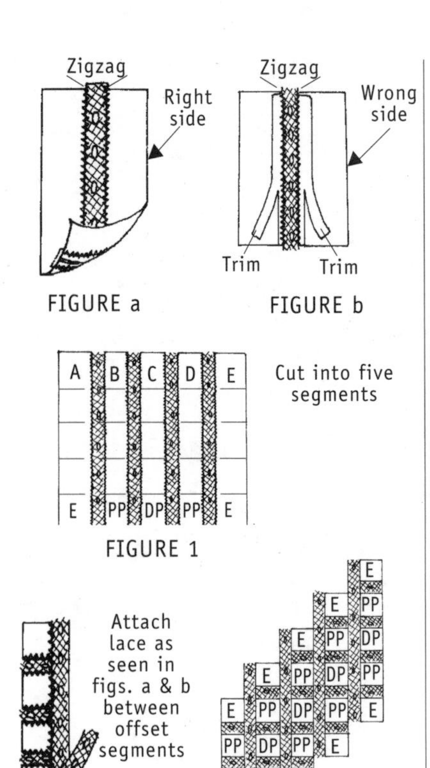

FIGURE a

FIGURE b

FIGURE 1

FIGURE 2a

FIGURE 2b

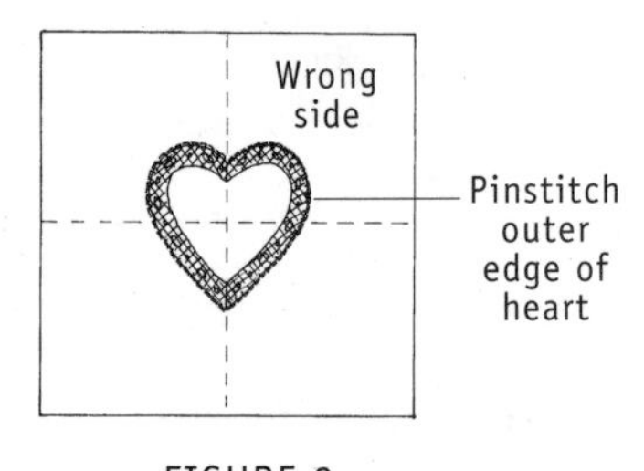

FIGURE 3

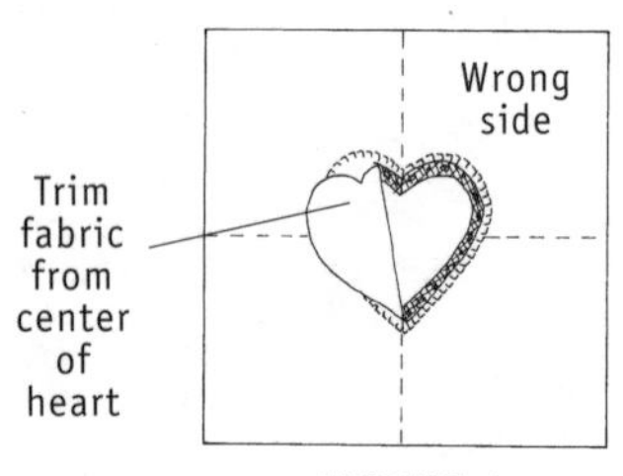

FIGURE 4

FIGURE 5

Seminole Lacework Heart

Block #7
Seminole Lacework Heart

Supplies

- One 11" dusty pink batiste square
- 1-1/2" strips of dusty pink, pale pink and ecru batiste to the measurements listed below in step 1
- Tear-away stabilizer
- #70 universal needle
- #120 universal or #100 wing needle
- Embroidery foot
- Wash-out marker
- Ecru lightweight sewing thread
- Glass head pins
- Lace shaping board
- Basic sewing supplies
- "Heart Template"
- 5/8" lace insertion

Constructing Block #7

1. Cut the following strips to measure 1-1/2" by 12":

- One strip (C) from dusty pink (DP)
- Two strips (B and D) from pale pink (PP)
- Two strips (A and E) from ecru (E)

2. Place a strip of lace insertion along the long raw edge of fabric strip A so that the raw edge of the fabric strip comes to the center of the width of the lace. The lace should overlap the fabric strip a little more than 1/4". Zigzag (W=0.8, L=2.0) the heading of the lace to strip A.

3. Zigzag (W=0.8, L=2.0) remaining fabric strip B to the other side of the lace insertion. The raw edges of the fabric strips should meet in the center under the lace *(fig. a)*.

4. Press the fabric raw edges away from the lace. Zigzag (W=1.5 – 2.0, L=1.5) along the lace heading and trim away the excess fabric from behind the lace *(fig. b)*.

5. Stitch the strips together with lace insertion between the strips to form a band consisting of fabric A, lace, fabric B, lace, fabric C, lace, fabric D, lace and fabric E *(fig.1)*.

6. Cut the band into five 1-1/2" segments.

7. Stitch the segments together in the same manner as the fabric strips *(fig. 2a)*, with lace between the segments and offsetting the colors as shown *(fig. 2b)*.

8. Press the panel of Seminole lace work and set it aside.

9. Place the pink square onto the heart template, aligning the centers, and trace the template lines.

10. Shape the lace around the inside of the template, mitering at the points. Pin the lace in place.

11. Place stabilizer beneath the square and pinstitch (W=2.0, L=2.0) the **outside edge** of the lace to the pink square *(fig. 3)*.

12. Remove the stabilizer and trim the fabric from behind the lace, leaving a heart-shaped opening in the center of the pink fabric *(fig. 4)*.

13. Center the Seminole lacework panel behind the heart opening. Pin in place.

14. Place stabilizer beneath the square and zigzag (W=1.5 – 2.0, L=1.5) the **inside edge** of the lace insertion to the Seminole lacework panel *(fig. 5)*.

15. Remove the stabilizer and trim the excess panel from behind the lace.

Ribbon & Puffing Heart

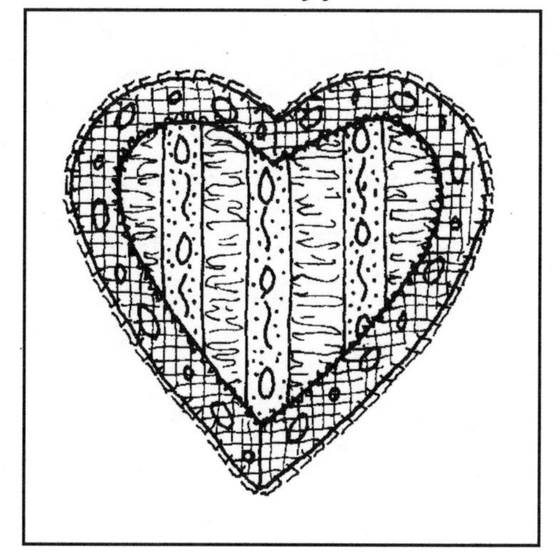

Block #8
Ribbon and Puffing Heart

Supplies

- One 11" pink batiste square
- One ecru rectangle 11" by 39"
- 1/2 yard of 1/2" wide embroidered ribbon
- Tear-away stabilizer
- #70 universal needle
- #120 universal or #100 wing needle
- Wash-out marker
- Ecru lightweight sewing thread
- Glass head pins
- Lace shaping board
- Basic sewing supplies
- Heart template
- 5/8" lace insertion

Constructing Block #8

1. Place the pink square onto the heart template, aligning the centers, and trace the template lines.

2. Shape the lace around the inside of the template, mitering at the points. Pin the lace in place.

3. Place stabilizer beneath the square and pinstitch (W=2.0, L=2.0) the **outside edge** of the lace to the pink square *(fig. 1)*.

4. Remove the stabilizer and trim the fabric from behind the lace, leaving a heart-shaped opening in the center of the pink fabric. Set the square aside *(fig. 2)*.

5. Fold the ecru rectangle in half to measure 5-1/2" by 39". Crease the fold. Open the piece and mark the crease with a wash-out marker.

6. Mark two additional lines on both sides of the center line, spacing the lines 1-1/2" apart *(see fig. 3)*.

7. Stitch a lengthened machine stitch slightly less than 1/4" to each side of the 5 drawn lines *(fig. 3)*.

8. Pull the threads up to gather the piece. Adjust the gathers attractively.

9. Cut the 1/2" wide decorative ribbon into three 6" pieces.

10. Place one piece of ribbon in the middle of the puffing panel over the center gathered rows. Pin in place.

11. Position the remaining two pieces of ribbon along the gathering rows on each side of the center, positioning them approximately 1" higher on the panel. This will ensure that the opening of the heart on the square will contain a complete piece of puffing/ribbon *(fig. 4)*.

12. Before stitching the ribbon, place the puffing/ribbon piece behind the open heart shape of the pink square. Be sure that the ribbon extends far enough so that the center of the heart opening does not contain the end of a ribbon piece. Adjust the ribbon pieces higher or lower as necessary.

13. Remove the pink square from the top of the puffing/ribbon piece.

14. Stitch the ribbon to the puffing piece with a narrow zigzag (W=1.5 – 2.0, L=1.5) along each long edge of the ribbon. Note that the first and last sets of gathering rows do not have ribbon on top of them. These will be cut away when the heart is attached to the puffing/ribbon piece *(fig. 4)*.

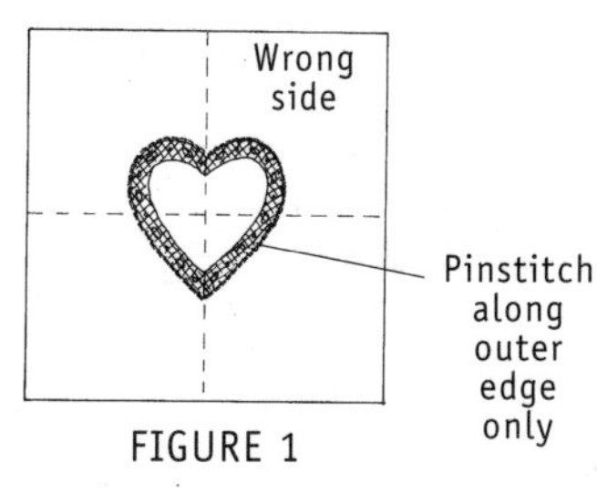

FIGURE 1

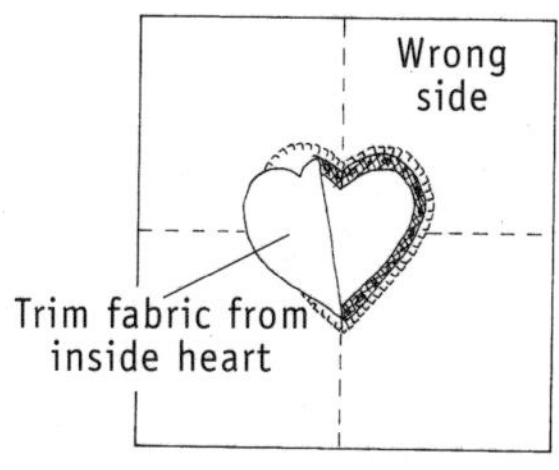

FIGURE 2

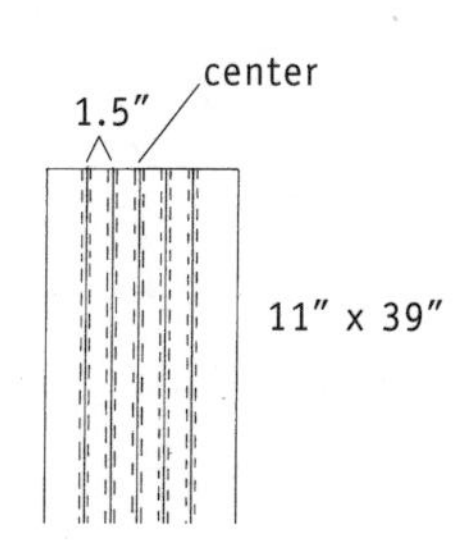

FIGURE 3

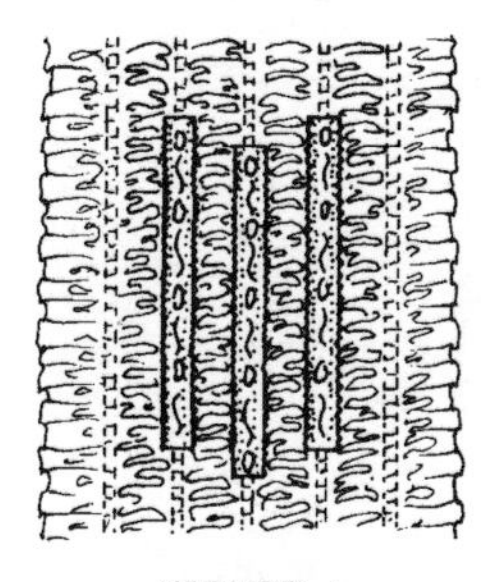

FIGURE 4

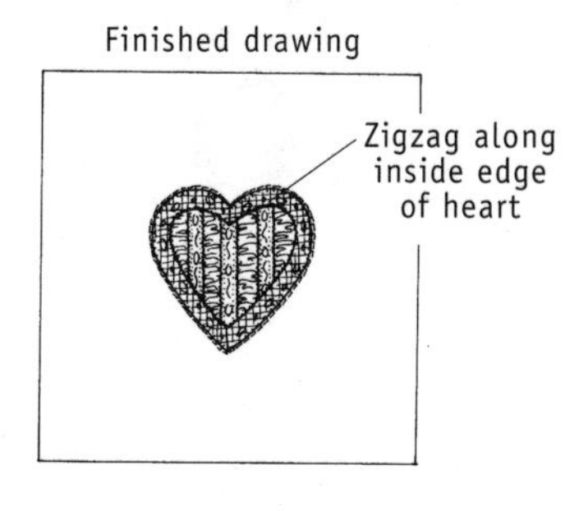

FIGURE 5

15. Center the open heart square onto the completed puffing/ribbon piece. Pin in place and stitch with a narrow zigzag along the heading of the lace insertion on the **inside** of the open heart *(fig. 5)*.

16. Remove the stabilizer and trim the excess panel from behind the lace.

17. Set the square aside.

FIGURE 1

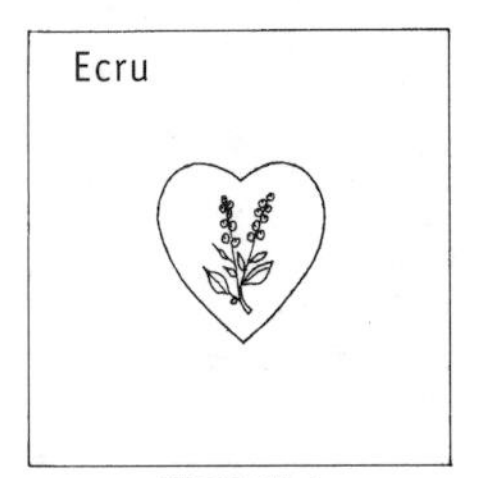

FIGURE 2

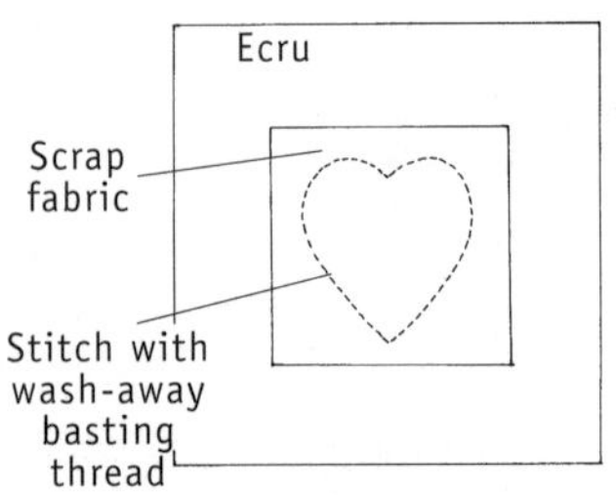

FIGURE 3

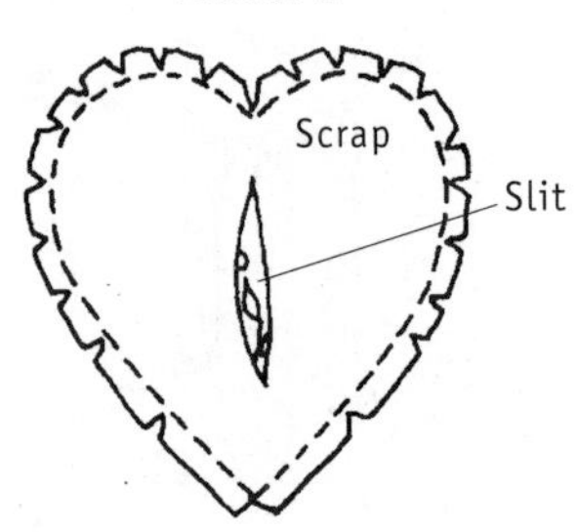

FIGURE 4

FIGURE 5

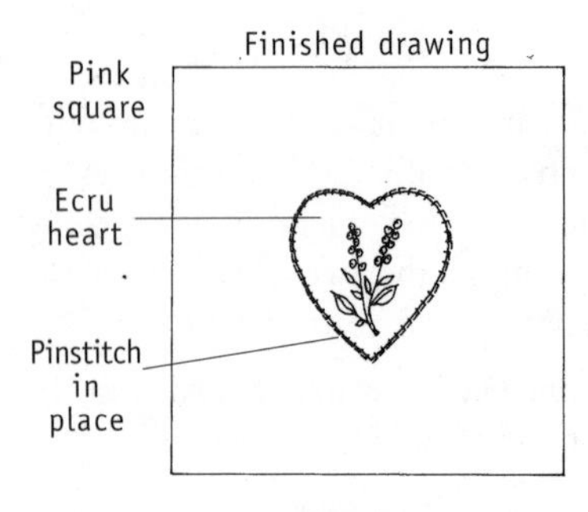

FIGURE 6

Embroidered Heart

Block #9
Embroidered Heart

Supplies

- One 11" pink batiste square
- One 11" ecru batiste square
- Tear-away stabilizer
- #70 universal needle
- #120 universal or #100 wing needle
- Embroidery foot
- Mauve, dark mauve, mint green, teal and sea foam green decorative threads
- Wash-out marker
- Ecru lightweight sewing thread
- Glass head pins
- Lace shaping board
- Basic sewing supplies
- Heart template
- Pfaff card 1, design #24 was used to embroider this block
- Wash-away basting thread
- Point turner

Constructing Block #9

1. Place the 11" ecru square and a square of stabilizer (cut stabilizer to fit into the hoop) into the machine's embroidery hoop.

2. Complete a floral embroidery no larger than 2-3/4" wide by 4" high in the center of the square using the pinks for the flower and the greens for the leaves and stem. When the embroidery is complete, remove the stabilizer and press the piece well *(fig. 1)*.

3. Place the ecru embroidered square onto the heart template (aligning the centers) and trace the template lines *(fig. 2)*.

4. Place a scrap square of fabric to the right side of the embroidered square. The scrap needs to be at least 1/2" larger than the traced heart.

5. With wash-away thread in the needle or the bobbin or both, stitch around the drawn template lines with a short straight stitch *(fig. 3)*.

6. Trim the seam allowance 1/4" from the stitching line. Clip curves and points *(fig. 4)*.

7. Cut a slit in the scrap fabric *(fig. 4)* and turn the heart right side out. Push out all curves and points and press well *(fig. 5)*.

8. Spray the edge of the turned heart with starch. Wait a few seconds and press until totally dry.

9. Pull the two hearts apart and discard the scrap piece. If the hearts do not pull apart easily, re-spray and press dry again.

10. Center the embroidered heart onto the pink square and pin in place.

11. Place stabilizer behind the pink square and stitch the embroidered heart to the pink square with a pinstitch (W=2.0, L=2.0). The straight portions of the pinstitch will be on the pink square and the "fingers" of the pinstitch will catch the edge of the heart *(fig. 6)*.

12. Remove the stabilizer and press the square well.

13. Set the square aside.

Constructing the Quilt Top

Supplies

- Lightweight sewing thread
- Basic sewing supplies

Construction

1. Starch and press each square. Cut each square down to measure 10" by 10", keeping the heart shape in the center of the newly cut square.

2. Attach a sashing strip to the left side of squares 1 and 2 and to both sides of square 3. Stitch the sashing/squares together to create a panel. If the design you chose for the sashing has a top and bottom, be sure to place the sashing pieces accordingly.

3. Repeat step 2 for connecting squares 4, 5 and 6.

4. Repeat step 2 for connecting squares 7, 8 and 9.

5. Attach a green 3-1/2" block to the left side of two sashing strips and to both sides of one sashing strip, creating a strip to be attached to the panels. Repeat this step to construct three more strips *(fig. 1)*.

6. Attach the strips constructed in step 5 to each long side of the panels. Sew all panels together, being very careful to match the seams.

7. This will complete the quilt top *(fig. 2)*.

Constructing the Quilt

Supplies

- Lightweight sewing thread
- Basic sewing supplies

Construction

1. Place the quilt backing on a flat surface. Place the batting on top of the backing. Place the quilt lining on top of the batting. Place the wrong side of the quilt top to the lining *(fig. 2)*. Pin everything well.

2. With the quilt pinned well, complete quilting lines as shown in *figure 3*. The quilting line around the heart in block 6 is done along the outermost pinstitching line. Refer to Stippling, page 111 for completing the stipple quilting for block 4.

3. Sew together the short ends of the six 1-3/4" by 33" dusty pink strips to make one long strip for the binding *(fig. 4)*. Fold in half lengthwise and press well.

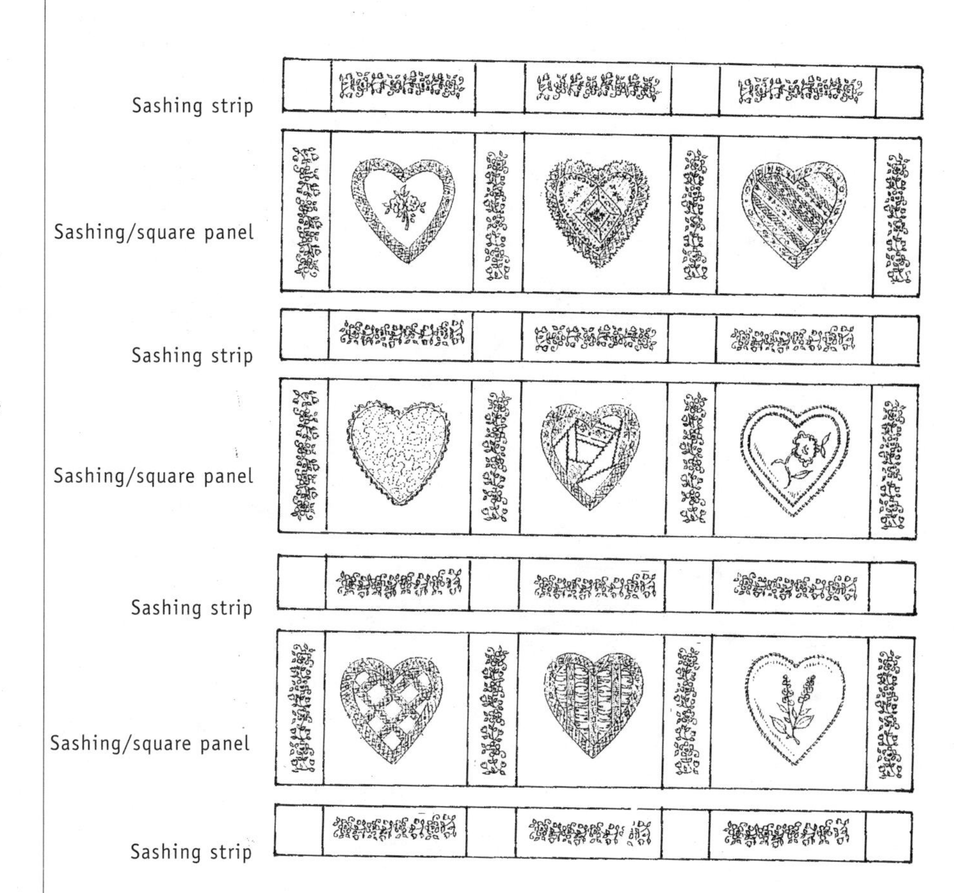

FIGURE 1

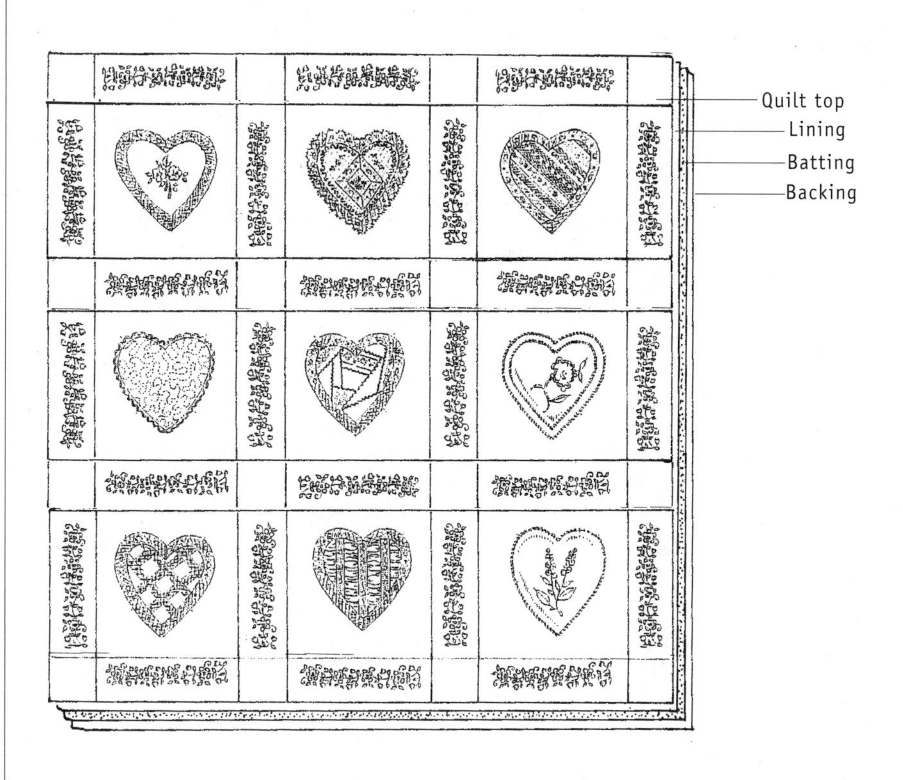

FIGURE 2

FIGURE 3

Stop stitching at miter line - backstitch

Start stitching 1" {

Flip pleat toward the stitching and stitch again along second side

FIGURE 4

FIGURE 5

FIGURE 6

FIGURE 7

4. Draw miter lines along each corner of the quilt. Beginning along one long edge of the quilt, pin raw edges of the quilt binding to the edges of the right side of the quilt.

5. Stitch using a 1/4" seam allowance, starting about 1" from the end of the strip. Stop stitching at the miter line and back stitch *(see fig. 5)*.

6. Fold a 1/2" pleat in the binding at the corner and begin stitching again along the second side of the binding, starting at the miter line *(see fig. 5)*.

7. Continue stitching, using this same technique at each corner. Stop stitching about 2" from the beginning. Overlap the beginning and the end 1/2" and trim away any excess. Fold one edge of the binding to the inside 1/4". Place the straight end into the folded end and continue stitching *(fig. 6)*.

8. Fold the binding over the edges of the

Serger Quilt

This precious quilt is sure to be one of your favorite sewing projects ever! Accented with silk ribbon beading, Swiss embroidery, and Swiss insertion, this delightful quilt looks as if it took weeks of effort to create. Would you believe that with the help of your serger, it can be made in just over ONE HOUR? Not only is this quilt easy to make, it is also versatile; for a little girl, pink can easily be substituted for the blue. What a perfect gift for that special baby in your life! It will be cherished for years, and everyone will think it took you almost that long to make! (Don't tell!)

SUPPLIES

- 1-7/8 yards embroidered insertion
- 1-1/3 yards lace insertion (3/4″)
- 1-1/3 yards faggoting
- 1-7/8 yards white batiste
- 5/8 yard blue batiste
- 1-1/3 yards blue ribbon to fit faggoting
- Thin quilt batting (crib size)
- Ruler, rotary cutter and cutting mat

Directions

1. Set the serger on three-thread rolled hem. The serger is used to create the heirloom center square and all quilt-as-you go piecing.

2. Cut the following pieces to 22″:

- two pieces of faggoting
- two pieces of lace insertion
- three pieces of embroidered insertion

3. Place the lace strips to each side of one embroidered insertion strip, right sides together with 1/8″ of the fabric extending beyond the edge of the lace. Place the pieces under the serger foot and serge so that the needle catches the lace edge and rolls in the extended fabric. A very small amount of fabric may be cut off as the pieces are serged together *(fig. 1)*.

4. Starch and press the rolled hem toward the fabric *(fig. 2)*.

5. Add the remaining strips of embroidered insertion to each side of the lace using the same technique described in step 3.

6. Place the faggoting strips on each side of the lace/embroidered insertion panel, right sides together. The fabric edge of the faggoting should meet the edge of the embroidered insertion piece. Place the pieces under the serger foot and serge so that the stitch is formed next to the ladder of the faggoting and the excess seam allowance is removed *(fig. 3)*.

7. Cut two rectangles of white fabric 9″ by 22″. Attach a fabric rectangle to the faggoting using the same technique described in step 6. This creates the embellished rectangle for the heirloom center square. Run ribbon through the faggoting.

8. Measure, square, and trim the embellished piece to 21″ square. Cut two squares of white fabric 21″, one for the lining and one for the backing. Cut a batting square 21″. Place the wrong side of the heirloom square to the right side of the lining square. Place the batting under the lining. Place the backing fabric piece under the batting. Pin all of the layers together about every 3″ with the pins 1″ from the edges of the fabric. Treat the four layers (backing, batting, lining and heirloom square) as one. This completes the heirloom center square. Set aside *(fig. 4)*.

9. Cut two blue fabric strips 6″ by 22″ and two blue fabric strips 6″ by 31″. Cut two white fabric strips 9″ by 22″ and two white fabric strips 9″ by 31″. Cut two batting strips 9″ by 22″ and two batting strips 9″ by 31″.

10. Center the short blue fabric strips to the top and bottom of the heirloom center square, right sides together. Center the short white strips to the back of the heirloom square, right sides together. Center the short batting strips behind the white strips. The layering will be (top to bottom) blue fabric strip, heirloom square, lining square, batting square, backing square, white strip and batting strip *(fig. 5)*. Match all long edges, pin often and serge using a 1/2″ to 5/8″ seam allowance. Remove the pins before they run under the serger foot. The larger seam allowance will insure that all layers are

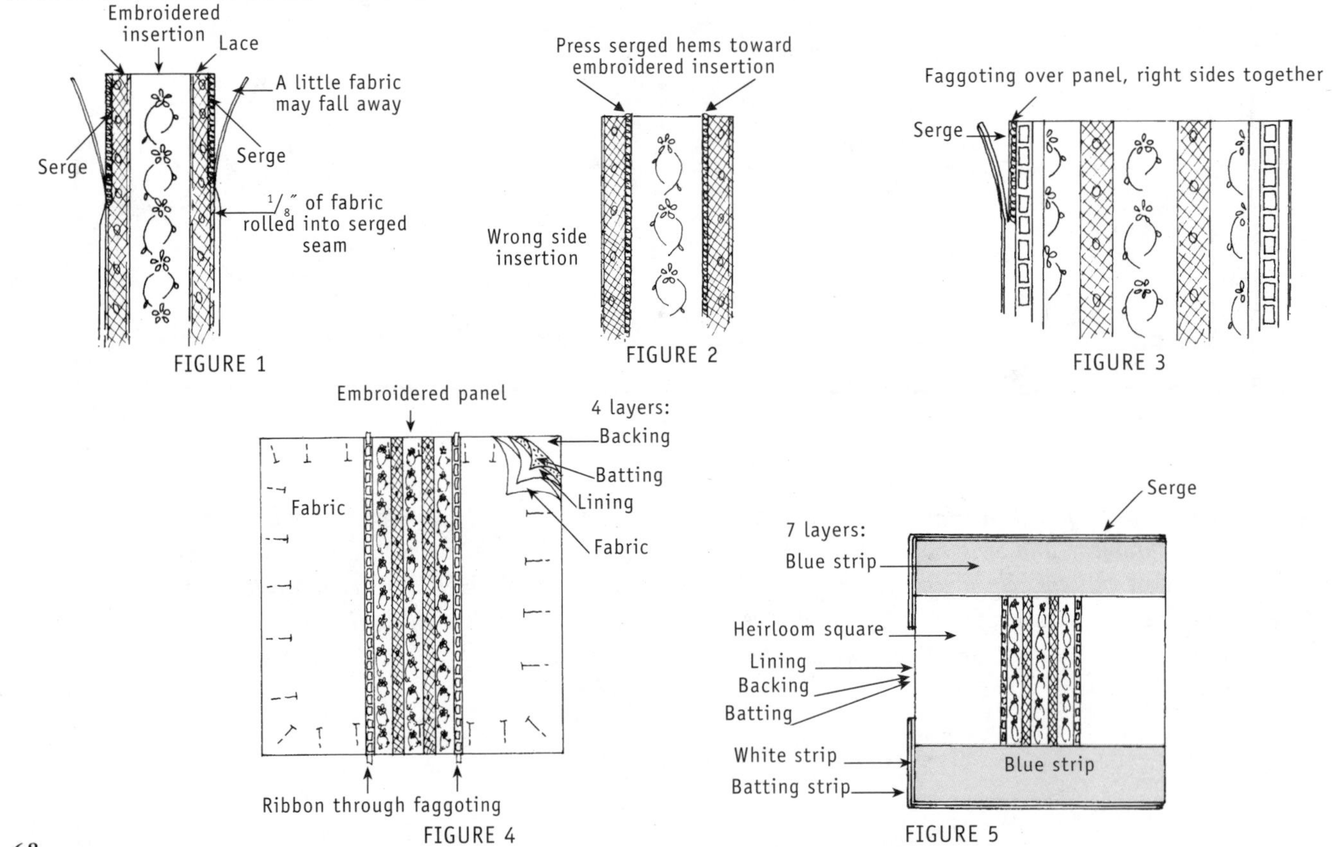

FIGURE 1

FIGURE 2

FIGURE 3

FIGURE 4

FIGURE 5

caught in the seam. Flip the blue fabric strips away from the heirloom center. Flip the batting/white strips away from the center. The batting and white fabric should extend beyond the blue strip by about 3″. Press well. Trim the outer edges of the fabric/batting/fabric strips even with the sides of the heirloom center *(fig. 6)*.

11. Add the longer fabric strips and batting strips to the sides of the quilt top, layering and stitching using the same technique as described in step 10. Flip the fabric/batting/fabric strips away from the heirloom center and press well *(fig. 7)*.

12. The binding will be formed from the extended white fabric and batting. Treat each corner in the following manner:

a. Trim the corner of the **batting** away at a 45° angle *(fig. 8)*.

b. Fold the outer edges of the white fabric/batting to the edges of the blue fabric *(fig. 9)*.

c. Fold the corner to the right side at a 45° angle *(fig. 10)*.

d. Fold each side on top of the blue fabric to form a miter at the corner. Pin the binding in place at each corner and along the sides *(fig. 11)*.

13. Topstitch along the inner fold of the binding. Hand stitch the opening closed at the corners. Topstitch through all layers along the outer edges of the faggoting to "quilt" the heirloom square *(fig. 12)*.

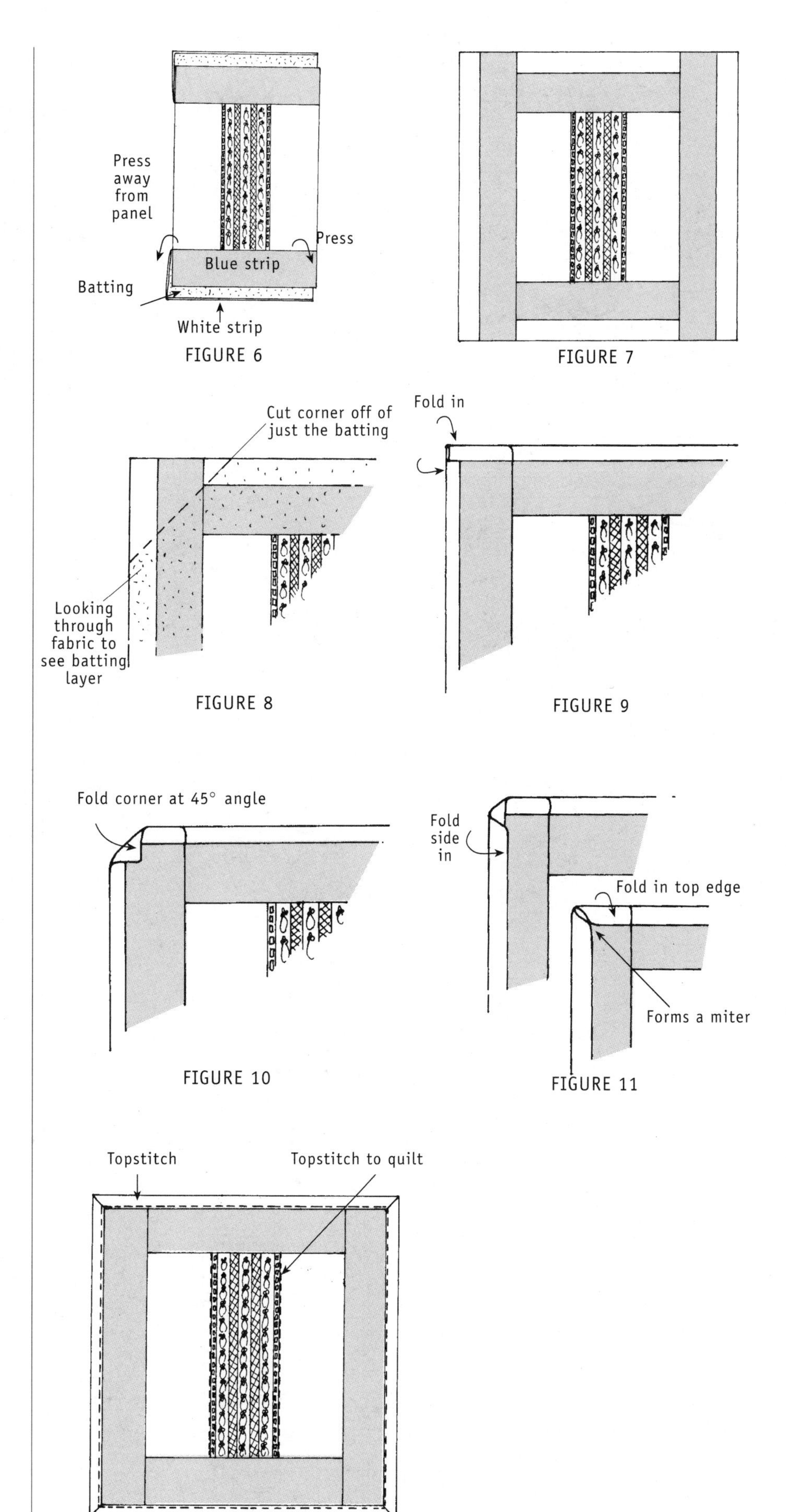

FIGURE 6

FIGURE 7

FIGURE 8

FIGURE 9

FIGURE 10

FIGURE 11

FIGURE 12

Joanna's Memory Quilt

This wonderfully happy quilt is made of 100% white cotton Swiss broadcloth and has heavy white 100% cotton French lace for the sections of the quilt, for the circles and for the gathered lace around the outside of the quilt. The circles are embroidered on Swiss Nelona. The batting is reasonably thick making it nice and puffy. Since Swiss broadcloth is almost impossible to find and very expensive, I suggest using 100% cotton Victorian batiste for the whole quilt; it is still advisable to use the thinner Swiss batiste for the circles since that will be an extra thickness of fabric in those areas.

When I first started discussing this quilt with Louise Baird, I knew I wanted it to be memories of Joanna's life to that point. Since she was still in college, I knew we would have to leave some of the spaces blank, such as engagement and marriage. We knew we wanted the quilt to be shadow appliquéd by machine and have some machine embroidery used for the flowers and the lettering. This quilt was on our 200 television series and was originally published in the book, Victorian Sewing and Crafts. It has been out of print for several years and we still get requests for directions on making the "Memories Quilt" which is the name that people remember it by.

Can I share what this quilt means to me about seven years after it was made? Actually I haven't looked at this quilt very much since Louise Baird keeps it with her to use in her shadow applique´ classes which she teaches all over the country. I wanted a detailed write up for this new quilt book, so I went back over each square to describe it for you. It was like living through special events in her life all over again. I remembered that all of the grandparents were alive at the time of her first birthday. My daddy was very sick but everybody else was in great health and came to the party. I remember so well the smocked dress she wore on her first day of school. It had a school bus on it and was a sundress made of red gingham. She wore two ponytails with huge navy ribbons on each pony tail. I traveled down memory lane with each square I was describing for you in this book.

I really recommend that you take the time to make a memory quilt for someone you love. It would be precious to use transfer photo techniques within the basic format of this quilt. That would make the quilt very, very quick and easy. You can program in the words and make the circles exactly like the ones used on this quilt, except for using a transfer in the center fabric.

I want to describe each square for you since each square is so special. Of course, you can make up your own squares depending on the occasions you want remembered. This quilt was created before the really big use of machine embroidery and the wonderful things we can do now with machine embroidery. One of the most significant improvements on machine embroidery is the ability to machine embroider names, dates and events to the point of even curving them on the computer. Even our titles, such as "First Spend the Night" and "First Step" were stitched in using machine decorative stitches such as tiny daisies, tiny flowers, tiny ovals, or tiny stems. In other words, whatever machine decorative stitches a machine has, make them very tiny and follow the outline of the written phrases. If you have a machine which makes beautiful letters, at least one inch tall, you can use your built-in embroidered letters and make this whole process much easier. We also curved our phrases and many of you know how to curve your letters on the computer so you can do the same thing.

For those of you who do not have a computer embroidery machine, you will be glad to know that you can use the methods given in this quilt for using the decorative stitches you have on your machine. Be sure to make them very tiny before you start stitching the letters of the phrases.

The quilt is made up of twenty squares with a circle within each square. Actually the quilt just looks as if it has twenty separate squares. The whole quilt top is one 74-1/2 inch piece of fabric with the "squares" being created by stitching white French lace insertion. We used sixteen of the square areas for phrases and four of the square areas for just embroidery within the square.

Each circular section is made on a square and everything cut away except the circular lace part and the portion within the lace circle. Then the circular sections are zig-zagged into the center of each section.

I would like to describe the individual phrase sections. The embroidery sections can be done by hand or machine on the four corners. A lot of the children's clothing had tiny, quilting type prints underneath to shadow through.

GOD GAVE US JOANNA

In this square is simply stitched (satin stitch), "God Gave Us Joanna-Feb. 23, 1976." Pink thread was used.

FIRST WORD

There is the cutest little bald-headed baby sitting beside a Jack-in-the-Box, saying "da da." Since those were Joanna's first words, those are the ones I used. The date below the little baby is July, 1976. The colors for the "First Word" are mint green and the shadow applique´ suit on the baby is a mint green tiny print. Behind the Jack-in-the-Box is a mint green print. The Jack-in-the-Box is brown and red. His hat is the same print used for the baby suit. The "First Word" is stitched with a very, very tiny daisy stitch.

FIRST TOOTH

The little baby has a cute blue print peeking through with shadow applique´ for the clothing. A brown and beige teddy bear is sitting beside the baby and she holds a red rattle. The words "First Tooth" are stitched in blue with a decorative stitch. August, 1976 is stitched in blue also.

BAPTISM

The shadow applique´ behind the Bible is white; the words on the pages are dark gray, some of the trim is medium gray; the outline of the book is brown and the bookmark has gold lame´ peeking through. There are flowers in the pot beside the Bible and the word "Baptism" is stitched in mint green. Pink, dark pink and yellow flowers are in the pot; green leaves surround the flowers. The date is Oct. 7, 1976.

FIRST PARTY

Joanna's first birthday party was for her friend, Chris DeRosier, on February 17, 1977. Chris had turned one and was born just one week before Joanna. The suit the baby is wearing as well as the bow has blue printed fabric; the cake is green and the plate is pink. The candle is yellow. The gift beside the cake has a lavender printed fabric behind part of the cake and lavender ribbons. The outlining stitch around the printed fabric on the box is yellow. The baby is holding a dark blue balloon with a gray string. The words "First Party" are stitched in pink with a decorative stitch.

FIRST HAIRCUT

This is such a cute square with the mother's hand reaching out with the gray scissors to cut the blonde curls on top of the baby's head. The mother's arm has a black and white printed quilting fabric shadowing through. Her cuffs and buttons on the dress are gray. The baby is wearing a cape around its shoulders which is a printed fabric underneath; the pants are baby blue and the shoes are dark brown. The words "First Haircut" are stitched using a decorative stitch made very tiny on any sewing machine.

FIRST BIRTHDAY

For Joanna's first birthday celebration we chose green thread to stitch Happy Birthday. The stitch selected is a tiny featherstitch. The cake is navy blue with red scalloped trims. The flowers are yellow and the candle is white with yellow flames and shadows around the flames. There is a yellow shadow appliquéd daisy-like flower with green stems and a green leaf beside the cake. The gift has a pretty little tiny flowered print underneath the square box shape; the ribbon is shadow appliquéd in pink. The date, February 23, 1977 is embroidered in blue.

FIRST STEP

The words "First Step" are embroidered using a yellow oval stitch very close together. The words, Feb. 1977, are embroidered in blue. The baby's pajamas are shadow appliquéd using a pretty red and green tiny flowered quilting fabric and the collar and buttons on the front are red. The baby's doll has a yellow quilting fabric underneath the dress and her hair is brown; her eyes are brown also.

FIRST RECITAL

Joanna's first dance recital was in June, 1979. The letters are stitched in dark pink; the ballet costume is pink with darker pink for the bodice; the tutu is white with pink stitching. Her hair is blonde, since Joanna has blonde hair. She has pink bows in her hair and dark pink toe shoes.

FIRST DAY AT SCHOOL

The letters for "First Day at School" are stitched in brown. There is a red schoolhouse with brown steps, brown roofs and brown door. There is a writing slate with blue in the middle and brown on the outside. There is a red apple with green leaves and a yellow pencil; the date is September, 1981.

FIRST SPEND THE NIGHT

There are two of the cutest little girls in sleeping bags with a teddy bear sitting right beside the little girls on this circle. One little girl has blue pajamas with a sleeping bag with green print underneath and green ovals to embellish the top of the sleeping bag. The other little girl has red pajamas and a yellow sleeping bag with blue flowers. The bear is brown.

FIRST DATE

Her first date stitching is in blue. There are pink and green flowers underneath those words. There is a brown box of candies with a blue ribbon tying the pink flower bouquet on top of the box of candy. The date is February, 1990.

FIRST PROM

The words "First Prom" are stitched in red. There is a picture frame with gold lame´ underneath the shadow applique´; the outline of the frame is stitched with gold thread. The girl is wearing a red dress and the man is in a black tuxedo. There is a red flower with green leaves and French knots in a pearlized thread beside the red flower.

GRADUATION

High school graduation for Joanna was May 25, 1994. The word "Graduation" is stitched in gray; there are pink flowers surrounding the May 25, 1994 date. The mortar board is dark gray; the tassel is red and white; gold thread ties the diploma which is white stitched in pale blue. A gold thread holds the tassel to the hat.

ENGAGEMENT

The word "Engagement" is stitched in pink. There is an engagement ring stitched in gold with a diamond, shadow embroidered in white. Pink, yellow and green flowers cradle the engagement ring. Since Joanna was not engaged when the quilt was finished, there is no date on the engagement. I need to hand embroider the date of her engagement in the square since putting it in by machine would require stitching through all of the layers.

WEDDING

The wedding circle has two gold rings intertwined. The stitching is in pink; there are pink, green and yellow sprays of flowers in-between the two wedding rings. Since Joanna was not married when this quilt was made, I must go back and embroider the date of her marriage on the quilt.

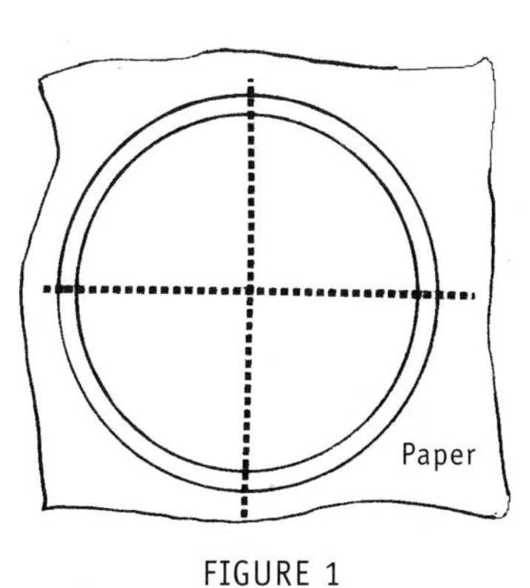

FIGURE 1

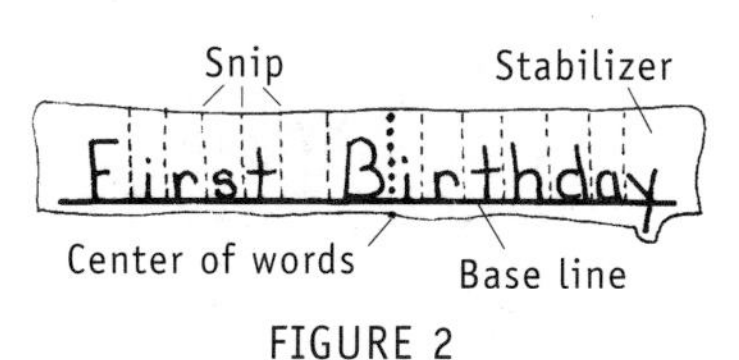

FIGURE 2

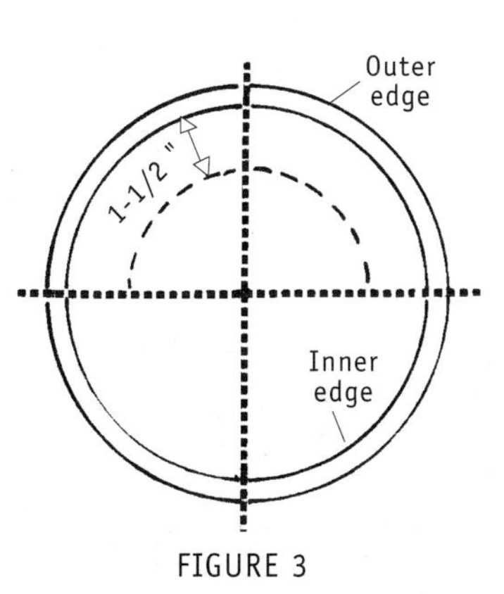

FIGURE 3

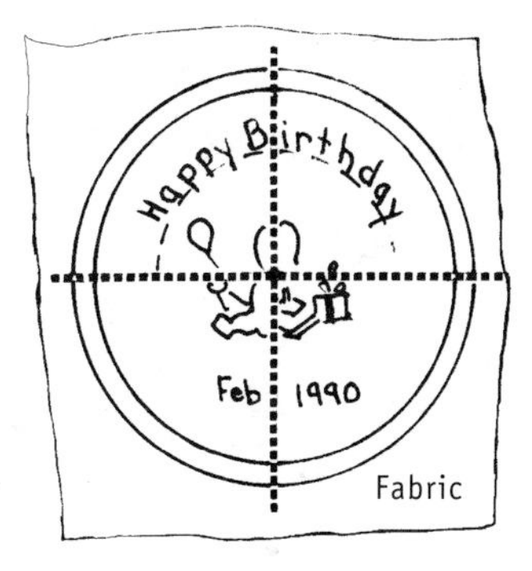

FIGURE 4

Supplies

- 1-1/2 yards Swiss batiste
- 7 yards Swiss broadcloth or Victorian batiste
- Extra loft batting (Single Bed - 72" x 90")
- 37 yards of 1" insertion lace
- 20 yards of 2-1/2" to 3" edging lace
- Machine embroidery thread, white and colors
- Various fabrics for shadow appliqué
- Open-toe appliqué foot
- Wash-out marker
- Water-soluble stabilizer (Solvy, WSS)
- Size 70 and 80 needles
- Spray starch
- Soft tear away stabilizer
- Pocket or kindergarten scissors
- Appliqué scissors

All Shadow Appliquéd Quilt templates and letters are found in the pattern section of this book. Refer to Shadow Appliqué technique on page 115.

Directions

There are 15 event squares, four flower squares and one square with letters only.

1. Cut or tear the batiste into twenty 10" squares. These pieces will be used for the designs in the center of the circles.

2. Spray starch each of the batiste squares to give them body.

3. Find the center of each square by folding in half and then in half again. Mark center and quarter divisions.

4. Trace both lines of lace circle template on a piece of paper or tear-away. Fold to find center and quarter points of the circle *(fig. 1)*.

5. EVENT DESIGNS - Use the following directions on 15 squares for the event designs.

a. On an extra piece of soft tear-away stabilizer, mark a baseline and write (trace) the phrase on the baseline, spacing as needed. Fold this in half and mark the halfway point. Trim close to the baseline and around the phrase. Snip in between each letter from the top to (but not through) the baseline *(fig. 2)*.

b. Mark a curved line 1-1/2 inches in from the inner line of the circle template. This is the line for the placement of the letters *(fig. 3)*.

c. Match the center line of the circle with the center of the phrase. Match the baseline with the line drawn, curving the phrase. Trace the letters to the paper or tear-away.

d. Trace the design in desired position within the circle. A date can be added, if desired.

e. Place fabric on top of paper or tear-away template and trace design onto the batiste matching centers of the fabric square and circle design. Use a wash-out pencil or a quilting pencil that can be erased if

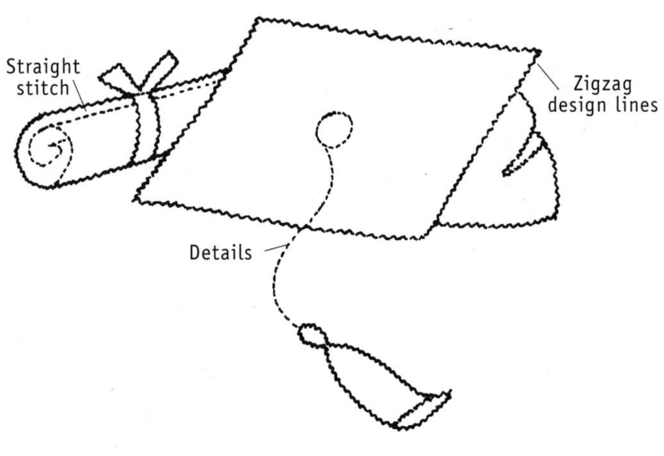

FIGURE 5

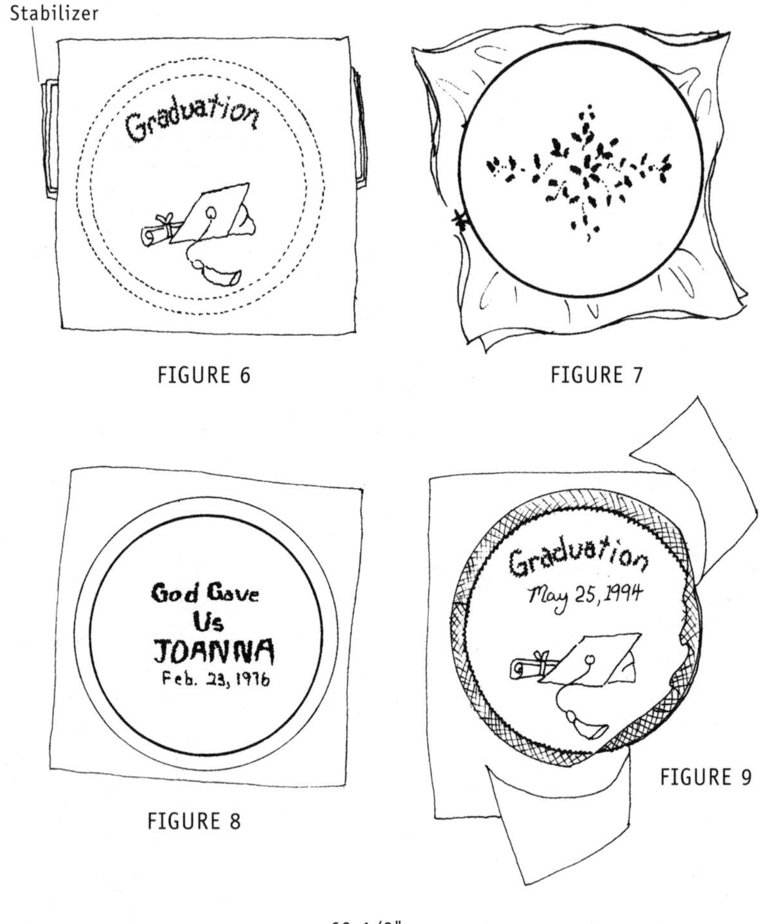

FIGURE 6

FIGURE 7

FIGURE 8

FIGURE 9

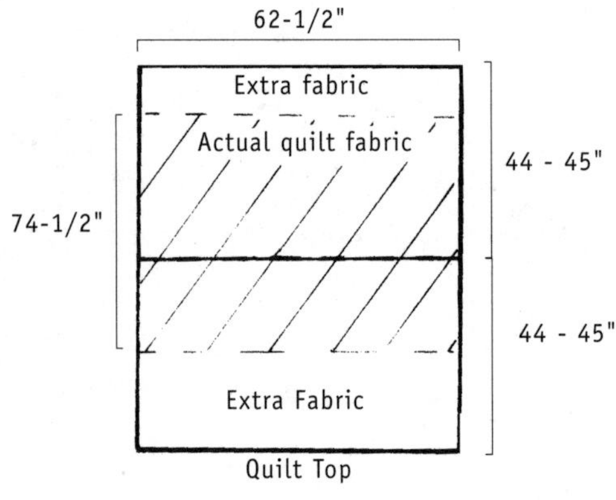

FIGURE 10

necessary. Trace outline of the circle onto fabric also *(fig. 4)*.

f. *Shadow appliqué*. Place different fabrics between two layers of batiste to see what they will look like (some prints were used on the sample). Prints with a white or light background and pastel colors worked the best. Match the top thread color to what shows through the top layer. Use white thread in the bobbin. Stitch along the design lines using a narrow open zigzag (W = .5-1, L=.75-1.25) *(fig. 5)*. Refer to the Shadow Appliqué directions in this book for specific instructions, page 115.

g. Use a very short straight stitch for detailing *(see fig. 5)*.

h. Use built-in decorative stitches to stitch the letters. Place several layers of WSS under letters to prevent puckering. On a scrap of the same fabric that is stabilized try your decorative stitches. The width and length will need to be decreased and tested to get correct proportions. When stitching on the letters, stitch slowly and watch how the stitch is formed. You should not pivot when the next move is a backward stitch. When turning curves or approaching a pivot, use the single pattern button if available *(fig. 6)*.

6. Embroidery Designs are done on 4 squares. For the squares with the embroidery designs, position and trace in the center of the circle.

a. Place the fabric in a hoop with several layers of WSS.

b. Use built-in stitches or a satin stitch zigzag changing the width to cover the flower or leaf design lines. The French knots are done with a narrow zigzag bar tack. The stems are a very narrow open zigzag *(fig. 7)*.

7. WORDS ONLY - 1 square.

a. For the square with words only, position within the circle.

b. Use a narrow satin stitch to cover all of the lines *(fig. 8)*.

Construction of Quilt

1. Shape the insertion lace along the traced circle of each quilt square. Zigzag (L=0.6, W-1.5-2.0) along the inside edge of the lace circle only. Refer to the Lace Shaping directions, page 109. Trim the excess fabric from under the lace close to the stitching. This will leave the lace circle and the inside design *(fig. 9)*.

2. Cut or tear four pieces of broadcloth 62-1/2" long. Put two pieces aside for now.

3. Stitch two of the long edges together using a 1/2" seam. Press the seam open. The quilt will be cut to the correct size in step 5 *(fig.10)*.

4. On the right side of the quilt top, measure three lines 14" apart above the seam and two lines 14" apart below the seam. These are the horizontal lace placement lines (dotted lines on *fig. 11)*. Add a line 2-1/4" from the last line on each side. This is the cutting line.

5. For vertical lace placement lines fold in half and mark this center line. Measure from this line and mark two lines 14" apart on each side of this center line *(slashed lines on fig. 11)*. Add a line 2-1/4" from the last line on each side. This is the cutting line. Cut on the cutting lines. The quilt top now measures 62-1/2" wide by 74-1/2" *(fig. 11)*.

6. Center lace insertion over the horizontal lines. Using a short narrow zigzag, stitch the lace to the fabric along both edges.

7. Repeat for vertical lace placement lines. At the ends of lace turn under about 1/4" before stitching *(fig. 12)*.

8. Center the finished design circles into the squares created by the horizontal and vertical rows of lace. Stitch along the outer edge of the lace circle using the same stitch as above *(fig. 13)*.

9. With the remaining two pieces of fabric, create the backing by stitching two pieces together, along the long sides, with a 1/2" seam. Press seams open. Place the quilt top on the backing piece centering the backing seam as shown on figure 14. Cut the excess backing away to match the top front *(fig. 14)*.

10. To form the quilt, layer on a large flat surface as follows *(fig. 15):* batting, backing (right side up), and quilt top (right side down).

11. Pin all layers together.

12. Stitch around the quilt using a 1/2" seam allowance. Leave 8-10" open.

13. Turn quilt to right side. Stitch opening closed.

14. Pin all layers together with safety pins. Use plenty of pins to prevent layers from shifting. Using a straight stitch, free motion or with the foot on, quilt as desired. This quilt is stitched on each side of the lace: lace circles, vertical lace lines and horizontal lace lines. *NOTE: Take care to prevent any pleats from forming on the back when quilting.*

15. Topstitch 1/8" from the edges of the quilt to flatten the edge. Refer to the finished drawing of the quilt.

16. Gather the lace edging to fit the outer edge of the quilt. Overlap the ends of the lace. Stitch the gathered edging to the quilt edge with an open zigzag. Zigzag the lace overlap *(fig. 16)*.

17. Wash to remove all of the markings and WSS.

18. Press if necessary.

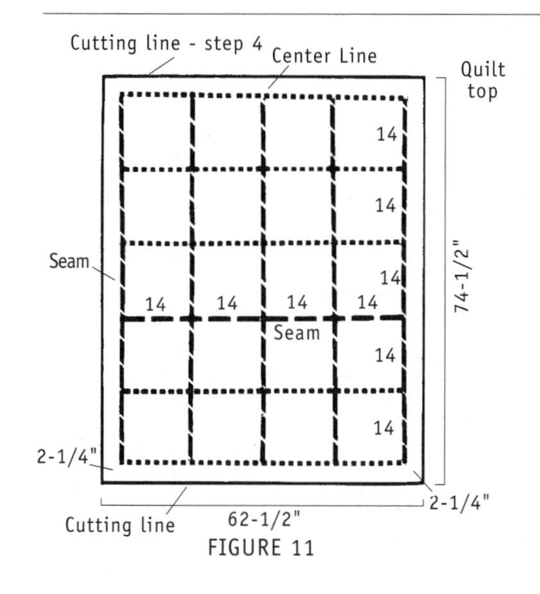

FIGURE 11

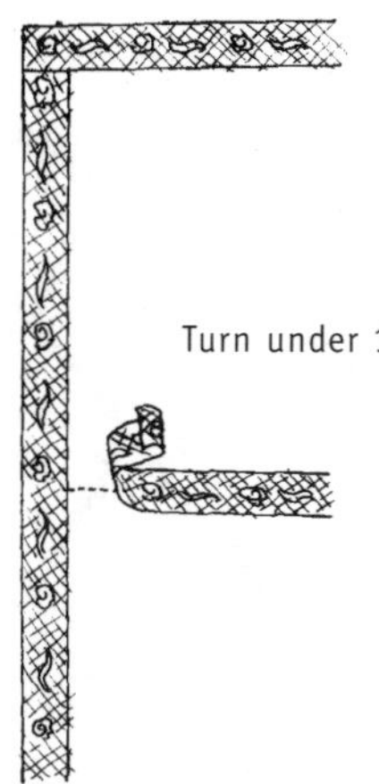

FIGURE 12

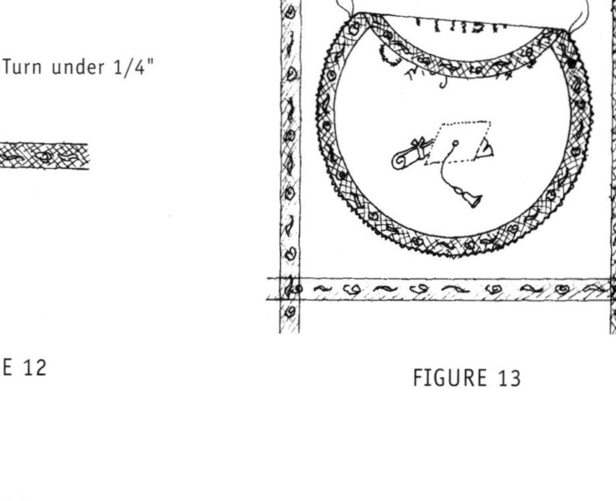
FIGURE 13

Cut away excess backing

44 - 45"

Backing seam

44 - 45"

Cut away excess backing

FIGURE 14

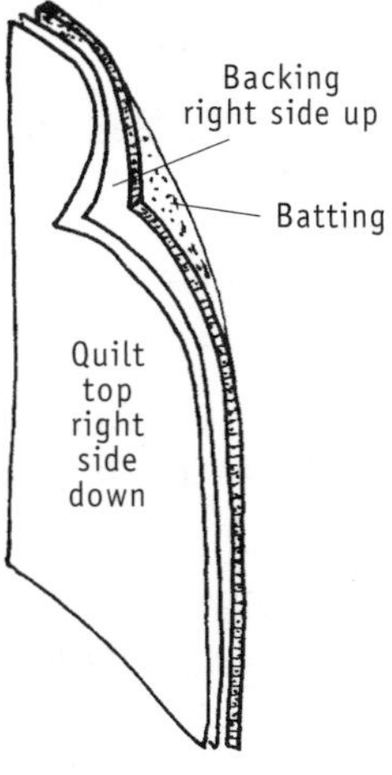

FIGURE 15

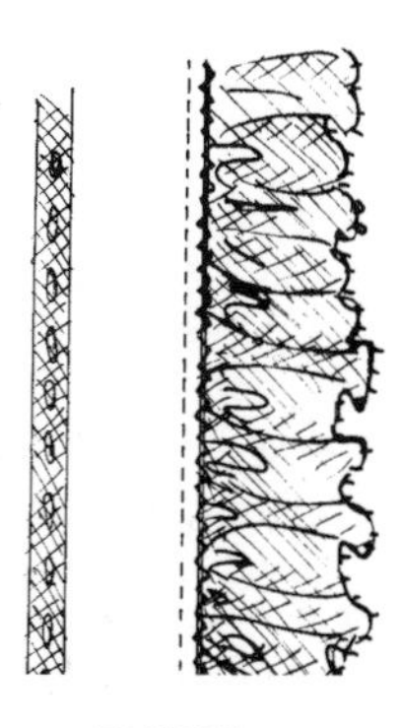
FIGURE 16

Crazy Patch Doll Quilt & Matching Pillow

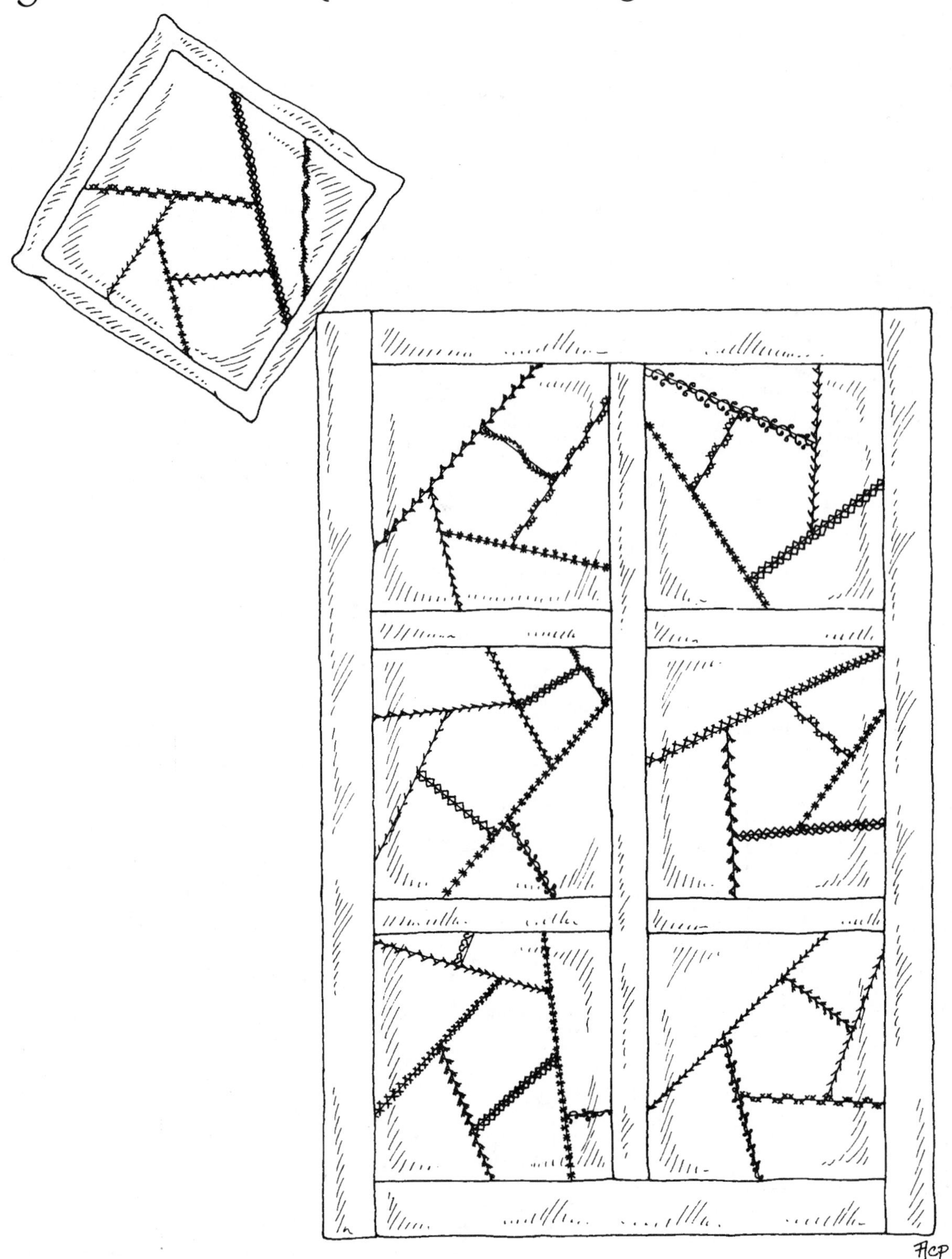

What could be happier than a brightly colored doll quilt and pillow to match? Using a mottled purple for the sashings and binding, the colors of the crazy patched squares are as bright as a rainbow. Machine decorative stitches embellish the different sections of the crazy patch. The back of the quilt is purple.

The pretty pillow is a miniature version of the quilt with the crazy-patched square of the pillow being the same size as one of the squares in the quilt. It is a very lucky doll who will sleep underneath this quilt. This would be a great project for a mother and daughter to stitch together.

SUPPLIES

Quilt and Pillow:

- Threads for decorative stitching
- 30 weight thread to match the backing (purple)
- Invisible thread
- 1/4 yard of seven or eight different fabrics for crazy patch
- 3/4 yard of purple for quilt backing and sashing
- 1/2 yard of light-weight muslin
- Quilt tack gun or safety pins
- Stuffing for pillow
- Wash-out marker

Cutting - Quilt

• Cut seven 7-3/8" squares of unbleached muslin (crazy patch base fabric) – one square will be for the pillow

• Cut one 19" by 26" for backing (purple fabric)

• Cut sashing strips (purple fabric) as follows:

Two strips 2" by 26"
Two strips 2" by 15"
One strip 1-1/2" by 23"
Four strips 1-1/2" by 8"

NOTE: Crazy patch pieces will be cut as needed.

Cutting - Pillow

• Cut one 10" square for the pillow back (purple fabric)

• Cut sashing strips (purple fabric) as follows:

Two strip 1-1/2" by 8"
Two strips 1-1/2" by 10"

Note: Crazy patch square will be completed with the quilt.

Creating the Crazy Patch Blocks

NOTE: Two crazy patch templates have been given. Each template can be turned to look like four different templates.

Repeat steps 1-11 for all seven muslin squares.

1. Trace Template #1 on 3 muslin squares. Trace Template #2 on 4 muslin squares. Find the center of the squares and mark with a fabric marker *(fig. 1)*.

NOTE: Template #1 is shown for all figure drawings. Refer to figure 11 for placement order for Template #2.

2. For the patchwork, start with a multi-sided fabric piece (patch "A") with at least five sides.

3. Pin patch "A" to the center of the muslin square *(fig. 2)*.

4. Cut a piece of fabric larger than area for patch "B". Place patch "B" to patch "A", right sides together. Line up one side of patch "B" with one side of patch "A". Patch "B" will overhang patch "A". Stitch using a straight stitch (L=3) and a 1/4" seam the length of the edge of patch "A" *(fig. 3)*. This stitching will be made through the two patch pieces and the muslin square.

5. Flip patch "B" to the right side and press *(fig. 4)*.

6. Place one of the straight sides of patch "C" overlapping patches "A" and "B". The edge of patch "C" may extend beyond the length of the patches underneath. The patches underneath may extend above the straight edge of patch "C" *(fig. 5)*.

7. Stitch along the straight edge of patch "C" the length of the under pieces. Trim

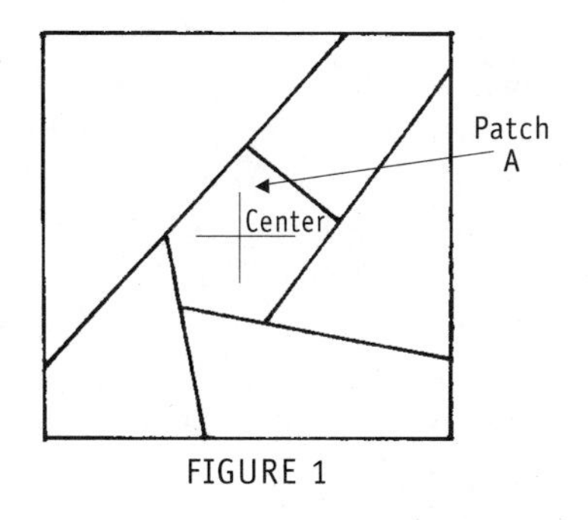

FIGURE 1

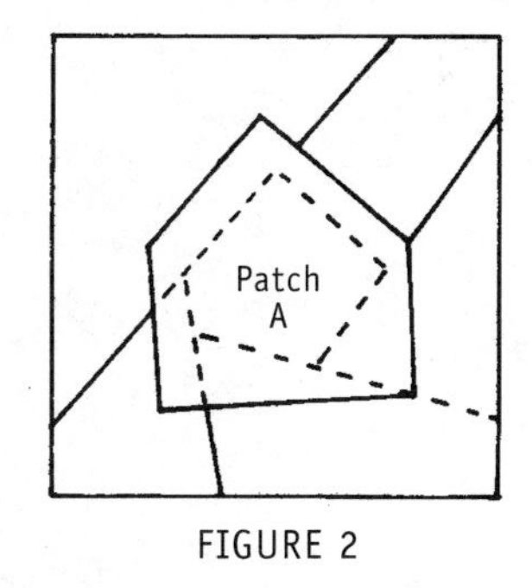

FIGURE 2

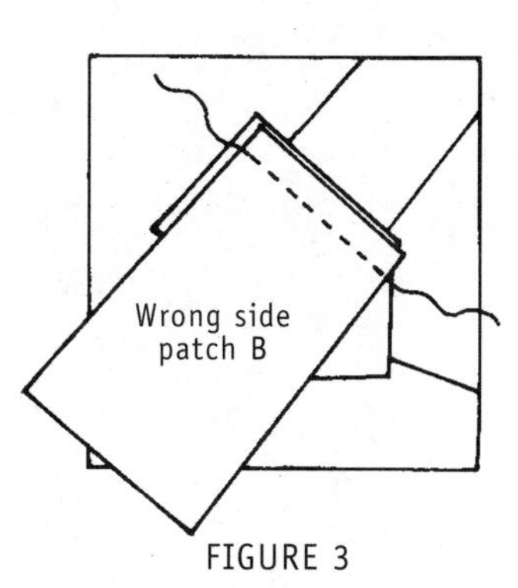

FIGURE 3

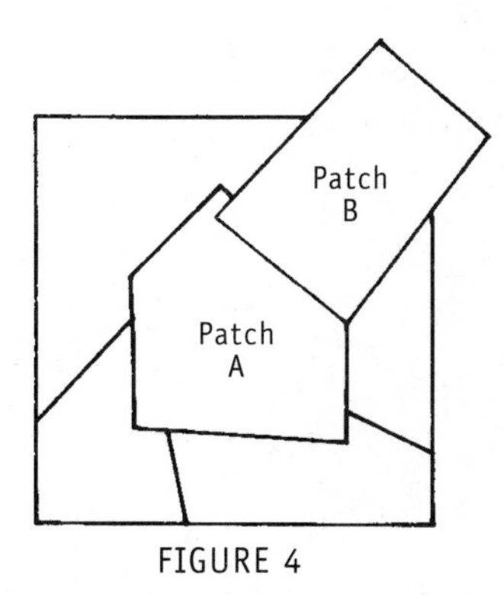

FIGURE 4

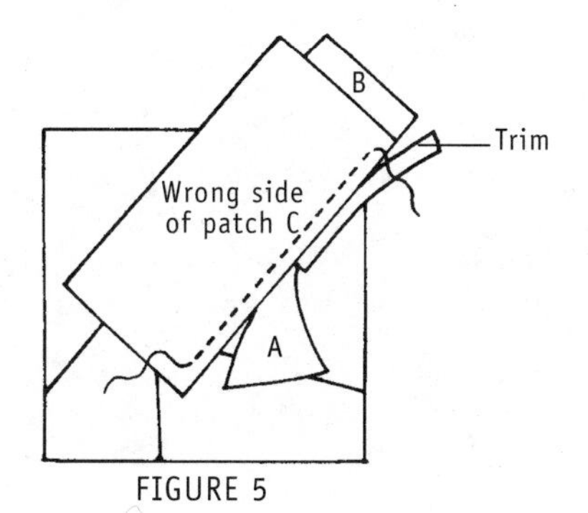

FIGURE 5

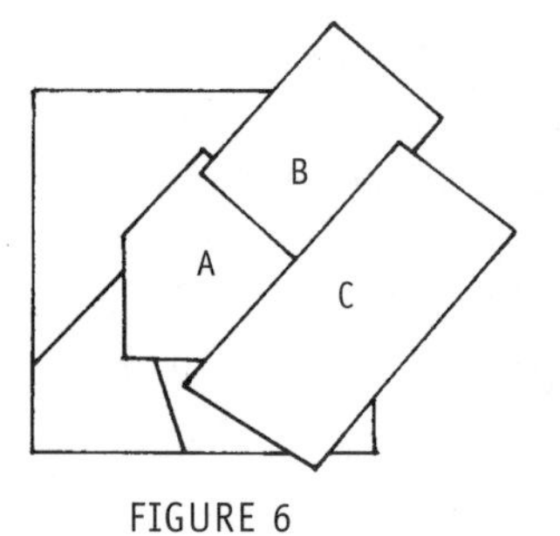

FIGURE 6

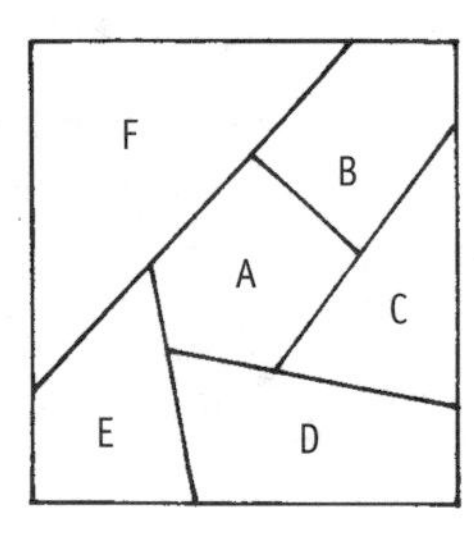

FIGURE 7

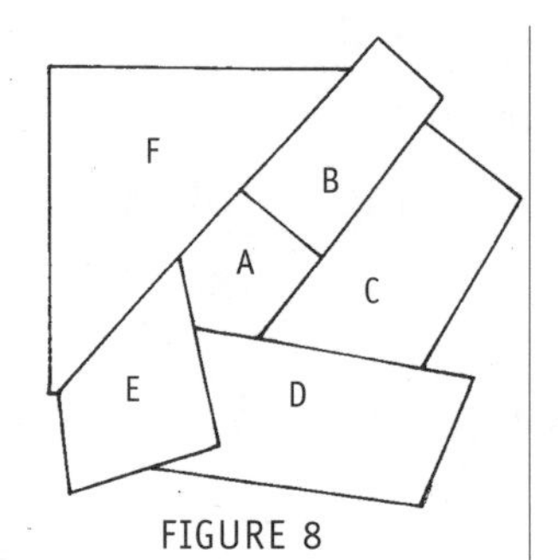

FIGURE 8

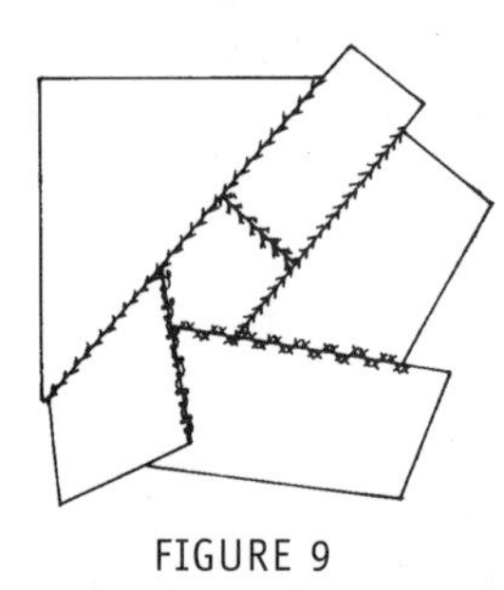
FIGURE 9

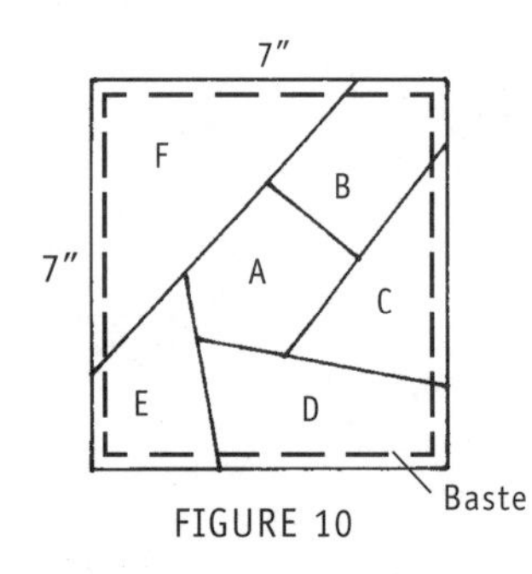

FIGURE 10

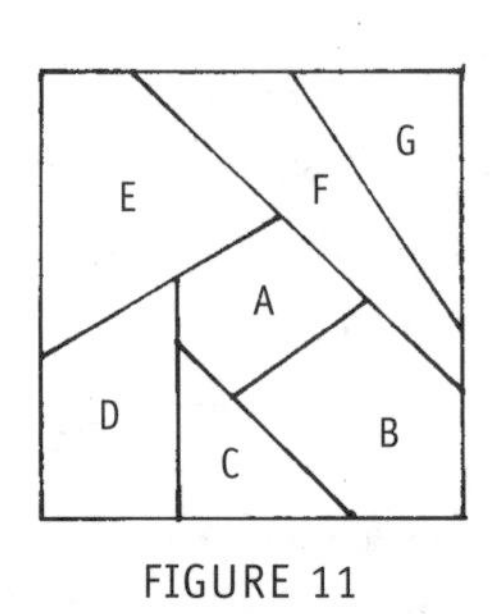

FIGURE 11

away any excess of the "A" and "B" patches *(fig. 5)*.

8. Flip patch "C" to the right side and press *(fig. 6)*.

9. Continue working in a clockwise direction adding patches in the order shown in *figure 7* until the muslin square is covered. The patches should extend beyond the edges of the muslin square. This will insure that the crazy patch design covers the entire square of the quilt *(fig. 8)*.

NOTE: Eventually, when stitching crazy patch, an unusual angle will develop or you will come to an unfinished space. A piece of fabric can be used to cover the space by turning the edge or edges of the fabric under and top stitching in the desired area.

10. Using contrasting threads, cover each seam with a decorative stitch *(fig. 9)*.

11. With the muslin side up, baste 1/4" from the muslin edge. Cut the block to measure 7" square *(fig. 10)*. Complete all squares as directed above using Template #1 and Template #2 *(fig. 11)*. Set one Template #2 block aside for the pillow.

Creating the Quilt Top

All seams 1/4" unless otherwise indicated.

1. Arrange six crazy patch squares, two across and three down. Label blocks 1-6 as shown *(fig. 12)*. Note the quilt top construction order: the blocks are stitched together in two long strips with sashing in between the blocks. Blocks 1, 3, and 5 make up one long strip and blocks 2, 4, and 6 make up the second long strip. The two long strips of blocks are stitched to a central sashing piece. Outer sashing is stitched around the four sides of the created quilt top to complete the design.

2. Stitch a 1-1/2" by 8" strip to the upper and lower sides of block #3. Trim the sashing even with the edges of the block.

3. Stitch block #1 to the upper sashing strip of block #3. Stitch block #5 to the lower sashing strip of block #3. This completes the first long strip.

4. Stitch a 1-1/2" by 8" strip to the upper and lower sides of block #4. Trim the sashing even with the edges of the block.

5. Stitch block #2 to the upper sashing strip of block #4. Stitch block #6 to the

lower sashing strip of block #4.

6. Stitch a 1-1/2" by 23" sashing strip to the inside edge of one of the long strips. Trim the sashing even with the edges of the long strip.

7. Stitch the second long strip to the remaining long side of the sashing strip. Make sure the blocks are directly across from each other.

8. Stitch the 2" by 15" sashing strips to each short end of the quilt top. Trim the sashing even with the edges of the quilt top.

9. Stitch the 2" by 26" sashing strips to each long side of the quilt top. Trim the sashing even with the upper and lower sashing pieces.

10. Press the quilt top well.

Finishing the Quilt

1. Place the backing and the quilt top right sides together. Trim the quilt back even with the quilt top *(fig. 13)*.

2. Stitch the two layers together leaving a 4" opening along one side *(fig. 13)*.

3. Turn the quilt to the right side through the opening. Press well.

4. Turn the edges of the opening to the inside 1/4" and stitch in place by hand *(fig. 14)*.

5. Pin the backing and the quilt top together around the edges of each crazy patch block.

6. Using 30-weight machine embroidery thread to match the backing in the bobbin and invisible thread in the needle, quilt around each crazy patch block, next to the sashing *(fig. 15)*.

Constructing the Pillow

1. Stitch the smaller sashing strip to the top and bottom of the remaining crazy patch square. Trim the sashing even with the edges of the block *(fig. 16)*.

2. Stitch the longer sashing strip to each side of the crazy patch square. Trim the side sashing pieces even with the edges of the upper and lower sashing strips *(fig. 17)*.

3. Place the pillow backing and the pillow top right sides together. Trim the pillow back even with the pillow top.

4. Stitch the two layers together leaving a 4" opening along one side *(fig. 18)*.

5. Turn the pillow to the right side through the opening. Press well.

6. Stuff the pillow with stuffing.

7. Turn the edges of the opening to the inside 1/4" and stitch in place by hand.

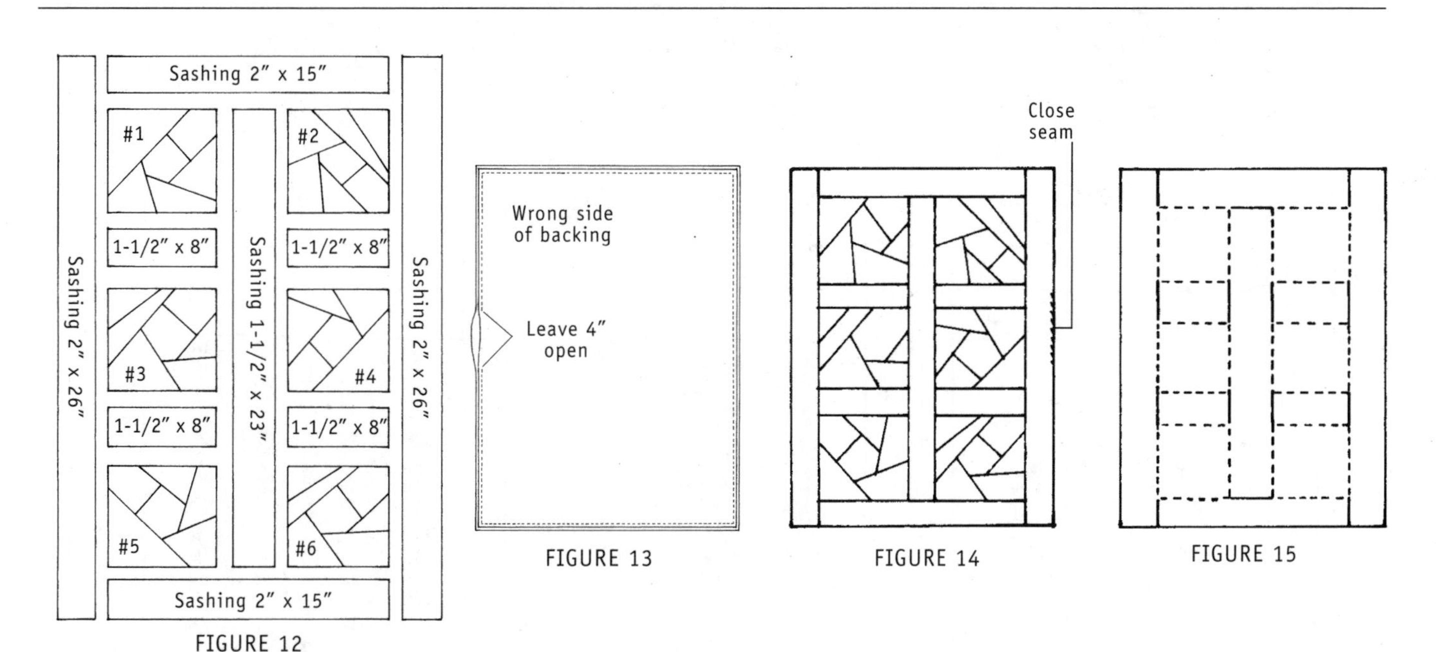

FIGURE 12

FIGURE 13

FIGURE 14

FIGURE 15

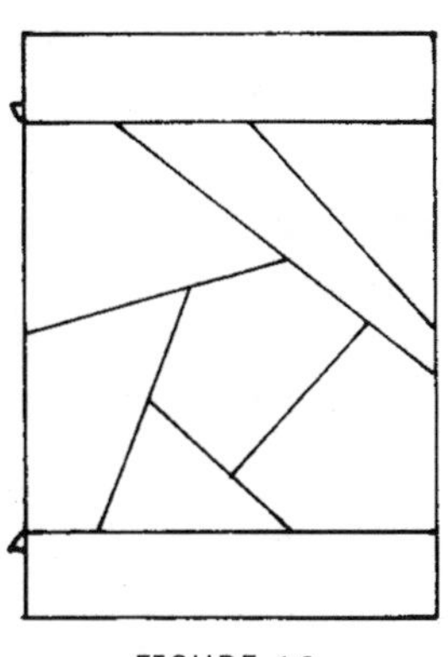

FIGURE 16

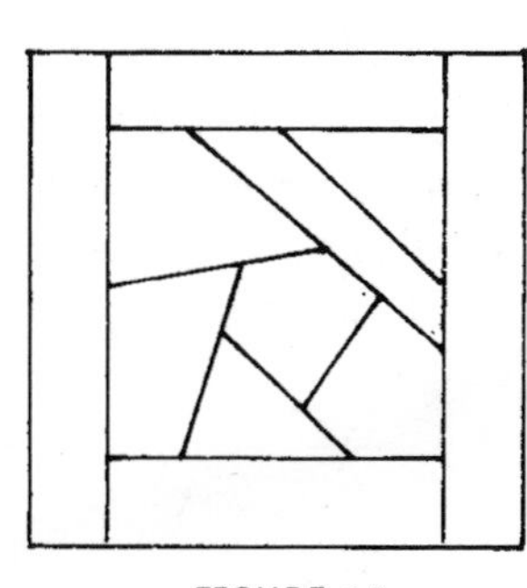

FIGURE 17

FIGURE 18

Blue Danube Quilt

Romantic is the word which best describes this quilt. When I think of romantic music, I think of waltzes; therefore, we named the quilt Blue Danube. How is that for Martha Thinking? Made of blue and ecru Victorian 100% cotton batiste, the quilt is beautiful. The squares are magnificently designed, with machine embroidery and other techniques used very elegantly on all nine of the squares. This is a great class for a block of the month club. Gorgeous pillows can be made from each square. This quilt in a larger size would be the most beautiful coverlet for any size bed.

Some of the backgrounds of the squares are ecru, some are blue. The upper left hand corner square has a very pretty technique called Organdy Madeira Windowpane. Inside the Madeira window is ecru Swiss organdy upon which delicate machine embroidery has been stitched. The flowers look like forget-me-nots in a pretty shade of lavender blue; the leaves are green and the outline stitching is of a darker ecru. Two rows of ecru pinstitching are found around the outline of the organdy. Little blue flowers with yellow centers and green leaves are positioned at four places around the organdy design. The square is quilted to the back of the quilt with straight stitching following the outline of the organdy. The upper middle square has a Seminole patchwork strip, bordered on either side with ecru lace insertions and blue Victorian batiste inside the two lace strips. One row of pretty machine-embroidered blue diamonds runs vertically beside the lace and batiste strips. Shades of blue, green and ecru are used for the Seminole patchwork in the center of this square, which has an ecru background. The upper right corner is so delicate and pretty, with the lace shaped in four petals of Celtic lacework. Four pretty machine-embroidered hearts are found within each section of the Celtic shaping; the colors in the hearts are blue, lavender, yellow, green and pink. A tiny row of featherstitching in ecru travels all the way around the shape. The square is quilted to the back of the quilt with straight stitching on both sides of the lace, which has been attached with a decorative pinstitch.

The middle left square has the same shape as the upper right but this time it is formed using shaped bias linen. Little flowers are scattered individually around and in between the bias lace shape. The background of this square is ecru. The middle square has a pretty circular shaping with four curved shapes inside each circle. The circles of "lace" have been made by stitching decorative stitching on English netting. Pretty machine scallops in ecru have been stitched on the outside of this circle. A circle of delicate flowers and bows has been stitched inside the middle of the circle. The far right square is stitched on ecru Victorian batiste. The shape is a diamond and there are satin ribbons of pink, green, ecru and blue within the diamond. The technique for the ribbons is crazy patch, and they are stitched together with ecru featherstitching. Two sprays of the blue, lavender and yellow flowers with green leaves are found on either side of this diamond.

The lower left corner has shark's teeth, three rows on each side of center, for its main embellishment theme. Ecru flowers and green leaves are on either side of the shark's teeth. The middle square features the technique French waterfall. What is French waterfall? Scallops of lace create an outline for the center panel which is machine embroidered with blue, lavender, green and ecru. Two blue Victorian strips with three rows of pintucks are on either side of this center strip. Two more rows of French scallops outline the blue strips. The quilting to the back of the quilt is done on all eight sides of the lace insertion with a straight stitch using ecru thread.

The bottom right quilt square is my very favorite and it features the wonderful technique of lace cathedral windows. Strips of ecru lace insertion are found on either side of the lace cathedral window strip which also has decorative stitching that looks somewhat like attached ecru ovals. These ovals are found on either side of the lace, on the inside lace as well as the outside lace. Beautiful ecru machine embroidery is found between the lace strips on either side of the lace cathedral windows.White sashing runs around some of the squares; blue runs around the others. There is a blue binding on the quilt and the backing is of ecru Victorian batiste.

Supplies

- 5-5/8 yards ecru Victorian batiste
- 2-1/2 yards blue Victorian batiste
- 1/8 yard green Victorian batiste
- 13 yards ecru insertion lace
- 10" x 10" ecru organza or organdy
- 10" x 10" ecru netting
- 7" x 12" batiste or muslin for crazy patch foundation
- Ecru lightweight heirloom sewing thread, 2 spools
- Invisible thread
- Wash-away basting thread
- 2 yards tear-away stabilizer
- 40-weight machine embroidery thread in blue, green, ecru, lavender, light yellow or desired colors
- Offray ribbon in coordinating colors
- Open-toe appliqué foot
- Rotary mat, cutter and ruler
- 1/2" bias tape maker
- Water-soluble fabric glue
- Glass head pins
- Wash-out marker
- #70/10 needle
- #100/16 or #110/18 universal or topstitch needle
- #1.6/70 or #2.0/70 twin needle
- Point turner
- Temporary spray adhesive (optional)
- Appliqué pressing sheet (optional)
- Pfaff (P) cards 1,28 and MP1004 (optional)
- Water-soluble stabilizer
- Safety pins or quilt tack gun and tacks

Cutting

- Ecru Batiste
  Ten 2-1/4" by 13-1/2" strips
  Ten 2-1/4" by 17" strips
  Two 15" squares
  Two 3-1/2" by 15" strips
  Two 4" by 15" strips
  Two 2-1/4" by 14" strips
  Two 45" by 55" rectangles
  Four 7" by 55" strips
  Four 7" by 45" strips
- Blue Batiste
  Five binding strips 1-3/4" by 45"
  Four 15" squares
  One rectangle 15" by 22"
  Two 1" by 15" strips
  One 1-3/4" by 14" strip
  Two 5-1/2" by 15" strips
  Eight 2-1/4" by 13-1/2" strips
  Eight 2-1/4" by 17" strips
  Two bias strips 2-1/2" by 17"
  Bias strips 1-1/8" wide to equal 2-1/2 yards
- Green Batiste
  One 3" by 15" strip
  Two 1-3/4" by 14" strips

NOTE: Use ecru lightweight heirloom sewing thread in the needle and bobbin unless otherwise stated.

Organdy Madeira Windowpane

Block #1

Organdy Madeira Windowpane

Supplies

- 15" square blue batiste
- 10" square ecru organza
- Wash-away basting thread
- Point turner
- #100/16 or #110/18 universal or topstitch needle
- Tear-away stabilizer
- P card 28, design #9, P card MP 1004, design #8 (optional)
- Reverse Madeira Appliqué Template

Construction

1. Starch and press the batiste square. Fold into quarters and finger press the fold lines. Trace half the template on the wrong side of the square with a wash-out marker *(fig. 1)*.

2. Fold the square right sides together with the template along the fold. Using wash-away basting thread in the needle or in the bobbin or both, stitch along the template line with a stitch length of about 1.5. Cut out the center of the fabric leaving a 3/16" seam allowance beyond the stitching line. Clip the curves and points of the seam allowance *(fig. 2)*.

3. Turn the square right side out. Push out the points and curves using a point turner and finger press along the seam.

4. Starch and press along the edge of the opening to dissolve the basting thread. Press until dry. Gently pull the layers apart. If the layers do not pull apart easily, starch and press again until dry *(fig. 3)*. Gently pull the layers apart creating an opening in the center of the square with the edges of the opening turned to the underside.

5. Place the organza square under the faced window, aligning the grain lines. Pin well *(fig. 4)*.

6. Place a tear-away stabilizer on the wrong side. Remove the wash-away thread and put ecru thread in needle and bobbin. Use a #100/16 or #110/18 universal or topstitch needle to stitch a pinstitch (L = 2.5; W = 2.0) along the "window" edge so that the straight part of the stitch is on the organza only and the "fingers" of the stitch bite into the batiste. Remove the stabilizer carefully *(see fig. 5)*.

7. Place another piece of stabilizer to the wrong side of the block. Stitch again 1/4" outside the previous stitching. This time, the fingers of the stitch will point toward the center. Carefully remove the stabilizer *(fig. 5)*.

8. On the wrong side, trim away the organza close to the outer row of pinstitching *(fig. 6)*.

9. Soak in water to remove the markings. Roll in a towel and press dry from the wrong side.

10. Use hand or machine embroidery to stitch a design in the center of the organza and outside the Madeira appliqué opening if desired (see finished drawing). P Card 28, #9 and P card MP1004, #8 were used for the pictured quilt.

Blue Batiste Square
Trace Madeira template
Wrong side

FIGURE 1

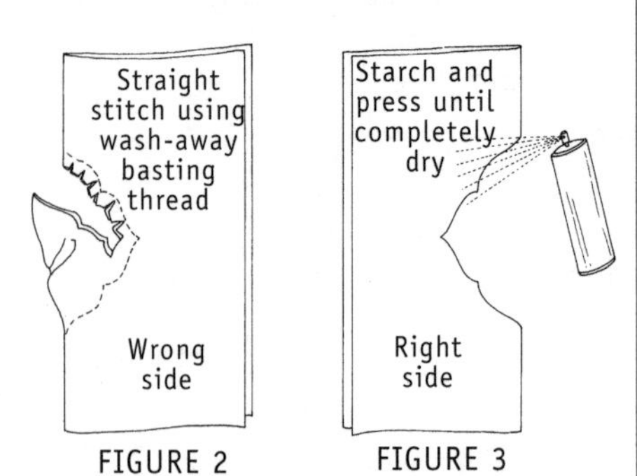

FIGURE 2 FIGURE 3

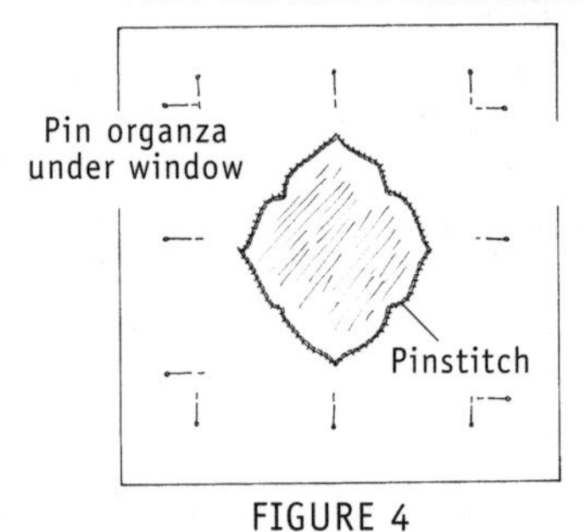

FIGURE 4

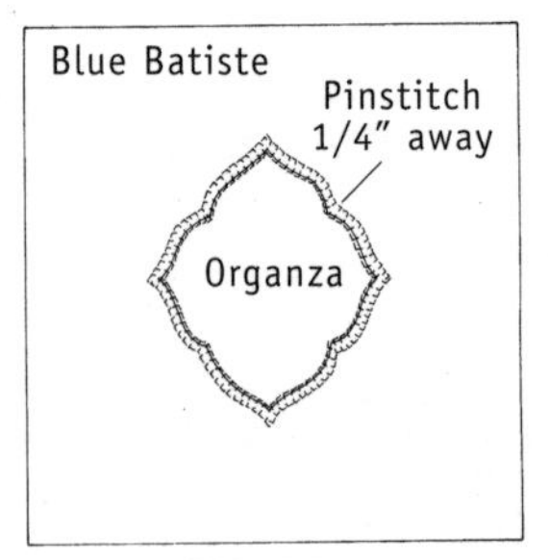

FIGURE 5

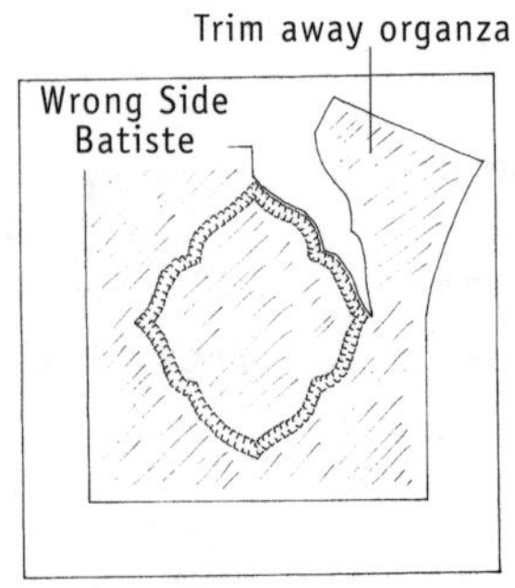

FIGURE 6

Seminole Lacework

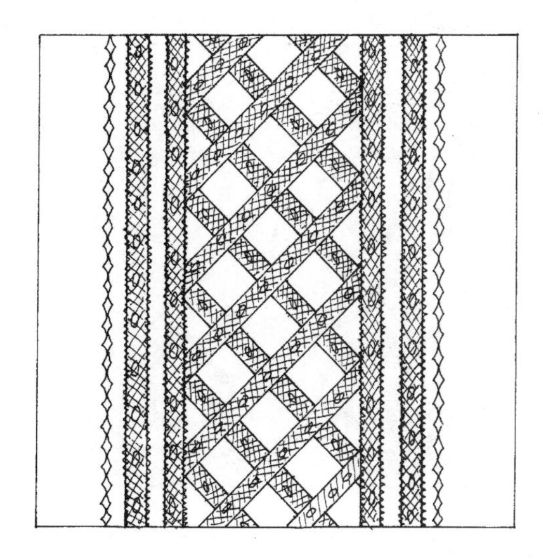

Block #2
Seminole Lacework

Supplies

- Two 2-1/4" x 14" strips ecru batiste
- Two 1-3/4" x 14" strips green batiste
- One 1-3/4" x 14" strip blue batiste
- Two 1" x 15" strips blue batiste
- Two 3-1/2" x 15" strips ecru batiste
- Insertion lace
- Rotary mat, cutter and ruler

Construction

General procedure for attaching lace:

Step 1) Use fine thread, #70 needle, and zigzag (W=0.8; L=2.0). Center lace insertion over the fabric raw edge; zigzag over lace heading. Zigzag the next fabric strip to the other side of the lace insertion. Fabric raw edges will meet at center under the lace (fig. a).

Step 2) Press the fabric raw edges away from the lace. Zigzag (W=1.5 – 2.0, L=1.5) along the lace heading and trim away the excess fabric from behind the lace (fig. b).

1. The five 14" strips of fabric are joined with lace insertion between the strips of fabric. Stitch in this order: ecru batiste, lace insertion, green batiste, lace insertion, blue batiste, lace insertion, green batiste, lace insertion and ecru batiste *(fig. 1)*.

2. Square one short end of the strip. Use a rotary cutter, mat and ruler to cut seven 1-3/4" wide segments. Zigzag insertion lace to one long side of each segment *(fig. 2a)*.

3. Offset the segments as in figure 2b and zigzag all seven strips together in a stair-step panel *(fig. 2b)*.

4. Square one short edge of the Seminole lacework strip by making a perpendicular cut through the strip. Place the small piece just removed on the opposite end of the lacework strip. Offset the segment and zigzag the segment to the lace of the larger piece *(fig. 3)*.

5. Using a rotary cutter, mat and ruler, trim off the little saw tooth points along both long sides, making sure that the cut is a consistent distance from the center of the strip on both sides and the strip is the same width along its full length *(fig. 4)*.

6. Zigzag the lace insertion to both long edges of each 1" x 15" blue batiste strip. Zigzag these to the long edges of the lacework strip. Zigzag the ecru rectangles to each side of the border. Stitch a row of decorative stitching (blue diamonds) approximately 1/2" from each outside edge of the lace strips (see finished drawing).

7. Trim fabric from behind the lace, starch and press the block.

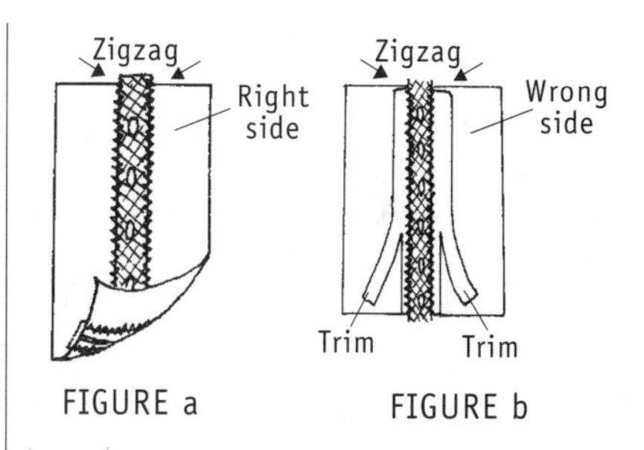

FIGURE a FIGURE b

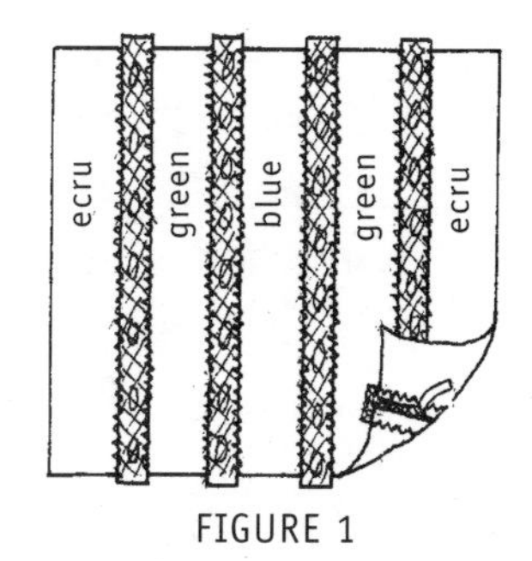

FIGURE 1

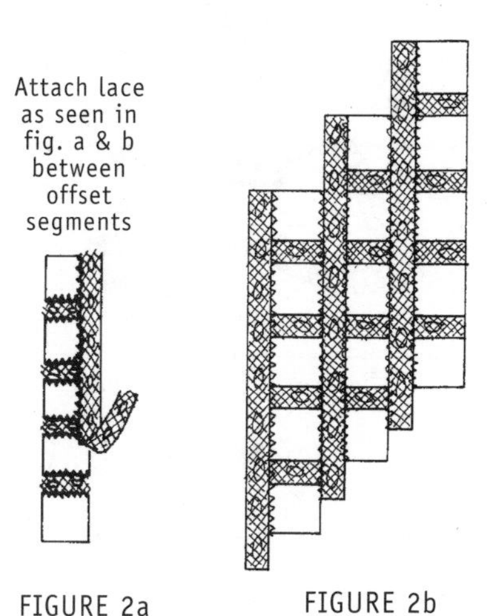

FIGURE 2a FIGURE 2b

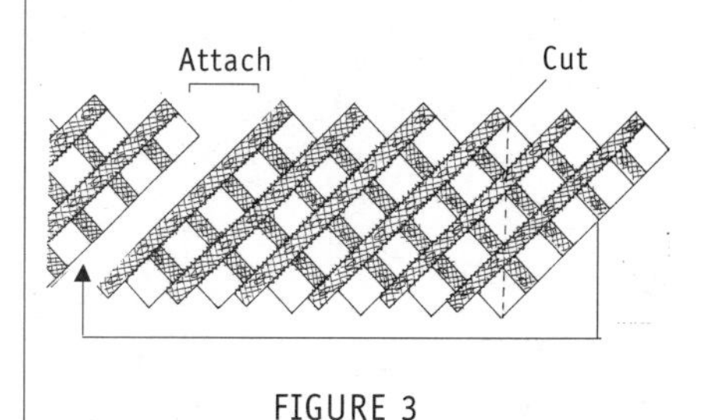

FIGURE 3

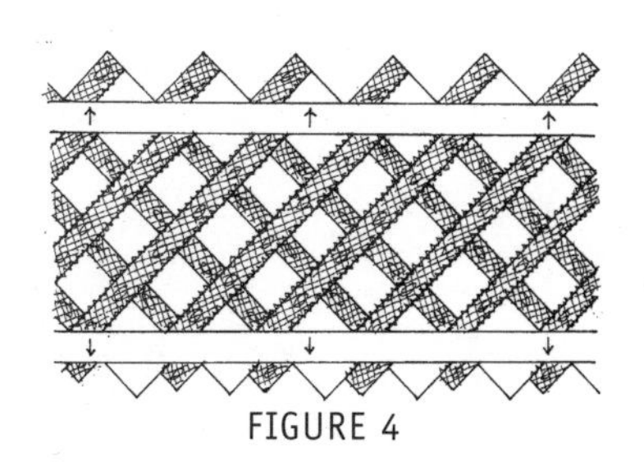

FIGURE 4

Celtic Lace

FIGURE 1

Place end of lace
under intersection

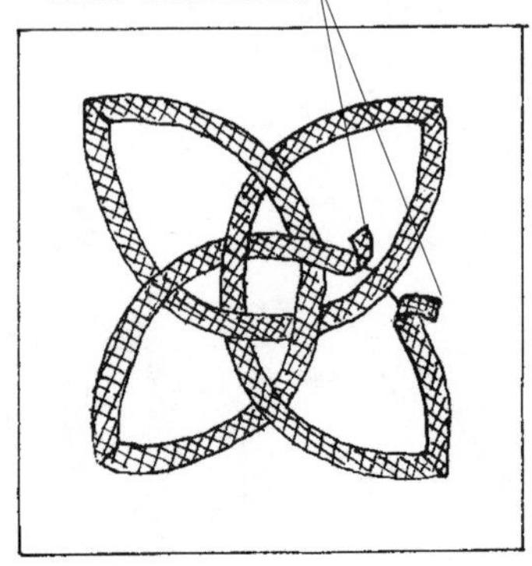

FIGURE 2

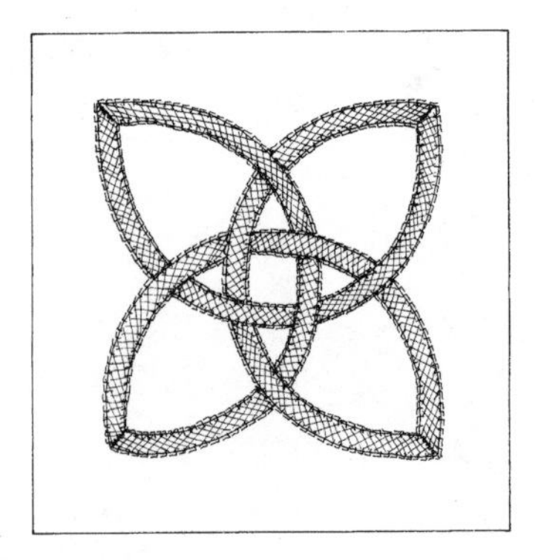

FIGURE 3

Block #3
Celtic Lace

Supplies

- 15" square blue batiste
- Insertion lace
- Stabilizer
- Shaped Bias/Celtic Lace Template
- #100/16 - #110/18 universal or topstitch needle
- P card 1, design #22 (optional)

Construction

1. Starch and press the batiste square. Fold in quarters and finger press the fold lines. With a washout marker, trace the template on each quarter of the square, making sure that the lines meet in each quarter *(fig. 1)*.

2. Starting at any intersection, center and shape the insertion lace over the lines, mitering the corners.

3. The lace should be shaped in an under-over-under pattern *(refer to fig. 3)*. Lace Shaping directions can be found on page 109. The cut ends of lace should meet under top lace at intersection *(fig. 2)*.

4. Use a #100/16 or #110/18 universal or topstitch needle to pinstitch (L = 2.5; W = 2.0) along both headings of the lace, following the piece of lace that falls on top at the intersections. Tear-away stabilizer should be placed to the wrong side before pinstitching *(fig. 3)*.

5. Embroider designs within the lace shapes by hand or machine if desired. P card 1, #22 was used on the pictured quilt (see finished drawing).

6. Add featherstitching around the outer edge of the shape.

7. Soak to remove the markings, roll in a towel to remove the excess water and press dry from the wrong side.

Shaped Bias

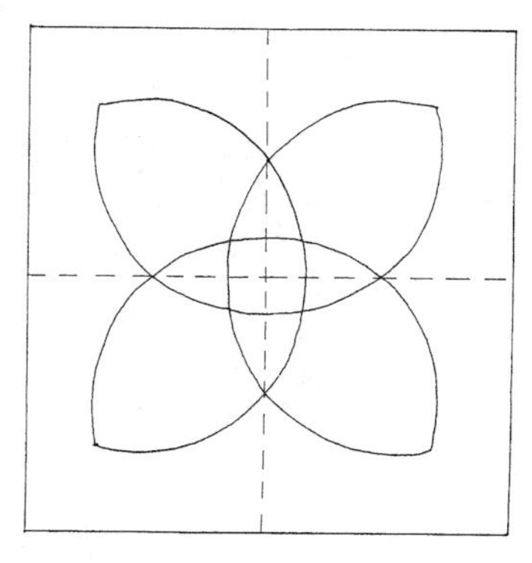

FIGURE 1

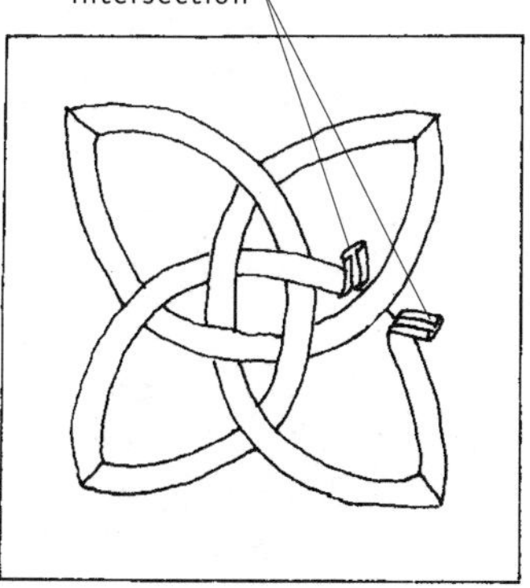

FIGURE 2

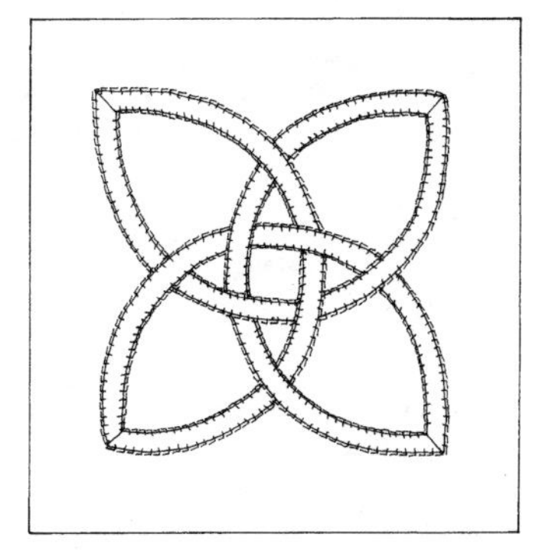

FIGURE 3

Block #4
Shaped Bias

Supplies

- 15" square ecru batiste
- 2-1/2 yards of blue bias strips, 1-1/8" wide
- 1/2" bias tape maker
- Water-soluble fabric glue
- Shaped Bias/Celtic Lace Template
- P card 28, design #16 (optional)

Construction

1. Starch and press the batiste square. Fold it into quarters and finger press the fold lines.

2. Trace the template onto each quarter of the square using a wash-out marker. Make certain that the lines meet correctly at the fold lines *(fig. 1)*.

3. Use a 1/2" bias tape maker to create the bias strips. It is not necessary to seam the bias strips together.

4. Square one end of a bias strip. Starting at an intersection, sparingly apply the water-soluble fabric glue along several inches of the marked template line. Center the bias strip along the marked line. Glue and apply another few inches, and continue following an over-under-over pattern at the intersections. Miter the corners just as in mitering lace. The bias strips can be pinned every 1" - 2" if glue is not used *(fig. 2)*. Cut ends should meet under bias at intersection (fig. 2).

5. Lightly starch and press.

6. Insert a #100/16 or #110/18 universal or topstitch needle and choose the pinstitch (L = 2.0-2.5; W = 2.0).

7. Place a square of tear-away stabilizer to the wrong side of the block. Stitch on both sides of the bias strips so that the straight part of the stitch is on the ecru batiste right next to the bias strips and the "fingers" of the stitch bite into the bias strips. Do not sew across the intersection if the strip that is being sewn goes under another strip. Instead, use the tie-off feature of the sewing machine or backstitch a few stitches to tie-off, then skip over the intersection and continue stitching. Remember to tie-on when beginning to stitch again. Carefully remove the stabilizer *(fig. 3)*.

8. After all of the stitching is complete, soak the block in water for a few minutes to remove the markings and dissolve the glue. Roll in a towel to remove the excess water. Press dry on the wrong side. If desired, embellish the block with machine or hand embroidery. P card 28, design #16 was used for the pictured quilt (see finished drawing).

"Shaped" Netting Lace

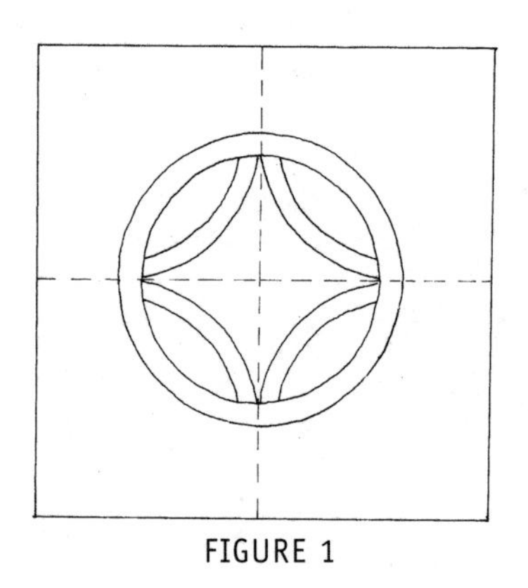

FIGURE 1

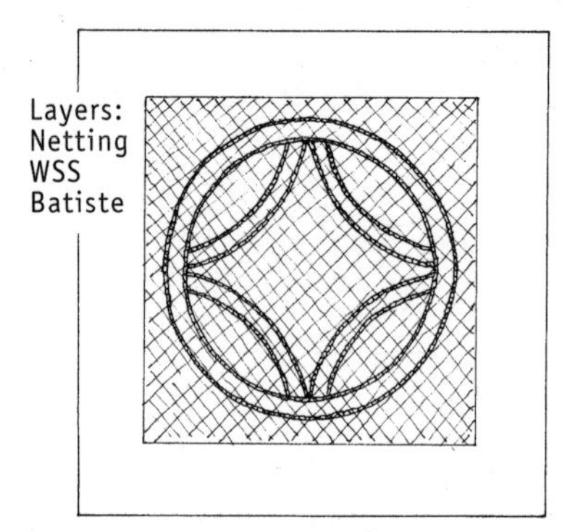

FIGURE 2

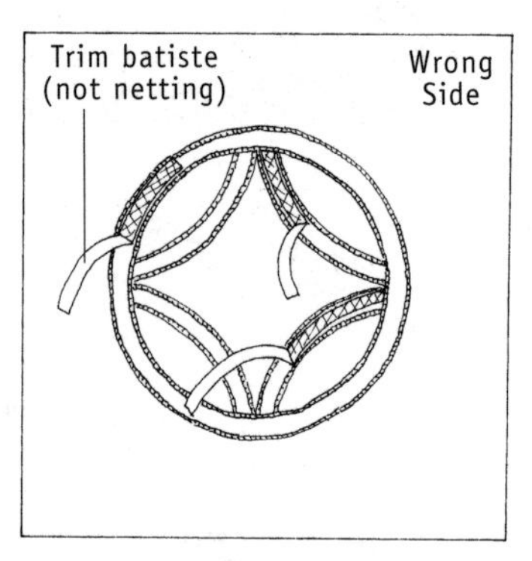

FIGURE 3

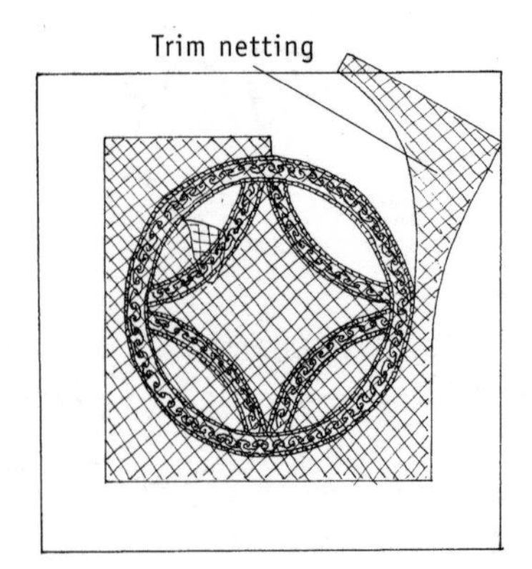

FIGURE 4

Block #5
"Shaped" Netting Lace

Supplies

- 15" square blue batiste
- 10" square ecru cotton netting
- Water-soluble stabilizer (WSS)
- Shaped Netting Lace Template
- Temporary spray adhesive
- Ecru decorative thread
- Tear-away stabilizer
- Appliqué pressing sheet (optional)
- P card MP1004 #23 (optional)

Construction

1. Starch and press the batiste and netting squares. Fold the batiste into quarters and finger press the creases. Trace the template onto the batiste using a heavy line with a wash-out marker *(fig. 1)*.

2. Iron a layer of WSS to the netting by placing the netting over a slightly smaller square of WSS, mist VERY LIGHTLY with spray starch and press dry. The netting and WSS can be sandwiched between two layers of an appliqué pressing sheet before pressing or the two can be glued together with a temporary spray adhesive.

3. Place the stabilized netting over the batiste so that the WSS is sandwiched between the netting and the batiste. The marked lines should be visible through the netting *(fig. 2)*.

4. With tear-away stabilizer to the wrong side of the fabric and using a #100/16 or #110/18 universal or topstitch needle, stitch an entredeux stitch along all marked lines. Remove the stabilizer *(fig. 2)*. Trim the batiste from between the rows of stitching on the wrong side, close to the stitching. The WSS will help to prevent cutting the netting *(fig. 3)*.

5. Between the rows of entredeux stitching, stitch a decorative open work stitch (not a satin stitch) with the ecru decorative thread. A scroll or snowflake decorative stitch would be a good choice. This stitching is done on the single layer of stabilized netting. Additional WSS can be added if needed to prevent puckering.

6. Soak to remove the markings and the WSS, roll in a towel and press dry.

7. Trim away the netting close to the entredeux stitching everywhere except between the entredeux stitching *(fig. 4)*.

8. Place a tear-away stabilizer behind the block. Using ecru decorative thread, stitch a satin stitch scallop or other design along the outer edge of the lace circle so that the inner edge of the scallop just touches the entredeux stitching. Remove the stabilizer.

9. Use hand or machine embroidery to stitch a design in the center of the square. P card MP1004, design #23 was used for the pictured quilt (see finished drawing).

Ribbon Crazy Patch

Block #6
Ribbon Crazy Patch

Supplies

- 15" square ecru batiste
- 7" x 12" batiste scrap or muslin for crazy patch foundation
- Insertion lace
- Satin ribbons, 6 - 8 various colors and widths
- Invisible thread
- Ecru decorative thread
- Diamond Template
- P card 28, design #17 (optional)

Construction

1. Starch and press the batiste square. Fold into quarters and finger press fold lines. Center and trace the Diamond Template onto the fabric with a wash-out marker *(fig. 1)*.

2. Shape the insertion lace along the traced diamond so that the outer heading of the lace is along the line. Refer to Lace Shaping, page 109.

3. Stitch only the outer edge of the insertion lace to the fabric using an entredeux stitch if available. Otherwise use a zigzag (L = 0.6 - 0.8; W = 2). Cut out the fabric from behind the lace close to the stitching, leaving a diamond-shaped hole in the block *(fig. 2)*.

4. Place invisible thread in the needle. Trace the lace shaping lines on the 7" x 12" piece of batiste or lightweight muslin. Use this as the foundation for the crazy patch. To create the crazy patch, start with one of the wide ribbons. Cut a 2" section with non-parallel and non-right-angle sides. Place the finished edge of another ribbon over one of the raw edges of the first ribbon so that it overlaps the raw edge about 1/4". Zigzag (L = 1.0; W = 2.0) along the finished edge of the top ribbon so that it extends a little beyond the first. Lift up the second ribbon and trim the edges of the first ribbon. Place another ribbon along the side of the first ribbon and covering the raw end of the second ribbon. Zigzag as above. Continue adding and overlapping ribbons, trimming excess ribbon on the wrong side *(fig. 3)* until the patch is large enough to fill the lace diamond. All of the stitching is done on the foundation piece *(fig. 4)*.

5. With ecru decorative thread, stitch a featherstitch (L = 2.0; W = 2.0) over all of the ribbon "seams". Use a stabilizer to prevent puckering if necessary.

6. Place the crazy patch block under the lace diamond. Pin in place and zigzag (L = 0.6 - 0.8; W = 2) along the inner edge of the insertion. *NOTE: Do not use the pinstitch or entredeux stitch because the ribbon is too bulky and tightly woven. Trim away the excess crazy patchwork on the wrong side close to the stitching (see finished drawing).*

7. Use hand or machine embroidery outside of the lace diamond if desired. P card 28, design #17 was used for the pictured quilt (see finished drawing).

8. Soak to remove markings, roll in a towel to remove the excess water and press dry from the wrong side.

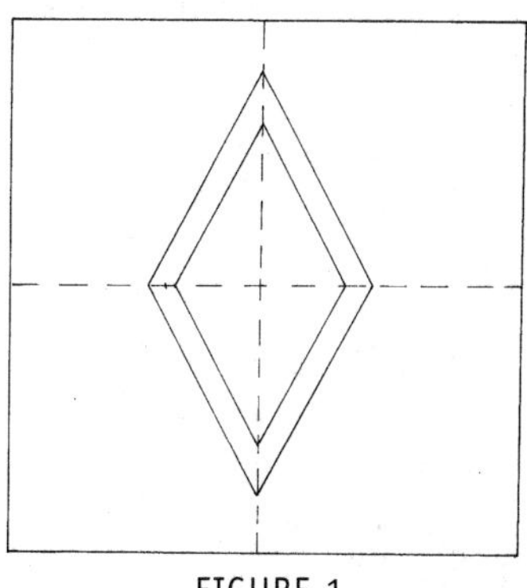

FIGURE 1

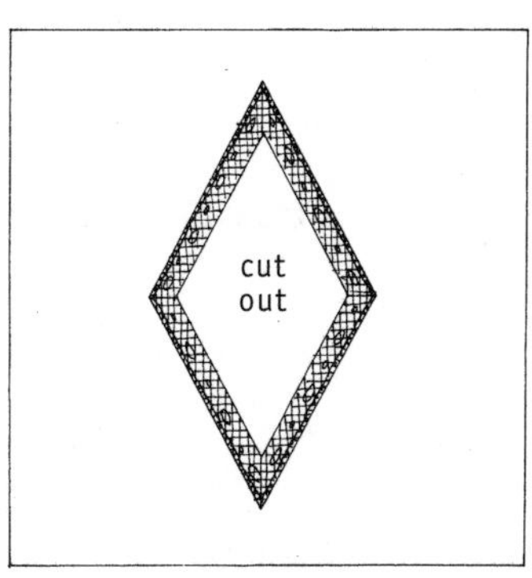

FIGURE 2

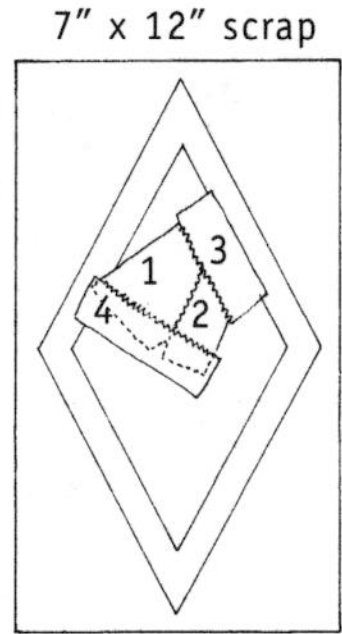

FIGURE 3

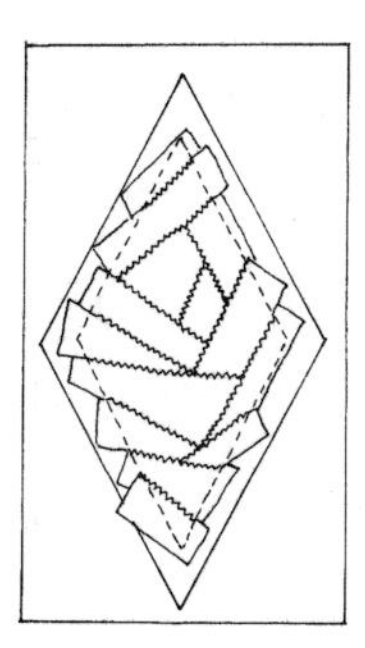

FIGURE 4

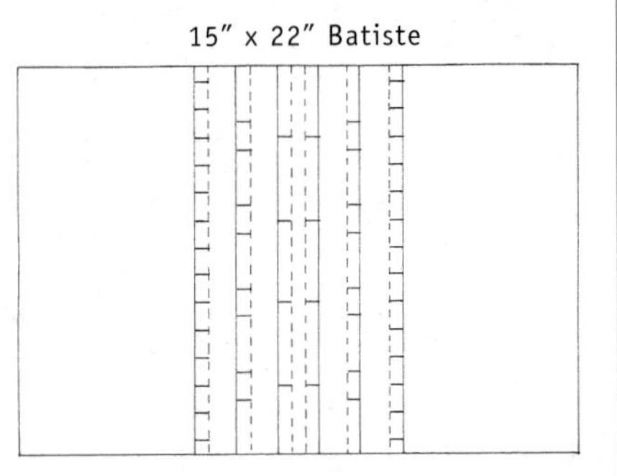

FIGURE 1

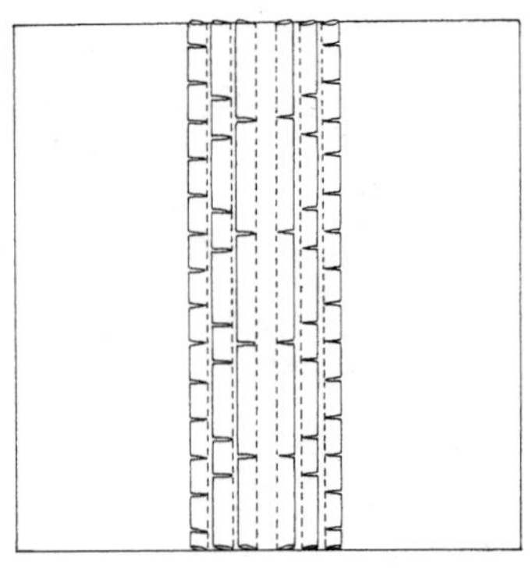

FIGURE 2

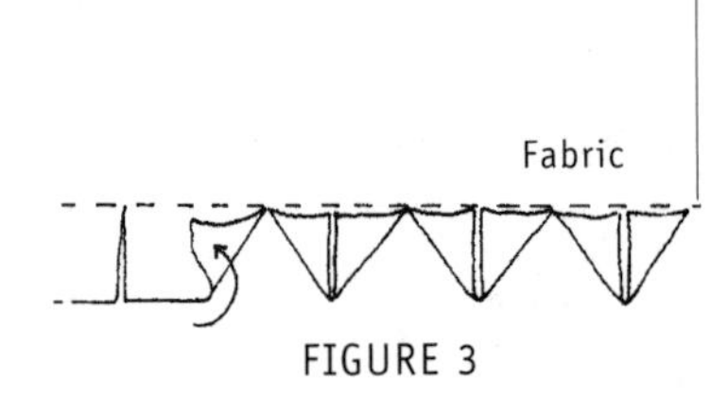

FIGURE 3

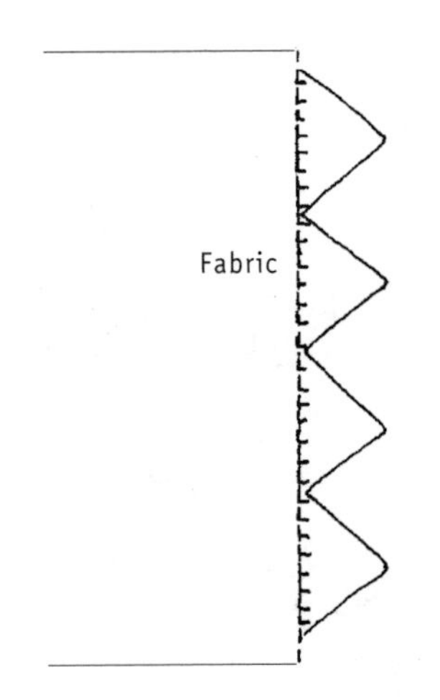

FIGURE 4

Shark's Teeth

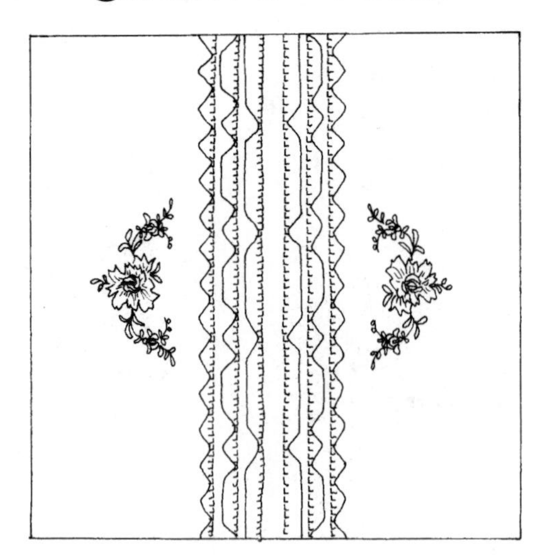

Block #7
Shark's Teeth

Supplies

- 15" x 22" rectangle blue batiste
- Ruler
- Wash-out marker
- Optional: water-soluble glue
- Shark's Teeth Template
- P card 1, design #10 (optional)

Construction

1. Starch and press the 15" x 22" rectangle of blue batiste.

2. Trace the Shark's Teeth Template onto the rectangle using a ruler and wash-out marker *(fig. 1)*.

3. Press a sharp fold directly along each marked fold line (solid lines).

4. Using a size #70/10 needle and a straight stitch (L = 1.5 - 2), stitch along the marked stitching lines (dashed lines) to form 1/2" tucks. Press the tucks away from the center *(fig. 2)*.

5. Clip, fold and stitch the shark's teeth one row at a time, working from the outer edge toward the center. Clip the tucks in one outside row on the short solid lines perpendicular to the fold. Clip just to, but not through, the stitching line *(fig. 2)*. At the ironing board, place the fabric so that you are looking at the underside of the tuck, with the fabric under the tuck folded back out of the way. At each clip, fold the fabric so that the raw edges of the clips lie directly along the stitching line forming fabric V's. Press firmly. A very small amount of water-soluble fabric glue may be used to secure the little flaps *(fig. 3)*.

6. Set up the sewing machine for a zigzag stitch (L = 1; W = 2.0), a pinstitch or picot stitch (L = 2.0; W = 2.0) or a blanket stitch (L = 1.0; W = 2.0). Stitch along the previous stitching lines from the right side, keeping all of the flaps folded under. Keep the fabric under the tuck folded out of the way. You will be stitching through the tuck only and not the fabric underneath the tuck. Stitch so that the left swing of the needle is directly on top of the previous stitching and the right swing of the needle bites into the tuck *(fig. 4)*.

7. Embellish the block with hand or machine embroidery on each side of the shark's teeth or as desired. P card 1, design #10 (see finished drawing).

8. Soak the square to remove markings and glue, roll in a towel to remove the excess water and press dry.

French Waterfall

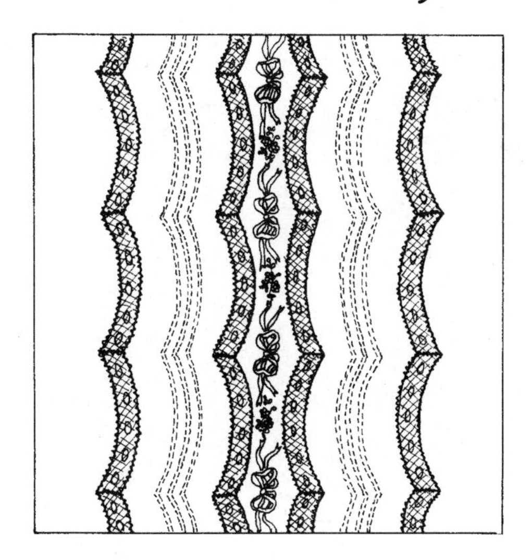

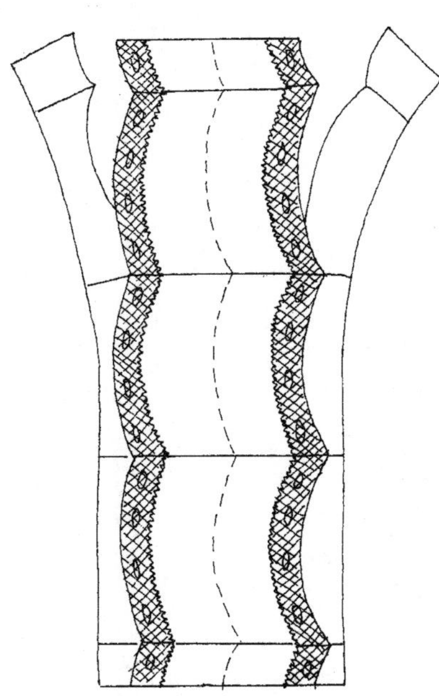

FIGURE 1

Block #8
French Waterfall

Supplies

- 3" x 15" strip green batiste
- Two 5-1/2" x 15" strips of blue batiste
- Two 4" x 15" strips ecru batiste
- Insertion lace
- Wash-out marker
- #1.6/70 or #2.0/70 twin needle
- Waterfall Lace Shaping Template
- P card MP1004, design #33 (optional)

Construction

1. Starch and press all of the fabric pieces (do not starch the insertion lace). Trace the lace shaping template, the pintuck line and the pivot lines onto the two pieces of blue batiste. Center the template on the fabric and extend the scallops to the edges of the fabric.

2. Mark the center of the green batiste strip. Stabilize the fabric and stitch a machine or hand embroidery design down the length of the green strip. P card MP1004, design #33 was used for the pictured quilt. Remove the stabilizer and press well.

3. On the two blue strips, shape the insertion lace on the lines as indicated on the template.

4. Zigzag (L = 0.6 - 0.8; W = 2.0) along the inner edges only of the lace scallops. These are the edges of the lace that are closest to the center of the fabric. Trim the excess fabric from behind the lace *(fig. 1)*.

5. Place the inner scalloped lace of the blue fabrics over the raw edges of the embroidered green strip so that the scallops point away from the center, are symmetrical and an equal distance the length of the strip. This creates the center strip of the block. Zigzag the inner unstitched edge of the scalloped insertion onto the green batiste strip *(fig. 2)*. Trim the green fabric from behind the lace.

6. Place the raw edges of the ecru strips under the remaining unstitched edges of the lace scallops. Zigzag the lace to the fabric and trim the fabric from behind the lace (see finished drawing).

7. Insert the twin needle into the machine, thread with two spools ecru lightweight thread, increase the needle thread tension slightly and set the machine for a short straight stitch (L = 1.5). Test stitch on a scrap fabric and adjust the tension until the pintucks pull up but do not pucker. If the fabric is too stiff from spray starch, it may need to be rinsed before the pintucks are stitched. If so, rinse, and remark the pintuck lines.

8. Stitch along the curved pintuck line until the pivot line is reached, stop needle down with the double needles straddling the pivot line, raise the foot, turn the fabric, and continue stitching along the drawn line, creating a scalloped pintuck *(fig. 3a)*. Stitch another pintuck on each side of the first one by placing the outer edge of the foot along the pintuck, pivoting as before at the pivot lines *(fig. 3b)*. Rinse, press, and trim the block to 14".

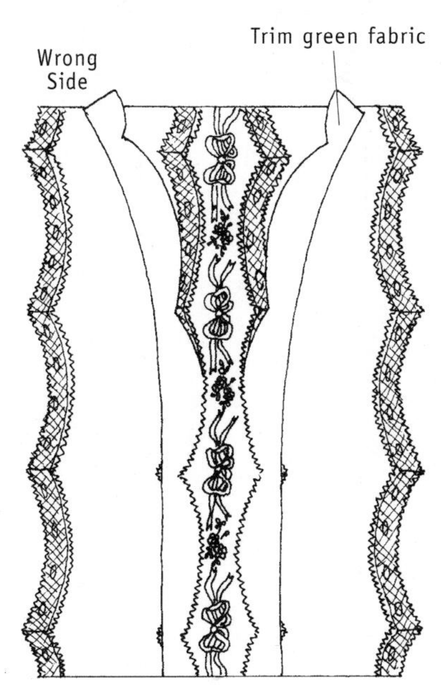

FIGURE 2

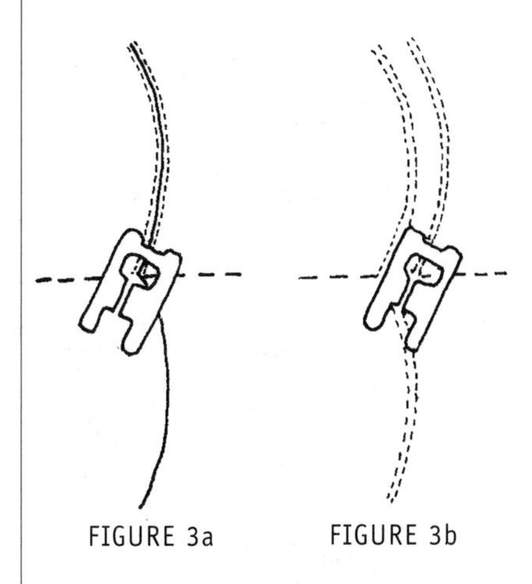

FIGURE 3a FIGURE 3b

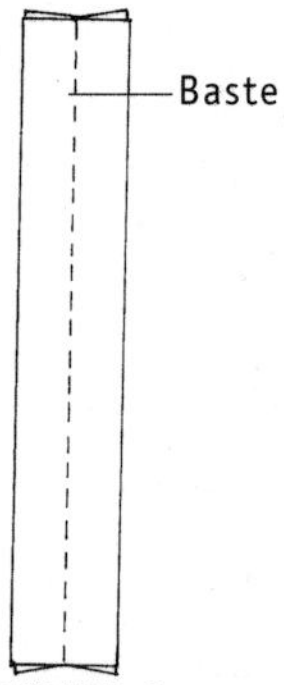

Cathedral Lace Windows

Block #9
Cathedral Lace Windows

Supplies

- Two 2-1/2" x 17" blue batiste bias strips
- 15" blue Batiste square
- Insertion lace
- Open-toe appliqué foot
- Tear-away stabilizer
- Optional: temporary spray adhesive
- P card MP1004, design #2 (optional)

Construction

1. Lightly mark the center of one of the bias strips. Place the two bias strips together with the marked strip on top and matching the raw edges. Stitch down the center of the pair of bias strips with a long straight stitch and a loosened needle tension or basting stitch *(fig. 1)*. Fold each strip on itself along the basting line *(fig. 2)*.

2. Center the lace insertion along the fold/basting line. A temporary spray adhesive can be used to hold the lace in place. This is the wrong side of the Cathedral Lace strip *(fig. 3)*.

3. Fold back the lower layer of fabric and stitch each side of the lace to one layer of fabric using a small zigzag (L = 1; W = 1.5) *(fig. 4a and 4b)*. Refold the lower layer of the bias in place and press *(fig. 5)*.

4. Using a rotary cutter, mat and ruler, trim the strip to an even 1-1/8" on both sides of the center seam.

5. Cut the blue batiste square in half. Stitch a 7" x 15" rectangle of fabric to both sides of the bias strip, right sides together, using a 1/4" seam (remember that the right side of the Cathedral Lace strip is the side without the lace). Trim this seam to 1/8" and zigzag (L = 1.5; W = 4.0) *(fig. 6)*. Press the seam toward the plain fabric blocks.

6. Place a strip of stabilizer under the seams. On the right side of the fabric, stitch a decorative satin stitch over the seam line using ecru decorative thread. The satin stitch oval or football shape mirrors the shape of the Cathedral windows. Remove the stabilizer and press *(see fig. 7)*.

7. Place a piece of lightweight tear-away stabilizer behind the Cathedral Lace strip. From the right side, place dots 2-1/4" apart along the fold/basting line.

8. Stitch each dot using a zigzag (L = 0; W = 2) with the feed dogs dropped and an open-toe appliqué foot. Pull the stabilizer away from the dots *(fig. 7)*.

9. Remove the basting thread from the fold/basting line.

10. Using the tip of the iron, press the center of each opening toward the satin stitching creating an "eyeball" between each set of stitched dots. Press well and pin if desired *(fig. 7)*.

11. Using the same decorative ecru thread as in step 6, straight stitch (L = 1.5) along the outer edges of the "eyeballs", stitching in an "s" pattern to complete the Cathedral Lace windows. Press well *(fig. 8)*.

Baste

FIGURE 1

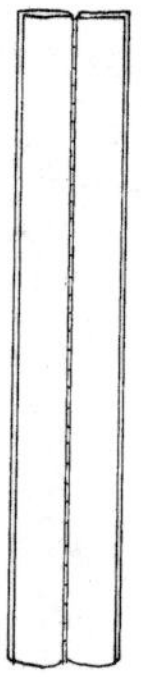

FIGURE 2

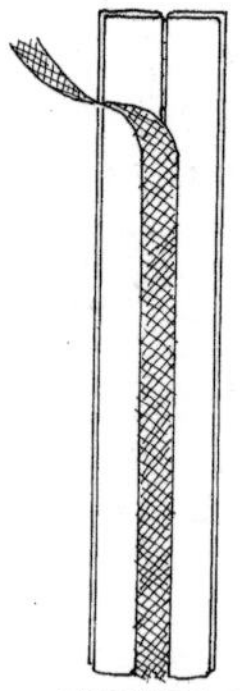

FIGURE 3

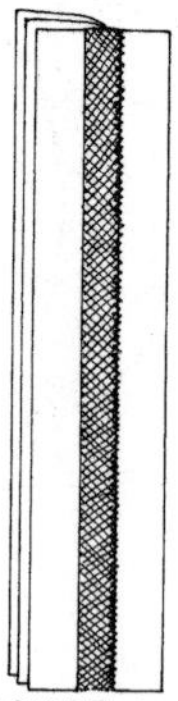

FIGURE 4a

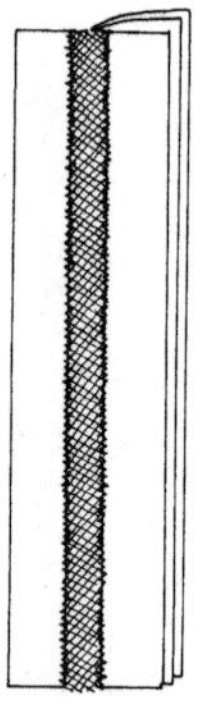

FIGURE 4b

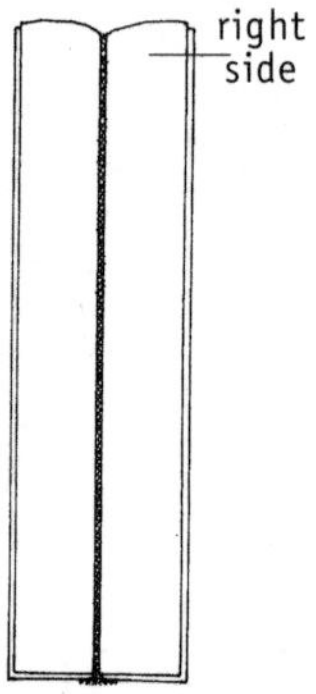

right side

FIGURE 5

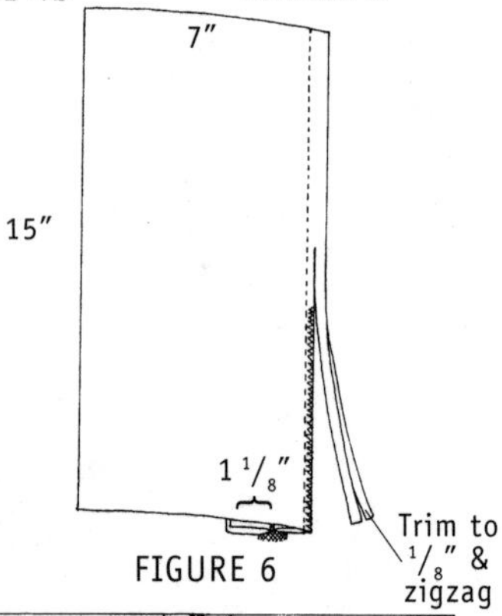

7"

15"

1 1/8"

Trim to 1/8" & zigzag

FIGURE 6

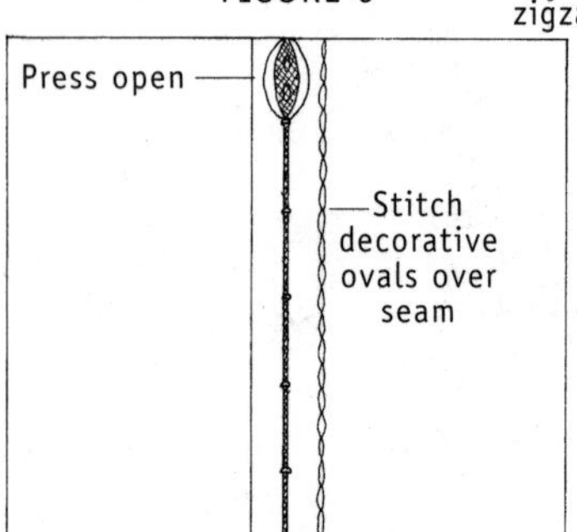

Press open

Stitch decorative ovals over seam

FIGURE 7

12. Draw lines 1/2" and 3-1/2" from the satin stitching on both sides of the window strip *(fig. 9)*. Pin insertion lace along all four lines so that the inner edge of the lace is along the drawn line. Place tear-away stabilizer to the wrong side of the block. Stitch along both headings of the lace strips with the same thread and decorative satin stitch used on the Cathedral Lace window strip (step 6). Trim the fabric from behind the lace.

13. Stitch hand or machine embroidery between the rows of plain insertion lace as desired. P card MP1004, design #2 was used for the pictured quilt (see finished drawing).

14. Soak to remove markings, roll in a towel to remove the excess water and press dry from the wrong side.

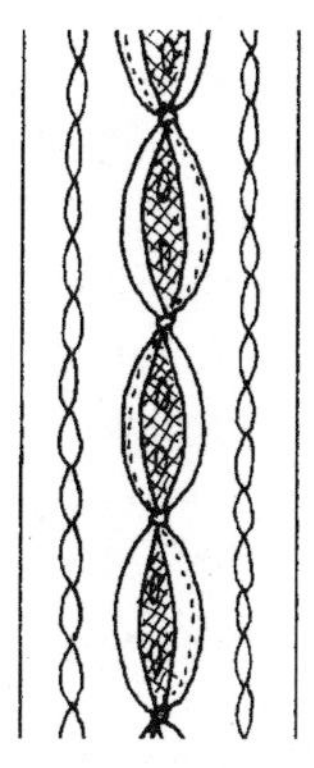

FIGURE 8

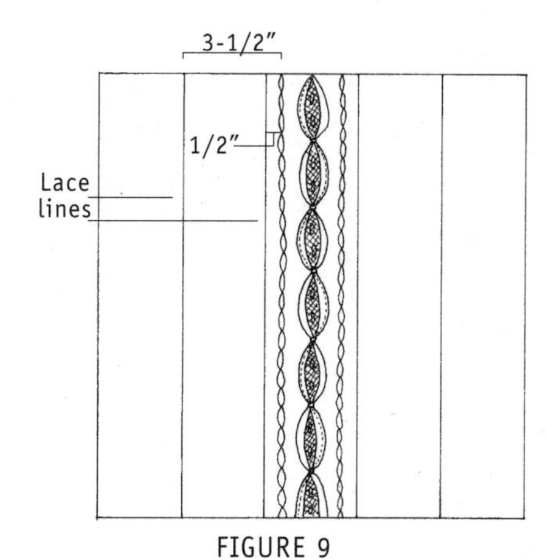

FIGURE 9

Construction of the Quilt

Supplies

- 10 ecru sashing strips, 2-1/4" x 13-1/2"
- 10 ecru sashing strips, 2-1/4" x 17"
- 8 blue sashing strips, 2-1/4" x 13-1/2"
- 8 blue sashing strips, 2-1/4" x 17"
- Three 55" x 45" rectangles of ecru batiste (backing and lining)
- 55" x 55" low loft batting
- Five blue batiste binding strips, 1-3/4" x 45"

NOTE: All seams are 1/4" unless otherwise specified.

1. Lightly starch and press all of the blocks.

2. Centering the design, trim each block to measure 13-1/2" square.

3. Stitch the 13-1/2" blue sashing strips to the top and bottom of all of the blocks. Press the seam toward the sashing.

4. Stitch the 17" ecru sashing strips to the sides of each sashing-block-sashing unit. Press the seams toward the sashing.

5. Arrange the blocks for the quilt with the blue blocks in the center and corners (see finished drawing). Stitch the blocks together in three rows of three blocks. Press the seams well and to one side. Stitch the rows together to complete the quilt top *(see fig. 4)*. Press all seams well and to one side.

6. Create the backing and the lining:

a. Trim off the selvage on both sides of each 55" by 45" piece of ecru batiste *(fig. 1)*. Lightly starch and press the rectangles.

b. Tear one of the pieces into four strips 7" by 55" *(fig. 2)*. Lightly starch and press.

c. Add one 7" by 55" ecru batiste rectangle to each side of the center rectangles (backing and lining) *(fig. 3)*. Press seams toward the center on one piece and toward the sides on the other pieces. Both rectangles should be approximately 55" square.

7. On a large flat surface, layer the backing wrong side up, then the batting followed by the lining, right side up and then the quilt top, right side up *(fig. 4)*.

8. Baste the layers together with pins, hand or machine basting or a quilt tack gun.

9. Machine or hand quilt as in *figure 5* or as desired.

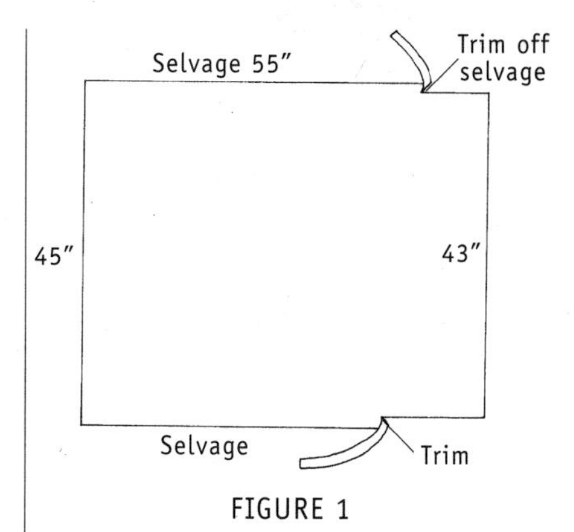

FIGURE 1

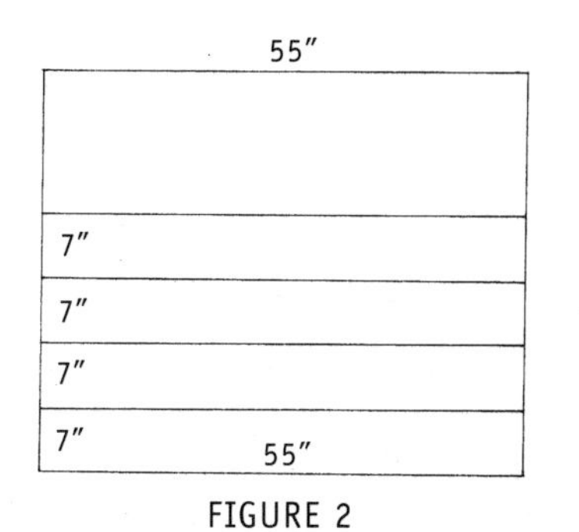

FIGURE 2

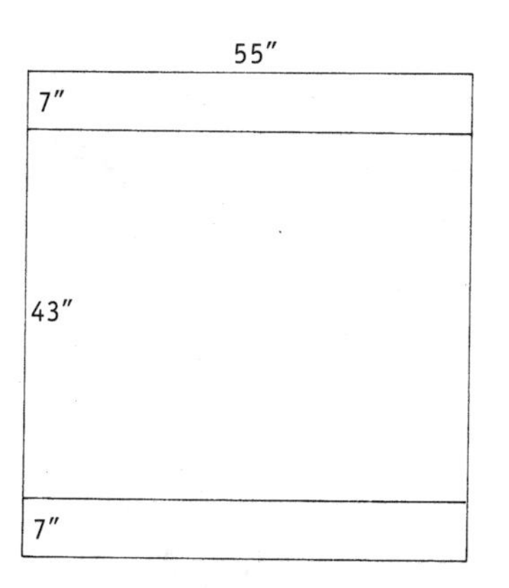

FIGURE 3

FIGURE 4

FIGURE 5

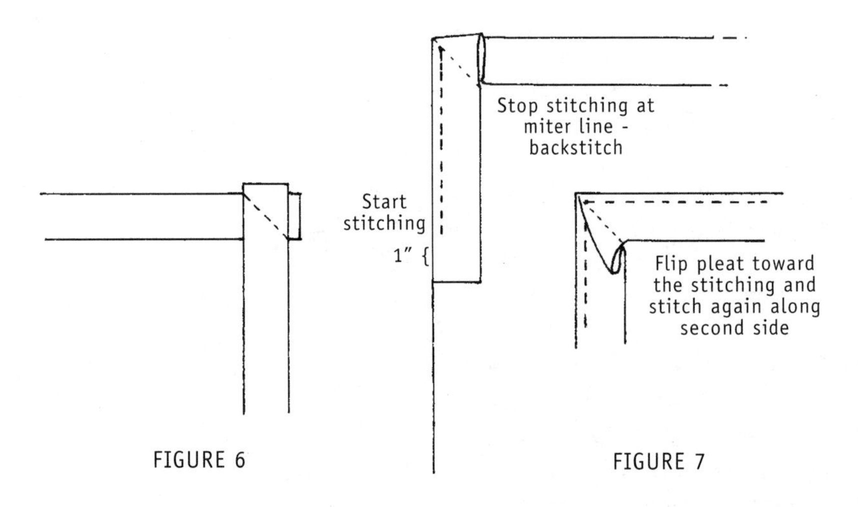

FIGURE 6

FIGURE 7

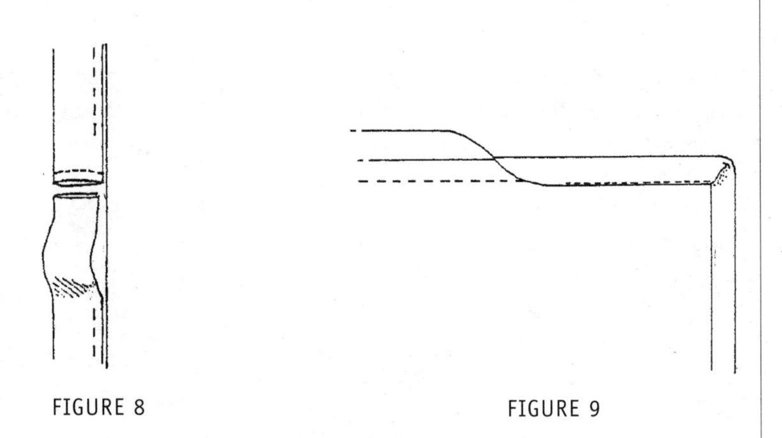
FIGURE 8

FIGURE 9

10. Machine stitch close to the outer edging of the quilt borders. Cut off extra batting and backing being careful not to trim any of the borders.

11. Remove the selvages from both end of each binding strip. Place two strips right sides together and stitch the layers together with a diagonal seam *(fig. 6)*.

12. Trim the excess fabric 1/4" beyond the stitched seam. Press the seam open or to one side.

13. Continue stitching the strips together until you have one long continuous strip of binding.

14. Fold the strip lengthwise, wrong sides together and press.

15. Draw miter lines along each corner of the quilt. Beginning along one long edge of the quilt, pin both raw edges of the quilt binding to the edges of the right side of the quilt.

16. Stitch, using a 1/4" seam allowance, starting about 1" from the end of the strip. Stop stitching at the miter line and backstitch.

17. Fold a 1/2" pleat in the binding at the corner and begin stitching again along the second side of the binding, starting at the miter line *(fig. 7)*.

18. Continue stitching, using this same technique at each corner. Stop stitching about 2" from the beginning. Overlap the beginning and the end 1/2" and trim away any excess. Fold one edge of the binding to the inside 1/4". Place the straight end into the folded end and continue stitching *(fig. 8)*.

19. Fold the binding over the edges of the quilt, enclosing the seam allowance. The folded edge of the binding should be placed just past the seam line. At the corners, the binding will be folded into a miter. Stitch the binding in place by machine or stitch by hand *(fig. 9)*.

Crayon Art Heart Quilt

ACP

This quilt is super easy to make and super fun to do. The motifs are done by cutting sandpaper shapes and coloring on the rough surface of the sandpaper with a crayon. Then, they are ironed onto the fabric. The fabric must be washed and pressed before you iron on the crayon hearts and the fabric must have some polyester in it. The quilt is pink and white striped fabric with a pink backing and a pink binding. The hearts and squiggles are of pink, purple and turquoise. The quilt is stippled with a pale pink thread after all of the ironing and coloring has been done. This quilt is a great project to do with a child.

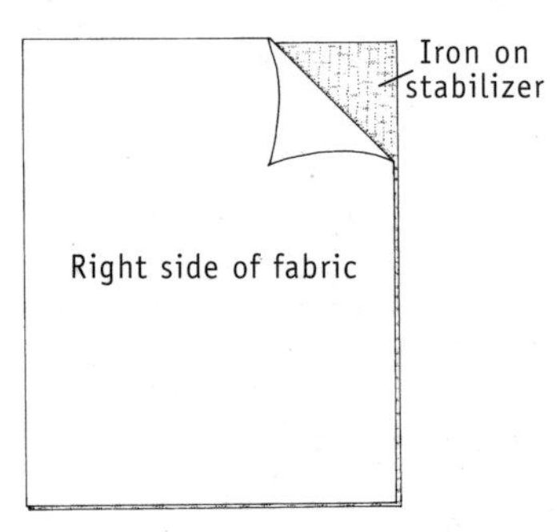

FIGURE 1

Lightweight tear-away stabilizer

FIGURE 2

FIGURE 3

FIGURE 4

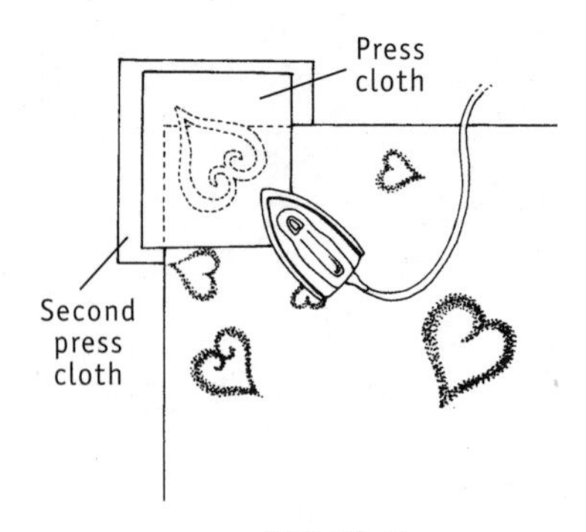

FIGURE 5

SUPPLIES

- 1-3/8 yards poly/cotton pink and white striped fabric for quilt front (washed and pressed)
- 1-7/8 yards poly/cotton or all cotton solid fabric for quilt back and binding
- Low-loft quilt batting
- 30 weight ecru machine embroidery thread
- Invisible thread
- Regular wax crayons or Crayola fabric crayons, not washable kind
- Crayon sharpener
- Coarse-grain sandpaper (available in hardware stores)
- New, inexpensive paint brush, 1" to 2" wide
- Old scissors to cut the sandpaper
- One large disposable pressing cloth or many small cloths from cotton or muslin
- Large Teflon pressing sheet
- Iron-on tear away stabilizer
- Lightweight tear away stabilizer
- Temporary spray adhesive
- Old cheese grater
- Safety pins or quilt tacks and quilt tack gun
- Heart templates
- Permanent black marker

Construction

1. Cut stripe fabric to the desired size (50" x 43").

2. Following the directions, press the iron-on, tear-away stabilizer to the wrong side of the striped fabric *(fig. 1)*. The stabilizer will prevent the crayons from bleeding onto your pressing surface.

3. Using a permanent black marker, trace the heart templates onto the lightweight tear-away stabilizer and cut out each heart just outside the marker line *(fig. 2)*. You do not need to cut away the inside of the heart.

4. Cut a piece of coarse sandpaper for each template, making sure that they are larger than the template.

5. Lightly spray the lightweight tear away stabilizer with a temporary spray adhesive. Adhere the stabilizer templates to the smooth side of the sandpaper *(fig. 3)* and roughly cut out.

6. Color the heart shapes on the sandpaper side, pushing hard so that the color of the crayon goes into the sandpaper *(fig. 4)*. *NOTE: To see the marker lines through the sandpaper, place the smooth side of the sandpaper against a sunny window or a light box. The colors used for the hearts were red, purple and bright blue. After coloring is complete, shake the sandpaper away from the project to remove any loose particles.*

7. Place the stabilized quilt top on a flat padded surface. Position one colored heart (crayon colored side down) onto the quilt top and brush away any crayon particles that may have fallen onto the fabric. Cover with a large disposable press cloth, fabric scrap or Teflon coated pressing sheet *(fig. 5)*.

NOTE: For the partial hearts on the quilt top, a second press cloth will need to be placed between the quilt top and the padded surface to prevent the colored sandpaper heart from transferring to the padded surface. Or, if you prefer, the portion of the colored sandpaper heart beyond the quilt top may be cut away.

8. With the iron set on the cotton setting, press (do not move the iron while it is on the fabric; lift the iron off the fabric each time before moving the iron) for about 10 seconds.

9. Gently remove the press cloth and sandpaper.

10. Repeat steps 6-9 reapplying crayons as needed to create the desired number of hearts (*see fig. 6*). Place the hearts randomly and use different colors. Use a clean press cloth each time and always have a press cloth when pressing over an already transferred heart.

11. Draw random swirls and curls over the quilt top *(see fig. 6)*.

12. Using the old cheese grater, grate the crayons and spread around loosely with the paintbrush (refer to finished drawing).

13. Use a Teflon coated pressing sheet or new press cloths to melt the pieces of crayon into the fabric.

14. Press the entire quilt top with a Teflon coated pressing sheet or new press cloths to make certain that all of the crayon pieces are melted.

15. Remove the iron-on stabilizer and wash the quilt top in a mild detergent. Line dry and press.

Layering and Quilting

1. Make a quilt sandwich by placing the quilt backing, wrong side up on a flat surface. Place the batting on top of the quilt backing. Center the quilt top on top of the batting, right side up *(fig. 6)*. Baste all layers together with safety pins, hand or machine basting, or quilt tack gun.

2. Using the ecru machine embroidery thread in the needle and invisible thread in the bobbin, stipple stitch the quilt with a loose meandering pattern (refer to Stipple Stitching, page 111) (see finished drawing).

3. Even up the raw edges of the quilt using a rotary cutter, mat and ruler.

Binding

1. Cut five 2-1/2" wide strips of solid fabric for the binding. Trim the selvages from both ends of each strip. Place two binding strips right sides together and stitch the layers together with a diagonal seam *(fig. 7)*.

2. Trim the excess fabric 1/4" beyond the stitched seam. Press the seam open or to one side.

3. Continue stitching the strips together until you have one long continuous strip of binding.

4. Fold the strip lengthwise, wrong sides together and press.

5. Draw miter lines along each corner of the quilt. Beginning along one long edge of the quilt, pin the raw edges of the quilt binding to the raw edges of the right side of the quilt top.

6. Stitch using a 3/8" seam allowance, starting about 1" from the end of the strip. Stop stitching at the miter line and backstitch.

7. Fold a 3/4" pleat in the binding at the corner and begin stitching again along the second side of the binding, starting at the miter line *(fig. 8)*.

8. Continue stitching, using this same technique at each corner. Stitch through all layers. Stop stitching about 2" from the beginning. Overlap the beginning and the end 1/2" and trim away any excess. Fold one edge of the binding to the inside 1/4". Place the straight end into the folded end and continue stitching *(fig. 9)*.

9. Fold the binding over the edges of the quilt, enclosing the seam allowance. The folded edge of the binding should be placed just past the seam line. At the corner, the binding will be folded into a miter. Stitch the binding in place by machine using a straight stitch or whipstitch in place by hand *(fig. 10)*.

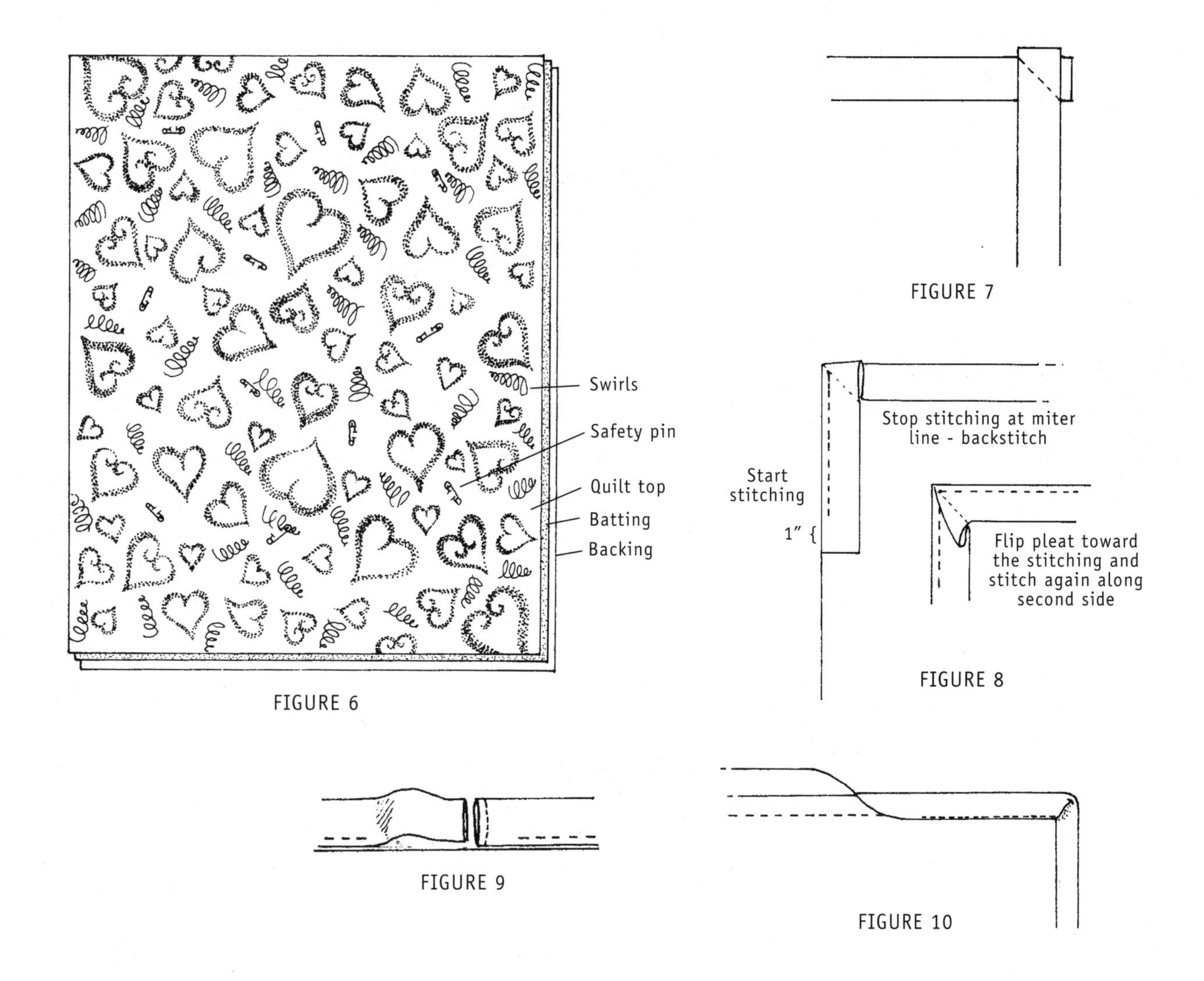

FIGURE 6

FIGURE 7

FIGURE 8

FIGURE 9

FIGURE 10

Bunnies By The Bay® Quilt

What a precious small quilt or wall hanging! Using Bunnies By The Bay® embroidery designs by Martha Pullen, this quilt can be made in any fabric to coordinate with any room. The quilt is 32 inches square. The center of the quilt has five squares, on point, with each square having a "magic Madeira" appliquéd heart in the middle. The four outside hearts have different bunnies embroidered in the center; the middle heart features the carrots peeking out of the ground with a little bumble bee flying overhead. The side and corner triangles and sashing are stipple quilted. The second border has corner squares featuring a blue bird from the Bunnies By The Bay® embroidery CD. The longer portions of the outside border feature straight stitch quilting in the form of hearts. The quilt is finished with a straight edge binding. The quilt has a thin, traditional batting and the backing is one piece of fabric. An adorable label is stitched in the matching fabric on the back of the quilt. It reads, "Bunnies By The Bay® Designs available from Martha Pullen Company, Made in the U.S.A." A carrot with one bite taken out of the carrot is also stitched on this quilt label. Just too cute!

SUPPLIES

- 1/4 yard for inner square background (blue)
- 1/4 yard for inner sashing (green)
- 1/4 yard for inner squares on point (pink print)
- 5/8 yard for outer sashing (blue floral circle bunnies)
- 1/2 yard for hearts and corner (yellow dots)
- 1/4 yard for binding (blue ladybugs)
- 1 yard for backing (bunny print)
- Optional: 1/8 yard for rod pocket (bunny print)
- 1/4 yard of cotton fabric (scrap fabric used for turning edges of the hearts)
- Tear-away stabilizer
- Wash-away basting thread
- White thread for piecing
- Thread to match inner background for stippling and quilting
- Thread for embroideries
- Batting at least 33″ square
- Temporary spray adhesive (KK2000)
- Quilt tack gun or safety pins
- Bunnies by the Bay® Embroidery CD
- Optional: Rod for hanging
- Invisible thread (optional)
- Bunny Quilt Heart Template

Cutting

1. Inner square background (blue): *For corner triangles:* Cut two squares 5-3/4". Fold the two 5-3/4" squares in half, point to point to form a triangle. Cut along the fold. *For middle triangles:* Cut two squares 8-3/4". Fold the two 8-3/4" squares in half, point to point to form a triangle. Cut along the fold. Cut four strips 1-1/2" by 8".

2. Inner squares on point (pink print): Cut five 8" squares.

3. Hearts and Corner Blocks (yellow dots): Cut nine 7" squares.

4. Inner sashing (green): Cut four 1-1/2" by 25" strips.

5. Outer sashing (blue floral circle bunnies): Cut four 4-3/8" by 25" strips.

6. Binding (blue ladybugs) : Cut three 2-1/2" by 45" strips. Remove the selvages from both ends of each strip.

7. Optional: Cut one strip 4-1/2" by 31-1/2" (bunny print) for the rod casing.

Template: Heart

NOTE: If the fabric is too small to fit into the desired hoop use the following steps:

1. Hoop a piece of stabilizer.

2. Spray the hooped stabilizer with a temporary spray adhesive (KK2000).

3. Secure the fabric to the stabilizer, align as needed. If an area is not secure, remove the fabric, spray again and secure the fabric.

4. Stitch the embroidery.

5. Remove the stabilizer.

Embroidery and Heart Appliqué

1. Stabilize, center and stitch the following bunny embroideries on four of the 7" squares of the yellow dot fabric: Buzzy and Bunny, Blueberry Bunny, Grandmother Bunny, Boy Bunny. Remove the stabilizer from the embroideries.

2. While the embroidery unit is attached to the machine, stabilize, center and stitch two Bluebirds as is and two mirror image on four of the 7" squares of the yellow dot fabric. Remove the stabilizer from each embroidered piece. Mark a 4" square centered around each bird. Place an "x" in the corner that the bird's beak points toward. This indicates the inner corner of the square. Draw cutting lines 1/4" beyond the two lines of the inside corner. Draw cutting lines 3/8" from the remaining two lines *(fig. 1)*. Cut along cutting lines. Set the bluebird squares aside. These will be used as the corner blocks.

3. Mark the vertical and horizontal center of one of the 7" squares of the yellow dots fabric. This will be for the carrot embroidery placement. Place a second set of marks 1/2" to the right of center and 1-1/2" up from the center *(fig. 2)*. This will be for the bee embroidery placement. Stabilize, center and stitch the Three Carrots embroidery on the center mark. Stabilize, center and stitch the Bumblebee embroidery on the upper mark.

4. Center the embroidery and trace the heart template on the wrong side of the bunny embroideries and the carrot and bee embroidery *(fig. 3)*.

5. Place a scrap piece of fabric to the right side of each piece of embroidery *(fig. 3)*. With wash-away basting thread in the bobbin or needle or both, stitch along the heart template line using a short, straight

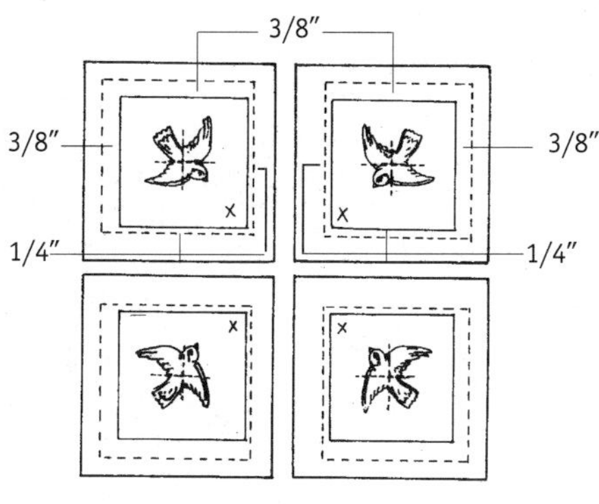

FIGURE 1

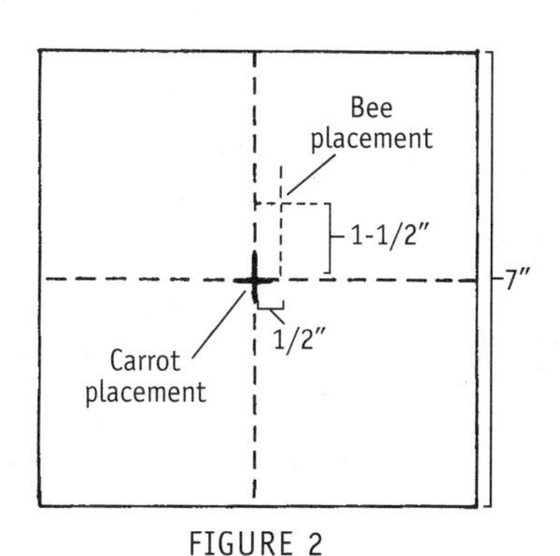

FIGURE 2

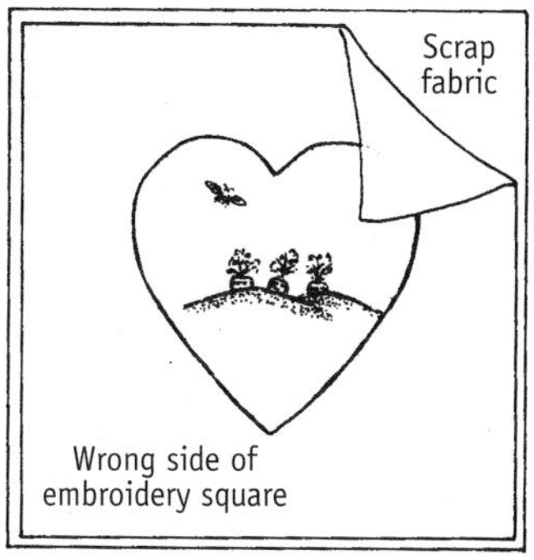

Scrap fabric

Wrong side of embroidery square

FIGURE 3

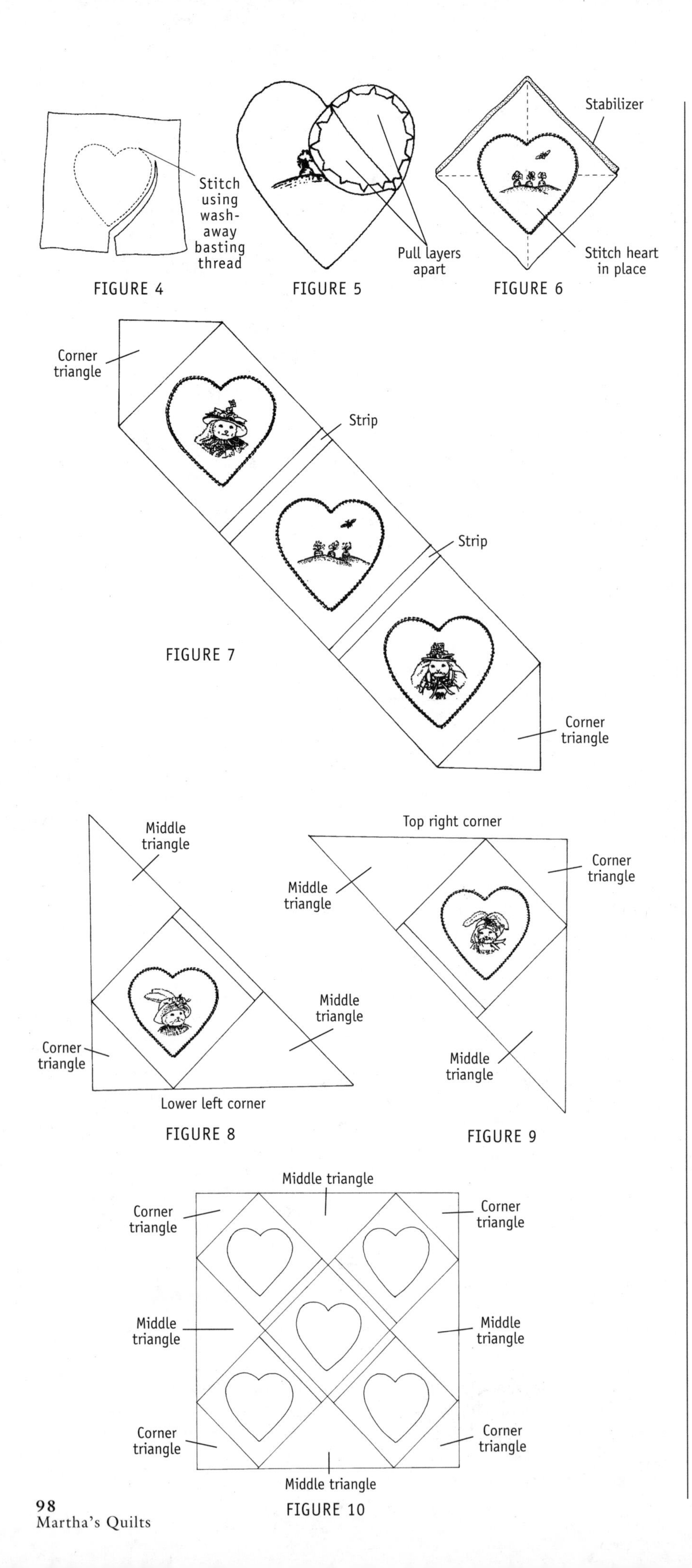

stitch (L=1 to 1.5). Trim away the excess fabric 1/4" to 1/8" from the stitching line *(fig. 4)*. Clip the angles and curves of the seam allowance. Cut an "X" in the scrap fabric. Turn the heart to the right side through the "X" . Using a point turner or dull stick, push out all points and curves. Press flat. Starch and press. Spray starch along the edges of the heart. Press again until dry. Gently but firmly pull the two heart layers apart *(fig. 5)*. If the layers are hard to pull apart, starch again, press until dry and pull apart. Discard the scrap. Repeat for each of the five hearts. Remove the wash-away thread and put white thread in the needle and bobbin.

6. Fold each of the 8" pink squares, point to point and again point to point. Center the heart on each of the pink squares with the point of the heart centered on the fold lines. Remember the pink square is on point or turned like a diamond. Pin the heart in place.

7. Place stabilizer behind the pink square and stitch the heart in place with a small zigzag (L= 1.5 - 2, W=1.5 - 2), a blanket stitch (L=2, W=2) or pinstitch (L= 2, W=2) *(fig. 6)*.

Constructing the Inner Square of the Quilt Top

1. The inner square consists of the following: five pink squares with yellow hearts, small connecting strips in between pink squares, four corner triangles, and four middle triangles. The construction order is as follows:

Step 1. Construction of the center diagonal strip.

Step 2. Construction of the lower corner piece.

Step 3. Construction of the upper corner piece.

Step 4. Attaching the upper and lower corner pieces to each side of the center diagonal strip.

2. To construct the center diagonal row (top left to lower right), stitch the center diagonal row in the following order: corner triangle, pink (Buzzy and Bunny) square, 1-1/2" by 8" strip, pink (Carrot/Bee) square, 1-1/2" by 8" strip, pink (Grandmother Bunny) square and the corner triangle *(fig. 7)*. Set aside.

3. To construct the lower left corner piece, stitch a 1-1/2" by 8" strip to the upper right side of the pink (Boy Bunny) square and a corner triangle to the lower left edge of the pink square. Stitch a middle

triangle to the top and bottom of the remaining sides *(fig. 8)*.

4. To construct the upper corner piece, stitch a 1-1/2" by 8" strip to the lower left side of the pink (Blueberry Bunny) square and a corner triangle to the upper right edge of the pink square. Stitch a middle triangle to the top and bottom of the remaining sides *(fig. 9)*.

5. Stitch the upper and lower corners to each side of the center strip making sure all pink squares are lined up diagonally. Even the edges as needed. This completes the inner square. Press well *(fig. 10)*. If colors in the fabric used differ greatly, remember to press the lighter color seam allowances toward the darker fabric.

Finishing the Quilt Top

1. Stitch inner sashing strips (1-1/2" by 25" - green) to each side of the inner square. Trim the ends of the strips even, top and bottom, with the inner square *(fig. 11)*.

2. Stitch inner sashing strips (1-1/2" by 25" - green) to the top and bottom of the inner square. Trim the ends of the strips even at the sides *(fig. 12)*.

3. Cut four 4-3/8" outer sashing pieces the same length as each side of the quilt top.

4. Stitch one 4-3/8" outer sashing piece to each side of the quilt top *(fig. 13)*.

5. Stitch a corner piece to each end of the remaining two outer sashing pieces with the bird's beak pointing to the seam as shown *(fig. 14)*. One strip is for the top edge of the quilt top and one strip is for the bottom edge of the quilt top.

6. Stitch the sashing/corner pieces to the top and bottom of the quilt top. The bird's beak should be pointing to the inner corner of the quilt top *(fig. 15)*.

7. Press the entire quilt top very well.

Constructing the Quilt

1. Place the backing onto a table top with the wrong side up.

2. Center the batting onto the backing.

3. Center the quilt top onto the batting. The backing and batting should be slightly larger than the quilt top *(fig. 16)*.

4. Pin the layers together with safety pins approximately 2" to 3" apart. Pin the layers together along the raw edges of the quilt top. A quilt tack gun, hand basting or

FIGURE 11

FIGURE 12

FIGURE 13

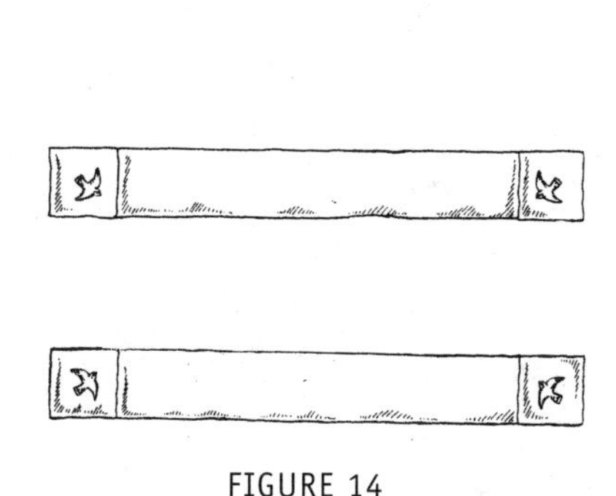

FIGURE 14

FIGURE 15

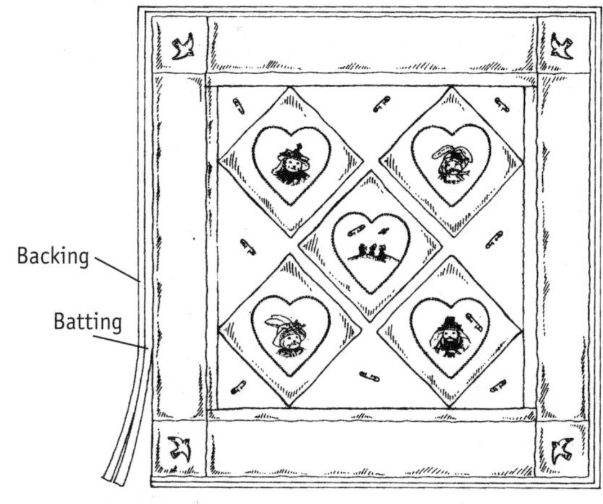

FIGURE 16

machine basting can be used to hold the layers together *(fig. 16)*.

5. Trim away the excess batting and backing even with the edge of the quilt top, being very careful not to cut away any of the quilt top *(fig. 16)*.

Quilting

NOTE: Machine embroidery thread to match the backing is used in the bobbin for all quilting. Machine embroidery thread to match the part of the quilt top being stitched is used in the needle. Invisible thread can be used in the needle when "stitching in the ditch".

1. With all layers of the quilt pinned well, stitch in the ditch along each side of the green inner sashing strip and along each of the pink inner squares. This can be stitched free-motion or stitched using a walking foot. Straight stitch quilting using invisible thread may also be added where desired in the embroidery designs of each square.

2. The blue background of the inner square is quilted using medium to loose stipple stitching *(fig. 17)*. Refer to the technique for Stippling, page 111.

3. Straight stitch hearts can be stitched randomly along the outer sashing strips.

Optional: Adding A Rod Pocket For Hanging

1. Fold each end of the strip for the rod casing 1/2" and 1/2" again and press *(fig. 18)*. Fold the strip in half lengthwise and press *(fig. 19)*.

2. Pin in place along the top edge of the back of the quilt matching the raw edges. Pin in place.

Binding

1. Using the 2-1/2" blue fabric for the binding, place two strips right sides together and stitch the layers with a diagonal seam *(fig. 20)*.

2. Trim the excess fabric 1/4" beyond the stitched seam. Press the seam open or to one side.

3. Continue stitching the strips together until you have one long continuous strip of binding.

4. Fold the strip lengthwise, wrong sides together and press.

5. Draw miter lines along each corner of the quilt. Beginning along one long edge of the quilt, pin the raw edges of the quilt binding to the edges on the right side of the quilt top *(fig. 21)*.

6. Stitch using a 3/8" seam allowance, starting about 1" from the end of the strip. Stop stitching at the miter line and backstitch.

7. Fold a 3/4" pleat in the binding at the corner and begin stitching again along the second side of the binding, starting at the miter line *(fig. 21)*.

8. Continue stitching, using this same technique at each corner. Stitch through all layers (including the rod casing layers along the top of the quilt). Stop stitching about 2" from the beginning. Overlap the beginning and the end 1/2" and trim away any excess. Fold one edge of the binding to the inside 1/4". Place the straight end into the folded end and continue stitching *(fig. 22)*.

9. Fold the binding over the edges of the quilt, enclosing the seam allowance. The folded edge of the binding should be placed just past the seam line. At the corner, the binding will be folded into a miter. Stitch the binding in place by machine using a straight stitch or whipstitch in place by hand *(fig. 23)*.

Finishing the Rod Pocket

1. Press the rod pocket flat to the back of the quilt.

2. Hand whip the lower fold and the inside of the opening to the quilt back. *(fig. 24)*.

3. Insert the rod through the casing for hanging.

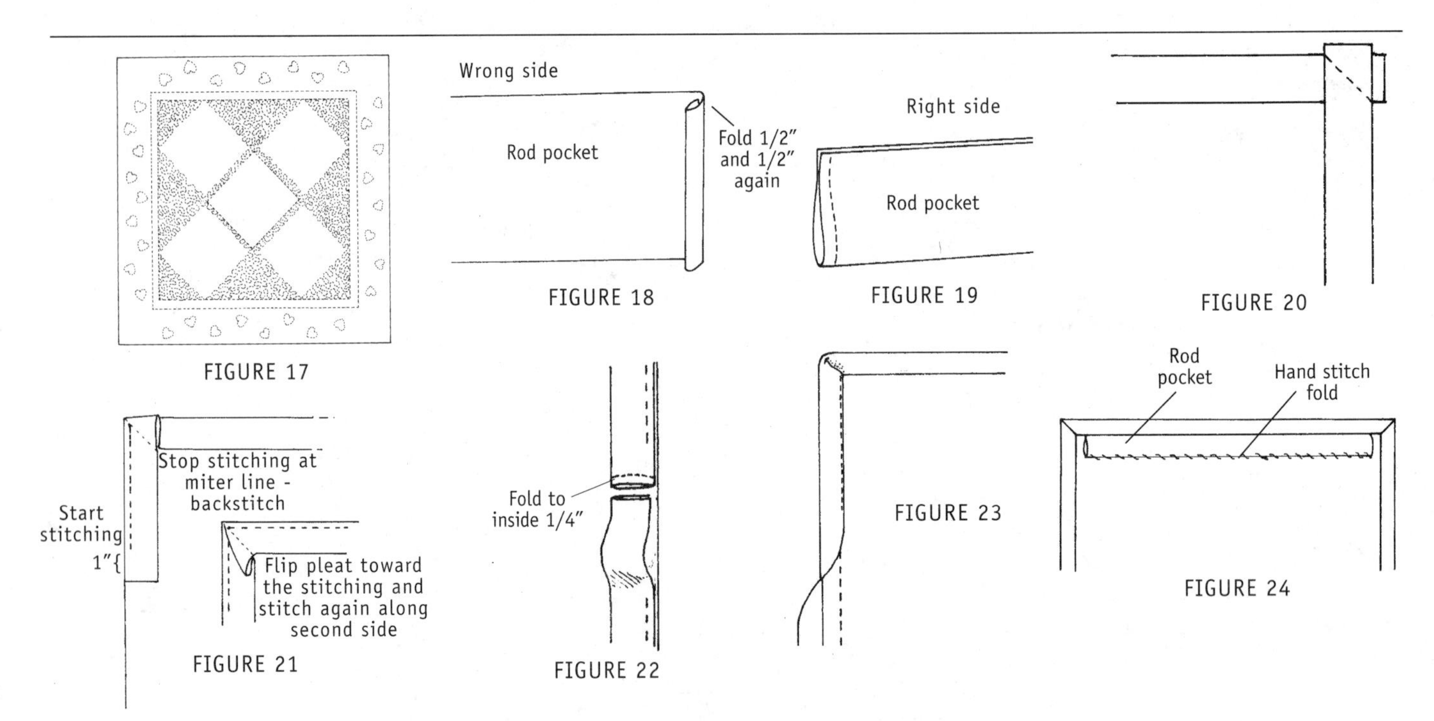

FIGURE 17

FIGURE 18

FIGURE 19

FIGURE 20

FIGURE 21

FIGURE 22

FIGURE 23

FIGURE 24

Mommy's Helpers Wall Panel

Acp

She has her own miniature sewing machine, a toy vacuum cleaner, and play-size kitchen with all the accouterments. Whenever she whips up an imaginary four-course meal, you can't hold back the hugs. She's Mommy's helper, and she's been pretending to be you for most of her little life. Capture cherished moments on a wall hanging or quilt by embroidering motifs that suit your child's personality.

The first panel features a little girl dusting, arranging flowers, cooking and sweeping. A little white dog with spots chases throughout the scenes. Dolls are found in many of the vignettes. The second panel has little girls going to market, little girls having a tea party, a little girl playing the piano for her dolls and another leading her dolls in singing. The third panel has a little girl bathing her doll, rocking her doll, putting her doll to sleep and drying dishes. On the back of the quilt there is an appliquéd circle with the words stitched in, "Mommy's Helpers, Designs available from Martha Pullen Company, Made in the U.S.A." Of course, you can stitch your information; however, it is so cute stitched onto a circle. There is also a little doll sitting in a chair with a hat stitched on the circular information appliquéd piece on the back.

Using the embroidery disk, Mommy's Helpers from Martha Pullen, this rendition of the 1920s or 1930s little girls has been beloved by people the world over. Fabric to match this embroidery disk is available from Martha Pullen (retail only) as well as Clothworks (wholesale only). Using a pretty flower print for the outside border and the quilt binding as well make this a little feminine quilt or wall hanging. The lining is also out of this flower fabric. Blue tone-on-tone fabric is sashed next to the flower print; red tone-on-tone fabric is found around the white stippled/embroidered panels. The finished measurements of the quilt are 25 by 36 inches.

SUPPLIES

(Finished size of sample is 25" by 36")

- 1-1/4 yards floral fabric (backing, borders, binding)
- 1/4 yard of blue fabric (inner border)
- 1/4 yard of red fabric (panel borders)
- 1/2 yard of ecru fabric (embroidered panels)
- 25 by 36 inch lightweight batting or fleece
- Rayon machine embroidery threads (colors listed in embroidery instructions)
- 80 weight white thread for bobbin
- Regular sewing thread to match fabrics (for construction and quilting)
- #70 universal needle or needle appropriate for chosen threads
- Stabilizer
- Mommy's Helpers Embroidery CD available from Martha Pullen Company

Cutting

Color/number	Width x Length
a. Red, cut six	1-1/2" x 8"
b. Red, cut six	1-1/2" x 17"
c. Blue, cut two	2" x 17"
d. Blue, cut two	2" x 28"
e. Blue, cut two	2" x 19"
f. Floral, cut two	4" x 29"
g. Floral, cut two	4" x 25"
Cut three binding strips	2" by 45"

Construction

(Finished size of sample is 25 x 36 inches)

1. Trace three panels onto ecru fabric, each 8" x 16". Choose embroidery designs and use templates or stitched samples to mark placement on panel; sample shows four motifs on each panel. When placing motifs, remember to allow 1/2-inch seam allowances on all sides of each panel *(fig. 1)*.

2. Stabilize, hoop, and stitch embroideries, changing colors as needed for each motif. The sample was worked with the Viking Designer I "Megahoop;" a 4-inch square hoop can also be used but re-hooping is necessary for each motif. Use 80 wt. white thread in bobbin to eliminate bulk and color changes.

3. After embroideries are finished, remove as much stabilizer as possible and press panels from wrong side on padded surface. Cut the three panels apart.

4. Cut border strips as directed in "Cutting" instructions.

5. Piece the quilt top in the following order using 1/2" seams and ecru sewing thread; press well after each step. Refer

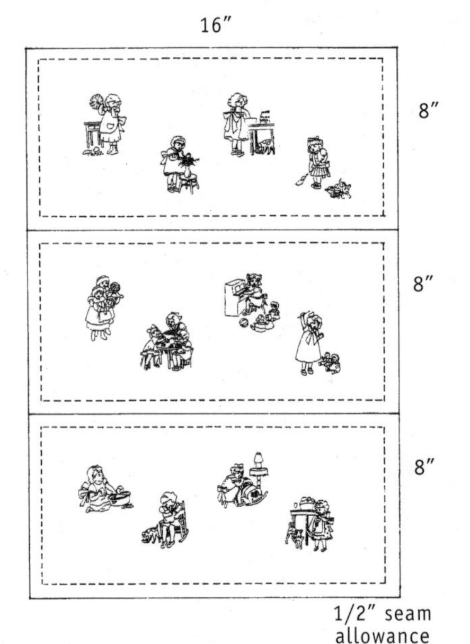

FIGURE 1

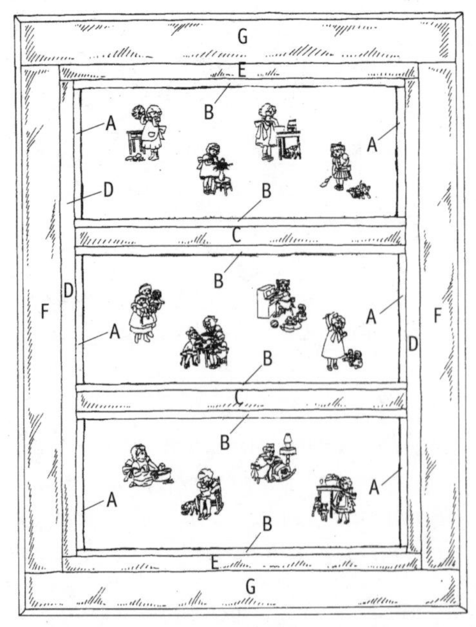

FIGURE 2

to *figure 2*; letters on figure correspond to letters in following steps.

a. Short red strips to short ends of panels

b. Long red strips across top and bottom of panels

c. Short (17-inch) blue strips between panels

d. Long blue strips to sides of joined panels

e. 19-inch blue strips at top and bottom of center panel

f. Long (29-inch) floral strips to side of center panel

g. Short (25-inch) floral strips to top and bottom of center panel

6. Press top and backing well. Place backing wrong side up on flat surface, with batting on top of it; place pieced top right side up over batting *(fig. 3)*. Pin or baste well to hold layers in place for quilting.

7. Stipple quilt inside each panel; outline each motif and stipple close to borders. *(fig 4)*. Refer to the technique for Stipple Stitching, page 111.

8. Quilt the rectangles by stitching "in

FIGURE 3

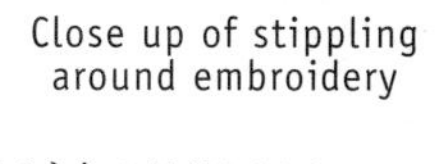

FIGURE 4

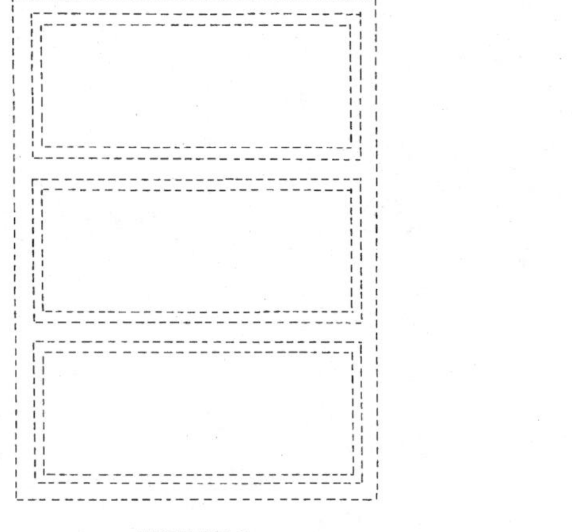
FIGURE 5

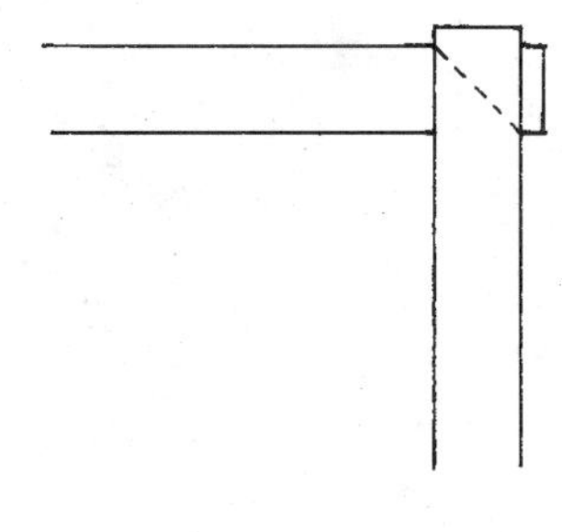
FIGURE 6

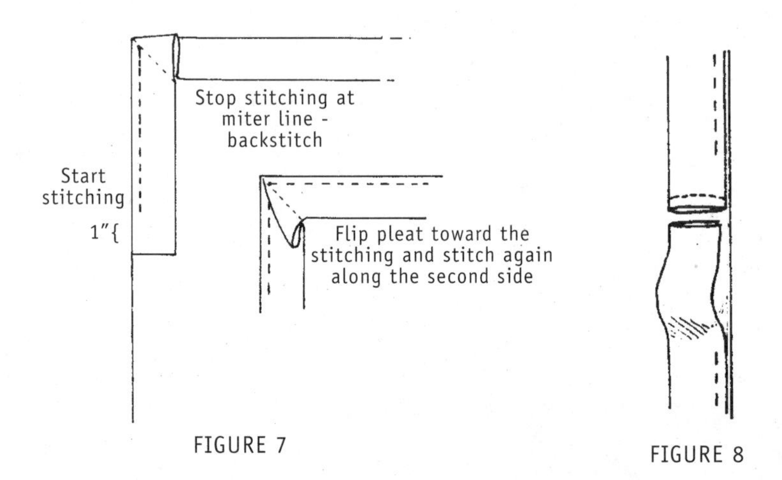

FIGURE 7

FIGURE 8

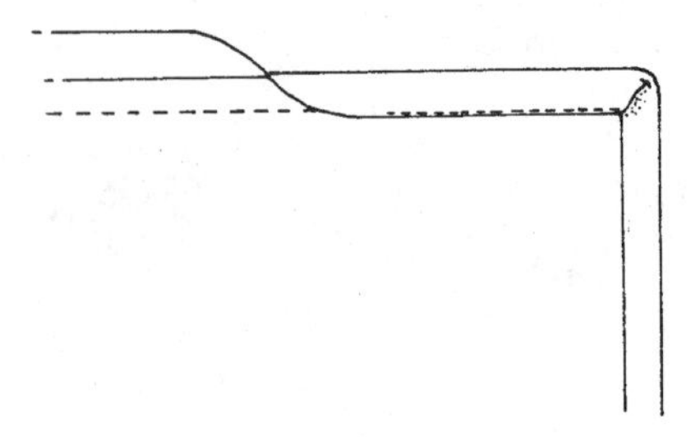
FIGURE 9

the ditch" of the seam lines connecting the strips using thread to match the quilt top in the needle and thread to match the backing in the bobbin *(fig. 5)*.

9. Press again and trim to measure 25" x 36".

10. Remove the selvages from both ends of each of the three binding strips.

11. Place two strips right sides together and stitch the layers together with a diagonal seam *(fig. 6)*.

12. Trim the excess fabric 1/4" beyond the stitched seam. Press the seam open or to one side.

13. Continue stitching the strips together until you have one long continuous strip of binding.

14. Fold the strip lengthwise, wrong sides together and press.

15. Draw miter lines along each corner of the quilt. Beginning along one long edge of the quilt, pin raw edges of the quilt binding to the edges of the right side of the quilt.

16. Stitch, using a 1/4" seam allowance, starting about 1" from the end of the strip. Stop stitching at the miter line and backstitch.

17. Fold a 1/2" pleat in the binding at the corner and begin stitching again along the second side of the binding, starting at the miter line *(fig. 7)*.

18. Continue stitching, using this same technique at each corner. Stop stitching about 2" from the beginning. Overlap the beginning and the end 1/2" and trim away any excess. Fold one edge of the binding to the inside 1/4". Place the straight end into the folded end and continue stitching *(fig. 8)*.

19. Fold the binding over the edges of the quilt, enclosing the seam allowance. The folded edge of the binding should be placed just past the seam line. At the corners, the binding will be folded into a miter. Stitch the binding in place by machine or stitch by hand *(fig. 9)*.

Mommy's Helpers Wing Needle Entredeux Quilt

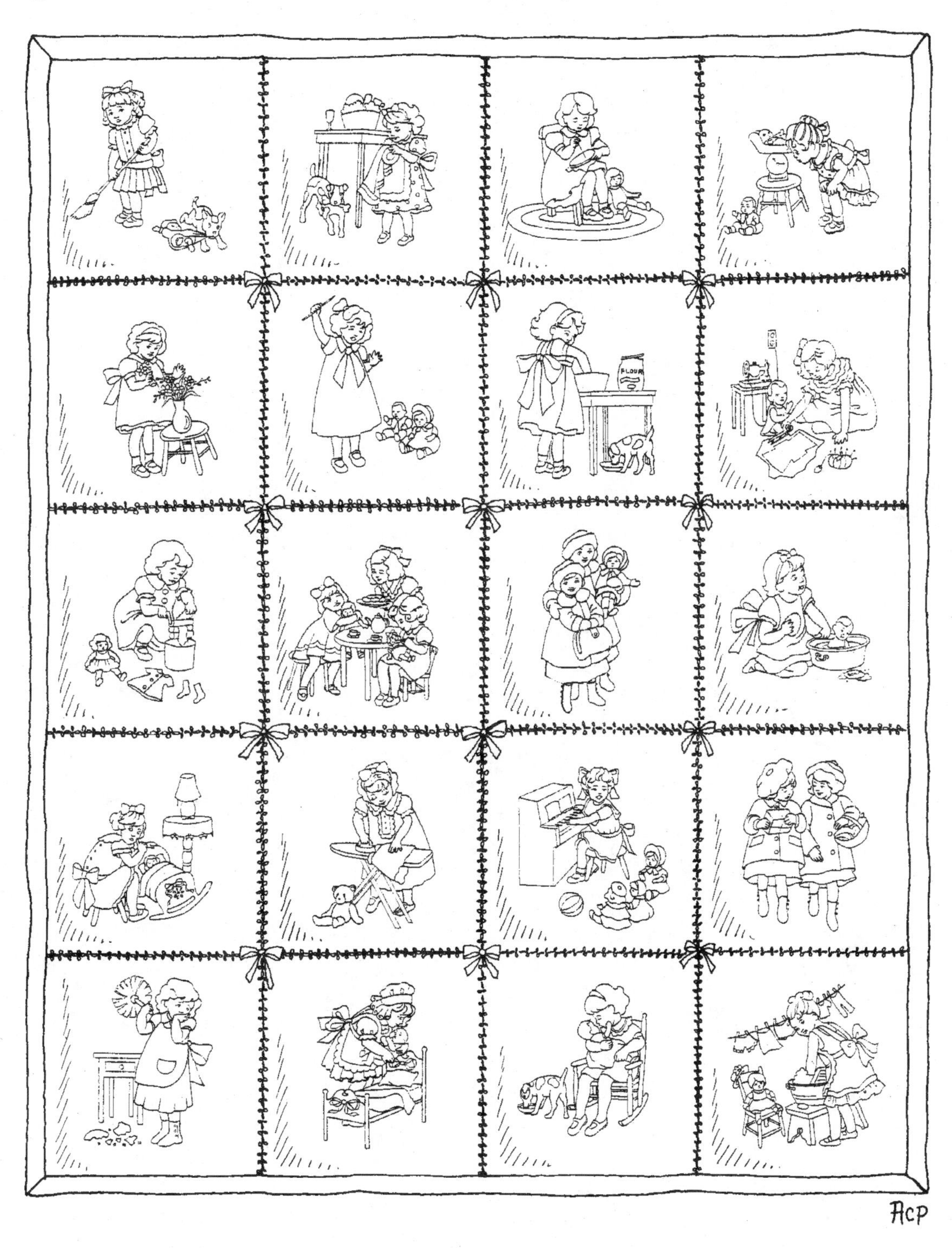

Each of the precious designs from the Martha Pullen embroidery CD, Mommy's Helpers, is stitched on the 20 sections of this quilt. Made of white linen for the front and the lining, the quilt is bound in the same white linen. There is a thin, traditional batting inside the quilt. The quilting is actually a wing needle entredeux stitch going through the front, the batting and the lining. At the points of each square of wing needle entredeux there is a little pink silk ribbon bow stitched and tied. The wing needle entredeux is stitched in white. The finished quilt measures 23 by 28-1/2 inches. This quilt is really easy and quick to assemble, after you have embroidered all of the helper designs. Mommy's Helper fabrics are now available to match these embroidery designs. It would be precious to use this fabric!

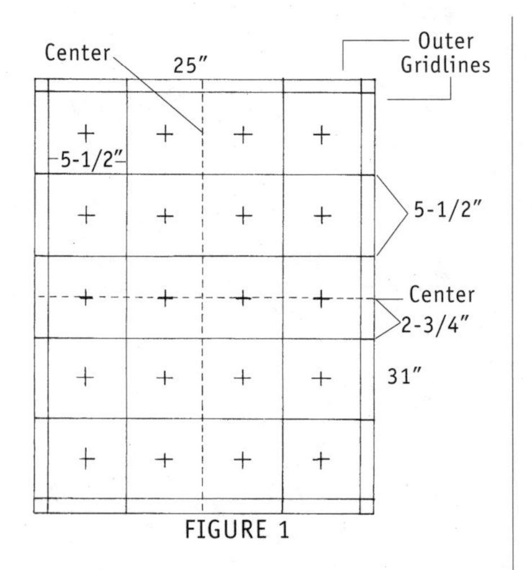

FIGURE 1

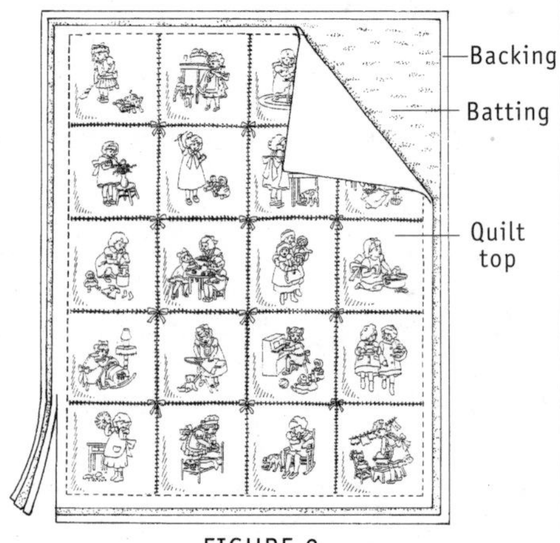

FIGURE 2

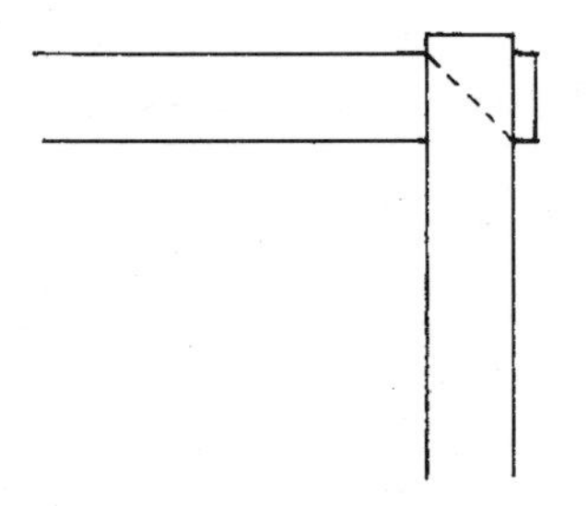
FIGURE 3

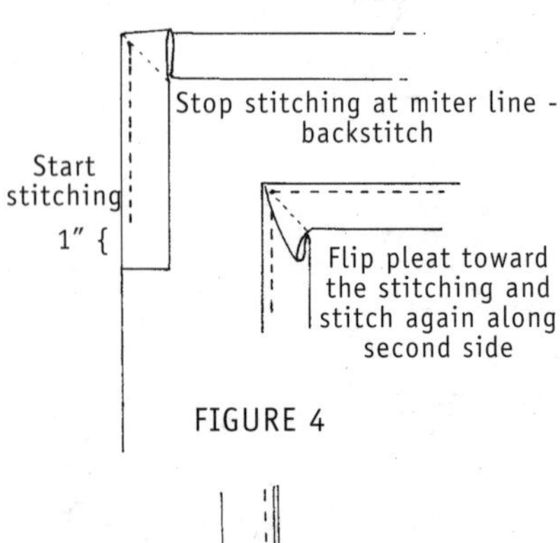

FIGURE 4

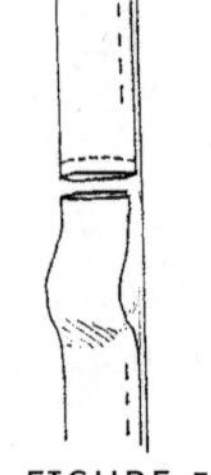
FIGURE 5

Supplies

- 1-1/2 yards of white linen/cotton blend (top, backing and binding)
- Low loft quilt batting
- Martha Pullen's Mommy's Helpers Embroidery Designs
- Machine embroidery threads for embroidery
- White lightweight thread for quilting
- #100 wing needle
- 3 yards of 2mm silk ribbon (pink)
- Tapestry needle
- Stabilizer
- Wash-out marker
- Optional: Temporary spray adhesive
- Safety pins or quilt tacks and quilt tack gun

Cutting

1. Cut two pieces of fabric 25" wide by 31" long. One piece will be for the quilt top and one piece will be for the quilt back.

2. Cut three strips 2-1/2" by 45" for the binding. Remove the selvages from both ends of each of the binding strips.

Embroidery

1. For the embroidery placement, mark the quilt top as follows:

a. Fold the 25" width of the quilt top in half to find the vertical center. Draw a line along the fold (*fig. 1*).

b. Place two vertical lines to the left of the center line and two vertical lines to the right of the center line spaced 5-1/2" apart (*fig. 1*).

c. Fold the 31" length of the quilt top in half to find the horizontal center. Press along the fold (*fig. 1*).

d. Place a horizontal line 2-3/4" on each side of the pressed center line (*fig. 1*).

e. Place two horizontal lines 5-1/2" above and two below the two lines drawn in step d (*fig. 1*).

2. The outermost lines are the outer gridlines. These will be the stitching lines for connecting the binding of the quilt.

3. Mark the center of each 5-1/2" square.

4. The Mommy's Helpers embroideries always start in the center of the hoop. Hoop, stabilize and stitch the embroideries in the center of each square. Refer to the finished drawing for specific embroideries.

5. Remove the stabilizer and press the quilt top.

Layering and Wing Needle Quilting

1. Make a quilt sandwich by placing the quilt backing, wrong side up on a flat surface. Place the batting on top of the quilt backing. Center the quilt top on top of the batting, right side up. Baste all layers together with safety pins, hand or machine basting, or quilt tack gun.

2. Insert a wing needle and place white lightweight thread in both the needle and the bobbin. Stitch along the lines of the grid using an entredeux stitch or small zigazg. Do not stitch along the outside lines of the grid (*fig. 2*).

3. Trim all layers of the quilt 3/8" from the outer grid lines (*fig. 2*).

Binding

1. Using the 2-1/2" strips for the binding, place two strips right sides together. Stitch the layers together with a diagonal seam (*fig. 3*).

2. Trim the excess fabric 1/4" beyond the stitched seam. Press the seam open or to one side.

3. Continue stitching the strips together until you have one long continuous strip of binding.

4. Fold the strip lengthwise, wrong sides together and press.

5. Draw miter lines along each corner of the quilt. Begin along one long edge of the quilt, pin the raw edges of the quilt binding to the edges of the right side of the quilt top.

6. Stitch using a 3/8" seam allowance, starting about 1" from the end of the strip. Stop stitching at the miter line and backstitch.

7. Fold a 3/4" pleat in the binding at the corner and begin stitching again along the second side of the binding, starting at the miter line (*fig. 4*).

8. Continue stitching, using this same technique at each corner. Stitch through all layers. Stop stitching about 2" from the beginning. Overlap the beginning and the end 1/2" and trim away any excess. Fold one edge of the binding to the inside

1/4". Place the straight end into the folded end and continue stitching *(fig. 5)*.

9. Fold the binding over the edges of the quilt, enclosing the seam allowance. The folded edge of the binding should be placed just past the seam line. At the corner, the binding will be folded into a miter. Stitch the binding in place by machine using a straight stitch or whipstitch in place by hand *(fig. 6)*.

Ribbon Embellishments

1. Cut the silk ribbon into 9" pieces.

2. Working from the quilt top, thread one piece of ribbon through a tapestry needle, take the needle down and back up at each intersection leaving the tails of the ribbon on the quilt top *(fig. 7)*. Tie the tails of the ribbon into a bow (see finished drawing). Trim the excess ribbon tails.

3. Repeat for each intersection.

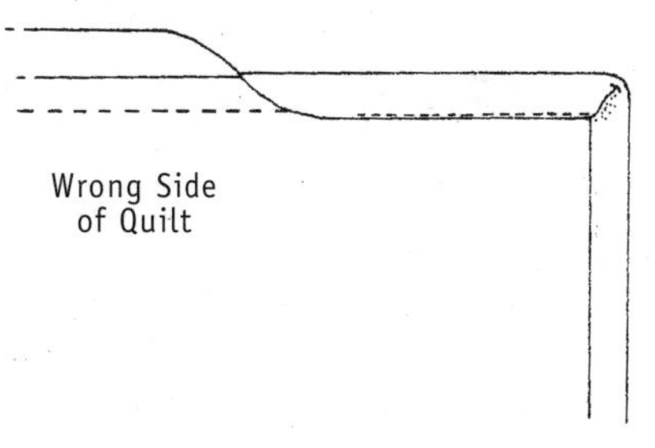

FIGURE 6

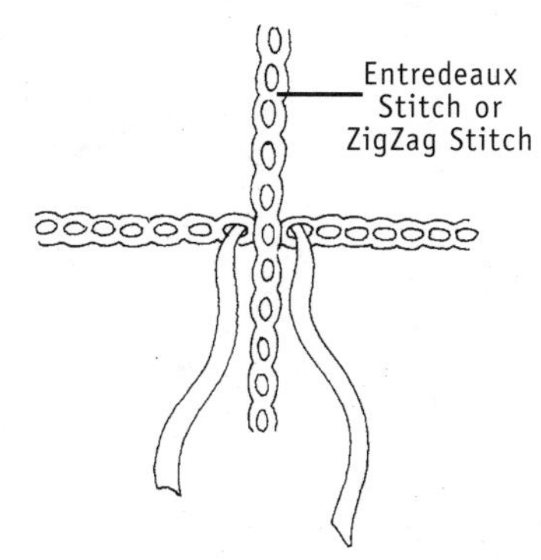

FIGURE 7

Beginning French Sewing Techniques

Lace to Lace

Butt together and zigzag.

Suggested machine settings: Width 2-1/2, length 1.

Lace to Fabric

Place right sides together.

Fabric extends 1/8" from lace.

Zigzag off the edge and over the heading of the lace.

Suggested Machine Settings: Width 3-1/2, Length 1/2 to 1 (almost a satin stitch).

Lace to Entredeux

Trim batiste from one side of the entredeux.

Butt lace to entredeux and zigzag.

Suggested Machine Settings: Width 2-1/2, Length 1-1/2.

Gathered Lace to Entredeux

Trim one side of the entredeux.

Gather lace by pulling heading thread.

Butt together and zigzag.

Suggested Machine Settings: Width 2-1/2, Length 1-1/2.

Entredeux to Flat Fabric

Place fabric to entredeux, right sides together.

Stitch in the ditch with a regular straight stitch.

Trim seam allowance to 1/8".

Zigzag over the seam allowance.

Suggested Machine Settings: Width 2-1/2, Length 1-1/2.

Entredeux to Gathered Fabric

Gather fabric using two gathering rows.

Place gathered fabric to entredeux, right sides together.

Stitch in the ditch with a regular straight stitch.

Stitch again 1/16" away from the first stitching.

Trim seam allowance to 1/8".

Zigzag over the seam allowance.

Suggested Machine Settings: Width 2-1/2, Length 1-1/2.

Optional: Top Stitch (to be used after Entredeux to Flat or Gathered Fabric)

Turn seam down, away from the lace, entredeux, etc.

Tack in place using a zigzag.

Suggested Machine Settings: Width 1-1/2, Length 1-1/2.

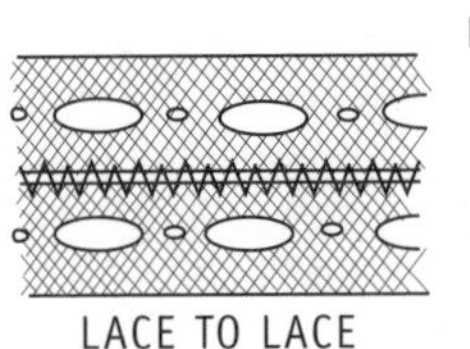

LACE TO LACE

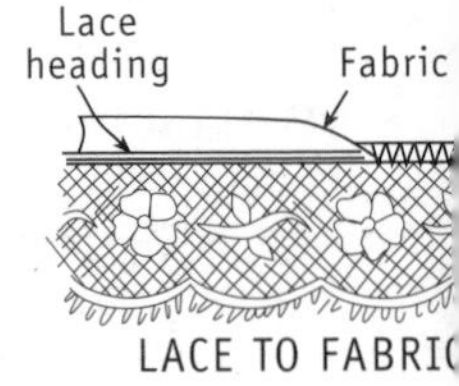

LACE TO FABRIC

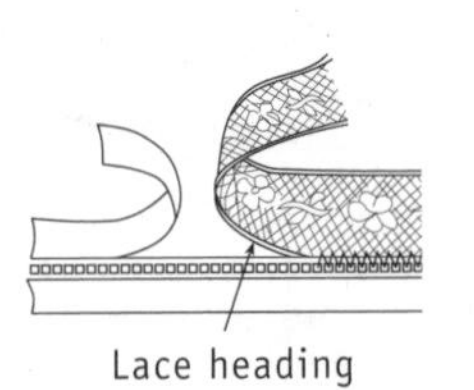

LACE TO ENTREDEUX

GATHERED LACE TO ENTREDEUX

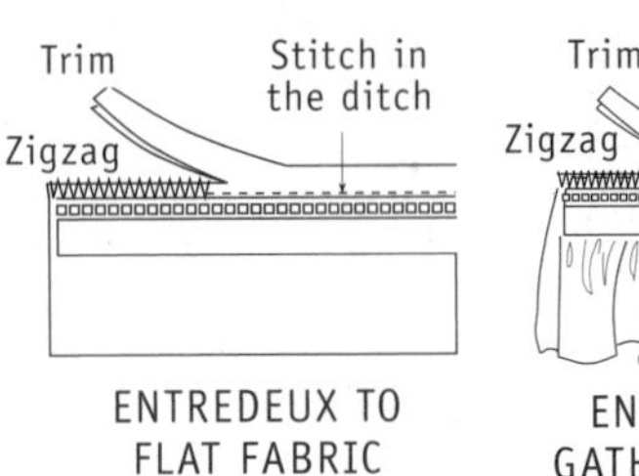

ENTREDEUX TO FLAT FABRIC

ENTREDEUX TO GATHERED FABRIC

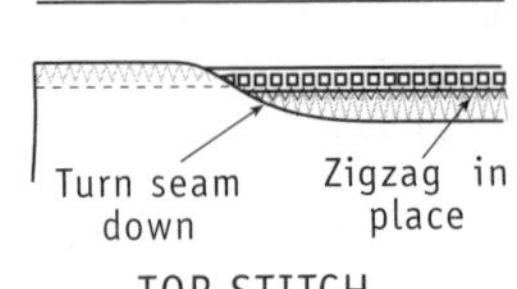

TOP STITCH

Extra-Stable Lace Finishing

1. If the lace is being attached to a straight edge of fabric, pin the heading of the lace to the right side, 1/4" or more from the cut edge, with the right side of the lace facing up and the outside edge of the lace extending over the edge of the fabric. Using a short straight stitch, stitch the heading to the fabric *(fig. 1)*.

2. If the lace is being attached to a curved edge, shape the lace around the curve as you would for lace shaping; refer to Lace Shaping, page 109. Pull up the threads in the lace heading if necessary. Continue pinning and stitching the lace as directed in Step 1 above *(fig. 2)*.

3. Press the seam allowance away from the lace, toward the wrong side of the fabric *(fig. 3)*. If the edge is curved or pointed, you may need to clip the seam allowance in order to press flat *(fig. 4)*.

4. On the right side, use a short, narrow zigzag to stitch over the lace heading, catching the fold of the pressed seam allowance *(fig. 5)*.

5. On the wrong side, trim the seam allowance close to the zigzag *(fig. 6)*.

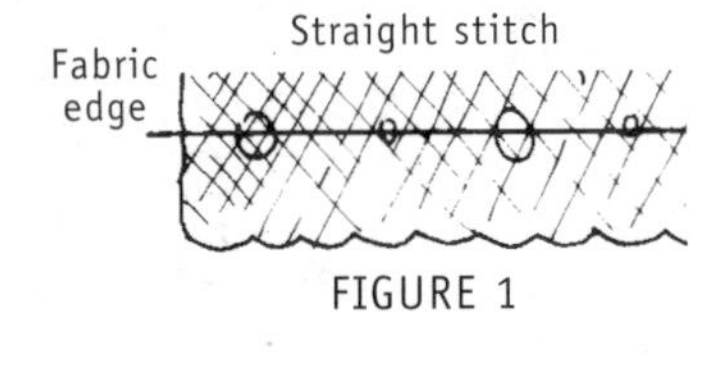

FIGURE 1

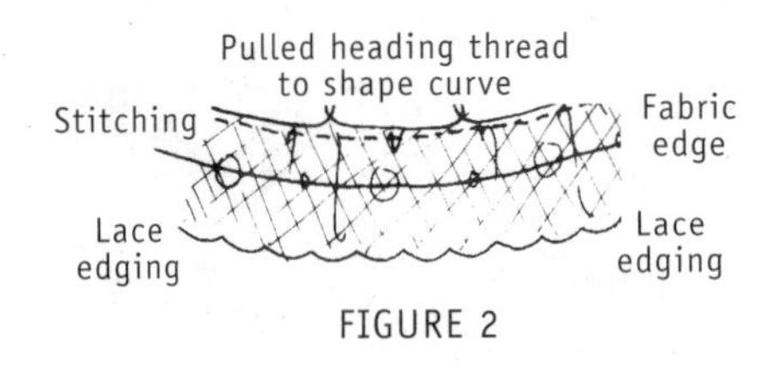

FIGURE 2

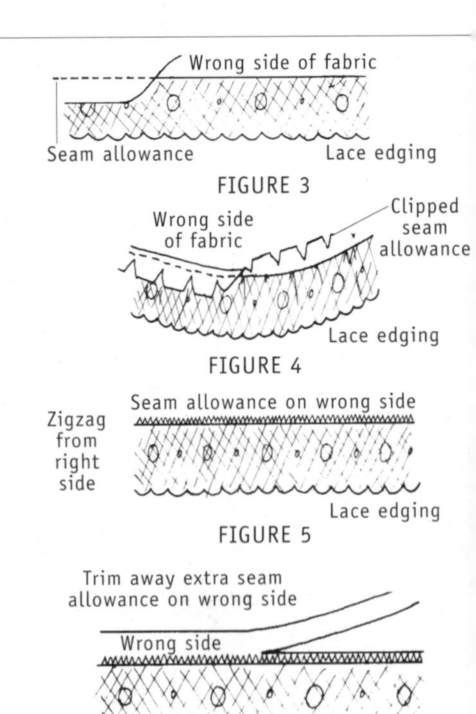

Lace Shaping

Curves, Miters, Hearts, Ovals and Diamonds

1. Trace the lace shape and miter lines onto the fabric with a wash-out pen or pencil (*see fig. 1*). Place the fabric on a padded surface, like a lace shaping board or ironing board.

Note: If only one line is given for the template, shape the lace on the inside of the template. For scallops, shape the lace above the curve as shown in fig. 1. Scallops contain both curves and fold-back miters and are used in the illustrations.

2. *To shape a curve* - place the outer edge of the lace along the outer template line. Pin the lace to the template line by pushing glass head pins through the lace and fabric at an angle, into the padded surface. (Do Not use plastic head pins because they will melt.) Pin only along the outer edge; the inner edge will be loose and curvy (*see fig. 1*).

3. *To miter* - let the lace extend past the point (miter line) in a straight line. Pin the lace to the miter line at points A and B (*fig. 1*).

4. Fold the extended end of the lace back on top of itself. Leave the pin at B just as it is; remove the pin at A and replace it through both layers (*fig. 2*).

5. Continue to guide the lace along the next section of the template. Pin along the outer lace edge as before (*fig. 3*). *Note: If part of the folded miter peeks out, just push it underneath the lace; it can be trimmed away later.*

6. To shape the inner edge, slip the point of a pin under the top heading thread of the lace at the point of the miter, or at the center of a section between the miters; refer to the illustration for gathered lace. Pull the heading thread just until the lace is flat against the fabric (*fig. 4*)

7. Lightly starch and press as each section is shaped or after the entire design is pinned. The iron can be placed directly over the glass head pins; press until dry. Remove the pins and pin flat through the lace and fabric only, removing it from the padded surface (*fig. 5*).

8. Stitch the lace edge(s) to the fabric using one of the following methods:

NOTE: The specific directions will indicate if one edge or both edges of the lace are to be stitched.

- small zigzag (L=0.5 – 1.0, W=1.5 - 2.0) (*fig. 6*)
- place tear-away stabilizer behind the design, use a large needle or wing needle and pinstitch (L=2.0 to 2.5), W=1.5 to 2.0). The straight side of the stitch should fall on the fabric while the "fingers" of the stitch will catch the lace (*fig. 7*)
- place tear-away stabilizer behind the design, use a large needle or wing needle and an entredeux stitch (*fig. 8*)
- extra stable lace (page 107)

9. Carefully trim the fabric from behind the lace, close to the stitching (*fig. 9*). Stitch along the lace miters with a small zigzag and trim the excess lace at the miters (*fig. 10*).

10. *To shape an oval* –Pin the outer edge of the lace along the template line. Overlap the ends of the lace by 1". Pull the heading threads along the inner edge of the lace (refer to step 6). Fold the top piece of lace under 1/2" (*fig. 11*). Lightly starch and press the oval and pin the lace to the fabric only (refer to step 7). Stitch as directed in the instructions (*refer to step 8*).

11. *To shape a diamond* – Place the lace inside the template with the outer edge of the lace along the template line. Allow the end of the lace to extend beyond the lower point placing pins at A and B (fig. 12). Continue mitering at each point (*refer to step 3*). When

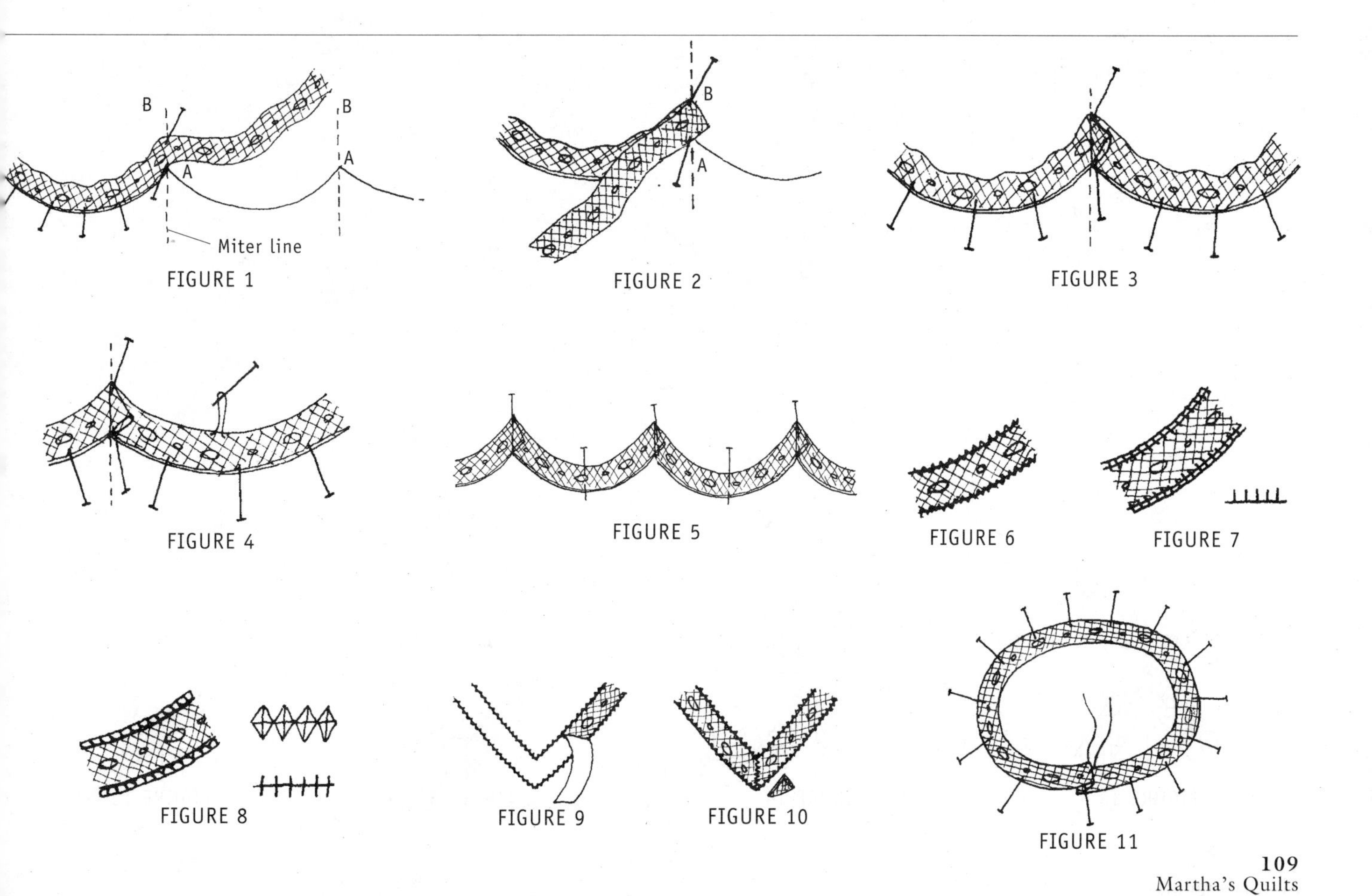

FIGURE 1

FIGURE 2

FIGURE 3

FIGURE 4

FIGURE 5

FIGURE 6

FIGURE 7

FIGURE 8

FIGURE 9

FIGURE 10

FIGURE 11

returning to the lower point, use the *fold back miter* method as follows: crisscross the ends of the lace at the miter line. Place pins through both layers of lace at B (fig. 13). Remove the pin at A and fold the tail of the upper lace under to lie directly on top of the beginning lace tail. Repin at A *(fig. 14)*. Lightly starch and press the diamond and pin the lace to the fabric only (refer to step 7). Stitch as directed in the instructions *(refer to step 8)*.). Carefully trim the fabric from behind the lace *(refer to fig. 9)*. Stitch along the lace miters with a small zigzag and trim the excess lace at the miters *(refer to fig. 10)*. Figure shows the lace diamond stitched to the fabric using a zigzag stitch.

12. *To shape a heart* - begin at the lower point (A). Pin the outer edge of the lace along one side of the heart template. Miter at the inner point (refer to steps 3-5). Pin the lace along the remaining curve. Pull the heading threads along the inner edge of the lace (*refer to step 6*) *(fig. 16)*. Lightly starch and press the heart and pin the lace to the fabric only (refer to step 7). Stitch as directed in the instructions (*refer to step 8*). Carefully trim the fabric from behind the lace *(refer to fig. 9)*. Stitch along the lace miters with a small zigzag and trim the excess lace at the miters *(refer to fig. 10)*.

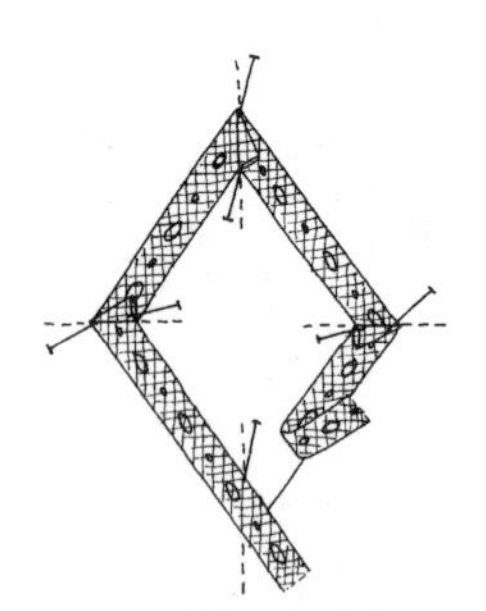

FIGURE 12

Settings For Entredeux (Hemstitch) And Pinstitch

Bernina 180 E
Pinstitch
-100 wing needle or 100 universal
-Stitch #330 as is or L=2.5,W=2.5
Entredeux
-100 wing or 100 universal
-Stitch #701 as is or L=2.5, W=3.0

Pfaff 7570
Pinstitch
-100 wing or 100 universal
-Stitch #112, tension 3, twin needle button, L=3, W=4
Entredeux
-100 wing or 100 universal
-Stitch #132, L=5, W=3.5
-Stitch #113, L=2, W=4
-Stitch #114, L=2.5, W=3.5
-Stitch #115, L=3, W=3.5

Viking Husqvarna, Designer I and 1+
Pinstitch
-100 wing needle or 100 universal
-Stitch #D6, L=2.5 - 3, W=2 - 2.5
Entredeux
-100 wing needle or 100 universal
-Stitch #D7 (as is)

Elna CE20
Pinstitch
-100 wing needle or 100 universal
-Stitch #149, L=2.5, W=2.5
Entredeux
-100 wing needle or 100 universal
-Stitch #36, L=1.5, W=2.5

Singer XL - 1000
Pinstitch
-100 wing needle or 100 universal
-Screen #6, Stitch #7
-Medium or Small (width changes with the length)
Entredeux
-100 wing needle or 100 universal
-Screen #6, Stitch #8
-Medium or Small (width changes with the length)

Janome 10,000
Pinstitch
-100 wing needle or 100 universal
-Stitch #87 or 88, L=1.5 - 2.5, W=1.5-2.5
Entredeux
-100 wing needle or 100 universal
-Stitch #97, L=1.0, W=3.5

Brother ULT 2001
Pinstitch
-100 wing needle or 100 universal
-Screen #3, Stitch #4, L=3.0, W=2.5
Entredeux
-100 wing needle or 100 universal
-Screen #3, Stitch #8, L=2.5, W=3.0

Baby Lock, Esanté
Choose Decorative Stitch - Heirloom
Pinstitch
-100 wing needle or 100 universal
-Stitch #4 (as is)
Entredeux
-100 wing needle or 100 universal
-Stitch #5 (as is)

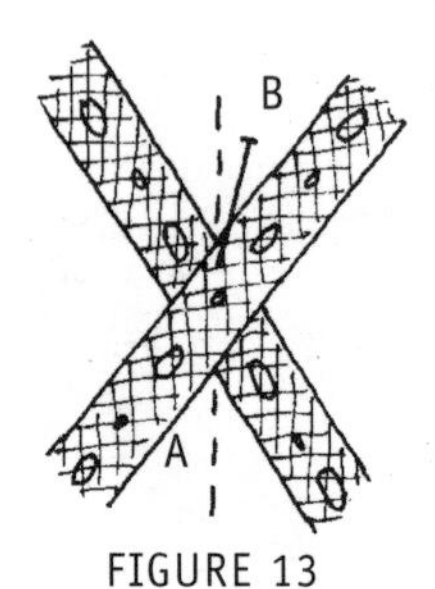

FIGURE 13

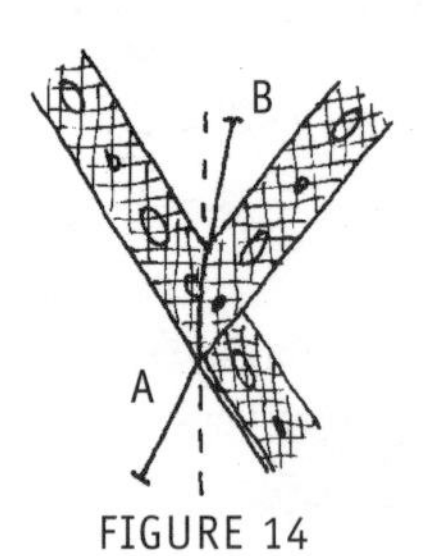

FIGURE 14

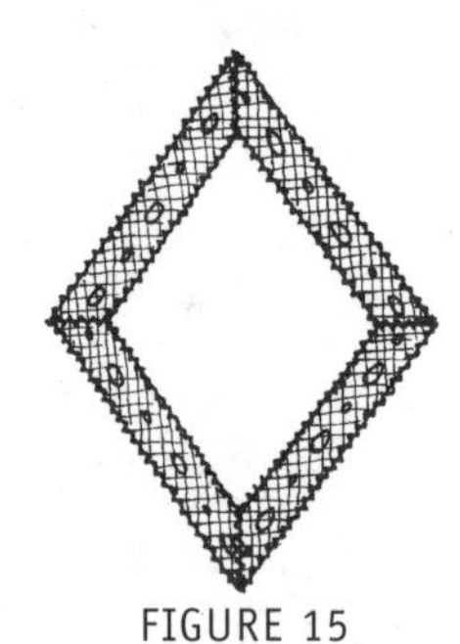

FIGURE 15

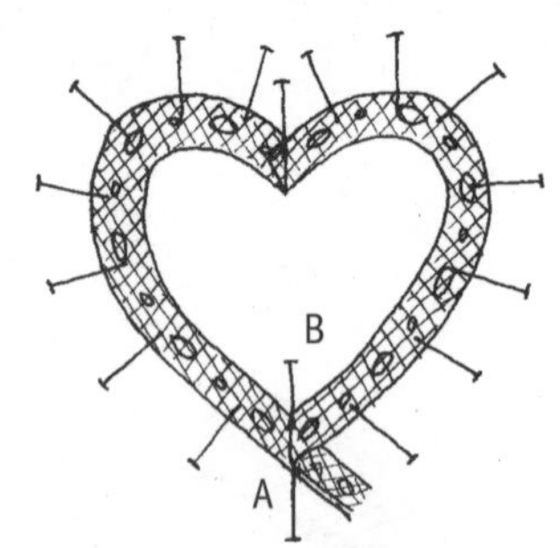

FIGURE 16

Stipple Stitching

Supplies

- Basted quilt sandwich consisting of the top, batting and backing (Stipple stitching can be done without the backing.)
- Thread to match the backing if used
- Thread to match top or invisible thread for the needle
- Machine embroidery, Metafil, Metallica or Quilting needle, size 75 to 90
- Free Motion quilting or embroidery foot

Optional: Sewing aids that will help in moving the quilt sandwich

Machine Set-up

1. Set up the machine for free motion embroidery by lowering the feed dogs and placing the free-motion quilting or embroidery foot on the machine (see machine instruction manual).

2. Place a new needle in the machine.

3. Thread the needle with desired thread or invisible thread.

4. Use desired thread in the bobbin to match the backing.

5. The tension should be adjusted so the top thread does not show on the back and the bobbin thread should not be visible on the topside. Use a sample quilt sandwich to test and adjust as needed.

Rules for Free Motion Quilting

1. The feed dogs are always lowered or covered (see machine instruction manual).

2. The foot should be lowered before sewing. Some newer machines will not allow stitching with the foot in the up position, but older machines do not offer this. Lowering the presser foot engages the needle thread tension. If using free-motion stitching and a "bird's nest" is created on the wrong side, it usually indicates that the foot is not down OR that the top thread is not in the tension disks.

3. YOU are the stitch length in free motion stitching. The stitch length as indicated on the sewing machine does not come into play since YOU have to move the fabric (quilt sandwich).

4. Push the machine away from the edge of the table. This will allow the sewer to place the elbows or forearms on the machine bed or table. With the elbows up in the air, the shoulder, neck and arms become tired rather quickly. By placing the elbows down, the fingers can be placed on the quilt sandwich with the wrists up, allowing for easier controlled movement.

5. Position yourself directly in front of the needle.

6. Run the machine at a moderately fast, steady speed. The steady part of this statement is more important than the moderately fast. The speed of the machine must be adjusted to the speed of moving the fabric to create even-length stitches. If the needle breaks in free motion stitching, it is often because the speed of the sewing machine is too slow for the speed of moving the fabric. To create even-length stitches, practice stitching until even stitches are achieved.

7. Stipple stitching generally indicates that the stitches do not cross over each other, but are rather like the pieces of a puzzle. The curves are rounded, not squared. Stitch randomly to prevent a structured row look to the stitching. The stitching can be in a tight design or stitched in a looser design depending on the desired finished effect.

8. Begin near the middle and work out toward the sides.

9. Do not press on the quilt top too hard. This will make moving it more difficult and uneven.

10. Always tie-on and off at the beginning and end of stitching. This will prevent the stitches from unraveling.

Stipple Stitching

NOTE: A template can be traced onto the fabric with a washout marker before beginning.

1. Position the quilt sandwich under the needle where the stitching will begin.

2. Sit comfortably directly in front of the needle with the elbows and fingers down and the wrists up.

3. Pull the bobbin thread to the right side by taking one complete stitch and pulling on the needle thread. Place the thread ends under your fingers and take several very tiny stitches to tie-on (*fig. 1*). Clip the thread ends.

4. Stitch at a moderately fast steady speed while moving the fabric in a smooth, even manner. There are many sewing aids that help in controlling the fabric although none are absolutely necessary: rubber finger tips, quilting gloves, hoops with rubber on the under sides (they look like a partial hoop – not enclosed in a circle – with handles on each side) and finger cots available at the drug store. Follow the directions on the product that you use. These sewing aids are not necessary, but they help in gripping the quilt sandwich so that it can be moved slowly.

5. Stitch in a random pattern that resembles puzzle pieces. Stippling may be stitched in a loose pattern (*fig. 2*) or a tight pattern (*fig. 3*). Stitching in vertical or horizontal rows becomes obvious. Change direction frequently, always rounding curves and keeping an even stitch length. It is important not to "paint yourself into a corner" and always leave an "escape route" when going into small areas. Practice with a pencil and paper to see how to stitch areas.

FIGURE 1

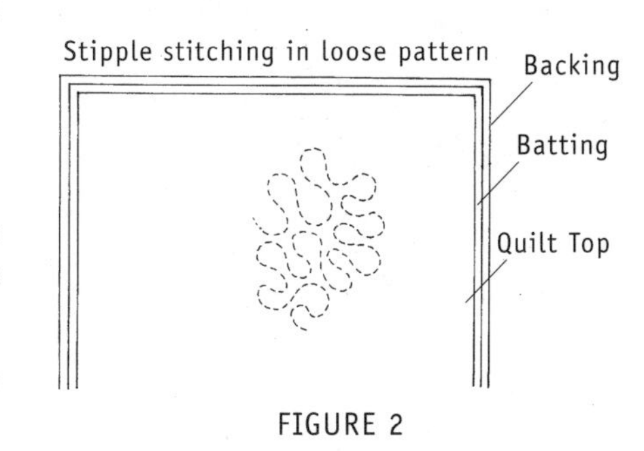

FIGURE 2

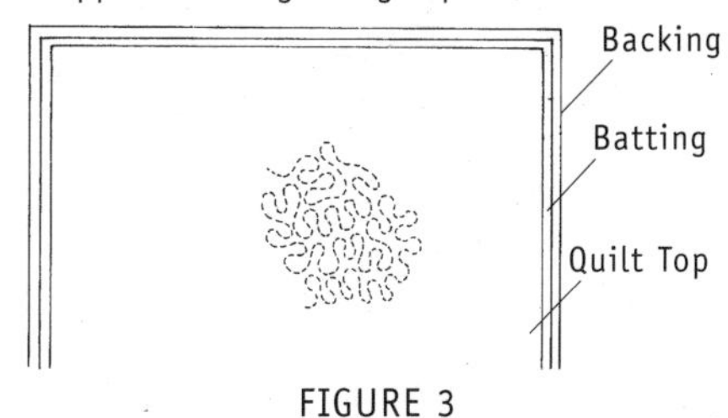

FIGURE 3

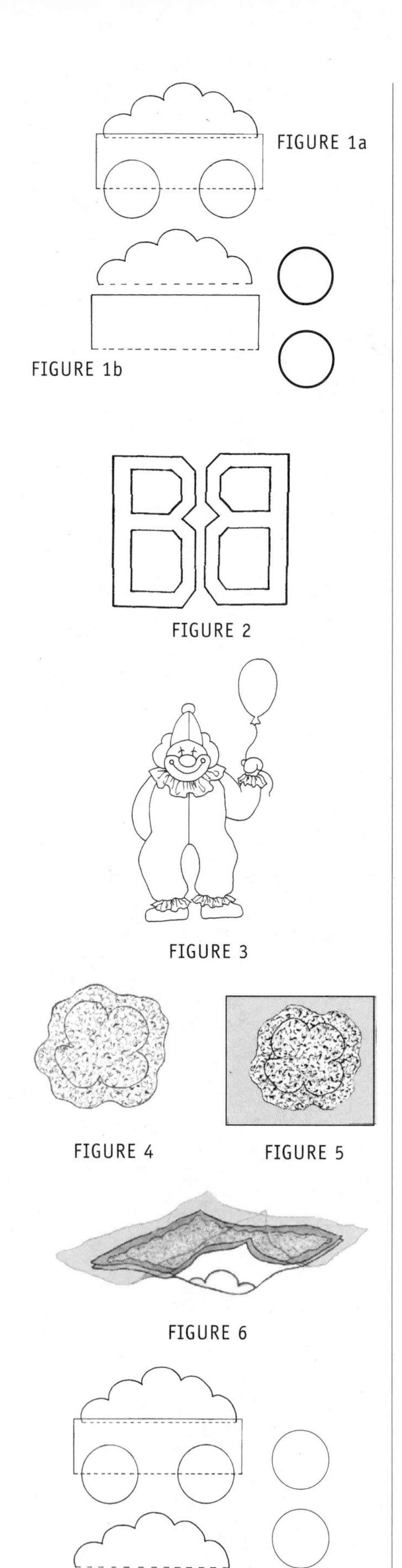

FIGURE 1a

FIGURE 1b

FIGURE 2

FIGURE 3

FIGURE 4

FIGURE 5

FIGURE 6

FIGURE 7

Appliqué

Using The Patterns

Each appliqué design can be dissected into smaller pieces. Some of the appliqué pieces may extend under other appliqué pieces. Some appliqué designs are drawn with a dotted line extending from the appliquéd piece. This shows that the fabric extension is under another piece. When dissecting these designs, watch for these dotted lines. When you are tracing your pattern which will later be used for cutting out your appliqué fabric, include the dotted extension as a part of your pattern.

For example, on a coal car of the train, the coal pattern piece extends under the body of the car and the body of the car extends under the wheels *(fig. 1a)*. This is the appliqué design. Here are the dissected pieces *(fig. 1b)*.

Some appliqué patterns have a definite right and left side *(fig. 2)*. For example, letters of the alphabet (B, E, R), or a clown holding balloons with his left hand *(fig. 3)*. Other patterns do not, such as the letter A (uppercase) or O. Keep this in mind when following the directions below.

Tracing Pattern On Bonding Agent

If Wonder Under™ or another paper-backed bonding agent is used, trace each individual pattern piece on paper backing, with a permanent fine-tip marker. Since the pattern is placed on the wrong side of the fabric, and if it has a definite right and wrong side, the pattern should be traced in reverse. Any design traced exactly as it is featured in this book will appear in reverse on the project.

Take the clown appliqué as an example. If the clown were holding balloons in his left hand and that is how you want it to look on the garment, the design would need to be traced in reverse. If the balloons on the completed project need to be in the clown's right hand, trace as is.

Tracing A Pattern In Reverse Image

1. Photocopy or trace the design from this book.

2. Hold the design to a window with the design facing outside.

3. Trace the design on the back of the paper.

4. This newly traced design is your reverse image.

Roughly Cut Pattern

Roughly cut out pattern pieces to separate leaving about 1/4 inch to 1/2 inch around pattern lines. Do not cut pattern on cutting lines at this time *(fig. 4)*.

Fusing

Follow the bonding agent instructions and fuse to the wrong side of a square of appliqué fabric. Be sure the bonding agent does not extend past the edges of the fabric to be appliquéd *(fig. 5)*.

Cutting Out Appliqué

Cut out appliqué pieces along cutting lines. Remember to use the dotted extensions where indicated as the cutting lines.

* Fine Fuse™ or Stitch Witchery™ *(fig. 6)*

a. An appliqué pressing sheet is required. Plastic coated freezer paper or lightweight iron-on stabilizer is also needed.

b. Trace pattern pieces onto paper side of freezer paper or stabilizer with a fine-tip permanent marker. Since the pattern is placed on the right side of the fabric the pattern should be traced as is, no reversal is necessary.

c. Press to right side of appliqué fabric.

d. Fuse bonding agent to wrong side of fabric using the pressing sheet between bonding agent and iron. Iron according to manufacturer's instructions.

e. Peel off pressing sheet. Cut out pattern pieces along lines traced on the stabilizer. There will be paper on the right side and the bonding agent on the wrong side of each piece.

Placing Appliqué Pieces

a. Place pattern pieces on base fabric in desired position, fitting pieces together as you would a puzzle. Remember when putting the pieces together, the background pieces may extend under foreground pieces (designated by dotted lines). This will help you to see how the final design will look, as well as decipher where each piece will be fused *(fig. 7)*.

b. Slide appliqué to the side, away from placement of design. While looking at the total design, remove paper backing from first piece to be fused. If paper is difficult to remove try scratching an X or a line in the paper backing with a straight pin or needle. This will help release the paper from the appliqué piece. Place stabilizer under base fabric in the area of the appliqué *(fig. 8)*.

Stitching

Satin stitch each piece, background to foreground. Satin stitch maneuvers, including straight lines, curves, corners, and points will be discussed in the following section, Stitch Maneuvers.

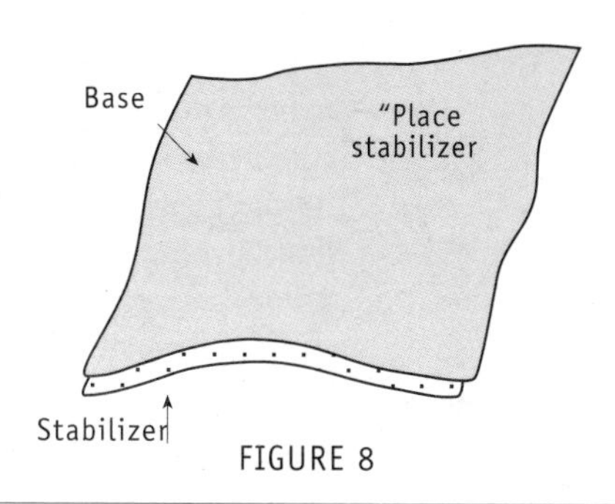

FIGURE 8

Stitch Maneuvers General Directions

1. Never start stitching at a corner or point; start at a straight side or curve.

2. Preferably, the appliqué piece should be positioned so that the left swing of the needle (zig) stitches on the appliqué piece and the right swing of the needle (zag) stitches off the appliqué piece *(fig. 1)*. All stitch maneuver directions are given with appliqué piece positioned on the left needle swing unless otherwise indicated. Sometimes the appliqué piece should be placed on the right needle swing *(fig. 2)*. Appliqué piece position is provided in such maneuvers.

3. Tie-On *(fig. 3)*. Using a short straight stitch, take one complete stitch on the fabric right next to the appliqué. Pull gently on the top thread, bringing the bobbin thread to the top side of the fabric. Place threads under and behind foot. Take several straight stitches on base fabric just off appliqué.

4. Set the machine for a zigzag, medium width and satin or buttonhole length. Slightly loosen the top tension to allow the thread to"wrap"to the wrong side. If "needle down" is available on your machine, it will be helpful in satin stitching and pivoting. Reposition appliqué so that zigzag stitches are placed mostly on the appliqué but extend completely off the edge of the appliqué. This will stitch the appliqué piece on in a neat fashion encasing the raw edges of the appliqué. If the entire stitch is taken on the appliqué, fuzzy may occur on the edge of the appliqué piece. If you don't stitch enough on the appliqué fabric, the appliqué may pull from the stitching.

5. Take all stitches perpendicular to the edge of the appliqué.

6. Stitch individual pieces and detail lines (that identify arms, legs, flower petals, etc.), working background to foreground.

7. Do not push or pull but simply guide the fabric through the machine. Let the machine do the work. A gentle nudge may be required when crossing over previous stitching.

8. Tie-Off *(fig. 4)*. Change to a short straight stitch, reposition appliqué, and take several straight stitches just beside the satin stitch.

9. Cut threads very close to the stitching.

10. Complete design using steps 1-8 on this page.

11. With a water-soluble marker, transfer any straight stitch detail not previously satin stitched (eyes, mouth, hair, nose, glasses). These will be stitched using free-motion embroidery or hand embroidery.

Straight Lines

Follow steps in General Directions *(fig. 5)*.

Curves - Outside and Inside

1. Zigzag along the appliqué as described in steps 1 - 7 of the *General Directions.* While stitching along a curve, the stitching will fail to be perpendicular to the appliqué, therefore pivoting is required. There is more area to cover along the outside edge of the curve, so the pivot must be taken with the needle down at this outside edge *(fig. 6)*.

2. To pivot on a curve, leave the needle in the outside edge of the curve (not specifically on the zig or the zag). Raise the foot and pivot very slightly, keeping the stitches perpendicular to the edge of the appliqué. It is better to pivot too often than not often enough. If the needle is left in the inside edge of the curve while pivoting, a V will occur in the stitching.

NOTE: When stitching around a curve, the tendency is to force the stitching without pivoting. This will cause the appliqué edge to be wavy, therefore pivoting is very important!

Pivoting Rule For Curves: To pivot on an outside curve, the needle is left in the fabric right next to the appliqué piece. To pivot on an inside curve the needle is left in the appliqué piece itself.

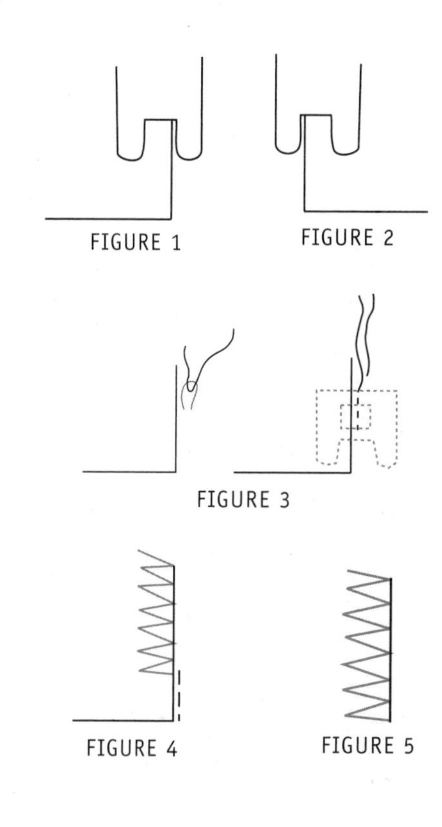
FIGURE 1 FIGURE 2

FIGURE 3

FIGURE 4 FIGURE 5

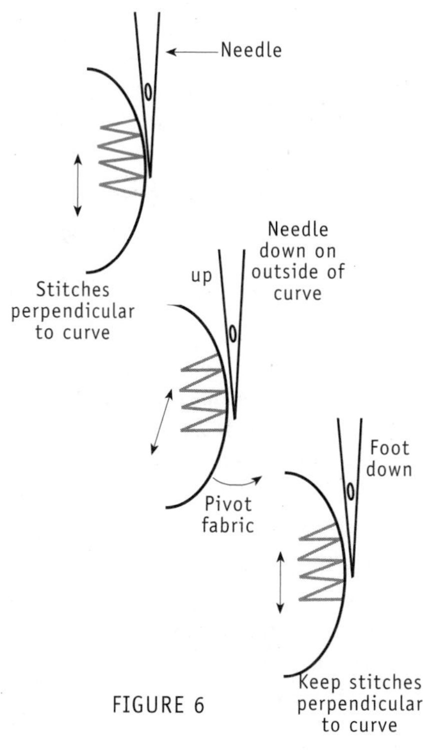

FIGURE 6

Corners - Block Corners

Any zigzag sewing machine will accomplish this very simple method of turning corners.

Outside Block Corner Method 1

1. Zigzag along the appliqué as described in steps 1 - 7 of the *General Directions.*

2. Stitch down first side to corner, stopping with the needle down at the point of the corner *(fig. 7).*

3. Pivot 90° *(fig. 8).* Walk the machine by using the fly wheel to take the first stitch that should be placed in the edge of the previous stitching.

4. Continue stitching along the second side *(fig. 9).* Some machines may need a little push to begin satin stitching the second side at the corner. To keep the machine from bogging down at this point, push gently by placing fingers along the sides of the foot to help move the stitching over the previous satin stitch at the corner.

Outside Block Corner Method 2

1. Zigzag along the appliqué as described in steps 1 - 7 of *General Directions.*

2. Stitch down first side to corner, stopping with the needle down on the left swing [not on the point of the corner (zag) but on the other side (zig)] *(fig. 10).*

3. Pivot 90°. Raise needle out of fabric, raise presser foot, and reposition so that the needle pierces the same hole of the last stitch before the pivot *(fig. 11).* Lower foot.

4. Continue stitching.

Inside Block Corner Method 1

1. Bisect corner using a water-soluble marker *(fig. 12).*

2. With appliqué on left needle swing, zigzag along the appliqué as described in steps 1 - 7 of the *General Directions.* Continue stitching until the left needle swing hits the drawn line *(fig. 13).*

3. With needle in fabric, raise foot, pivot 90°, walk the machine by using the fly wheel to take the first stitch that should be placed in the edge of the previous stitching *(fig. 14),* lower foot and continue stitching along the second side.

4. Some machines may need a little push to begin satin stitching the second side at the corner. To keep the machine from bogging down at this point, push gently by placing fingers along the sides of the foot to help move the stitching over the previous satin stitch at the corner.

Inside Block Corner Method 2

1. Bisect corner using a water-soluble marker *(See fig. 12).*

2. With appliqué on left needle swing, zigzag along the appliqué as described in steps 1 - 7 of the *General Directions.*

3. Continue stitching until the left needle swing hits the drawn line *(fig. 15).*

4. On the next stitch, leave the needle down on the right swing *(fig. 16).* Raise foot, pivot 90°, lower foot, raise needle out of fabric, raise presser foot, and reposition so that the needle pierces the same hole of the last stitch before the pivot *(fig. 17).*

5. Continue stitching along the second side.

Mitered Corners

Before beginning the maneuvers of miters and points it will be helpful to practice on stabilized scrap fabric, increasing and decreasing the stitch width with the right hand while guiding fabric with the left. Watch where the needle is stitching, not the stitch width knob or lever. Also practice this stitching method using right and left needle position, if available.

Mitering corners can be done if your machine has the capability of changing needle positions (right, left or both) and being able to change the stitch width while stitching in any of these needle positions. Note: Once the needle position is changed, it may stay in that position to continue stitching until the next maneuver (corner or point) is reached.

Points

All points are stitched in center needle position.

Outside Point

1. Appliqué piece on left needle swing.

2. Zigzag along the appliqué as described in steps 1 - 7 of the *General Directions.* Zigzag toward point until needle is stitching off both sides of the appliqué piece. Leave needle down on left side *(fig. 18).*

3. Raise foot, pivot so that point is directly toward you *(fig. 19).*

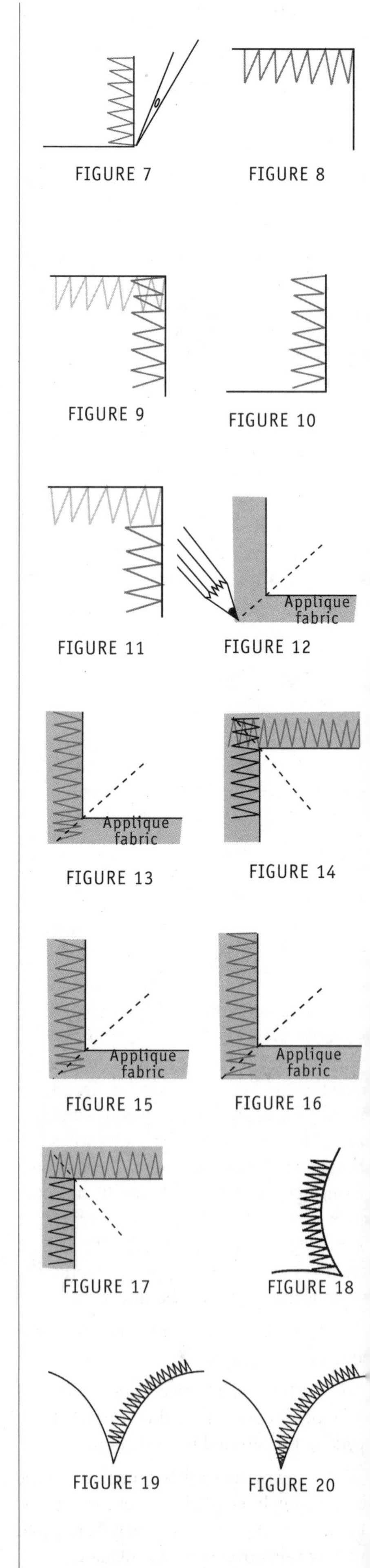

FIGURE 7 FIGURE 8 FIGURE 9 FIGURE 10 FIGURE 11 FIGURE 12 FIGURE 13 FIGURE 14 FIGURE 15 FIGURE 16 FIGURE 17 FIGURE 18 FIGURE 19 FIGURE 20

4. Note stitch width. Continue stitching to the point guiding the fabric with your left hand, while decreasing stitch width with your right hand to cover appliqué piece.

a. For a sharp point it will be necessary to take the stitch width down to 0 *(Fig. 20).*

b. For a blunt point, taking the width to 0 is not necessary *(fig. 21).*

5. Lower needle, raise foot, pivot 180° (the point of the appliqué piece is pointed away from you) *(fig. 22).*

6. Lower foot, raise the needle and reposition so that the first stitch will re-enter the hole of the last stitch.

7. Continue stitching away from the point, guiding the fabric with your left hand, while increasing the stitch width with your right hand to the original width. Continue stitching *(fig. 23),* pivoting as necessary to keep the satin stitches perpendicular to the appliqué edge.

Inside Point

1. Appliqué piece on left needle swing.

2. Bisect the point using a water-soluble pen *(fig. 24).*

3. Zigzag along the appliqué as described in steps 1 - 7 of the *General Directions.* Continue stitching until the right swing of the needle is off the appliqué at the point *(fig. 25).*

4. Note original stitch width. Guide the fabric with your left hand, so that the right needle swing hits the bisected line as you decrease stitch width gradually to 0 *(fig. 26).*

5. With the needle down, raise the foot, pivot approximately 180° positioning unstitched edge of appliqué under the foot. Lower the foot and continue stitching as you gradually increase the stitch width to the original width keeping the right needle swing butted up against the edge of the previous stitching. Continue stitching *(fig. 27),* pivoting as necessary to keep the satin stitches perpendicular to the appliqué edge.

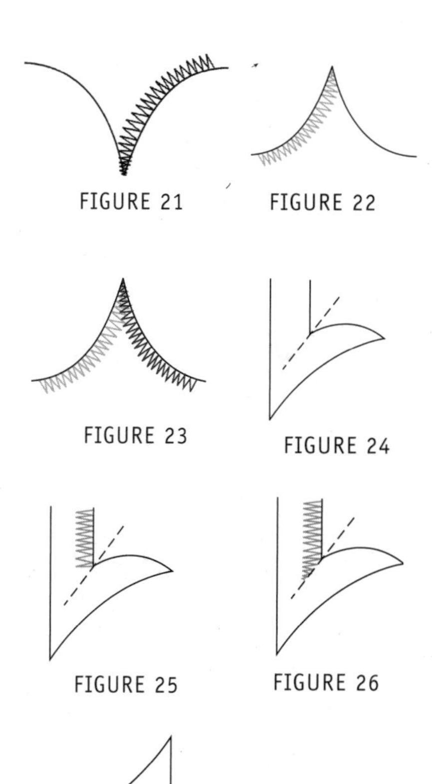

FIGURE 21 FIGURE 22

FIGURE 23 FIGURE 24

FIGURE 25 FIGURE 26

FIGURE 27

Shadow Appliqué

Different colored fabrics can be applied to the wrong side of a sheer fabric to give a shadow effect. This simple technique can be applied to collars, blouse fronts, cuffs, and skirt hems. An open zigzag, blanket stitch or other decorative stitch can be used to apply the colored fabrics to the base fabrics.

Supplies

- Sheer Base Fabric (blouse, collar, etc.)
- Bright or Dark Appliqué Fabric
- Open Toe Appliqué Foot
- Machine Embroidery Thread
- Size 70 to 80 Needle
- 6" to 8" Hoop (Wooden machine embroidery or spring tension)
- Marking Pens or Pencils, Water or Air Soluble
- Small, Sharp Pointed Scissors Appliqué Scissors

Shadow Appliqué Fabrics

1. Base Fabric

The base fabric should be a sheer fabric so that the fabric appliqué will show through from the wrong side. If a fabric other than white is used, experiment to see how it will change the color of the appliqué fabric. The appliqué will show more distinctly after it is lined.

2. Appliqué Fabric

The appliqué color should be bright enough to show through base fabric. Some colors will look "muddy" under the base fabric. Always test appearance of color by placing a single layer of appliqué fabric between two layers of the base fabric.

General Shadow Appliqué Directions

1. To determine the size of base fabric to be shadow appliquéd, consider the position of the appliqué. The fabric should extend beyond the appliqué design in all directions, so that it may be placed in the hoop. For example, when doing shadow appliqué on a pocket edge, even though the pocket pattern itself is small, you must start with a piece of fabric large enough to fit in the hoop *(fig. 1).* Another example would be when placing shadow appliqué near the edge of a collar, the base fabric must be large enough to contain the whole collar pattern plus enough fabric on the edges to hold in the hoop *(fig. 2).*

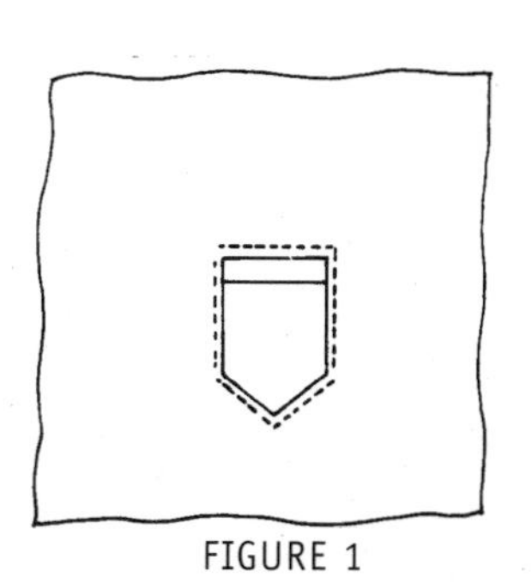

FIGURE 1

FIGURE 2

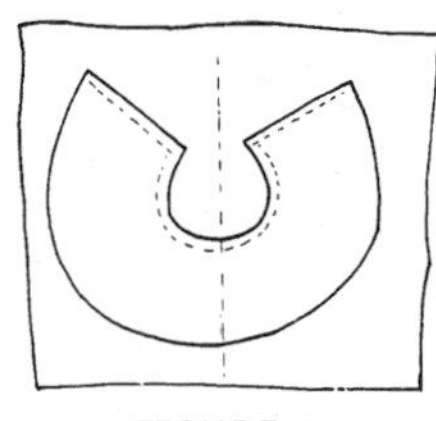

FIGURE 3

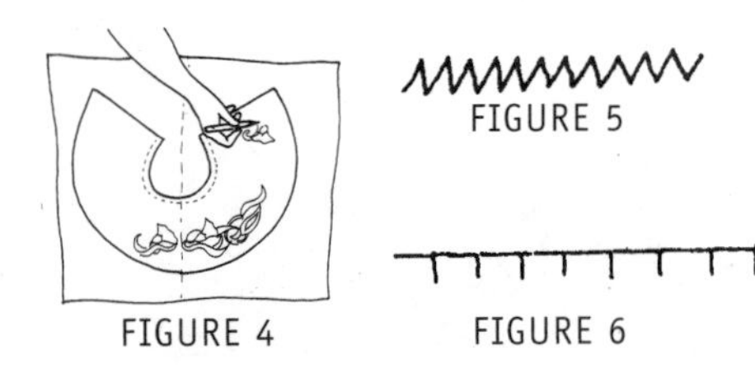

FIGURE 4 FIGURE 5 FIGURE 6

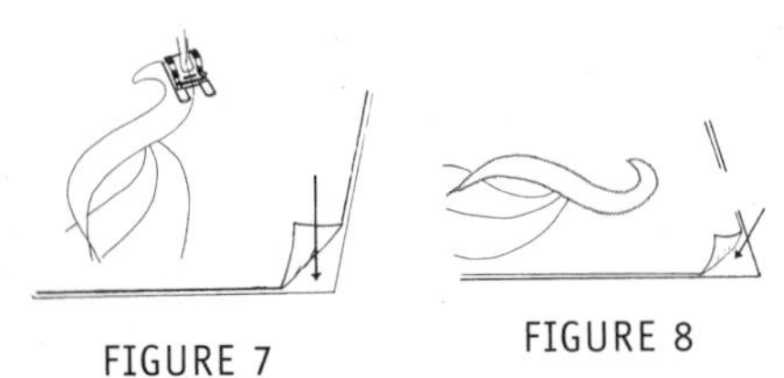

FIGURE 7 FIGURE 8

FIGURE 9 FIGURE 10

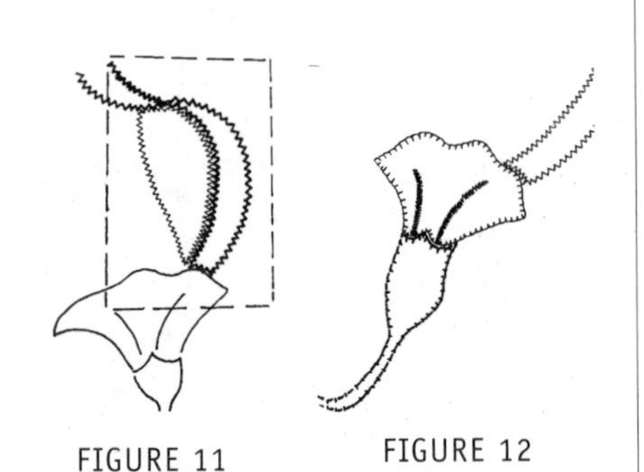

FIGURE 11 FIGURE 12

2. Press and starch the pretreated fabric to remove all of the wrinkles and give the fabric some body. Several applications of starch can be used.

3. Trace the pattern piece (cutting lines, seam lines and center front line and all other necessary markings) *(fig. 3)*. Trace the design, within the pattern stitching lines, to the base fabric in the desired position *(fig. 4)*. When tracing, especially the design for the appliqué, maintain as fine a line as possible since you will be stitching ON this line. A washable marking pencil with a sharp point is helpful. To trace the design, place the base fabric in a hoop large enough to encompass the design. This will help to hold the fabric flat and keep it from shifting while tracing. Don't pull fabric too tight in hoop.

4. To determine the thread color to use, place a piece of each of the appliqué fabrics between two layers of base fabric. Match the thread to the color that shows through the base fabric. It will be lighter than the actual appliqué fabric. Use this color for the top thread. White or base fabric color thread can be used in the bobbin throughout the project.

The upper thread tension should be loosened so that the bobbin thread will pull the top thread to the wrong side. It should not be so loose that the bobbin thread forms a straight line on the wrong side. Test to make correct adjustments.

5. Decide what stitch to use to attach the appliqué fabric to the base fabric. There are several choices.

a.A narrow open zig zag can be used, a stitch width of about 1 mm and a length of 1 mm *(fig. 5)*. This is not a satin stitch, but a short, narrow zig zag stitch.

b.A pin stitch or blanket stitch can also be used if your machine has this capability *(fig. 6)*. The pin stitch generally has a heavier look than the blanket stitch. The stitch width should be narrowed to about 1 mm and the length may also need to be adjusted. Test on a sample to make adjustments.

6.With machine shadow appliqué, the appliqué fabric is placed to the wrong side of the base fabric and you must work from foreground to background (opposite from regular machine appliqué). Place both fabrics in a hoop, layered with the right side of the appliqué fabric to the wrong side of the base fabric.

When learning to do shadow appliqué by machine, have the appliqué fabric large enough to be placed in the hoop with the base fabric. As you become more accustomed to this technique it is not necessary to place the fabrics in a hoop *(fig. 7)*. When the stitching is done, care should be taken to keep the appliqué fabric from shifting or wrinkles being stitched in. Pin in place if necessary or use a touch of water soluble glue stick to hold the fabric in place. Spray starching the appliqué fabric again will help it to remain flat.

Decide on the starting point, generally not a corner or a point. Pull up bobbin thread and tie on by taking several tiny straight stitches on the drawn line of the appliqué pattern. Stitch on design line to completely enclose area in that color *(fig. 8)*. When using the pin stitch or blanket stitch, the straight part of the stitch should be on the design line and the "fingers" part or "ladder steps" of the stitch should be INTO the appliqué *(fig. 9)*. You may need to engage "mirror image" if your machine has this capability or stitch in the opposite direction to place the stitch correctly.

6.Trim the appliqué fabric close to the stitching lines, being careful not to cut the stitches *(fig. 10)*. If both the base fabric and the appliqué fabric are in the hoop, remove the hoop, and re-hoop just the base fabric. Trimming will be easier if the base fabric remains in the hoop.

7. Working foreground to background, place the next color to be appliquéd under the base fabric as above and stitch. For areas that touch each other, the stitching must be done on BOTH sides of the appliqué *(fig. 11)*. Allow the regular zigzag stitches to just touch each other (not overlap) or the straight part of the pin or blanket stitch to be beside each other *(fig. 12)*.

8. Continue in this manner until all of the appliqué pieces are attached and trimmed.

9. Wash fabric to remove all of the markings.

10. Press with the right side down on a towel.